The Problem with Evangelical Theology

Early Christian thought is biblical, and one of the lasting accomplishments of the patristic period was to forge a new way of thinking, scriptural in language and inspiration, that gave to the church and to Western civilization a unified and coherent interpretation of the Bible as a whole. Needless to say, this means that any effort to mount an interpretation of the Bible that ignores its first readers is doomed to end up with a bouquet of fragments that are neither the book of the church nor the imaginative wellspring of Western literature, art, and music. Uprooted from the soil that feeds them, they are like cut flowers whose vivid colors have faded. . . . Yet, and this is the central point, the biblical narrative was not reduced to a set of ideas or a body of principles; no conceptual scheme was allowed to displace the evangelical history.

R. Wilken
The Spirit of Early Christian Thought
(New Haven: Yale University Press, 2003), xvii, 24

The Problem with Evangelical Theology:
Testing the Exegetical Foundations of Calvinism, Dispensationalism, and Wesleyanism

Ben Witherington III

Baylor University Press
Waco, Texas

Cover Design: Keith Saunders of Marion Design

Library of Congress Cataloging-in-Publication Data

Witherington, Ben, 1951-
  The problem with evangelical theology : testing the exegetical foundations of Calvinism, dispensationalism, and Wesleyanism / by Ben Witherington III.
      p. cm.
  Includes bibliographical references (p.   ).
  ISBN 1-932792-42-2 (pbk. : alk. paper)
    1. Evangelicalism. 2. Theology, Doctrinal. 3. Calvinism. 4. Dispensationalism. 5. Wesley, John, 1703-1791. I. Title.

  BR1640.W58 2005
  230'.04624--dc22

                                    2005021029

Printed in the United States of America on acid-free paper

To Carey Newman, a good friend in all seasons, and to Jerry
Walls the instigator and deal maker of this project.
Thank goodness the Red Sox finally won the World Series!

CONTENTS

OVERTURE

The Legacy of the Reformers

There were two battle cries associated with the Protestant Reformation—"semper reformanda" and "sola Scriptura." These cries were heard not only in the works of Luther, Calvin, and Zwingli, but also in the later English Reformation of the Wesleys and George Whitefield. But what does the commitment to these two principles (having only Scripture as the final authority in matters of faith and practice, and at the same time always being committed to reforming) ultimately amount to at the end of the day? How successfully have those of us who have embraced the legacy of the Reformers really been in implementing the game plan, so to speak? One thing is for sure: none of the original Reformers could have imagined modern-day Evangelicalism. Evangelicalism is a many-splintered thing with more denominational expressions than one can count, and like much of the rest of the church is to a large extent biblically illiterate or semiliterate.

I am, by trade, a New Testament scholar, but I am also an ordained minister involved every week with the church. What I see in the church's proclamation, and in what passes for its theology, are not just glaring weaknesses but real problems of exegesis. For an Evangelical there is an ultimate litmus test for good preaching and teaching: is it well grounded in and illuminating the biblical text? If it is not, it requires revision or reformation.

As we are now well into the twenty-first century it would be a good thing to take stock of our Reformation theological heritage and ask the hard question—to what extent is its current shape actually biblical, actually well grounded in God's Word? Three examples, two from popular Evangelical literature and one from a popular recent film widely embraced by Evangelicals, will illustrate why I am concerned.

Rick Warren's *The Purpose-Driven Life* (followed by *The Purpose-Driven Church*) has sold millions of copies and has become regular study-material for Sunday schools all over the Protestant church. But when one looks more closely at the theology and exegesis that undergird this work what do we find? We find a sort of radically individualistic Calvinism. What God demands of us is far more than to realize he has plans for our individual lives, plans for good and not for harm. In fact God demands of us a less narcissistic focus on ourselves and our own needs. When we actually examine the use of the phrase "the will of God" in the only two places it appears in Paul's writings (1 Thess 4:3; 5:18) it has to do with the mandates to maintain a holy life and to take up and practice regularly the three major forms of prayer (adoration, intercession, thanksgiving). It has little to do with finding some more particular purpose or calling in one's life when it comes to our tasks in life or our occupation.

Take another example. The megamillion-selling *Left Behind* series of LaHaye and Jenkins in some respects falls at the other end of the spectrum from Warren's work in regard to its eschatology. Unfortunately, one has to ask, what sort of future eschatology is being served up? The answer is a Dispensationalism that is miles away from the intent of Jesus, Paul, and John of Patmos when it comes to understanding and using biblical prophecy, and in particular apocalyptic prophecy. Even worse, these novels promulgate a sort of American Zionism, by which I mean a belief that Americans, or at least believing Americans, have become God's chosen people in a special sense that gives them a special role to play in matters eschatological, ignoring entirely that our primary theological DNA is to be found in our pan-national, Christian identity rather than our national identity.

But alas for Dispensationalists, the truth is that America and its modern capitalistic concerns about oil, our standard of living, Islamic terrorists, and the like are nowhere to be found in the Bible. Indeed, America and Islamic terrorists were not even on the edge of the imagination of the biblical writers.[1] This whole approach to prophecy ignores the most important principle of interpretation that the Reformers insisted on—namely, sticking with the plain, originally intended, sense of the text.

Hermeneutical principle number one is this: what the text could not have possibly meant to the original inspired biblical author, it cannot possibly mean today. For example, John of Patmos was addressing first-century churches in Asia Minor at the end of the first century A.D. *in terms they could understand.* I must insist that what it meant then is still what it means today; that is the very nature of treating the Bible's authors with the respect they deserve and letting them have their say in their own words, rather than trying to put words in their mouths. It is the height of arrogance to assume that only we in the twenty-first century are really in a position to understand these texts, and that two thousand years of interpreters before us were all in the dark.

Last, there is Mel Gibson's *The Passion of the Christ*, embraced with great fervor by Evangelicals across the country. But what happens when one points out how at least one-third of this film is found nowhere in the Bible, and indeed at various points it introduces some unsettling and even unbiblical notions? Why in the world would one draw on the writing of Anne Katherine Emmerich's *The Dolorous Passion of Our Lord Jesus Christ* if one knew that so much of that work is profoundly anti-Semitic? While it is a mercy that little of the anti-Semitic material from that source made it into the movie, we still have the very troubling nonbiblical scene of Jewish children wearing their kepas and turning into demons badgering Judas into hanging himself. What is the Jewish community supposed to think about such scenes, and what are they to think of Evangelicals who so vigorously supported this film? Such scenes are severely problematic, and, for a Protestant whose cry is "sola Scriptura," they should have raised considerable concerns. But it was not Evangelicals, by and large, protesting the unbiblical character of a good deal of this movie.

These three examples illustrate very well the ethos of Evangelicalism at this juncture in regard to the matter of concern for this study, namely how biblical it is. Evangelicalism has lost touch with its Reformation principles and in particular with its necessary rigorous attention to the details of the Bible and the need to stick to the text and heed the cry "sola Scriptura." It is my hope that those who read the following critique will understand what I am concerned about, and will perhaps take up that other cry of the Reformation—"semper reformanda." You may find one aspect or another of the critique too strident, but my hope is you will embrace the underlying and overarching concern about biblical illiteracy. Strange as it sounds, the problem with Evangelical theology at this juncture is that it is not nearly biblical enough.[2] And for a Bible-centered form of Christianity, that is a very dangerous place to be indeed.

CHRISTMAS 2004

PART ONE

AUGUSTINE'S CHILDREN:
THE PROBLEMS WITH REFORMED THEOLOGY

CHAPTER 1

Oh Adam, Where Art Thou?

THE PROBLEM WITH TULIPS — AND OTHER PROTESTANT FLOWERS

Popular Evangelicalism has three main theological tributaries. Each of these three tributaries ultimately goes back to the Bible in one way or another and each has made serious and lasting contributions— the Augustinian-Lutheran-Calvinist juggernaut kept Evangelicalism focused on soteriology or the way of salvation. Dispensationalism renewed our focus on and thinking about the future in eschatological ways. Wesleyanism/Pentecostalism stressed the experiential dimensions of Christian thought and life and the need for holiness of heart and life. However, each of these contributions came at a price—individualism and determinism in the case of the Augustinian heritage; systematic ahistoricism in the case of Dispensational reading of prophecy; and the raising of experience to a norm, sometimes even above the Bible, in the case of Wesleyanism/Pentecostalism. My concern is not just to point out the problems with each of these theological streams, but rather to clean up the streams by passing these theological tributaries through a more purifying and rectifying biblical filter. We will begin with the children of Augustine after a few necessary preliminary remarks.

In Evangelical theology today, it is hard to tell who the players are without a program. Sometimes scholars in the Reformed tradition sound remarkably like John Wesley, and sometimes scholars in the Arminian tradition talk about things like total depravity and "once saved always saved," when they are not busy toying with nonbiblical notions like openness theology.[1] My concern in this portion of the book, however, is with those Evangelicals who deliberately articulate their biblical theology in a way that reflects their deep indebtedness to

Luther or Calvin or both, and to their successors as well (e.g., in the Calvinistic tradition that would include the Hodges, Warfield, Berkhof, Berkower, and the like, to name but a few).

My interest is in the big ideas that serve as building blocks for looking at the biblical text in a certain kind of way and that undergird Evangelical theology in this tradition. My concern is that various of these seminal and interesting ideas are simply not biblical. For example, the idea of "once saved always saved," or the idea that it is impossible for a "saved person," a true Christian, to commit apostasy, is simply not an idea to be found in the NT. More to the point, much in the NT flatly contradicts such an idea.

It must be said from the outset to their eternal credit that scholars who look to Calvin and Luther and their legacy pride themselves on being biblical and giving meticulous attention to the biblical text. This is not a surprise since both Calvin and Luther were formidable exegetes and theologians, and they set examples that many have sought to follow ever since. Calvin did not just write *Institutes*, he did the painstaking work of exegeting inch by inch almost the entire corpus of the canon. Luther as well wrote some remarkable commentaries. These were not armchair theologians, nor those who deliberately ignored exegetical particulars. To be honest and to be fair, they would be ashamed of a good deal of what passes for good theology in some Reformed Evangelical pulpits and pamphlets and books today. Would that they were here to discipline their offsprings' unruly use of their heritage! I do not intend, however, to get bogged down with popular expressions of this theology. My plan is to deal with the problem at its roots—at the level of the underlying exegesis and theological system.

Sometimes with Reformed exegetes, indeed all exegetes, the problem is reading the text outside of its proper original contexts—historical, rhetorical, social, theological, and so on. Proof-texting and what I call the strip-mining of the text are endemic problems with Biblicists who cannot wait to get to the theological or ethical implication or the application pay dirt. Sometimes, of course, the problem is more hermeneutical than it is exegetical, and sometimes it is more presuppositional than it is a matter of careful exposition of texts. Sometimes the problem is a matter of imposing a theological grid on the schema of interpretation and assuming that if text A cannot possibly mean that (since it would be inconsistent with one's prior theological commitments), then text B surely does not mean that either. And sometimes one's theological system is so carefully worked out that one assumes that anything that does not fit the system must be a misinterpretation of the text. But it is perfectly possible to argue consistently and logically about something, but draw the circle of argumentation too narrowly, and so wrongly exclude some of the most important data. I believe the latter is often the case with Reformed exegetes.

Reformed exegetes have a hard time coming to grips with the paradox of a God who is both sovereign and free, and yet somehow so exercises that sovereignty and limits his own freedom that he has made it possible for human beings to have and exercise a measure of freedom as well, including in matters of salvation. They have a hard time understanding that holy love does not involve determinism, however subtle. Indeed love, if it is real love, must be freely given and freely received, for God has chosen to relate to us as persons, not as automata. They have a hard time dealing with the idea that God programmed into the system a certain amount of indeterminacy, risk, and freedom. And maybe, just maybe the good old Evangelical lust for certainty leads us all to too quickly fill in gaps and silences of Scripture, driving us to bad exegesis.

There are in fact profound exegetical problems with the T.U.L.I.P. theology of Calvinism and to a lesser extent of Lutheranism. These theological ideas are linked, and, with the exception of the "T" and the "L," are necessary corollaries of each other. For example, if one believes that God has predetermined from before the foundation of the world people to be saved, then of course election is unconditional, grace is irresistible, and perseverance is inevitable. These three linked ideas do not necessarily require the notion of total depravity or limited atonement (e.g., God could have predetermined to save everyone, and original sin might not have had as extensive an effect as sometimes thought).

There is then a logical consistency to this cluster of linked ideas, and it is the logic and coherency that seem to make it compelling, rather than its real exegetical viability. And of course the danger of any such necessary linking of ideas is that if one link in the chain is dropped off then the chain ceases to hold. For example, if it can be demonstrated that apostasy from the true faith is not merely possible but is an idea that Christians are regularly warned against in the NT, then there is something wrong not only with the notion of perseverance but also with the ideas of irresistible grace and predetermination. But there is more. The hermeneutic that seeks to see salvation history as various administrations of just one covenant and continues to seek to see Christians as under various parts of old covenants which have been renewed in the new covenant is severely problematic, especially in light of Paul's remarks about the Mosaic covenant being obsolescent. The older covenants do not determine the character of the new one, as it turns out. In fact the older ones are read in light of the new and final one. There is an indirect critique here not only of Reformed biblical theology but also its child—certain forms of canonical criticism.

Lest this criticism seem one-sided I would stress there is a similar kind of problem with Dispensationalism. If one takes the rapture out of the system, then the rest of the eschatological schema falls to the ground as well. There will not be two second comings, there are not two fulfillments of final prophecy—one in Israel and one in the church—there are not two peoples of God, and so on. The Dispensational hermeneutic applied to the OT is in fact denied in the NT, where all the promises of God are yea and amen in Jesus Christ.

Once more, there is a similar sort of problem with Wesleyan and Pentecostal theology. The theology of prevenient grace, not well tethered to sound exegesis, is allowed to vitiate the concept of being a slave or addicted to or in bondage to sin. This idea then is linked with "free will" or a kind of voluntarism that is not found in the NT. It makes salvation more of a self-help program rather than a radical rescue mission. And then there is the problem with the theology of subsequence, whether it takes the form of "the baptism of the Holy Spirit" or "perfection." Such ideas on the one hand suggest that conversion is inadequate to save a person and on the other hand, that it is possible to divide Christians into two major categories—Christians and super-Christians. But no such twofold division of Christians can be found in the NT—the dividing line between weak and strong, immature and mature Christians has to do with progressive sanctification and growth in Christ. It is apparently not linked to a second-blessing theology, though the NT does not rule out the idea of crisis experiences subsequent to conversion. The point I am making is just this—all these Evangelical theological systems *in their distinctives* are only loosely tethered to detailed exegesis of particular texts.

My modus operandi in this chapter will be to deal with some of the key texts of the Reformation, showing the problems with the traditional Reformed exegesis of the materials. Romans more than any other source has determined Evangelical exegesis when it comes to the nature of salvation. It is time then to dive into the deep water of Romans, all the while seeking to keep our heads above water and our eyes on the safe parameters of the pool.

BACK TO REFORM SCHOOL—SHOULD OUR TEACHERS BE AUGUSTINE AND LUTHER?

Adam was the beginning of it all in more ways than one. For Reformed theology, Adam is a crucial starting point because particular notions about the fall, total depravity of humanity because of the fall, loss of any sort of free will, and general human lostness are bound up in this story. The "T" in T.U.L.I.P. is all about certain kinds of conceptions about Adam and his legacy to us all. But the story of Adam in Genesis 1–3 is not simply read by itself in Reformed theology, it is read through the eyes of Paul (particularly in light of texts like Rom 5 and 1 Cor 15), and furthermore, it is read through the eyes of Augustine as he viewed those Pauline texts. We must keep all this in mind as we focus on the most crucial Adamic texts in Romans.

There is no text more commented on in the entire Bible than Romans, and within the text of Romans, there is no text more commented on than Romans 7. One would think with all the ink spilt on this text that we could get it right. Yet there are almost as many views of this text as there are major commentaries and dissertations on it. Oddly enough, one of the most fundamental problems in Evangelical exegesis of Romans is the failure to read Romans cumulatively, rather than sound-byting it. This failure manifests itself when Romans 7 is read as if it has little or no connection with Romans 5. But the story told in Romans 5:12–20 is the very story that underlies and undergirds Romans 7, as we shall see. In order to set up the discussion, it is necessary to speak briefly about Augustine's views on Romans 5–7 and their influence on Luther and others.

T. J. Deidun aptly summarizes the key points of Augustine's mature interpretation of Romans, and we turn to this in a moment, but first we need to bear in mind that his interpretation immediately had enormous weight in the West and was to be, in effect, canonized for the Roman Catholic tradition at the Council of Carthage in A.D. 418 and of Orange in A.D. 529.[2] It was to be canonized, so to speak, for the Protestant line of interpretation by Luther and Calvin. It must be stressed that Augustine's interpretation of Romans, and especially Romans 7, seems to be in various regards an overreaction to Pelagius who argued that sin comes from human beings' free imitation of Adam, and can be overcome by imitating Christ. Pelagius also suggested that justification, at least final justification, is through determined moral action.

Consider now Deidun's summary of Augustine's main points on Romans:

> 1) The "works of the Law" which Paul says can never justify, mean moral actions in general without the grace of Christ, not Jewish practices as Pelagius and others maintained. 2) The "righteousness of God" is not an attribute of God but the gift he confers in making people righteous; 3) Romans 5:12 now became the key text for Augustine's doctrine of original sin: all individuals (infants included) were co-involved in Adam's sin. As is well known, Augustine's exegesis of this verse largely depended on the Latin translation *in quo* ("in whom") of the Greek *eph hoi* ("in that," "because") and on the omission in his manuscripts of the second mention of "death," with the result that "sin" became the subject of "spread": sin spread to all (by "generation," not by "imitation").[3] 4) Romans 7:14–25, which before the controversy Augustine had under-

stood to be referring to humanity without Christ, he now applied to the Christian to deprive Pelagius of the opportunity of applying the positive elements in the passage (esp. v. 22) to unredeemed humanity. To do this, Augustine was obliged to water down Paul's negative statements: the apostle is describing not the bondage of sin but the bother of concupiscence; and he laments not that he cannot do good (*facere*) but that he cannot do it perfectly (*perficere*). 5) During this period Augustine came to express more boldly his teaching on predestination. It does not depend on God's advance knowledge of people's merit as Pelagius and others maintained in their interpretation of Romans 9:10ff. nor even on his advance knowledge of "the merit of faith" as Augustine had supposed in 394 in his remarks on the same passage: it depends rather on God's "most hidden judgment" whereby he graciously chooses whom he will deliver from the mass of fallen humanity. Everything is pure gift (1 Cor 4:7).[4]

Of course all of these points of Augustine are today under dispute among interpreters of Romans, and some are clearly wrong, such as the conclusions based on the Latin text of Romans 5:12. For our purposes it is interesting to note that Augustine, having changed his mind about Romans 7:14–25 in overreacting to Pelagius, must water down the stress on the bondage of the will expressed in this text in order to apply it to Christians. Luther takes a harder and more consistent line, even though in the end he refers the text to the wrong subject—namely everyone including Christians. It is also noteworthy that Pelagius does not dispute God's destining of persons, only that God does it on the basis of his foreknowledge of the response of believers. It is also important that Augustine talks about God's gift of making people righteous. The later forensic emphasis comes as a result of the translation work of Erasmus.

It is interesting that the discussion of merit which Pelagius introduced into the conversation about Romans resurfaces in the medieval exegetes after Augustine. Paul's doctrine of "justification" is filtered through Aristotelian thinking, so that grace becomes a *donum super additum,* something added on top of God's gift of human faculties (see Aquinas). "Divine *charis* became 'infused grace.'"[5] The nominalist school of William of Occam focused on merit, even in a Pelagian way, and it was to this repristinization of Pelagius's case that Luther, an Augustinian monk much like his founder, was to react in his various lectures and then in his commentary on Romans. But it was not just Pelagius he was reacting to. In due course Luther came to see self-righteousness as the most fundamental of human sins (not concupiscence), and his polemics were directed against both Judaism and Catholicism, which he saw as religions embodying this besetting sin, as well as being preoccupied with "merit." Luther thought that Romans 7:14–25 was about that sin of self-righteousness.

Deidun notes, rightly, that Luther's exploration of what Augustine says about the righteousness of God led him to criticize Augustine for not clearly explaining about the imputation of righteousness. But in fact, as Deidun says, Augustine's "understanding of justification is thoroughly incompatible with the notion of imputation."[6] Luther gets this idea from Erasmus, but he is not afraid to critique Erasmus at other points. For instance, drawing on his understanding of Romans 7:14–25 validating the notion of the Christian as being *simul justus et peccator* ("at the same time justified and sinner"), he argues against Erasmus and other humanists in regard to human freedom of the will. It is also noteworthy that Luther's influential two-kingdom theory (spiritual and temporal) is derived from his exegesis of Romans 13. Christians are subject to earthly powers out of respect and love, but in the spiritual sphere only subject to God, not to human authorities such as the pope. Calvin was to follow Luther's line on justification and predestination, except that he at least more explicitly highlight the notion of double predestination, based on a certain reading of Romans 8:29 (cf. the 1539 edition of Calvin's *Institutes*).

The English Reformation or Revival of the eighteenth century did not produce any great commentaries on Romans, not by Wesley, or Coke, or Fletcher, nor later in the Wesleyan tradition by Clarke, Watson (though he offers much exposition on Romans in his *Institutes*, as a rebuttal to Calvin) or Asbury. This helps explain why the Protestant tradition of interpretation of the nineteenth and twentieth centuries continued to be dominated by Lutheran or Calvinist interpreters. This all too cursory summary shows us the context in which we should read Luther's interpretation of Romans 5–7. The especially crucial notions of the influence of Adam on all humanity in terms of total depravity, the bondage of sin, the necessary predetermining of some of the lost for rescue, the imputation of righteousness come from Luther's reading (and sometimes misreading) of Augustine and his indebtedness to Erasmus. But is this really a cogent reading of Paul, if we view the discussion of Romans without an Augustinian lens?

We are perhaps by this time all too familiar with Luther's own wrestling with his Augustinian heritage, especially when it came to the problem of sin, and particularly sin in the life of the believer. But before we too quickly join that wrestling match, leaping into the fray and shouting *simul justus et peccator* as a description of the normal Christian life, it will be well to ask if in fact Romans 7 describes the Christian life at all. My answer will be—on further review no it does not. Christians are not in the bondage to sin as non-Christians may be said to be. But to understand Romans 7, we must hear Paul's explicit telling of Adam's tale in Romans 5 first. Let us attend to the text itself, carefully working through the exegetical particulars.

ROMANS 5 — ADAM'S TALE REVISITED

In a piece of rhetoric like Romans, the effect of the comparison here is rather like a Rembrandt painting; the dark backdrop of Adam's sin serves to highlight the brightness and clarity of God's grace gift. The comparison by contrast also brings to the fore another key point— namely, that those who are in Christ and feeling the effects of the reign of his grace in their lives are no longer in Adam, and do not labor under the reign of sin in the way Paul describes the human condition between Adam and Moses (and beyond until Christ). Thus, by this comparison, Paul has prepared the way for the contrast between the "I" described in Romans 7 and the person in Christ described in Romans 8. The former is laboring under the bondage of sin, while the latter has been set free by the Spirit from that bondage, as we shall see.[7]

Quintilian, the Latin rhetorician, says that comparisons of this sort are to be done on the basis of the character of the two parties (*Inst.* 4.2.99). In this case it is not just the characters of Adam and Christ which are contrasted, but also all those in Adam and all those in Christ. Paul's argument here would likely have been recognized as a sophisticated form of rhetorical comparison that moves from the dark to the light, the lesser to the greater. The psychological dynamics of the technique are that if the listener grants the premise in regard to the example of Adam (namely that his sin affected all humanity), there is a strong pull to grant the conclusion when the comparison is made with Christ. It was important that one conclude the argument on the positive, or "greater" side, which is of course what Paul does with a flourish in Romans 5:21 where the duel between sin and grace, and death and eternal life is won, with grace and life reigning longer and more profoundly in the life of the believer. Consider now a rather literal translation of what Paul says in Romans 5:12–21:

> So it is that through one human being sin entered the world, and through sin, death, and thus death spread to all human beings, because all sinned. For until the Law, sin was in the world, but sin was not reckoned, not being against the Law. But death reigned from Adam to Moses, even upon those who did not sin in the same likeness of the trespass of Adam, who is a type of Coming One.
>
> But not like the trespass is thus also the grace gift. For if through the trespass of the one the many died, how much more the grace of God and the gift in grace of the one human being Jesus Christ abounded to the many. And the gift is not like the sin by the one. For on the one hand the judgment from the one unto condemnation, but on the other hand, the grace gift after many trespasses unto acquitting judgment. For if death reigned because of the trespass of the one through that one, how much

more those receiving the abundance of the grace and the gift[8] of righteousness will reign in life through the one Jesus Christ. So then, as through one trespass unto all humans unto condemnation, thus also through one human being's act of justice/righteous deed unto all humans for the putting right of life. For as through the disobedience of the one human, many were made sinners, thus also through the obedience of the one many were constituted righteous. But the Law intruded in order to increase the trespass. But where the sin increased, the grace superabounded, in order that just as the sin reigned in death, so also the grace reigned through righteousness unto everlasting life through Jesus Christ our Lord.

The logic of argumentation found in Romans 5:12–21 will seem strange to many moderns, for it deals with the concept of how one can affect many, for ill or good, and not only affect them but determine their destiny to a real extent. Paul can say in the midst of such an argument that death spread to all humans because they all sinned, but then turn around and say that death reigned over even those who did not trespass in the same fashion Adam did. Some have drawn an analogy with the notion of federal headship over a group of people (e.g., when the president declares war on another nation, whether the citizens of the United States will it or not, they are affected by this decision and are in effect also at war with the nation in question). This analogy does get at some of the dimensions of Paul's argument. But there is a dimension of corporate personality—or, better said, incorporative personality—to Paul's argument as well.

Paul says that death reigned (because of Adam's trespass) through Adam unto all of his progeny, just as through Christ those receiving grace will reign in life. All those in Adam feel the effect of that incorporation, while all those in Christ experience the very resurrection life of Christ through him. This notion goes well beyond the modern concept of federal headship, and it is not a surprise that this passage became a mainstay in later arguments about original sin and its taint and effect.

It is important to note two more things before looking at the details of each verse in the argument: (1) Adam is viewed as not merely sinning, but disobeying a direct commandment of God. Therefore his sin can be called a trespass or transgression—a willful violation of a known law, which becomes important when we consider Romans 7:7–13. Notice also that Paul nowhere blames Eve for original sin here. (2) Paul is using a form of reasoning involving typology, which he has used previously (cf. for example 1 Cor 10). Adam is said to be a type of Christ, in that his action affects all those who are "in him." This is not the same sort of trope as an allegory, such as we find in Galatians 4. Typology is reasoning by analogy using historical examples, therefore

Paul does not attempt to suggest some aspects of the Adam story are symbolic in some sense. This is a historical form of reasoning, based on Paul's reading of salvation history and its most seminal figures.

Romans 5:12–21 does not stand in isolation but indicates some further conclusions to be drawn from the previous argument in Romans 5:1–11. The *dia touto* of v. 12 must surely refer back to the material in the first eleven verses of this chapter, and should be translated "because of this." In other words, vv. 12ff. take the argument to a further stage, based on what had been said in 5:1–11.[9] Here we are dealing with some of the more difficult material in all of Romans in terms of grammar and interpretation.

This whole section is comparing Adam and his progeny and Christ and those in him. It is not about comparing Adam and all other humans. Notice that the phrase "through him" is in the emphatic position in the first part of the leading sentence, which suggests that Paul is going to tell us in the last part of the sentence what is true through another one. It is not unusual for Paul to start a sentence and then digress, or qualify the sentence, as he does here.[10]

Thus, I take it that Paul's argument here is more difficult than the idea that each person is their own Adam and that because of their individual sins like Adam's, their deaths result.[11] At issue is whether or not Paul subscribed to some sort of notion of original sin being passed down to and/or through the race of humanity.[12] The final clause of v. 12 is heavily debated, especially in regard to how to translate *eph ho*. There are at least six possibilities, but we may boil things down as follows: (1) one of the basic questions is whether we should take these words as a conjunction and translate them "because" or whether we should take the *ho* as a masculine relative pronoun referring either to death or to "one man";[13] (2) ruled out as an antecedent by case ending is *hamartia* (feminine noun), i.e. sin; (3) notice that in 2 Corinthians 5:4 and Philippians 3:12 and 4:10 *eph ho* is used causally—meaning because of something,[14] not "in which" or "to which." Thus I must follow Chrysostom—the Greek words mean "because." Thus the phrase means "because all sinned," and here concrete acts of sin would be in view. Some have argued that what is meant is not our individual sinning, but rather our participation in Adam's sin. On this view not merely do humans imitate Adam's sin, they do so in consequence of Adam's original sin. This view seems closer than some to what Paul is trying to suggest here. Human beings in general sin because Adam has had an influence on them, but in the end they are judged not just because Adam sinned, but because they all sinned willingly as well.

Paul is not suggesting that Adam and Christ are alike in all respects, not even in the way they affect the race that flows forth from them. The point of comparison is simply this: that the act of the one man had far-reaching consequences for all those who came after him and had integral connection with him. In all other respects, and at some length in vv. 13–17 Paul wishes to distinguish Adam and Christ. Thus, it is not necessary to argue that Christ's salvation must pass to or affect everyone in the exact same manner as Adam's sin, for as Paul says, the gift of salvation is in many ways not like the trespass. Paul's "universalism is of the sort that holds to Christ as the way for all."[15]

Paul begins by stating that because of the action of one man, the destiny of the whole race was affected. *Kosmos* probably means "humanity" here, though it could mean "world." Notice that Paul is clear that death enters the world because of sin. It is not viewed as a natural occurrence, at least insofar as humanity is concerned. As 1 Corinthians 15 makes clear, Paul sees death as an enemy, not a friend. Paul is quite clear that death spread to all because of Adam's sin, but it was not as though this negative result was not deserved because all did in fact sin. Thus, while it is true that humans die because of the sin of Adam, it is also true that death is a just outcome in view of the fact that all have sinned. Humans do not die simply because of Adam's sin, but because of Adam's and their own sin.

There can be no question that Paul believed in a historical Adam who affected the whole historical process. It is also possible that like his contemporary, the author of *4 Ezra*, he believed in a seminal transmission of a fallen identity passed from Adam to his offspring (see *4 Ezra* 3:7–22). It is interesting to compare and contrast other early Jewish remarks on the story of Adam. *Jubilees* 3:17–32 blames Adam, Eve, and the serpent equally for sin and death entering the world. By contrast Paul says nothing here about Eve. Sirach 25:24 is even a greater contrast with Romans 5, for it says that Eve was the cause of sin and death entering the world, an opinion also found in *Life of Adam and Eve* 3. Wisdom of Solomon 2:24 blames the devil for death entering the world. The famous remark found in *2 Baruch* 54:19 says "Adam was responsible for himself only; each one of us is his own Adam." By contrast *4 Ezra* 7:48 complains: "O Adam what have you done? For though it was you who sinned, the fall was not yours alone, but ours also who are your descendants."[16]

Romans 5:13 somewhat abruptly introduces the idea of the Law. Paul says until the Law (surely the Mosaic Law), sin was in the world. Sin is almost personified here, as death was in v. 12.[17] Sin was in the world, but it was not reckoned or counted, since there was no Law. Paul cannot mean that God simply ignored sin since he surely knows the story of Noah. Thus what Paul seems to mean is that sin was not reckoned[18] as transgression, for the latter involves a willful violation of a known law. Transgression then, in the case of all of humanity (except

Adam), does not come on the scene until the time of Moses. This explains why it is that death still reigned between Adam and Moses, even over those who had not sinned in the form of transgression, as Adam did. Death as a consequence for sin still held sway even before the Law of Moses, but a different sort of punishment entered the picture with Moses, just as a different view of sin enters the picture with the Mosaic Law.

In v. 14 we hear that Adam is the type of the Coming One.[19] The word *homoiomati* refers to likeness (the mark made by striking or an impression made by something, or the form or pattern of something made by a mold), but the term *tupos* is even more important. A *tupos* refers to something or someone that prefigures something or someone else, in this case someone or something that belongs to the eschatological age. C. E. B. Cranfield says "Adam in his universal effectiveness for ruin is the type which . . . prefigures Christ in his universal effectiveness for salvation."[20] Notice that it is Adam's transgression which makes him that type of Christ. In short it is his one deed which affects all, just as the Christ event affects all. "Paul sees history gathering at nodal points and crystalizing upon outstanding figures . . . who are notable in themselves as individual persons, but even more notable as representative figures. These . . . incorporate the human race, or sections of it, within themselves, and the dealings they have with God they have representatively on behalf of their [people]."[21]

Having initiated the analogy, Paul in v. 15 proceeds to clarify by saying that the trespass is in fact not exactly like the gift of grace. Again we have a "how much more" argument. If the trespass affected many and many died, how much more will the grace of God and the gift that comes through the one man Christ abound to many all that much more. While it is true that *polloi* can be used to mean "all," it may be significant that Paul at this juncture switches to using *polloi* whereas before he had used *pantes*. Paul does *not* wish to convey the notion of automatic universal salvation.[22] While Paul and his coworkers do not have a problem with the idea that Jesus died for the sins of the whole world, not just for the elect (see, e.g., 1 Tim 2:5–6—"for there is one God and one mediator between God and human beings, the man Christ Jesus, who gave himself *a ransom for all persons*"), Paul does not believe that this automatically means all will be saved. There is the little matter of responding in faith to God's work of salvation in Christ and receiving the gift of God's grace. Still it is a crucial Pauline theme as early as Galatians and as late as the Pastorals that God's desire is for all to be saved, and that Christ's atonement is to cover the sins of the world, not just of the elect. We see this most clearly in the Pastorals, and it is worth digressing here just for a moment to make this point clear.

1 Timothy 2:3–4 provides the sort of context in which we should view this matter, namely that God desires that "all people be saved and come to the full knowledge of the truth," a theme we also find in 1 Timothy 4:10 where we hear of "the living God who is the Savior of all people, especially of the faithful." Notice that the limitation comes at the point of those who respond in faith, not at the point of God's desire or will. It is in this context that we must evaluate what is said in Titus 3:5–6 about how this salvation happens "according to his mercy, he saved us through the washing of rebirth and renewal by the Holy Spirit, which is poured out on us in abundance through Jesus Christ, our Savior."[23] The language of election is used in a corporate sense in these letters, and when salvation is spoken of, God's desire for universal salvation is expressed while at the same time making clear that only those are saved who respond in faith to the message of salvation, are reborn, and receive the Holy Spirit.

1 Timothy 2:5 stresses the oneness of God, the basic Jewish claim, and thus multiple mediators to God are ruled out as well. There is said to be only one mediator between God and humankind—the human being Jesus. This has several implications. First of all, a human being is the mediator. He could not represent human beings unless he was one, but equally he could not fully represent God unless he was divine as well. The mediatorship goes in both directions (cf. Job 9:32–33 LXX).[24] A mediator was a person who went between two parties in conflict with each other, seeking to reconcile them. The admission that he is a human being in no way compromises the statement in Titus 2:13 that he is God the Savior. The point is that he is both, and so he is the perfect choice to represent God to human beings and human beings to God. There is one mediator, and thus the one means of salvation and reconciliation between God and humankind. Notice that this reference to Jesus being a mediator immediately leads to a comment on his death, probably drawing on Mark 10:45. Of course Jesus' death was in some ways his most human act.

Here his death is said to be an *antilytron* for all. The word is found only here in the NT, though its cognate *lytron* is used in Mark 10:45 and elsewhere, and Paul uses *apolytron* in much the same sense (Rom 3:24; 8:23; 1 Cor 1:30; Col 1:14).[25] It means either a ransom, and therefore a payment of some sort, or redemption, and thus some sort of deliverance from bondage, perhaps mainly the latter here. It should be noted however that we do have here hints of substitutionary atonement.[26] Christ gave himself on behalf of all. The prefix *anti-* here probably suggests replacement, Christ in the place of all.[27] The accent or emphasis in the Greek here is on the word "all."[28] What is especially interesting about these verses is that our author is relating the oneness of God to the idea of salvation for all, not just for one people or ethnic group. Not only is there only one God for all peoples, that one God desires the salvation of all peoples and all people groups and has sent one mediator to bring about that reality. This is clearly a different sort of theology than that found in some quarters in early Judaism (e.g., at Qumran) which suggested that the one God had one chosen people, and the only way one could be saved would be to be born into or to join that chosen people. Here the theology is a "one for all, and all for one" theology.[29] L. T. Johnson is right to stress: "Nowhere in the New Testament is such an inclusive hope for humanity comparably expressed."[30] What is intimated in Romans is made quite explicit in the Pastorals. The tulip begins to wilt when one reads Romans in light of the Pastorals rather than through the much later lens of Augustine, Luther, and Calvin.

Returning to Romans 5 we find the same principle is stated but with an added factor. Here we learn that judgment followed only one misdeed and resulted in the condemnation of all, whereas the grace gift followed many misdeeds and resulted in a judgment of acquittal and in fact in salvation, potentially for all. In the former case we have an act that followed as punishment for a deed; in the latter case we have an act following God's long patience with many more sins, and it was not an act of condemnation.

Thus, as Paul was trying to say, there is almost no comparison between the trespass and the grace gift. The one trespass led to death reigning through the one misdeed, but how much more did the grace and the gift of being set right by God and acquitted accomplish, for it will result in believers reigning in life through Christ? Paul may be drawing on the old apocalyptic notion of the reign of the saints, possibly in connection with millennial ideas (cf. 1 Cor 15). The important thing to note is that this reigning is envisioned as happening sometime in the future, not in the present. The life Paul is referring to is also something received in the future, and so not at conversion. It is part of the hope previously mentioned.

Romans 5:18 expands the notion a bit further, speaking of the *dikaiosis* of life. Some have translated this as if it were two ways to refer to the same thing (the right standing, i.e., Life), but it is perhaps more likely that Paul is referring to a *dikaiosis* which results in life, or perhaps, if we translate the phrase as "the setting right of life" we can get at the gist of the matter. Adam's act led to the condemnation of all, but Christ's righteous act led to the setting right of life for all. There is a problem with translating *dikaiosis* here as "right standing," because in fact Paul did not believe that Christ's death automatically gave all humans right standing with God apart from a faith response.

It appears then that what Paul has in mind is the fact that Christ's "act of justice" wiped the slate clean, and so life was set right. Humans were then in a position to once again have a right relationship with God, whereas there was not even that potential before Christ died. In this entire context Paul has been discussing the vast superiority of Christ and his effect to that of Adam and his effect on humankind. The condemnation of Adam is reversed in Christ. In Christ, human destiny changed. The emphasis on the effect for and upon all in the case of both Adam and Christ is noteworthy. At the very least this implies that Paul does not believe it was God's intent to send Christ to die for the select few. Christ's act of justice was for the whole human race. This argument here, however, does not state the conditions under which all might receive the benefit of Christ's act.[31] Notice that Paul talks about this blessing as a "gift," and a gift is something which has to be received and unpacked. It is not something that has an automatic effect, and of course it can be rejected.

In v. 19 we hear of the obedience of the one man Christ, and here Paul surely has in mind his obedience unto death on the cross, which made possible the righting of things, as he earlier stated. It was Christ's obedience, earlier in Romans 3 called his faithfulness,[32] which constituted or made many to be set right insofar as their relationship with God is concerned. The verb here does not mean "to reckon," but rather "to make." This is to be contrasted with the disobedience of Adam which "made" many sinners. As J. Fitzmyer rightly says, Adam's act not merely made humans liable to punishment, it constituted them as sinners.[33] The effect of Adam's sin is both relational and personal. The action of one person has drastic effects on many. As P. Achtemeier puts it, those who belong to the race of Adam are under the power and reign of sin. The only way to escape this is to join another race of humanity—those who are in Christ.[34] C. K. Barrett argues "But the words 'sinners' and 'righteous' are words of relationship, not character."[35] But this dichotomy cannot be made between the relational position and condition of a person when Paul chooses to use the verb *made* rather than *reckoned*. Paul believes that Christ's death not only affects the believer's position in relationship to God, but also his condition, as Romans 5:1 makes perfectly clear.

At v. 20 we learn that the Law intruded into the historical process. The verb *intrude* is an interesting choice. Just as Paul has personified sin and death in this discussion, so here he personifies the Law, treating it as an actor on the historical stage, who could intrude into some process.[36] There is a *hina* clause here which could be purpose or result— the Law intruded for the purpose of increasing sin, or more likely the Law intruded with the result that sin increased (cf. Gal 3:19). How so?

There are at least three points to be made: (1) the Law revealed and made evident sin; (2) sin increased in the sense that it became more sinful for sin was turned into trespass—a willful violation of a known law; (3) sin increased in the sense that the Law gave sinful humanity a target. It gave ideas of more things to rebel against or to try and do as acts of rebellion against God. Perhaps then Paul sees the Law as deliberately sent by God to reveal human sin to humanity.[37] The Law could count sin, but it could not counter it.[38] But however much sin increased as a result of the Mosaic Law coming into the historical process, grace abounded even more with the inbreaking of the Christ event into the historical process. So just as sin reigned in death, so grace reigned through righteousness unto eternal life through Jesus Christ.

Here in Romans 5:21 we have a parallel construction. The question is, to what does "righteousness" refer? The debate has been between divine righteousness and human right-standing. But if this is a true parallel construction (which the *hosper* at the beginning of the clause suggests), then righteousness may be an elliptical way to refer to Christ's death. Just as sin reigned through the death that Adam brought into the world, so also grace reigned through the death/act of justice/expression of righteousness that happened through Jesus with the result of life eternal.[39] Paul then would be concluding his rhetorical comparison by comparing the effect of the death Adam brought into the process and the effect of the death Jesus brought into the historical process. The aorist tense of the verb makes very good sense if the referent for righteousness is to Christ's act of justice—his death. It makes far less sense if we take him to be referring to human right-standing with God, which of course had only been established for some by the time Paul wrote.

What does it mean to say sin reigned in death? Perhaps Paul refers to the notion that since we are all going to die, there comes a certain fatalism into human thinking. Sin becomes the attempt to have as much pleasure as one can while alive—to eat, drink, and be merry knowing that death is coming. The hovering cloud of death leads those under it to look for diversions and ways to distract themselves from the inevitable, and also ways to spit into the prevailing wind. Because death is inevitable, sin becomes a live and appealing option. As Ecclesiastes suggests, what is the point of being good if it all ends in death? Thus the finality and reality of death cause sin to reign in human life. Thus, in order to deal with the human sin problem, Christ also had to deal with the death problem. Eternal life had to be on offer if the reign of sin was to be ended. Once again we see what a very negative and highly theological view of death Paul has.

It is interesting that, as Fitzmyer points out, this section and also the next three major sections in Romans all end with a reference to the lordship of Christ. This may be because, as Fitzmyer avers, Paul is stressing throughout this section of the discourse that Christ has established his lordship over the human process, eclipsing the lordship of sin, death, and the Law.[40] The Law, while being holy, just, and good, unfortunately can be death dealing rather than life giving when its recipients are fallen human beings.

C. K. Barrett in reflecting on the human condition outside of Christ says this:

> The ruin of the old creation, as of the old man, Adam, was sin. Sin could never be a private matter, but corrupted the whole race, which consisted of men born out of true relation with God and condemned constantly to worsen their relationship, whether they carelessly ignored it or self-righteously essayed to mend it. Like planets robbed of the centre of their orbit they could not possibly keep a proper course. The more they sought life for themselves, the more they forsook God and plunged into death. Their lot could be changed only by a new creation, from a new beginning.[41]

This is the dark backdrop, or one might say the Rembrandt-like framework, in which one needs to understand Romans 7, but we must realize that there is a series of closely related concepts (sin, death, the Law vs. grace, life) which were introduced once Paul began to tell the story of Adam in Romans 5:12–21. It needs to be seen that Paul will address in Romans 6–7 a series of questions that arise out of his telling of the Adam story as it was compared to the Christ story in Romans 5. The story of Adam and those in Adam, and the story of Christ and those in Christ continue to undergird and underlie the discussion throughout the material leading up to Romans 8. J. D. G. Dunn puts it this way: "Paul's thought is still determined by the Adam/Christ contrast of 5:12–21. The death here spoken of is the death of Adam, and those in Adam and of the Adamic epoch."[42]

In one large argument in four parts encompassing all of Romans 6–7, Paul will discourse on human fallenness in the light of the Christ event. His thought does indeed move from solution to plight. Thus, some of what Paul will say about life outside of Christ he will say looking at things through the eyes of Christ rather than through the lens of the Law. And certainly some of the things Paul is prepared to say in this letter about sin, death, and the Law he would have put differently when he was a Pharisee. His conversion changed his perspective on these matters in various respects. To some extent Paul must forestall some possible false conclusions that one might draw from the previous argument in Romans 5:12–21. This he begins to do in Romans 6:1–14. Our concern however must be with Romans 7:7–25. We turn to the latter text in our next chapter.

Here, however, we must reiterate several crucial points: (1) It appears clear from a close reading of Romans 5 that neither Augustine, nor Luther, nor Calvin understood the trajectory of Paul's argument properly. We can see where that argument is leading in texts like 1 Timothy 2:3–6. Paul is his own best interpreter; (2) the incorporative nature of life in Adam or life in Christ does not in either case alleviate individuals of their own responsibilities for their own sin, nor for the need for their own response to the offer of salvation. As for God's desire, God desires that none should perish or fall short of eternal life.

CHAPTER 2

Squinting at the Pauline "I" Chart

PRELUDE TO A FALL

The degree to which the material in Romans 7 has been influential in western history can hardly be overestimated. It has not only fueled whole schools of thought about Pauline theology, it has informed scientific theories about human psychology. Unfortunately, especially in the latter case what was assumed was that Augustine's interpretation of this text was correct. We have already seen in the previous chapter reasons to doubt the cogency of Augustinian exegesis of Romans 5–7. For our purposes, what is especially crucial about Romans 7:7–25 is that: (1) it is not about the Christian life, but rather is (2) a Christian view of Adam's plight (vv. 7–13) and of the pre-Christian condition in general (vv. 14–25).

This on the one hand means that Augustine and Luther were wrong about the bondage of the will when it comes to Christians (cf. 1 Cor 10:13), but they were right about life in Adam. The person described in Romans 7:14–25, while he knows better, in his preconverted state is not able to do better. This speaks against both voluntarist notions of absolute free will, and perhaps also against the notion of universal, prevenient grace. How can this "I" say that he is unable to will or do the good, unless his will is in some sort of bondage condition? In other words, this text and its interpretation, while crucial to both Augustinian and Arminian theories of anthropology, has been seriously misread by both theological traditions. This calls for a careful walking through of this text one more time, for all of Protestant theology about human fallenness and the nature of life outside and inside the Christian sphere hangs on this text to some degree.

Impersonation, or *prosopopoia*, is a rhetorical technique which falls under the heading of figures of speech and is often used to illustrate or make vivid a piece of deliberative rhetoric (*Inst.* 3.8.49; cf. Theon, *Progymnasta* 8). This rhetorical technique involves the assumption of a role, and sometimes the role would be marked off from its surrounding discourse by a change in tone or inflection or accent or form of delivery, or an introductory formula signaling a change in voice. Sometimes the speech would simply be inserted "without mentioning the speaker at all" (*Inst.* 9.2.37). Unfortunately for us, we did not get to hear Paul's discourse delivered in its original oral setting, as was Paul's intent. It is not surprising then, having only Paul's written words left to us, that many have not picked up the signals that impersonation is happening in Romans 7:7–13 and also for that matter in 7:14–25.[1]

"IMPERSONATING" THE FOUNDING FATHER

Quintilian says impersonation "is sometimes introduced even with controversial themes, which are drawn from history and involve the appearance of definite historical characters as pleaders" (*Inst.* 3.8.52). In this case Adam is the historical figure being impersonated in Romans 7:7–13, and the theme is most certainly controversial and drawn from history. The most important requirement for a speech in character in the form of impersonation is that the speech be fitting, suited to the situation and character of the one speaking. "For a speech that is out of keeping with the man who delivers it is just as faulty as a speech which fails to suit the subject to which it should conform" (3.8.51). This rhetorical technique also involves personification, sometimes of abstract qualities (like fame or virtue, or in Paul's case sin or grace— 9.2.36). Quintilian also informs us that impersonation may take the form of a dialogue or speech, but it can also take the form of a first-person narrative (9.2.37).

Since the important work of W. G. Kummel on Romans 7, it has become a commonplace, perhaps even a majority opinion in some NT circles that the "I" of Romans 7 is not autobiographical.[2] This however still does not tell us what sort of literary or rhetorical use of "I" we do find in Romans 7. As S. Stowers points out, it is also no new opinion that what is going on in Romans 7 is the rhetorical technique known as "impersonation."[3] In fact, this is how some of the earliest Greek commentators on Romans, such as Origen, took this portion of the letter, and later commentators such as Jerome and Rufinus took note of this approach of Origen's.[4] Not only so, Didymus of Alexandria and Nilus of Ancyra also saw Paul using the form of speech in character or impersonation here.[5]

The point to be noted here is that we are talking about church fathers who not only knew Greek well but who understood the use of rhetoric and believed Paul was certainly availing himself of rhetorical devices here.[6] Even more importantly, there is John Chrysostom (*Hom. Rom.* 13), who was very much in touch with the rhetorical nature and the theological substance of Paul's letters. He also does not think that Romans 7 is about Christians, much less about Paul himself as a Christian. He takes it to be talking about: (1) those who lived before the Law, and (2) those who lived outside the Law or lived under it. In other words, it is about Gentiles and Jews outside of Christ. But I would want to stress that since the vast majority of Paul's audience is Gentile, and Paul has as part of his rhetorical aims effecting some reconciliation between Jewish and Gentile Christians in Rome,[7] it would be singularly inept for Paul here to retell the story of Israel in a negative way, and then turn around in Romans 9–11 and try and get Gentiles to appreciate their Jewish heritage in Christ, and to be understanding of Jews and their fellow Jewish Christians. No, Paul tells a more universal tale here of the progenitor of all humankind, and then the story of all those "in Adam," not focusing specifically on those "in Israel" that are within the Adamic category.[8] Even in Romans 7:14–25, Paul can be seen to be mainly echoing his discussion of Gentiles in Romans 2:15, who had the "Law" within and struggled over its demands.[9]

But who is the "I" then who is speaking here? In my view the I is Adam in vv. 7–13, and all those who are currently "in Adam" in vv. 14–25. Adam, it will be remembered, is the last historical figure Paul introduced into his discourse at Romans 5:12, and we have contended that the story of Adam undergirds a good deal of the discussion from Romans 5:12 through Romans 7. Suffice it to say here that the old traditional interpretations that Paul was describing his own pre-Christian experience, or alternately the experience of Christians more generally in this text, fail to grasp the rhetorical finesse and character of this material, and must be deemed very unlikely not only for that reason, but for others we will discuss in due course.[10]

Listen to a rather literal translation of this material in Romans 7:7–13:

> What then shall we say? Is the Law sin? Absolutely not! But I didn't know sin except through the Law, for I should not have known desire except the Law said: "You shall not desire/covet." But sin taking opportunity through the commandment produced in me all sorts of desires, for without the Law sin is dead. But I was living without the Law once. But with the coming of the commandment, sin was awakened/lived anew. But I myself died, and the commandment which was unto life turned out for me unto death. For sin taking opportunity through the commandment deceived me and killed me through it. So the Law is holy, and the commandment holy and just and good. Did then the good become to me

death? Let it not happen! But sin, in order to reveal itself as sin, through that which was good produced in me death, in order that sin might become exceedingly sinful through the commandment.[11]

Three things are crucial if one is to understand this text. First of all, Paul believes that Moses wrote the Pentateuch, including Genesis; (2) the "law" in Moses' books includes more than the Law given to Moses and with the Mosaic covenant. It would include the first commandment given to Adam and Eve.[12] (3) It appears that Paul saw the "original sin" of coveting the fruit of the prohibited tree as a form of violation of the tenth commandment (cf. *Apoc. Mos.* 19:3). It is also crucial to bear in mind that Paul has already stated flatly in Romans 7:5–6 that Christians before their conversion were controlled by sinful inclinations but now are no longer in that condition, having been released from the Law, dying to what once bound them, and now serving in the new way of the Spirit. It is life in the Spirit and freedom from the Mosaic Law which characterizes the Christian, as Romans 8:1–2 will also stress. What is most notable about Romans 7:7–25 is that the person or persons who speak nowhere mention the Spirit and seem to have no access whatsoever to the power of the Holy Spirit.

I would suggest an expansive rendering of vv. 8–11 that takes into account the Adamic story which is being retold here as follows:

> But the serpent [Sin], seizing an opportunity in the commandment, produced in me all sorts of covetousness. . . . But I [Adam] was once alive apart from the Law, but when the commandment came, Sin sprang to life and I died, and the very commandment that promised life proved deadly to me. For Sin [the serpent] seizing an opportunity through the commandment, deceived me and through it killed me.

Here indeed we have the familiar primeval tale of human life which began before the existence of the Law, and apart from sin, but then the commandment entered, followed by deception, disobedience, and eventually death. We must consider the particulars of the text at this juncture.

First of all, those who claim that there is no signal in the text that we are going into impersonation at Romans 7:7 are simply wrong.[13] As Stowers points out:

> The section begins in v. 7 with an abrupt change in voice following a rhetorical question, that serves as a transition from Paul's authorial voice, which has previously addressed the readers explicitly . . . in 6:1–7:6. This constitutes what the grammarians and rhetoricians described as change of voice (*enallge* or *metabole*). These ancient readers would next look for *diaphonia*, a difference in characterization from the

authorial voice. The speaker in 7:7–25 speaks with great personal pathos of coming under the Law at some point, learning about desire and sin, and being unable to do what he wants to do because of enslavement to sin or flesh.[14]

It is indeed crucial to see what we have here as not only a continuation of Paul's discussion of the Law, but a vivid retelling of the fall in such a manner that he shows that there was a problem with commandments and the Law from the very beginning of the human story. Paul has transitioned from talking about what Christians once were in 7:5–6 before they came to Christ,[15] to talking about why they were that way and why the Law had that effect on them before they became Christians, namely because of the sin of Adam. This is the outworking of and building upon what Paul says when he compares and contrasts the story of Adam and Christ in Romans 5:12–21.

Furthermore, there is a good reason to not simply lump vv. 7–13 together with vv. 14–25, as some commentators still do. In vv. 7–13 we have only past tenses of the verbs, while in vv. 14–25 we have present tenses. Either Paul is somewhat changing the subject in vv. 14–25 from vv. 7–13, or he is changing the time frame in which he is viewing the one subject. Here it will be worthwhile to consider the issue of the "I" as it has been viewed by various commentators who do not really take into account Paul's use of rhetoric and rhetorical devices, nor note the Adamic narrative subtext to Paul's discourse here.

THE PAULINE "I" CHART

Vv. 7–13	Vv. 14–25
1. the "I" is strictly autobiographical	1. the "I" is autobiographical, referring to Paul's current Christian experience
2. the "I" reflects Paul's view of a typical Jewish individual	2. the "I" is autobiographical, referring to Paul's pre-Christian experience, as he viewed it
3. the "I" reflects the experience of Jews as a whole	3. same as #2 only it is as he views his Jewish experience now
4. the "I" reflects humanity as a whole	4. the "I" presents the experience of the non-Christian Jew as seen by himself
5. the "I" is a way of speaking in general, without having a particular group of persons in mind	5. the "I" presents how Christians view Jews
	6. the "I" reflects the so-called "carnal" Christian

7. the "I" reflects the experience of Christians in general
8. the "I" reflects a person under conviction of sin, and at the point of conversion (thus Rom 7:14–25, provides a sort of narrative of a conversion)

There is no consensus of opinion whatsoever among scholars who do not take into account the rhetorical signals in the text, and who do not recognize the echoes and allusions to the story of Adam in vv. 7–13. Sometimes, too, we have combinations of some of these views. E. Käsemann argues that 7:14–20 reflects the pious Jew, while 7:21–25 reflects all fallen humanity.[16] The very fact that there are so many varied conjectures about these texts counts against any of them being very likely.

The fact that many commentators through the years have thought Paul was describing Christian experience, including his own, we owe in large measure to the enormous influence of Augustine, including his influence especially on Luther, and those who have followed in Luther's exegetical footsteps. P. Gorday says: "This entire section of Romans 7:14–25 is absolutely omnipresent in Augustine's work, and is linked with every other passage in the epistle where the concern is to reinforce the complex interplay of grace and law that Augustine saw in Romans."[17] Furthering the impact of this view is that Augustine shared his opinions on this text in his most influential work, his *Confessions*, as well as in later works relating the text to his own experience.[18]

Various important later expositors, such as Luther, resonated with this approach. This fact, however, does not constitute any sort of proof that this was what Paul had in mind when he wrote Romans 7. It probably says more about Augustine and Luther than it does about a rhetorically adept first-century Jewish Christian like Paul, who, K. Stendahl was later to aptly say, does not much seem to reflect the introspective consciousness of the West.[19] Paul hardly ever talks about his own personal guilt feelings or repentance, and when he does so, it is a discussion of his pre-Christian period when he persecuted Christians, not about any internal moral conflict he struggled with as a Christian.[20]

What are the markers or indicators in the text of Romans 7:7–13 that the most probable way to read this text, the way Paul desired for it to be heard, is in the light of the story of Adam, with Adam speaking of his own experience?[21] Firstly, from the beginning of the passage in v. 7 there is reference to one specific commandment: "thou shalt not covet/desire." This is the tenth commandment in an abbreviated form (cf. Exod 20:17; Deut 5:21). Some early Jewish exegeses of Genesis 3 suggested that the sin committed by Adam and Eve was a violation of the tenth commandment.[22] They coveted the fruit of the tree of the knowledge of good and evil.

Second, one must ask oneself, who in biblical history was only under one commandment, and one about coveting? The answer is Adam.[23] Romans 7:8 refers to a commandment (singular). This can hardly be a reference to the Mosaic Law in general, which Paul regularly speaks of as a collective entity. Third, v. 9 says "I was living once without/apart from the Law." The only person said in the Bible to be living before or without any law was Adam. The attempt to refer this to a person being before the time of their bar mitzvah, when they take the yoke of the Law upon themselves at twelve to thirteen years of age, while not impossible, seems unlikely. Even a Jewish child who had not yet personally embraced the call to be a "son of the commandments" was still expected to obey the Mosaic Law, including honoring parents and God (cf. Luke 2:41–52).

Fourth, as numerous commentators have regularly noticed, sin is personified in this text, especially in v. 11, as if it were like the snake in the garden. Paul says "Sin took opportunity through the commandment to deceive me." This matches up well with the story about the snake using the commandment to deceive Eve and Adam in the garden. Notice too how the very same verb is used to speak of this deception in 2 Corinthians 11:3 and also 1 Timothy 2:14. We know, of course, that physical death was said to be part of the punishment for this sin, but there was also the matter of spiritual death, due to alienation from God, and it is perhaps the latter that Paul has in view in this text.

Fifth, notice how in v. 7 Paul says, "I did not know sin except through the commandment." This condition would only properly be the case with Adam, especially if "know" in this text means having personal experience of sin (cf. v. 5).[24] As we know from various earlier texts in Romans, Paul believes that all after Adam have sinned and fallen short of God's glory. The discussion in Romans 5:12–21 seems to be presupposed here. It is however possible to take *egnon* to mean "recognize"—I did not recognize sin for what it was except through the existence of the commandment. If this is the point, then it comports with what Paul has already said about the Law turning sin into trespass, sin being revealed as a violation of God's will for humankind. But on the whole it seems more likely that Paul is describing Adam's awakening consciousness of the possibility of sin when the first commandment was given. All in all, the most satisfactory explanation of these verses is if we see Paul the Christian rereading the story of Adam here, in the light of his Christian views about law and the Law.[25]

Certainly one of the functions of this subsection of Romans is to offer something of an apologia for the Law. Paul is asking: Is then the

Law something evil because it not only reveals sin, but has the unintended effect of suggesting sins to commit to a human being? Is the Law's association with sin and death then a sign that the Law itself is a sinful or wicked thing? Paul's response is of course "absolutely not!" Verse 7 suggests a parallel between *egnon* and "know desire," which suggests Paul has in view the experience of sin by this knower. Verse 8 says sin takes the Law as the starting point or opportunity to produce in the knower all sorts of evil desires.[26]

The story of Adam comes to the fore here. The basic argument is how sin used a good thing, the Law, to create evil desires in Adam. It is important to recognize that in Romans 5–6 Paul had already established that all humans are "in Adam," and all have sinned like him. Furthermore, Paul has spoken of the desires that plagued his largely Gentile audience prior to their conversions. The discussion then just further links even the Gentile portion of the audience to Adam and his experience. They are to recognize themselves in this story, as the children of Adam who also have had desires, have sinned, and have died. The way Paul illuminates the parallels is seen in Romans 7:14–25, which I take to be a description of all those in Adam and outside of Christ.[27]

Paul then is providing a narrative in Romans 7:7–25 of the story of Adam from the past in vv. 7–13, and the story of all those in Adam in the present in vv. 14–25. In a sense, what is happening here is an expansion on what Paul has already argued in Romans 5:12–21. There is a continuity in the "I" in Romans 7 by virtue of the close link between Adam and all those in Adam. The story of Adam is also the prototype of the story of Christ, and it is only when the person is delivered from the body of death, only when a person transfers from the story of Adam into the story of Christ, that one can leave Adam and his story behind, no longer being in bondage to sin, and being empowered to resist temptation and walk in newness of life, as is described in Romans 8. Christ starts the race of humanity over again, setting it right and in a new direction, delivering it from the bondage of sin, death, and the Law. It is not a surprise that Christ only enters the picture at the very end of the argument in Romans 7, in preparation for Romans 8, using the rhetorical technique of overlapping the end of one argument with the beginning of another.[28]

Some have seen Romans 7:9b as a problem for the Adamic view of vv. 7–13 because the verb must be translated "renewed" or "live anew." But notice the contrast between "I was living" in v. 9a with "but Sin coming to life" in v. 9b. Cranfield then is right to urge that the meaning of the verb in question in v. 9b must be "sprang to life."[29] The snake/Sin was lifeless until it had an opportunity to victimize some innocent one, and had the means, namely the commandment, to do so. Sin deceived and spiritually killed the first founder of the human race.

This is nearly a quotation from Genesis 3:13. One of the important corollaries of recognizing that Romans 7:7–13 is about Adam (and 7:14–25 is about those in Adam, and outside Christ), is that it becomes clear that Paul is not specifically critiquing Judaism or Jews here, any more than he is in Romans 7:14–25.[30]

Verse 12 begins with *hoste*, which should be translated "so then," introducing Paul's conclusion about the Law that Paul has been driving toward. The commandment, and for that matter the whole Law, is holy, just, and good. It did not in itself produce sin or death in the founder of the human race. Rather Sin/the serpent/Satan used the commandment to that end. Good things, things from God, can be used for evil purposes by those with evil intent. The exceeding sinfulness of sin is revealed in that it will even use a good thing to produce an evil end: death.[31] This was not the intended end or purpose of the Law. The death of Adam was not a matter of his being killed with kindness or by something good. Verse 13 is emphatic. The Law, a good thing, did not kill Adam. But sin was indeed revealed to be sin by the Law, and it produced death. This argument prepares the way for the discussion of the legacy of Adam for those who are outside of Christ. The present-tense verbs reflect the ongoing legacy for those who are still in Adam and not in Christ. Romans 7:14–25 should not be seen as a further argument, but as the last stage of a four-part argument which began in Romans 6, being grounded in Romans 5:12–21, and will climax Paul's discussion about sin, death, and the Law and their various effects on humankind.

THE DELIVERANCE OF THE WRETCHED ONE

Perhaps the largest problem some have with seeing Romans 7:14–25 as referring to the non-Christian life is Romans 7:25a. But in fact Paul is following a well-known rhetorical technique at that point. By an especially adept rhetorical move, before concluding the argument of Romans 6–7, Paul will introduce an interjection by Paul himself (answering the cry of the lost "I") praising Christ as the deliverer from the bondage to sin. Verse 25a introduces the following argument in Romans 8 about life in Christ, about which Paul will speak in the authorial voice, and then the previous argument is concluded in v. 25b.[32]

In *Institutio Oratoria* 9.4.129–30 Quintilian explains the use of the overlap or chain-link technique when moving from one argument or "proof" to the next. Quintilian says this sort of A, B, A, B structure, which he calls a rhythmical structure, is effective when one has to speak with force, energy, and pugnacity (i.e. with pathos), and he reminds that when one is recounting history or narrative this "does not so much demand full-rounded rhythms as a certain continuity of motion and connexion of style. . . . We may compare its motion to that of men, who link hands to steady their steps, and lend each other their mutual support" (9.4.129). So then, there is the passing of the baton. Failure to recognize this rhetorical way of introducing the next argument before concluding the previous one has helped lead to the incorrect conclusion that Paul is speaking about Christians in Romans 7:14–25, a mistake various early Greek fathers who knew rhetoric did not make.[33] Having been forewarned, there is no reason for us to make this mistake either. Consider now the translation of 7:14–25:

> For we know that the Law is spiritual. But I am fleshly, sold under sin. For, I do not understand what I do. For I do not practice what I want, but I do what I hate. But if I do not do what I want, I agree that the Law is good. But now it is no longer I myself who does it, but the sin which dwells within me. For I know that nothing good dwells in me, that is in my flesh. For to will is present to me, but to do the good is not. For the willing to do good is not there, but the evil I do not will, this I practice/commit. But if I do not wish to do this, and nevertheless I do it, then it is sin dwelling in me. For I find then it to be the rule/law with my willing to do the good, that the evil is ready to hand for me. For I rejoice in the Law of God in my inner self. But I see another law in my members at war with the law of my mind and making me captive in the rule of sin which is in my members. I am a miserable human being. Who will deliver me from the body of this death? Grace/thanks to God through our Lord Jesus Christ. So then I myself while on the one hand with mind I am a slave to the Law of God, but on the other hand the flesh [is a slave] to the rule/law of sin.

There is an ever-growing body of opinion, led by the reassessment of early Judaism offered by E. P. Sanders and his disciples, that Paul could not possibly be describing the experience of the Jew as the Jew himself would have described it. If we take for example Psalm 119 as any sort of transcript of Jewish experience of the Law, they delighted in it, and saw the wrestling with the Law and striving to keep its commandments as a joy, even if it was always a work in progress. Nor will it do to suggest that this is how at least a very rigorous Pharisaic Jew, like Paul, would have described his experience under the Law, for in fact Paul tells us in Philippians 3:6 that in regard to righteousness in the Law, Paul was blameless. As Stendahl says, the evidence is that Paul had a quite robust conscience as a Pharisaic Jew.[34] Romans 7:14–25 does not describe that experience.

Now of course it is true that Philippians 3:6 does not say that Paul was sinless. This is an important point. Paul is not claiming there that he was a perfect person. He is simply saying that according to the standard of righteous behavior the Law required, no one could fault him for being a lawbreaker.[35] Blameless before the Law and sinless are most certainly two different things. Galatians 1:14 only further supports this reading, for in that text Paul says he was making good progress in his faith, and he was very zealous and excited about keeping the traditions of his ancestors. Furthermore, as we have said, as a Christian Paul also manifests a robust conscience, not a sin-laden one, if the subject is what he has done since he became a Christian. His anxieties are about and for his fellow Christians, not about his own spiritual state.

This becomes especially clear in Romans 9 when Paul says that he could wish himself cut off from Christ if it would produce a turning to Christ by many of his fellow Jews! In fact, one would be hard-pressed to find many *mea culpas* of any kind in any of Paul's letters when he is describing his experience as a Christian, much less evidence that he saw himself as burdened by the body of death and the bondage to sin. If Paul when a Jew did not feel like the person described in Romans 7:14–25, is there any good reason to suppose other devout Jews like Paul felt this way? It is time to stop reading Romans 7:14–25 through the lens of Augustine and Luther, not least because it keeps fueling skewed views of both early and modern Judaism, which in turn fuels anti-Semitism.

Instead, we have here a Christian analysis of the general malaise of fallen humanity when it comes to sin, death, and Law; and the truth is that only when someone comes to the point of being convicted, convinced, and converted is it likely for fallen persons to see themselves as here described. In other words, we need to take seriously that Paul here is describing a crisis experience that leads to a crying out for help. He is not speaking of the day-to-day mind-set of the fallen person, whether devout or not, and whether Gentile or Jew. What we have then in Romans 7:14–25 and continuing into the next argument in Romans 8 is a narrative of a conversion and its theological and spiritual implications seen after the fact and from a Christian perspective.

Paul begins Romans 7:14 with his familiar "for we know" formula, a rhetorical technique in which he tries to include the audience as being "in the know," even if they have not yet quite seen it that way. It may mean "for as we all ought to know." The phrase does signal what is or ought to be common knowledge among Christians (see Rom 8:22; 2 Cor 5:1). In this verse we have a straightforward contrast: the Law is spiritual, but this person is in some respect fleshly, sold under sin. It is very difficult not to relate this to Romans 7:5–6 where it was said that there is a group of persons who were in the flesh, but are no more. Even more directly in Romans 8:9, Paul says to Christians, "you are not in the flesh." This builds upon Romans 8:2 where it says that the law of the Spirit of life (clearly not the Mosaic Law) has freed you from the law of sin and death. The verb "freed" there is in the aorist, speaking about a particular event in the past of the Christian. That is the very event Paul is describing in Romans 7:14–25—the event of conversion where freedom from bondage to sin happens. It will be noted that the person in question in Romans 7:14–25 is not as bad as he might be.

Paul has picked up the narrative of a surprising conversion after it was already the case that the person in question both knows the Law is good, and in his mind wants to be obedient to it. This is rather different than the general description of Gentile life in Romans 1:18–32. There the knowledge of God and his will is being rejected or ignored. Here it is being acknowledged, but the striving to conform is failing because of the other "law" in one's members, the ruling passions of the flesh. The person in Romans 7:14–25 is in a moral dilemma, for he recognizes the goodness of the Law and wants to obey it, but his fallen nature leads him to do what his mind condemns. He is then a person with a guilty conscience.[36]

It is Paul's view, as Romans 8 will show, that the Christian is in some ways like pre-fallen Adam. He is not immune to sin, and he may be inclined to sin on various occasions, but it is not inevitable that he do so. Like Adam before the fall, the Christian believer is *posse peccare* and *posse non peccare* (able to sin, able not to sin) by the grace of God, as for instance the discussion of temptation in 1 Corinthians 10:11–13 shows. But the fallen person is *non posse non peccare* (not able not to sin). This latter is what is described here in Romans 7:14–25. The theology of *simul justus et peccator* promulgated by Luther amounts to a very inadequate view of Paul's understanding of grace in the believer's life, and the power by that grace the believer has to resist temptation, having been set free from the rule or bondage of sin and death. In other words, *simul justus et peccator* ignores Paul's understanding of sanctification, which while not a counsel of sinless perfection,[37] is nonetheless an assertion about the ability to resist temptation and have victory over sin. While the danger of sin remains for the believer, it no longer reigns. There is no longer the bondage of the will, which is indeed described in Romans 7:14–25.

As v. 16 makes clear, the person in question agrees that the Law is good; he just does not do what he wills to do. There seems to be a power outage. Philosophers may want to debate what it means to say that a person wills one thing, but does another. Surely the willing is the starting point or agency through which doing happens. But if one is a deeply conflicted person, or in the thrall of strong passions to do something else, then that is another matter.

What Paul seems to mean is that this person with his mind wants to do one thing, but there is another force at work in his personality which actually controls his willing and doing. Paul is not talking about the Christian who tries hard, but whose deeds do not match up with his intentions. The point here is not the falling short or imperfection even of Christian good deeds, but the exceeding sinfulness of sinful deeds. Romans 7:17 makes evident that Paul is talking about the person who has indwelling sin such that the person is a slave to sin or his passions. Verse 18 says no good dwells in my flesh, and we must compare the closely similar phrase in Romans 7:6. This person intends to do good, but is simply unable to carry out such an intention.

Is v. 20 an attempt to exculpate the individual in question, since he cannot help himself, being in the bondage to sin? Probably not, as Paul's point is the bondage of the will, not the excuse making or excusability of the sinner's behavior. Barrett puts it this way: "Evil behavior is caused by sin, a personal power residing in and dominating the flesh."[38] The language here is strong, bordering on a concept of being possessed. But Paul says nothing of demons here, only of sin and its power over fallen human beings.

S. R. Llewelyn thinks that slavery is the controlling metaphor for Paul in this passage, and that Paul is drawing an analogy with the experience of the slave, whose mind may be free to think one way, but whose body is enslaved to obey his master.[39] Seneca, a contemporary of Paul, and Stoic philosopher, puts the matter this way:

> It is an error to think that slavery penetrates to the whole person. The better part is excluded: the body is subject to and at the disposition of its master; the mind however, is its own master and is so free and able to move that it cannot even be restrained by this prison, in which it is confined, from following its own impulse, setting in motion great ideas and passing over into infinity as a comrade to the gods. And so it is the body that fate surrenders to the master; he buys this, he sells this—the inner part cannot be given by purchase. Whatever issues from this is free." (*Ben.* 3.20)

The inner/outer contrast in Seneca's text is similar to what we find in Romans 7:14–25, especially when we see that the contrast distinguishes between what one thinks and what one does. The person that Paul describes in Romans 7:14–25 is as surely enslaved to sin as the person Seneca describes is enslaved to a human master.[40] Käsemann's theory that the pious Jew is meant in vv. 14–19, is based on understanding *nomos* as a reference exclusively to the Mosaic Law.[41] But if *nomos* could refer to a commandment given before Moses in vv. 6–13, it can have a wider reference here as well, or perhaps better said, Paul believes all persons (whether through the law written on the heart or on the tablets—see Rom 2:15) are under the Law of God. There need be no specific reference to Jews here, and indeed as Stowers shows, Paul seems to have Gentiles in view, in the main.[42] It needs to be borne in mind that the original prohibition to Adam incorporates all humanity under its condemnation, for all humans, in Paul's view, are "in Adam."

At Romans 7:21 Paul seems to use the term *nomos* in a different sense, which is perfectly possible, as Paul is rhetorically adept enough to play on words and use them in slightly different senses in the same context. Thus, it is perfectly possible that here and in 8:2 Paul is indeed speaking of another law (as he says here). I suspect the appropriate translation here is "rule," or less preferably "principle," so that Paul would be saying "I find it to be a rule/principle . . ." and in 8:2 he would be saying "the rule/principle of the Spirit of life has set me free from the rule/principle of sin and death."[43] If this is true, Paul is not really speaking about the Mosaic Law in these verses.

Romans 7:22 gives us some clues as to Paul's anthropology, though the verse should not be overpsychologized. The "I" says he rejoices in the Law of God (the Mosaic Law, or the Adamic commandment is likely in view), in his inner being. What is the "inner person"? Cranfield wishes to equate it with "my mind" mentioned in vv. 23 and 25, and in Romans 12:2.[44] However, at this juncture one needs to compare 2 Corinthians 4:16. Cranfield's bottom line is that the phrase "inner person" means the person as renewed by the Holy Spirit. If that were the case, Paul would necessarily be talking about Christians here. But against this view, if one looks carefully at 2 Corinthians 4:16 it becomes clear that the inner person is not equivalent to the renewed person in Christ. Paul says of the inner person in that text that the inner person is being renewed while the outer person (i.e., the body) is wasting away. Now the inner person must first exist before it can be renewed, and there is nothing to suggest that Paul is talking about something that exists only in Christians. Paul is clear enough that the mind exists before conversion; thus, if there is a parallel between mind and inner self, or an overlap between the two as Paul views it, it does not necessarily imply a mind renewed by the Spirit. Philo, for example, equates the mind with the inner person, without throwing in the notion that it is the enlightened person he has in mind (see *Plant.* 42; *Congr.* 97).

Paul says, of course, in Romans 2 that the Law can be written on the heart/mind of a Gentile nonbeliever.[45] Romans 7:22 thus means no more than that this person rejoices in the Law in their innermost being. It needs to be recognized that Paul does not identify the "flesh" with the "I." Rather, in a limited dualistic way, he distinguishes the "I" and its mind and will on the one hand, and the "flesh" which is associated with misdeeds. It is a mistake to see Paul as arguing for a divided I or a divided Law, or both (as if all the uses of the term *nomos* here must refer to the Law of God).[46]

Käsemann at this juncture wishes to interpret the phrase "law of the mind" as a reference to human conscience,[47] which was certainly referred to earlier in Romans 1–2. This may well be correct, but the law of the mind seems to be paralleled with the Law of God here, which could be a reference to the Mosaic Law as an external authority. In Romans 7:23 *nomos* may mean Law, or again it may simply be as in v. 21 that "I see another rule/principle at work within me. . . ." The person in v. 23 has two principles at work within him at the same juncture: one is of God, and one is not, and war is going on inside this person. The crucial point to note is that at present this person is fighting and losing the battle. He cries out that he is a miserable person, and cries, Who will deliver me from this body of death? This must be contrasted with Romans 8:2 where Paul speaks of freedom from such death in the Christian. It is interesting that even Augustine felt he needed to downplay the idea of the bondage of the will here, reducing it to the problem of concupiscence,[48] when he decided this was referring to Christian life. Cranfield's, like Luther's, attempt to see the Christian as the one experiencing this anguish of the bondage of the will is forced, and does not comport with the context or the rest of the content of these verses.

The language about the wretched person actually has a very close parallel to be found in Epictetus, which again suggests that Paul is arguing in a way that his audience would find intelligible, for the vast majority of them are Gentiles. Epictetus (*Diatr.* 1.3.3–6) says:

> since these two elements were commingled in our begetting, on the one hand the body, which we have in common with the animals, and on the other reason and intelligence, which we have in common with the gods, some of us incline toward the former relationship, which is not blessed by fortune and is mortal, and only a few toward that which is divine and blessed. . . . For what am I? "A miserable paltry man" say they, and "Lo, my wretched paltry flesh." Wretched indeed, but you also have something better than your paltry flesh. Why then abandon that and cling to this?"

For Paul, there is an anthropological tension in both the non-Christian's and the Christian's life (see the inner/outer discussion in 2 Cor 4–5). They differ in that what once was merely an anthropological tension in a fallen person, has become in the Christian an eschatological tension between Spirit and flesh, as Galatians 5 makes apparent. It is thus incorrect to pit eschatological tensions over against anthropological ones, or to read salvation historical tensions of already and not yet too strongly into Paul's anthropological tensions.[49] The tension in the Christian life is not between old person and new person (an anthropological tension), as if one could be both persons at once, and at least part of the self still be in bondage to the old and fallen ways. It is rather between the inner person which is now being renewed, and the outer self or body which is not, and between flesh or sinful inclination and the leading of the Holy Spirit.

Romans 7:25a is most naturally seen as the anticipation of what Paul is going to say in Romans 8. Paul anticipates the deliverance he will discuss in Romans 8 and celebrates it here in advance, as a sort of preview of coming attractions. This is effective rhetoric because he has been dealing with a very heavy and serious matter throughout Romans 5–7, and the audience will need some relief. So Paul here lets them know that relief from the lengthy discussion of the bondage of sin, death, and the Law is coming. This way he keeps his audience from despairing or tuning out.

Romans 7:25b then serves as a return to the theme of Romans 7:14–25, bringing this lengthy argument to closure. Here Paul sums up before turning to the joyful news of Romans 8. Thus like so many of the contrasts in Romans 6–7 which need to be taken seriously, Paul ends with one last contrast: "I myself while with my mind am a slave to God's Law, but with my flesh a slave to the rule of sin." This surely cannot be the same person described in Romans 8:2, unless Paul is guilty of a very schizophrenic view of Christian life. No, Paul has here described those living in the shadow of Adam, knowing something of God's will or Law, but unable by willpower or by the guidance of that Law to free themselves from the bondage of sin and death. His largely Gentile audience would recognize this discussion about enthrallment as not simply a description of what the life of a Jew might be like apart from Christ,[50] but what the life of any creature of God, including Gentiles and Jews, is like apart from the liberation in Christ. Here we have a narrative of a crisis in the life of such a person, not their ordinary day-to-day experience. This person has reached the point of despair over human inability to please God and to do his will and cries out for help. Paul describes that help found in Christ in Romans 8.

It appears then that Paul is describing in Romans 7–8 the anatomy of a conversion, and in Romans 7:14–25 we find a person under conviction of sin, but still in its bondage, and crying out for conversion. For our purposes it is sufficient to sum up and say that we have shown that Paul is not talking about the tensions in the Christian life here. Indeed, Paul believes that Christians have been set free from the bondage of sin and death as Romans 7:5–6 and Romans 8:1–2 make perfectly clear. The primary moral tension in the Christian life is a tension between the leading of the Spirit and the inclinations of the "flesh" as described in Galatians 5, and between the inner self which is being renewed daily and the outer self which is wasting away, and not the tension between old person and new person, much less the tensions within the old person as described here.

Along the way in this discussion we have seen some important points that call in question the Reformed (especially the Lutheran) way of looking at these texts: (1) not only is Romans 7:7–25 not about the Christian life, for Christians are no longer in the bondage to sin (they are to live without excuses), but (2) Paul does not affirm a theology of Jesus dying for the elect. The Adam-Christ contrast as well as various other Pauline texts make evident that Jesus died for the sins of all. That all are not saved is not a comment on God's intent, plan, or predeterminations. It is a comment on human response. (3) The righteousness of Jesus is not simply transferred to believers. They are in fact enabled and expected to behave in a holy manner, being empowered by the Holy Spirit. Christians are set right with God at the point of conversion, but they are also given the resources to live righteously thereafter, and they are expected to do so.

This whole discussion above immediately raises the issue of the place or role of the Mosaic Law in the Christian life. On the one hand there was Luther, who had what can only be described as an allergic reaction to the idea of Law ruling a life that had been justified by grace through faith, and on the other hand there was Calvin, who could not imagine God simply discarding Law in favor of grace, in some sort of antinomian overreaction. Calvin, as it turns out, had the better and more biblical view of the matter in some respects, but where he went wrong was in suggesting that the new covenant turned out to be a renewal of the old ones, including the Law covenant. In other words, he failed to take the measure of the radical nature of Paul's rhetoric about Law and new covenant in Galatians and elsewhere. To this we must turn in the next chapter, for the entire Evangelical tradition has often based its view of ethics on one or another way of viewing the Christian's relationship to the Mosaic Law.

CHAPTER 3

Laying Down the Law with Luther

Without a doubt, American Evangelicals have strong opinions about the Mosaic Law. Just look at the recent controversies all over the nation about the posting or removing of the Ten Commandments from courthouses or courthouse lawns throughout the nation. Who is it that is raising the big stink? Not Jews for whom those commandments were originally written. It is mostly Evangelicals who somehow feel Moses' Law belongs to them in America, and that if it is removed from the public forum a part of an American Evangelical's identity has been stripped away. Yet, oddly, at the other end of the spectrum there are Evangelicals who seem to think that the term "Law," including the Mosaic Law, is a cipher for legalism—something to be avoided at all costs. Should we agree with the Puritans and other forms of the Reformed tradition that we are still under the Mosaic Law, in one way or another? Should we take a radically libertarian approach such that any time anyone suggests obedience is required to one or another imperative we see this as antithetical to the gospel? Or has the Evangelical tradition often misread the character of the new covenant? What does Paul really tell us about the Mosaic Law?

OUTLAW TO MOSES, IN-LAWED TO CHRIST:
THE RHETORIC OF GALATIANS

In our discussion of Romans in the previous two chapters, several important things came to light about the Law, which we have reserved for mention until this juncture. Paul nowhere in Romans spends any real time on the story of Moses. This is largely true of his other letters as well (though cf. 2 Cor 3:7–18). This is because Paul believes that the story of Moses and those involved in the Mosaic covenant is not the generating narrative for Christians, whether Jew or Gentile. The Adam story, the Abraham story, and the Christ story are generating narratives for Christians—stories with lasting impact on their lives.

The story of Moses, like the Mosaic covenant and the Mosaic Law, is seen by Paul as *pro tempore*. It was a story meant to guide God's people between the time of Moses and Christ. But once the eschatological age dawned through the Christ event, the Moses story could no longer be the controlling narrative of God's people, precisely because now is the era of the new covenant. The Mosaic story thus becomes a story about a glorious anachronism, or as Paul puts it in 2 Corinthians 3, a fading glory. That story is to be respected and honored as a temporary part of God's plan for his people, but it is not a story that one is *required by Law* to obey any more, for Christ came to redeem even those under the Law out from under the Law.[1] Such is the nature of the radical eschatological theology of Paul. This raises interesting questions as we move to one of Paul's most polemical letters and his second most influential missive—Galatians.

Galatians, of course, was the stick of dynamite that Luther used to blow up the late medieval theology he was reacting against. Luther even said he was married to this epistle! And Luther, in a way that Calvin was never quite able to bring himself to do, realized that there was a radical view of the Mosaic Law in this document. Ultimately, Luther ended up closer to the antinomian end of the spectrum where Paul could not go, for the apostle, as we shall see, is happy to talk about Christians being under the Law of Christ (which is not simply a cipher for justification by grace through faith).

So we need to come to grips with what Paul actually says about the Mosaic Law, and we will do so by considering some of the foundational evidence in Galatians 3–6 and also 2 Corinthians 3 where Paul explains that the Mosaic Law, while glorious, is now a glorious anachronism that Christians are no longer obligated to keep. He goes further to explain that the Mosaic covenant was like a *paidagogus*, a slave child-minder, until the fullness of time came and Christ was born. Paul's is a theology of multiple covenants, not just one covenant in various administrations, and he will connect the Abrahamic one with the new covenant as promise and fulfillment, bypassing the Mosaic one altogether. We need to listen in on the scholarly discussion about Paul's view of the Law to understand all of this.

It is quite impossible to say all that needs to be said about Paul's view of the Law in a short span of pages when whole books continue to be devoted to this controversial subject,[2] and so we must settle for speaking here almost exclusively about Paul's view of the Law as it is revealed in Galatians. One cannot avoid all discussion of Paul's treatment of the Law in other letters, particularly Romans and 1 Corinthians, but methodologically I agree that we must study this issue in the context of the particular letters and their agendas and not in the abstract. Paul does not offer us a treatise on Law, only letters where the Law comes up as an important subject of discussion from time to time. F. Thielman is right to proceed carefully in his study, looking at the material letter by letter. There is no letter where the Law is a more crucial or central subject than Galatians, and most scholars would agree that Galatians is the earliest Pauline letter where Paul discusses the matter somewhat fully.[3]

No one would disagree with the assessment that Paul's views on this subject are complex, and they are related closely to his views on a host of other key subjects. To ask Paul's view of the Law is to ask his view of God, salvation, anthropology, and human relationships, to mention a few related topics. Some of the problems in the discussion of the Law have arisen because the subject has been isolated from other aspects of Paul's thought world. In my view one of the most crucial oversights is the failure to recognize the narrative character of Paul's thought world and the role Law plays in it. Paul asserts repeatedly in Galatians, using a variety of means and metaphors (e.g., the "pedagogue") that the Mosaic Law had an important but temporary role to play in the ongoing story of God's people. That role will not be understood unless one grasps the larger story and the way Paul understands its development.

If we ask why it is that Paul argues in the fashion he does about the Law, we are pushed back to Paul's own story, in particular to his conversion which he sees as a matter of pure grace, and to the Copernican revolution that happened in Paul's way of viewing the world as a result of that conversion.[4] I would point to three aspects of changed thinking which came out of his conversion and led to Paul's new view of the Law and its role in the life of God's people:

(1)   As a result of his conversion, Paul had a totally different estimate of Jesus of Nazareth than he had before—in particular, he saw Jesus as not only the messiah of Jews but also as the redeemer of Gentiles.

(2)   Since he believed messiah had come, he also believed that the eschatological situation was different than he had thought before Damascus road. The age to come and the new creation had broken into the present evil age and changed a host of things. Christ rather than the Law was now the mediator and means of the ongoing relationship between God and God's people.

(3)   Paul now viewed the world, the life of the believer, and the Scriptures through the eyes of Christ rather than through the lens of the Law.

In my view, Paul's critique of the Law in Galatians is not merely about legalism, though he has no love for that either, nor is it merely about the so-called badges of the Law (circumcision). It is about the impotence of the Mosaic Law itself when it comes to saving people, and so it is about how the eschatological timetable has passed by the age in which the Mosaic Law is any longer binding or useful for God's people, now that Christ has come.

The age of spiritual maturity had arrived for God's people, and this meant they were no longer "under the Law," they were no longer obligated to keep it.[5] The issue here is not merely the means of salvation, though that is an important part of the issue at least by implication,[6] but the means by which saved persons should live so as to please God. Not "getting in," or "staying in," is really at issue in Galatians, but the means of "going on" in Christ. By what rule or standard will the Christian community live and be shaped? Paul's answer is that the community is to be cruciform and christological in shape. It is to follow his example and the pattern of Christ and walk in and by the Spirit. It is, in short, to follow the Law of Christ which is not identical with the Law of Moses (on which more in a moment).

In Galatians 3:19 we see that Paul's assessment of the Law is certainly not entirely negative. In fact it is not very helpful to try to divide Paul's statements about the Law into negative and positive categories. Paul does not think the Law is against God's promises, he just does not think that Law-keeping is the means through which those promises come to fulfillment. He does not see it as a negative thing that the Law points out our sin, or better said turns sin into transgression for those under it.[7] It is true that the effect of the Law on fallen people is not pleasant—it involves condemnation rather than commendation. But the effect, and the purpose and intent of the Law are not one and the same.

It is true that Paul sometimes uses the term *nomos* to mean the Pentateuch in general (cf., e.g., Gal 4:21) or even the Hebrew Scriptures more broadly conceived (1 Cor 14:21—here citing Isa 28:11), but he is also capable of distinguishing between the Law of the Mosaic covenant which Jews are under, and the larger role of Scripture. Scripture assigned all, both Jew and Gentile, under sin (Gal 3:22), but for those under the Mosaic covenant and its Law there was the further problem that sin had been turned into transgression. It had been made clear that a Jew's sin was against God and was a willful violation of his revealed intentions for God's people, Israel (3:19). Much confusion would have been avoided in the interpretation of the Galatians passages dealing with Law if closer attention had been paid to Paul's careful use of pronouns ("we" Jews, as opposed to "you" Gentile Galatians).

In Paul's view the problem with the Law as a means of Christian living is at least sixfold. (1) Its actual effect is to imprison those who are under it in a form of slavery, the Law acting as a rather strict guardian (Gal 3:23–4:7). (2) The Law involves God's elementary principles which a believer, as s/he grows up in the faith needs to get beyond. (3) The Law is a temporary expedient given by God until he sent his Son. To go back to it is not only to be anachronistic, but it is tantamount to a denial of the efficacy of the work of Christ and the Spirit. (4) The Law is quite incapable of giving what Christ and the Spirit give—life, freedom, fruit, gifts, and the like. The Law is not seen as a bad thing, it is simply seen as impotent, unable to give someone the power or ability to keep God's commandments and unable to deliver the eschatological blessings of salvation and inheritance. It then becomes a question of whether or not it is right to complain about the Law for not doing what it was never intended to do. (5) The Mosaic Law was intended for Jews, and quite specifically meant to separate them from the other nations not only in social practice (e.g., Sabbath observance, circumcision, food laws), but also to make them stand apart in moral behavior and theological belief (standing against immorality and idolatry). It must be borne in mind that the Ten Commandments and the Shema were at the very heart of the Law, something Paul was well aware of, and yet Paul was still willing to place the Law in the categories of a ministry of death and a form of fleeting and fading glory *while talking about those very Ten Commandments* (2 Cor 3).

Paul says in Galatians 3:4–5 that Christ was born under the Law in order to redeem Jews from under the Law and give them adoption as children. This suggests that they did not have such adoption because of the Law or because of being Jews, but rather because of grace coming through Christ. (6) Paul opposes the mandatory observation of the Law by any Christians whether Jews (cf., the Antioch incident and Paul's reaction to Peter's and Barnabas' withdrawal from table fellowship with Jews) or Gentiles. No doubt the main reason he does so is that if some choose to be consistently and permanently Torah true, this will divide the community (as it had already done in Antioch), into clean and unclean, sinner and holy one, first- and second-class citizens. If fellowship is defined by the Law, then it requires Law observance by all so all can eat and live together. But in the Christian community the basis of association is simply being in Christ in whom there is no Jew or Gentile (Gal 3:28). There is a sense in which Christ came not to renew Jewish or Gentile religion but to get beyond both and form a "more perfect union" between all peoples and classes, and both genders. This is what Paul calls "a new creation." If both Jew and Gentile are children of Abraham through faith in the Faithful One, Jesus Christ, the Seed of Abraham, then the Israel of God or people of God has been reconfigured in a new fashion and with a new charter or covenant. This is sectarian thinking and involves a sectarian reappropriation of familiar terms in a new way.[8]

Something should be said about the difference in Paul's mind between being under the Law covenant and listening to any and all parts of the Hebrew Scriptures as God's Word, which reveals God's will. Paul's covenantal theology allows him to affirm that the Law tells the truth about human nature and about God and about their interrelationship. It reveals various of the fundamental things God expects of his people. It does not cease to be the Word of God just because God's people cease to be under a particular covenant spoken of in part of God's Word and cease to be obligated to keep *that particular covenant's* various requirements and to obey its various stipulations. Paul does not think there is only one continuous covenant, in various forms, between God and his people, as is made quite clear in Galatians 4:24. Paul's view is that God is perfectly capable of giving both situation-specific advice and contractual arrangements as well as more permanent ones.

Paul talks about the whole Law and its essential requirements as being "summed up" in a single commandment—to love neighbor as self (Gal 5:14). In his view the Mosaic Law can be boiled down to its bare essence, and will and should be reflected in the life of the Christian believer, not because Christians have placed themselves under the Law and committed themselves to obey it all, but because the Spirit produces the essential qualities the Law demanded in the life of the believer.[9] To put it another way, the eschatological age is the age of fulfillment, and the essential requirements of the Mosaic Law are fulfilled in the life of the Christian "not because they continue to be obligated to it but because, by the power of the Spirit in their lives, their conduct coincidentally displays the behavior the Mosaic law prescribes. In this verse then, Paul is claiming that believers have no need of the Mosaic law because by their Spirit-inspired conduct they already fulfill its requirements."[10] In fact, Paul will go on to suggest that when the Spirit shapes Christian character, giving it fruit, Christians are in fact going beyond what the Law requires in a positive direction (Gal 5:23).[11]

Not surprisingly there is considerable principle overlap between the Mosaic Law and the Law of Christ since God has given them both. But this does not mean that Paul sees the "Law of Christ" as simply Christ's interpretation of the Law. Indeed not. The phrase *Law of Christ* first and foremost refers to the cruciform and resurrection pattern of the life of Jesus, which is to be replicated in the lives of Christ's followers by the work of the Spirit and by imitation. They are to clothe themselves with Christ and immerse themselves in his life and lifestyle. This pattern of a crucified and risen Savior is not enunciated in the Mosaic Law and certainly not enunciated there as a pattern for believers to imitate. The Law of Christ also entails various teachings of Christ, both the portions of the OT he reaffirmed during his ministry (such as love of God and neighbor) and the new teachings he enunciated, which Paul draws on and sometimes even quotes (cf., 1 Cor 7; Rom 14). It furthermore involves some early Christian teaching such as we find in Galatians 6, including Paul's own paraphrasing and amplifying of the teachings of Christ (see Gal 6:1 and 6:6, where he paraphrases sayings of Jesus).

Thus, Paul's answer to the question "How then should Christians live?" is not "Adopt Christ's interpretation of the Mosaic Law and follow it," but rather "Follow and be refashioned by the Law of Christ" and "walk in the Spirit." Paul's letter to the Galatians is neither antinomian in character nor is it an attack on legalism. It is a salvation historical argument about recognizing what time it is, and what covenant God's people are and are not now under. The Law of Christ is not the Mosaic Law intensified or in a new guise. It is the new eschatological dictums appropriate for those living as new creatures, albeit in an already and not yet situation. The above constitutes my constructive proposal on how to read Paul's complex view of the Law, particularly as it is expressed in Galatians. It remains to critique some of the other major proposals in the rest of this excursus. We will focus here on the contributions of three other scholars: E. P. Sanders, F. Thielman, and J. D. G. Dunn.

It is fair to say that the recent renewed interest in Paul's view of the Law has in large part been sparked by the watershed study of E. P. Sanders entitled *Paul and Palestinian Judaism*, which appeared in 1977. The study challenged a great deal of what passed for common assumptions about early Jews and the way they viewed and related to the Mosaic Law. In particular it challenged the assumption that Jews were bogged down in legalism and that they thought they obtained or maintained right standing with God through punctilious observance of the Law. Rather, as Sanders argued, covenantal nomism instead of works of righteousness is a fairer description of how early Jews viewed and related to the Law. Covenantal nomism was a response to the gracious saving work of God for his people, not the cause of that work or the means of appropriating it in the first place. Sanders is reacting against the still ongoing effects of Luther's analysis of Galatians and Romans and the stereotypes of early Judaism that that analysis produced. It is ironic then that he himself is indebted to that same sort of soteriological analysis in that he chooses to frame the discussion in terms of "getting in" and "staying in."[12] But this is not in the main what Galatians and the discussion of the Law in this letter are about.

Paul is concerned not with Jews but with Christians, in particular Paul's Gentile converts in Galatia, submitting to the Law as an addition to their already extant faith in Christ. Nor does it appear that Paul is countering the position that Law-keeping was the means of maintaining their salvation or staying in the Christian community. Paul is attacking the view that submitting to the Law is the means of going on to maturity in Christ, indeed even "finishing" or "completing" one's Christian life and so showing oneself approved at the final judgment (cf., Gal 3:3 and 5:4).[13] If covenantal nomism is the grateful response of God's people to what God has already done in their lives, it would not appear that this is what Paul is discussing or trying to oppose in Galatians 3:3 and 5:4. The Galatians were looking to future benefits that accrued for submitting to the Law, not looking for a way to properly thank God for what they had already received in Christ.

Another major pillar in Sander's edifice is that it is wrong to assume that the Law was unkeepable and that if it was not all kept there was no forgiveness for sins. On the former point Sanders refers to Philo (*Rewards* 80), but one might also want to point to Philippians 3:6.[14] On the latter note Sanders refers to all the material in the Pentateuch which stresses that atonement could be made for sin. Two things need to be said about this sort of argument.

First, what Philo or other Jews may have said about whether one could keep the Law or not is one thing. Whether the Law was actually keepable by fallen human beings is quite another. Second, it is not at all clear that the Mosaic Law indicates that atonement was possible for any and all sorts of sins. In particular, it is not clear that "sins with a high hand" could be atoned for. Compare, for instance, what is said about sin in Numbers 15:22–31. Here there are specifications made for when a person unintentionally fails to observe *all* the commandments that the Lord spoke to Moses or when he or she transgresses unintentionally.[15] Sacrifices could be offered and forgiveness could be granted in such cases. But then the text goes on to say, "But whoever acts high-handedly, whether an Israelite or an alien, affronts the Lord, and shall be cut off from among the people. Because of having despised the word of the Lord and broken his commandment, such a person shall be utterly cut off and bear the guilt." There is certainly no thought of forgiving the intentional sinner in this text, so Sanders's failure to really deal with these sorts of exceptions to the possibility of atonement and forgiveness makes his case quite weak. In fact, Acts 13:39 makes perfectly clear that it was understood that not all kinds of sins could be atoned for under Mosaic Law.

Sanders in general is able to provide us with abundant evidence about the views of early Jews about the Law, but what he cannot and does not do is show that early Jews had in general correctly understood the Law and its purpose. The issue is not whether early Jews *felt* or *believed* the Law was too onerous a burden to bear, or whether it was believed that all sins could be atoned for, or whether it was believed that God did or did not require perfect obedience to all the Law.[16] The issue is whether the Law actually said these things or made these sorts of claims. Paul says that those who get themselves circumcised commit themselves to keeping the whole Mosaic Law, a perfectly plausible conclusion based on a close reading of what the Pentateuch actually says about obedience (see, e.g., Num 15:22). In Paul's view, the Law is a corporate entity (cf. Gal 5:3 and 3:10 and the continual use of *nomos* in the singular, never the plural), and Deuteronomy 27:26 is paraphrased to make clear that all the words of the Law must be kept. Paul seems to believe that the Law has not in general been kept by God's people and so they need to be redeemed from under the Law (Gal 4:5). The question is whether Paul is justified in his interpretation of the OT.

There are other flaws in Sanders's treatment of Paul's discussion of the Law, not the least of which is that he does not attend to the differences between what Paul says about "we" and "you" in Galatians 3–4. Paul does not think that everyone is under the Mosaic Law automatically; the Law is seen as but one form of the divine law. It must be stressed that Paul does not think that the Mosaic Law was given to the world, but rather to God's first chosen people as the rule of life for their community. This is why the "we Jews" and "you Gentiles" are such important distinctions in this letter when the Law is under discussion. Paul does not want his converts to submit to a condition which Paul himself has left behind; as he says in Galatians 2:18, these are the very things, the very barriers, he tore down when he became a Christian. It may also be said that while I agree with Sanders that one must take into account the difference between Paul's arguments about the Law and the reasons for his arguments, and also the fact that he is speaking in a polemical mode, using various rhetorical tactics, it does not follow from any of this that Paul is not arguing on the basis of a well-thought-out position. A good deal hangs on the way we interpret small turns of phrase.

For example, should we translate Galatians 3:11, "But it is obvious that no one is justified before God by the Law because 'the just shall live by faith,'" as most do, including Sanders?[17] But as Thielman shows, it is perfectly possible to translate the sentence, "But because no one is justified before God by the Law, it is obvious that 'The just shall live by faith.'"[18] In fact, this translation is far more likely, in which case Paul is not using the OT quote as a proof text at all, but rather v. 11 as a whole indicates the solution to the plight described in v. 10. In other words, the reasoning here is not from solution to plight, but rather the other way around, with the OT being allowed to state the major thesis that the "just shall live by faith." Sanders is, however, right that Paul's arguments are not merely socially motivated;[19] they have theological roots, and theological as well as social aims.

Enough has been said to show that Sanders's views are not without their problems, though he has quite rightly challenged us all to recognize that obedience in response to God's redemption of Israel from bondage, an obedience that is a response and so a form of covenantal nomism, is not the same as attempts to earn right standing with God by performing works of the Law. He has also rightly countered various caricatures of the *views* of early Jews about the Law and of how they viewed their own condition under the Law.[20] It must be said once more that Paul is countering neither legalism nor Jewish covenantal nomism in Galatians; he is trying to forestall his Gentile converts from submitting to the Law as a means of going on in Christ, as a means of making themselves fit subjects for final justification.

Our next dialogue partner is F. Thielman, who in many ways has provided the clearest and most exegetically careful exposition of Paul's view of the Law, including the views expressed in Galatians. I would like to focus on one aspect of his treatment that sheds fresh light on the discussion, namely his treatment of "the Law of Christ" as not merely Christ's interpretation of the Mosaic Law, but rather the new eschatological Law meant for those who are new creatures entering the kingdom of God. Thielman rightly points out that the terms *transgressor* and *transgression* have a quite specific nuance in the NT. These terms do not refer to sin or wickedness in general, but rather to violation of a particular Law or command (cf. Rom 2:23; 4:15; Gal 3:19; Heb 2:2; 9:15; and on transgressor Rom 2:25, 27; Jas 2:9, 11). This means that we must ask why Paul says withdrawing from table fellowship with Gentiles in Galatians 2:18 would make him a transgressor—that is, a violator of some law.

As Thielman goes on to say: "This cannot, however, be the law of Moses, since that law builds a boundary between Jews and Gentiles, the crossing of which is sin (2:17; compare 2:5). The law that Paul would transgress if he did not associate with believing Gentiles then is another law, and the 'law of Christ' of 6:2 that incorporates the Mosaic injunction to love one's neighbor seems the most likely candidate."[21] Thielmann also rightly points out that one must compare the phrase "the Law of Christ" in Galatians 6:2 to what we find in 1 Corinthians 9:21, where the Law of Christ is both *distinguished* from the Mosaic Law and at the same time *identified* with the law of God in 1 Corinthians 9:19–23.[22] Paul does not see himself as beyond all law since he became a Christian. He sees himself as both no longer under the Mosaic Law, but at the same time "in the Law of Christ."

Paul is no antinomian, and freedom in his view does not amount to exchanging obedience to the Mosaic Law for a condition in which no objective restrictions or requirements are placed on one's life. Paul believes that freedom in Christ means freedom from slavery, but it also means freedom for "obeying the truth" of the gospel,[23] which is but another way of saying freedom to keep the Law of Christ; and as Thielman says, "the Law of Christ is something new."[24] This new Law is more understandable if one looks carefully at Galatians 6:2.

Fulfilling this new Law amounts to "bearing one another's burdens." This is not a quotation of the Mosaic Law but rather a paraphrase of an idea found in the Jesus tradition. The idea is found in a specific commandment said by the Fourth Evangelist to have been given by Christ: "This is my commandment that you love one another as I have loved you. No one has greater love than this, to lay down one's life for one's friends" (John 15:12–13). One may wish to point to John 13:14: "you also ought to wash one another's feet," and perhaps also the specific exhortation about burden carrying in Matthew 5:41: "if anyone forces you to go one mile, go also the second mile."[25] What is interesting about all this material is that it shows up in the context where Jesus is saying something about loving one's neighbor or even one's enemy. Matthew 5:41 is followed in vv. 43–44 with the discussion about loving one's neighbor and even enemy, and loving one's neighbor is defined in John 15:13 as being willing to die for them and in their place, the ultimate form of bearing of another's burden. As we shall see,[26] the Law of Christ refers not just to the pattern of Christ's life, which should be emulated, but to the teachings of Christ which flesh out this pattern. Thielman has helped us by pointing us in this direction.

Thielman is also quite correct that in Galatians Paul is operating with a very different definition of what constitutes a sinner than is found in the Mosaic Law. Galatians 2:17–21 demonstrates this fact. Paul insists that Christ is no servant of sin and that Christ desires Jews and Gentiles to fellowship together without Gentiles being required to keep kosher food laws. Paul realizes that by his eating unclean food with "unclean" Gentiles he might be "found to be a sinner" by other Jewish Christians, but he rejects this definition of sinner. "The implication of . . . [2:17–21] . . . is that by eating with 'Gentile sinners' Paul does not become a sinner, although the Mosaic law might define his action as sinful."[27] This is not a mere modification of what the Mosaic Law says about boundary markers or identity badges. Paul is offering a new definition of what constitutes sin and what constitutes transgression. He also makes regular comments suggesting that Christians are free from the Mosaic Law not just in its condemning function or its boundary-defining function but in other ways as well. The Mosaic Law is seen as a pedagogue whose time of guardianship is over; the ministry of Moses, though glorious, has now been set aside because of the greater and more permanent glory that has come through the ministry of Christ (cf. Rom 7:6; 2 Cor 3:9–11).

Equally telling is Thielmann's treatment of the question of whether Paul regarded all Jews as legalists, or Judaism in general as a legalistic religion. Paul's argument, rather, is that any Jew familiar with Scripture will know the record of Israel's unfaithfulness to the Mosaic covenant and will be aware that the Scriptures themselves say that no one can be justified before God on the basis of their deeds or, as Paul puts it, by "works of the Law" (cf. Gal 2:15–16). Thus:

> far from attributing to most Jews a notion of salvation by works, these passages assume that most Jews understand that works of the law do not justify. Paul hopes that once reminded of the standard Jewish position on the plight of Israel, Judaizing Christians and unbelieving Jews will realize that . . . the Mosaic covenant is obsolete and they should embrace the Gospel of God's redemptive work in Christ.[28]

PAUL AND THE LAW COME UNDONE

Though I find myself in essential agreement with Thielman's approach, the same cannot be said about the views of J. D. G. Dunn. My view is that Dunn ultimately makes Paul sound as if he were one of the Judaizers or agitators, though holding to a less rigorous application of the Mosaic Law than they did. In short, Dunn sees Paul as yet another reformer of Judaism, not one who takes a sectarian approach to the issue of the community of God's people. I would disagree.

It is easy to be beguiled by Paul's use of the OT into thinking that Paul is simply offering one more revision of the argument for continuity between God's OT people and his people now. Some Scriptural continuity should not be confused however with what we may anachronistically call "ecclesial" continuity between "Israel" then and now. Paul's view is that the way to obtaining the benefits of the promise to Abraham is through Abraham's true and ultimate seed Christ, not through continuing to keep the Mosaic Law. It is Jew and Gentile united in Christ who are viewed by Paul as the people of God.[29] In short, Paul is arguing that the people of God were narrowed down to the elect one, Christ, the seed, after which those who are in the seed, the elect one, are in the people of God. One must quickly add that Paul does not think that Israel according to the flesh is broken off from the people of God forever, as Romans 9–11 makes clear. They have not stumbled so as to fall permanently, but Paul envisions their reintegration into the people of God on the same basis as Gentiles had entered, by grace through faith in God's Messiah, Jesus.

Some of Dunn's basic views can be summed up as follows:

(1)   Paul was converted from Judaism not in the sense in which we now use the term, but in the narrower sense as it was defined in the Maccabean literature (2 Macc 2:21; 8:1; 14:38; 4 Macc 4:26) "as the label coined or used to identify the national religion trying to define and defend itself over against the influences of Hellenism."[30]

(2)   Paul was converted from zeal for these Jewish traditions, zeal like that of Phineas, which caused him to persecute the church.

(3)   Paul was converted from a belief in the role of the Law as properly hedging around Israel and protecting it from outsiders, to a less restrictive view of the Law.

(4)   Paul was converted to the recognition that the gospel of Jesus must be taken to the Gentiles.

(5)   The phrase *works of the Law* in Paul refers to the deeds required by the Law and should be exegeted in light of 4QMMT. It has a limited sense.

(6)   The term *sinner* in Galatians 2:15–17 is used in a limited and factional sense as a means of distinguishing Jews from non-Jews and from other Jews who are perceived to be not as observant of the Law.

(7)   In general, one must assume that wherever one finds the term *nomos* in Paul's letters it refers to the Mosaic Law, even in the case of the phrase, "the Law of Christ," or of phrases like, "the law of faith" (Rom 3:27), or "the law of the Spirit of life" (Rom 8:2–4). In other words, Paul sees that the Mosaic Law has a variety of facets and functions, and he believes that only some of these facets and functions are obsolete.[31]

Thus, Dunn's basic approach has to do with limiting the scope of what Paul means by certain of the key terms in the debate. Paul has not converted to a new religion; he does not think that the Mosaic Law as a whole is obsolete; he does not distinguish radically between the Abrahamic and the Mosaic covenants; and in general Dunn wishes to stress that there is still much continuity between Paul's views and those that are held by other early Jews on a variety of important issues, though he does not deny discontinuity as well. Paul is in essence protesting not against the Mosaic Law itself in Galatians but rather "against the ethnic divisiveness which Paul saw as a consequence of Jewish over-evaluation of the role of the Law."[32] The problem is with particular views of the Law and particular social uses or aspects of the Law and not with the Law itself per se.

Now, on the one hand, Dunn is probably right that Paul would have been opposed to a legalistic misuse of the Law, but in fact Paul knows very well that it is not a misuse of the Law to insist on God's people being set apart both ritually and morally from the outside world. Indeed this is the very essence of the Levitical code, and is at the heart of the larger Mosaic code as well. The aim of the Law is holiness, which inherently requires being set apart from all uncleanness and unholiness—whether that involves unclean food, things, places, or persons. According to the Mosaic Law, acceptance of *goyim* (Gentiles) within Israel's community requires that the Gentiles abide by various parts of the Mosaic Law. This is precisely what Paul is denying repeatedly and vehemently in Galatians when he says that Gentiles do not need to keep the Mosaic Law in order to be members in good standing in, and an ongoing part of, the Christian fellowship.

In the second place, as Thielman points out, it is the Law itself, not its misuse, to which Paul is denying justifying power.[33] Only Christ justifies either those under the Law or those outside it. This is the very point of Paul's modification of Psalm 143:2, which he cites in Galatians 2:16. In regard to the phrase, "works of the Law," Dunn is right that Paul is not attacking in Galatians 2:15ff. works, or works of righteousness, or human attempts to earn salvation in general. Dunn is also right that Paul knows that his fellow Jews by and large understand the Law was not given as a means to obtain right standing with God but rather was seen as a means of living rightly before God. Dunn is also quite right that Paul is concerned with the social consequences of keeping the Law, namely the separation of Jews and Gentiles. Dunn is helpful then in defining what the phrase probably does not mean for Paul.

The problem comes when Dunn tries to define the positive content of the phrase. For instance, it is more than doubtful that "works of the Law" can be limited to mean some of the deeds required by the Law, or the social function of the Law focusing on particular ritual requirements. Nor is it adequate to say that this phrase sums up "the attitude against which Paul was protesting."[34] The focus of this phrase is surely on actions, not attitudes about actions. Furthermore, it was not just an "attitude" of Jews about the Law that led to their maintaining separation from Gentiles. Not only does the Law insist on such separation or set-apartness from the nations (cf., e.g., Exod 19:5–6ff.), but in the visions of the prophets about the restoration of Jerusalem and Israel we hear, "Put on your beautiful garments O Jerusalem, the holy city; for the uncircumcised and the unclean shall enter you no more. . . . The Lord has bared his arm before the eyes of all the nations; and all the ends of the earth shall see the salvation of our God. Depart, depart, go out from there! Touch no unclean thing; go out from the midst of it, purify yourselves, you who carry the vessels of the Lord . . ." (Isa 52:1–12).[35] Similar pronouncements about the problems of mixing with Gentiles or adopting Gentile practices can be found in Ezekiel and other prophets as well.

Notice the very similar way Paul puts things in Galatians 2:16 and 5:3–4. In the former text Paul denies that one can be justified at all by works of the Law. In the latter text he speaks of those desiring to be justified by the Law as being required to obey all of it. Works of the Law surely means all of the works of the Law that one is obliged to keep if one submits to the sign of the Mosaic covenant—circumcision. For Paul the Law is a package deal, and one cannot separate out one portion of its commandments from another. All must be obeyed if one is under the Mosaic Law.

What then of Dunn's strong stress on the new evidence about the phrase, *the works of the Law*, from 4QMMT? At first blush, this material looks quite promising to help us understand Paul's meaning.[36] Here we find a discussion of works of the Law by the sectarians at Qumran, and what they are discussing in this document is boundary marker issues, issues of clean and unclean, issues of what is holy and what is profane—in other words, issues about what amounts to a trespassing of the community's boundaries (e.g., rules about the cleansing of lepers, the admitting of the blind and deaf into the temple, the permitting of intermarriage with Ammonites and Moabites, the transmission of impurity by a flow of water, the cooking of sacrificial meat in unclean vessels). The key phrase comes at the very beginning of the document as part of the title, which probably should be read to mean "pertinent (or important) works of the Law."[37] M. Abegg then suggests that what Paul is rebutting in using the phrase *works of the Law* is the sort of sectarian thinking such as we find at Qumran. Especially intriguing is the fact that the final remarks of 4QMMT involve an allusion to Psalm 106:30–31, where being reckoned righteous is said to come about because someone has been zealous like Phineas in upholding the Law and protecting the boundaries of the community. Righteousness is reckoned on the basis of deeds or works of the Law.

Now as intriguing as this material is, there are some major question marks to be raised about it. Notice that the key introductory phrase is not simply *the works of the Law* but rather *pertinent or important works of the Law*. In other words, in this phrase, the unit "works of the Law" describes a larger entity, a subset of which is the important or pertinent works of the Law. This means that "works of the Law," is no more a technical phrase for some specific legal works in 4QMMT than it is in Paul's Galatians. The second major flaw in this argument is that, as is well known, the sectarians at Qumran had long since anathematized the present Jerusalem and its religious regime and had set themselves apart in the desert. This seems to be quite the opposite of the agenda of the agitators in Galatia, whose aim is to get the Galatians better connected with Jerusalem, the Jerusalem church, and the form of Judaism that was centered in Jerusalem. There is nothing at all sectarian about their insistence that the Galatians be circumcised and submit to the Mosaic Law. This is precisely what mainstream Judaism expected proselytes to do. I see no evidence that the agitators were urging on the Galatians' multiple water ablutions or other of the super-erogatory works that the Qumranites insisted on. The Judaizers or false brothers or agitators were not sectarians, if by sectarian one means a group self-consciously separating itself from some larger religious group.

On the contrary, they were trying to stress as much as possible the continuity or connectedness between Jewish Christianity and Judaism in general, not least because they wanted to avoid persecution for the beliefs that they held which were distinctive (e.g., Christ's death on the cross—Gal 6:12). Thus, the comparison between Paul and 4QMMT does not suggest that Paul is using the phrase in some limited or narrow or sectarian way. Paul provides us with no list of important "works of the Law," unlike 4QMMT, and when he does mention circumcision, he connects it with obedience to the whole Law (Gal 5:3)! Thus, while the boundary-defining rituals and identity markers are certainly a part of what Paul means by the works of the Law, they are by no means all that he means by the phrase, nor need we think he is especially focusing on such things. As J. Barclay points out, since Paul talks about dying to the Law himself, and he does not qualify this remark in any way, it is hardly likely when he is talking about wanting his converts to avoid works of the Law that he means something less than all the deeds required by the Law, whether ritual or otherwise. He does not want them to raise up a way of living in the Christian community in Galatia that he himself has left for dead.[38]

Let us consider for a moment why Paul objects to the agitators' view of the Law. The problem Paul has with the Law lies not only in its effect on fallen human beings, or its social effect of separating Jews and Gentiles, or even in its inability to give life and power to those under it, though all of these things are part of the problem. Paul's most basic problem with the Law is that it is obsolete, and therefore following it is no longer appropriate. It is not the rule of the eschatological age, and it is not to be imposed in the new creation which is already coming to be. If Christ came even to redeem Jews out from under the yoke of the Law, if the Law was a pedagogue meant to function only until Christ came, if the Law was "set aside" as 2 Corinthians 3:11 says, then it is a mistake—indeed, a serious mistake—to go back to keeping it, or in the case of Gentiles to begin to submit to it in any form or fashion. The Law had an important function and role to play in the divine economy, but the rule of the Mosaic Law has had its day and ceased to be. But it is not just the anachronism that bothers Paul about insisting that Christians, whether Jew or Gentile, must keep the Mosaic Law. What bothers him most is that keeping the Law implies in Paul's mind that Christ's death did not accomplish what in fact he believes it did accomplish. To submit to the Mosaic Law is to nullify the grace of God (Gal 2:21) and to deny that justification or righteousness, whether initial or final, comes through the death of Christ.

A further problem with Dunn's approach is his attempt to subsume all the Pauline uses of *nomos* (or at least all the ones crucial to the Law debate) under the one heading of the Mosaic Law, when in fact this is quite impossible to do. For example, in Romans 7:22–23 Paul is able to distinguish between the Mosaic Law and *another* law or principle resident in a person's members. Or again in Romans 8:2 Paul distinguishes between the law of sin and death and the law or principle of the Spirit of life. Now this latter cannot be a reference to the Mosaic Law at all, because Paul says quite clearly that the Mosaic Law cannot give life. Only God in Christ through the work of the Spirit can (cf. Rom 8:3; Gal 3:21). He is equally clear that those led by the Spirit are not subject to the Mosaic Law (Gal 5:18), but rather to the Law of Christ (6:2), which most certainly does involve good works, as 6:4–5 makes clear.

Finally, it is doubtful that Dunn's account of Paul's conversion is adequate. Paul was not simply converted from Maccabean-type zeal for the Law to some other less exuberant or stringent view of the Law. Clearly enough, zeal characterizes Paul's arguing about the Law and the faith in Galatians just as it had likely done before his conversion. What we are stressing is, it really was a conversion. Paul had left Judaism behind when he became a follower of Christ, which meant that in the eyes of any normal Torah-true Jew, Paul would have been seen as apostate, as one beyond the pale, one who was now to be classed with the Gentile sinners. Also, Paul saw himself as no longer obliged to keep the Mosaic Law (1 Cor 9), something with which no observant Jew would agree. Saul before and Paul after the conversion likely saw a fundamental antithesis between Jesus Christ and the Law being the basic means of defining the boundaries of God's people. In other words, Paul the convert took a radical or sectarian approach to his Jewish heritage. In particular, his views of the role, function, purpose, and applicability of the Mosaic Law to God's people now that Christ had come changed dramatically.

More could be said along these lines, but we may sum up by saying that for the Christian Paul, the Mosaic Law was a good thing, something that came from God, but that it was limited—limited in what it was intended to and could accomplish, limited in the time-span for which it was meant to be applicable, and limited in the group to which it was meant to be applied (namely, Jews and converts or adherents to Judaism). It was but one form of the *nomos* and it was something Christ's coming had rendered no longer in effect. The people of God were no longer to be under the guardian, now that the eschatological age had broken in and those in Christ could be new creatures and walk in the Spirit and according to the newly established Law of Christ.

Thus far we have pointed out that there are major problems with the Lutheran and Calvinistic view of Romans 7 and related texts, as well as the Lutheran and Calvinistic readings of Paul's treatment of the Mosaic Law. We have noted along the way that the misreading of Adam's story leads to a misreading of Moses' story, which in turn leads to a mistaken covenantal theology and a failure to come to grips with the radical nature of what Paul was proposing about the new covenant, which includes a misreading of Paul's atonement theology, as if Jesus only died for the elect, rather than—as Romans 3 and other texts make clear—dying for sinners in general.

But in some ways the heremeneutical problems with Lutheranism and Calvinism are larger than the exegetical ones. For the Christian, the story of God's people must in the first instance be read backwards, not forwards, and the whole OT revelation be read through the lens of the Christ event. When one does this, one realizes that the new covenant is not merely a renewal of older ones, and that the new Law is not merely the old one refurbished, any more than the new understanding of God, which incorporates Christ into the Godhead, is just a natural extension of what the OT says about such matters.

No, 1 Corinthians 8:6 shows how the Godhead is reinvisioned in light of Christ and the Christ event, as is all the previous history of God's people (see 1 Cor 10:4). Nowhere is this clearer than in the allegory of Sarah and Hagar in Galatians 4 where the Mosaic Law, Mt. Sinai, the earthly Jerusalem, and Hagar the slave girl are all put on one side of the ledger whereas Sarah, her offspring, the Jerusalem from above, freedom, and ultimately the new covenant are all put on the other side of the ledger—with Paul siding with the latter. The failure of Calvin and his successors to come to grips with this radical argument has skewed their reading of Paul for generations, and this involves both Pauline theology, and also, especially in the case of Luther, Pauline ethics.

Luther's instincts were right about Paul taking a radical approach to the Mosaic Law, but he was wrong about Paul eschewing law altogether. Paul was no libertarian, and he did not see all law as mere legalism. Calvin was right that Paul affirmed "law" in some sense. He was wrong in assuming that Paul thought there was just one covenant renewed through many administrations, with some permutations and combination. But even more skewed than their views of the biblical law is the theology of election that arises out of the Reformed reading of various Pauline texts, such as Romans, Ephesians, and 1 Thessalonians. This is the subject for our next chapter.

CHAPTER 4

Awaiting the Election Results

Evangelicals certainly have opinions about the concept of election. Some break out in a rash when you even mention the concept, and others think it necessarily means that God has predetermined everything in advance. Some think God is still awaiting the election results (about which it is assumed we have a vote since the issue is personal salvation), and others think that if God did not determine things in advance no one would be saved. But in fact election and absolute predetermination are not necessarily inherently linked concepts, and in early Judaism they were not necessarily linked ideas. To understand how Paul (and other NT writers) understood these complex ideas we must first consider how they were discussed in early Judaism.

THE CHOSEN PEOPLE'S VIEW OF ELECTION: PREDESTINATION, ELECTION, SALVATION, AND APOSTASY IN EARLY JUDAISM

Paul's concepts of election, salvation, predestination, and the like are not examples of *creatio ex nihilo*. Paul is writing out of and into a rather specific social and historical context. Some of the vocabulary he uses, such as the verb *pro-oridzo*, is not found in previous Greek literature, including the Septuagint. The related term *proginosko* ("to foreknow") is found with a little more frequency—for example in Philo, *Somn.* 1.2—and the concept and term is also present in Wisdom of Solomon 8:8. It is probable that lying in the background here are the OT references to God knowing his people, which at times connote his inclination toward or love for them, and at other times connote something like the concept of election (cf. Amos 3:2; Deut 9:24; Exod 33:12, 17; Gen 18:19; Deut 34:10). It is, however, a mistake to simply draw conclusions about Paul's views on these matters on the basis of word studies of certain key terms in earlier literature, not least because Paul has reenvisioned whatever he believed as a non-Christian Jew about such matters in the light of Christ and in the light of his new found eschatological beliefs, since he thinks the Christ event has inaugurated the end times. Furthermore, the language about God knowing and determining in the OT does not stand in isolation but needs to be correlated with the discussions about Israel's apostasy, rebellion, and falling away. Such discussions can be found especially in the prophetic literature (see e.g., Hosea), but also in the later Jewish literature such as in *Jubilees* 23:14–23, where, as in Paul, they are connected with certain eschatological and apocalyptic ideas. It is interesting then that in the very texts where God's sovereignty is stressed, there is also a stress on viable human choice when it comes to moral matters.

On this last point consider for example Sirach 15:11–17: "Say not it was the Lord's fault that I fell away . . . say not, He led me astray. . . . He made man from the beginning, and left him to his own counsel." Or again in *Psalms of Solomon* 9:4: "Our deeds are in the choice and power of our soul, to do righteousness and iniquity in the works of our hands." In 4 Esdras 8:55–56 we find: "Ask no more about the multitude of those who perish . . . for they themselves having freedom given them, spurned the Most High, and despised his law and abandoned his ways."

If we wish to pursue the discussion with specific rabbis, there is the famous saying of Rabbi Akiba: "Everything is foreseen (by God), and freedom of choice is given (to man), and the world is judged with goodness, and all depends on the preponderance of (good or ill) doing" (*P. Abot* 3:15). Simeon ben Azzai, a younger contemporary of Akiba says the same thing (*Mek.* on Exod 15:26). It is interesting that the usual proof texts for the idea that freedom of moral choice has been given to human beings are Proverbs 3:34 along with Exodus 15:26. R. Hanina says: "Everything is in the power of Heaven, except the reverence of Heaven (i.e. God)" (*B.T. Ber.* 33b). Especially telling is *B.T. Niddah* 16b which says that God in his providence determines beforehand what a person will be and what will befall him but *not* whether he will be godless or godly, wicked or righteous. G. F. Moore, in his summary of the evidence from early Judaism, says: "Religion is the one thing that God *requires* of man; He does not *constrain* him to it. It is unnecessary to multiply examples further; there are no dissentient voices."[1] This is perhaps a bit of an overstatement, as an examination of Josephus's account of the various sects of Judaism shows.

Josephus indicates that determinism, or fate, or predestination, was an issue very much in dispute in early Judaism, and the dispute was chiefly between Paul's former sect, the Pharisees, and other dominant sects. In regard to the matter of destiny or foreordination,

Josephus says the Essenes exempted nothing from its control, while the Sadducees took the opposite end of the spectrum, denying there was any such thing as foreordination, while the Pharisees held the middle ground, namely some things, but not all things, are the work of divine destining. Some things, such as whether one responds to divine grace, or whether one continues in one's faith, are within the control of human beings.

Yet Josephus recognizes there is some tension within Pharisaic thought on this matter. For example, in *Jewish War* 2.8 and 14, he says that the Pharisees ascribe everything to destiny and to God, except that to do right or wrong lies mainly in the hands of human beings, though God's hand can be seen as an auxiliary force involved in these choices as well. There is a fuller statement of the matter at *Jewish Antiquities* 18.1–3 where we hear: "While the Pharisees hold that all things are brought about by destiny, they do not deprive the human will of its own impulse to do them, it having pleased God that there should be a co-operation, and that to the deliberation (of God) about destiny, humans in the case of the one who wills should assent, with virtue or wickedness."

The relevance of this discussion of Pharisaism for what Paul says should be clear. Paul was a Pharisee before his Damascus Road experience; he affirms God's foreknowledge, his destining of some things, and also he affirms human responsibility for sin, and the awful possibility of radical rebellion against God by a believer, namely apostasy.

It is not an either/or matter for Paul when it comes to viable human moral choices and God's sovereignty, but rather a both/and situation. Among other things, this means that while he certainly affirms that all human beings are sinful, and have sinned and fallen short of God's highest and best for them, he also affirms the possibility by grace and through faith to avoid sin. He stands directly in the line of the early Jewish discussion by affirming that in the most important matter of all—one's salvation and the possibility of virtuous behavior—humans must respond to the initiative of grace freely, and continue to do so freely after initially becoming new creatures in Christ. The divine and human wills are both involved in such matters.

In sum, it is important to set Paul in the context of early Jewish discussions of such matters, especially early Pharisaic ones, to the extent we can discern them. When we do so, we find that Paul sounds rather like various of his contemporaries who certainly affirm divine providence, election, and destining, and also human sin and viable human choice, especially about the crucial matters of salvation and moral rectitude.

Early Returns and Late Losses

The concept of election is of course intertwined with the concepts of predestination and perseverance. Put another way, how one views election will affect, if not determine, how one views perseverance of the saints. If one thinks that God before the foundation of the world chose some individuals to be saved, come what may, then of course one has to believe that apostasy is impossible for a real Christian person, someone who is truly elect. But does God's destining, choosing, calling, saving really work that way? Is it really true that God's grace makes one an offer that one cannot ever refuse? Or is it the case that one is not eternally secure until one is securely in eternity? These are good questions that great minds have debated for centuries, and I am not naïve enough to think that anything I say here will stop that ongoing debate.

What I would hope, however, is that the discussion could be put on more sound exegetical footing, especially from the Reformed side of the equation, because frankly there are just too many warnings in the NT that Christians can and do fall prey to temptation, can make shipwreck of their faith, can grieve or quench the Holy Spirit in their lives, and can even commit apostasy or the unforgivable sin. If this can happen to genuine Christians, those whom God has called and given the Holy Spirit to, and destined or intended in advance for them to be conformed to the image of the Son, then frankly something is wrong with the Reformed concept of election.

Note that I did not say that there is *no* concept of election or of God's choosing people in the NT. Of course there is. However much this may make some of my voluntarist Arminian friends uncomfortable, it has to be frankly admitted that there is a concept of election in the NT that must not be ignored. The question is: what sort of concept of election? We need to work through various relevant texts about election and perseverance, and once again, Paul's letters are the real source of the material that is most often debated, especially by Evangelicals. Let us turn now to these texts. We begin with the earliest place, chronologically, in which Paul speaks of these matters: 1 Thessalonians.

The language of election and being beloved by God does not appear, of course, for the first time in the Bible in 1 Thessalonians, but it is quite common in the Pauline corpus. For example, the connection between God's love and election that we see in 1 Thessalonians 1:4 we also find in 2 Thessalonians 2:13, Romans 9:11–13, and Colossians 3:12. Paul is simply applying to the Christian assembly election-language that had previously been used of Israel on numerous occasions (see, e.g., Deut 32:15; 33:12; Isa 44:2). Note, for example, how election statements originally made only of Jews (Hos 2:25) are now applied by Paul to Jews and Gentiles united in Christ (Rom 9:28).[2]

Election for Paul is a corporate thing. It was in ethnic Israel; it is now "in Christ."[3] From Paul's viewpoint, which is simply an adaptation of views found in early Judaism, "election" does not guarantee the final salvation of individual Christian converts any more than it guaranteed the final salvation of individual Israelites in the past. We must caution that Paul's hermeneutical use of texts like Hosea 2:25 does not mean he operates with a replacement theology, as if God has reneged on his promises to Jews, but it does mean that those promises are now and in the future to be fulfilled through and by the Lord Jesus, the Jews' and Gentiles' Messiah. The church has not replaced Israel. Rather, Jews like Paul who believe in Jesus are viewed as the true Israel, the true descendants of Abraham, and those Gentiles who join them have become part of the people of God, grafted into the true olive tree.[4] Paul's is a fulfillment rather than replacement theology. But it is not just that Paul carries over concepts of corporate election from early Judaism into his theologizing about the Christian assembly. Just as apostasy was and could be committed by individual Israelites, whom God then broke off from the people of God, at least temporarily (see Rom 11:11–24), so there was also the same danger for individual Christians, hence all the warnings about falling away in 1 and 2 Thessalonians.

In his detailed discussion of the use of the term *eklektos* found in the Septuagint as well as in Paul's letters (cf. 2 Thess 2:13, 16; Rom 8:33; Col 3:12), I. H. Marshall rightly asks the question: Does the term simply refer to an action of God, perhaps a premundane action of God ("the people upon whom God has set his choice"), or does the phrase in fact refer to "the people upon whom God has set his choice and who have responded to the call"?[5] The answer he gives is that an "examination of the usage in the OT and in Judaism shows that the phrase 'the elect' is used of those who *have* become members of God's people and never of individuals *before* they have become members of God's people."[6]

This is correct, and we may add that apart from its occasional application to the king (cf. later the application to Jesus), the language of election in the OT is applied corporately to a people, not to an individual. The word "elect" (*bahir*) is normally used in the plural, and so collectively of Israel. And lest we think that being elect guarantees salvation, we even have texts like 2 Kings 23:27 where we hear of God rejecting Jerusalem after having chosen it. There are also, of course, texts that speak of God choosing and anointing persons for specific historical purposes (e.g., Cyrus in Isa 45:1), but these are not soteriological texts. In fact it must be stressed that texts which refer to Pharoah or Cyrus or someone else being chosen for some particular historical task, positive or negative, are really of no relevance to this discussion, because they are not about God picking those persons to be saved or to have eternal life. This is the general context in which one must view the references to election in 1 and 2 Thessalonians, to which we now turn.

In this discussion we interact with two dialogue partners, I. H. Marshall and J. M. Gundry Volf, who come to opposite conclusions in regard to the meaning of Paul's election, perseverance, and apostasy language.[7] Let us start with 1 Thessalonians 3:5 where Paul speaks of fearing that he may have been laboring in vain due to the dangers of loss of faith facing the Thessalonian church because of their many tribulations.

Gundry Volf on the one hand argues that while this *sounds* like Paul's genuine worry that his converts might fall away or commit apostasy, in fact what he was worried about was himself, his legacy, his own potential unfaithfulness to his calling, and whether in the end his own ministry was rooted in God's saving power.[8] She puts it this way: "Paul thus feared being robbed of his 'hope and joy or crown of boasting . . . before our Lord Jesus at his coming' if his converts fell in persecution. . . . Paul is thus uncertain whether or not some of his converts will be numbered among the saved at the day of Christ."[9] In her view, Paul also worried that perhaps some of his converts had actually falsely professed faith in the first place.

It would be hard to describe how many things are wrong with this sort of argument. In the first place Paul has no uncertainty at all about whether God's power was active amongst the Thessalonians and converted them when Paul preached there. He is in fact emphatic about this at 1 Thessalonians 1:5; the word came to them with power and in the Holy Spirit and with full conviction. He does not say it came to just *some* of them in this way. There is no shred of evidence in these letters that Paul worried that *some* had falsely made a profession of faith. Psychologically and socially it is hard to imagine someone doing that anyway in a social environment where there was considerable pressure and persecution *not* to convert to this new "Jewish superstition."

In the second place, as Marshall says, this explanation:

> fails to do justice to the fact that Paul's remarks are undoubtedly motivated by genuine concern for the welfare of his readers and not by personal concern for his own reputation at the parousia. Moreover, the language used shows that the purpose of sending Timothy to them was not to see whether they were truly converted, but rather to encourage converts to stand firm in the midst of persecution and to see what was the state of their faith. Paul's language deals with standing firm despite tribulation (3:3, 8) and repairing any weaknesses in their faith (3:10), not with the question of whether the readers actually possess faith.[10]

The worry and anxiety and pastoral concern of Paul in 1 Thessalonians about the spiritual danger his converts are truly in is hard to discredit or pass off as mere rhetorical flourish, much less to suggest it was really worry about himself.

Returning to 1 Thessalonians 1:4, what must be stressed is that "Paul's claim to knowledge of their election is related to his knowledge of their conversion."[11] "He wants to say both that the choice of God to save them was expressed in the fact that the Gospel came to them in power and that their response of faith shows that they now belong to the 'elect.'"[12] Notice too that Paul says that not only he but also the Thessalonians can "know" that the Thessalonians are God's chosen. There is nothing here about the invisible elect amongst the mass of churchgoers. This "knowing" comes from the recognizing of the positive response to the gospel received with joy and the changed lives turning from idols to the living God. Indeed the chosen are all too visible and are enduring persecution because of it. What Paul certainly does not say, or want to say, is that the Thessalonians have believed because God chose them and caused them to do so.

Our next text of interest is 1 Thessalonians 5:9—"For God did not purpose/appoint/ arrange things for/assign us to suffer wrath but rather to receive salvation through our Lord Jesus." The "us" here is those who are already Christians, and this text is thus closely parallel to what is said in Romans 8:28–30.[13] It has to do with the final destiny of human beings who are either lost or saved. The same antithesis may be found in Romans 5:9–10. Now there can be no doubt that the verb *tithemi* here in the middle with the preposition *eis* means to "purpose for/unto" or to "appoint for/unto." We may compare for example the same language in Acts 13:47 quoting the Septuagint of Isaiah 49:6 where we hear of a people who were appointed for or to be a light to the Gentiles. Of course in individual cases, some Israelites failed to fulfill the destiny or purpose that God intended for them. This was not because they were not chosen or purposed by God for such a task or end. In fact, if we compare John 15:16, we will see that the words for purposing and electing or choosing are used as virtual synonyms. What can be said about purposing can also be said about electing or choosing.

Gundry Volf argues on the basis of 1 Thessalonians 5:9 that Paul means that God has purposed for individual persons to receive final salvation and that this divine purpose will infallibly be brought to conclusion and completion. She stresses that the use of the verb "receive" here indicates the actual reception of something, which she takes to mean pure passivity, not allowing for any positive effort toward the goal or purposed end by the recipient.[14] She says, "Paul's statement that God has not destined Christians to wrath relativizes human action,"[15] but then she adds, "God's appointment to salvation does not make human obedience superfluous."[16] But if it is not superfluous or incidental to the outcome, then surely it is essential to the outcome!

The fact that final salvation is a gift that must be received when Christ returns does not in any way relativize the importance of believers here and now persevering in the faith so that they might "be in that number when the saints go marching in." Nothing in 1 or 2 Thessalonians suggests otherwise, and indeed much suggests that persevering is something that Christians must actively purpose and engage in, for it is possible for them to fall or commit apostasy. This is why in the very same context in 1 Thessalonians 5:11 Paul warns the Thessalonians to be alert and watchful, lest they be caught napping or even stumble in the dark.

This text in 1 Thessalonians 5:9 may also be compared to 2 Peter 3:9, which says that God does not desire that any should perish but that all should come to repentance. God's desires are one thing, the outcome is another. Similarly God's purpose, design, or intent for Israel to be a light to the nations was one thing. Whether they fulfilled that purpose or not in individual cases was not merely up to God; it also required willing human participation. Especially the text in Acts 13:47 should be seen as parallel to our text in 1 Thessalonians 5 when it comes to the force of the language about God's purposes or appointments.[17]

It is worth adding as well that since the very same instance of the very same Greek verb *etheto* ("appoint") in 1 Thessalonians 5:9 applies to those who are heading for wrath as well as to those being saved, it may be asked whether Gundry Volf really wants to argue that God infallibly and inevitably appointed some for wrath from before the foundation of the world, come what may and do what they will? The answer is apparently no, she does not want to argue that case. But then accordingly, whatever "appoint" means for the lost is also what "appoint" means for the saved in this text, and in neither case is unilateral predestination apart from human response or willing participation in view.

There is, in addition to the language of election, the language of calling. The question is, what does it mean when Paul talks about being called or God calling a person? The issue for this discussion is whether calling means "effectual calling" (i.e., an action of God which includes and indeed prompts and necessarily assures the response of the one called). 1 Thessalonians 2:12 is a good example of how Paul can use this language. He speaks of living a life "worthy of the one who calls you into his dominion and glory." Here the term *calling* does not refer to something retrospective but rather something prospective. It refers to the fact that believers are being invited or called to enter the eschatological dominion in the future. Clearly this text is not about "effectual calling" as a past event in the believer's life.

What about 1 Thessalonians 4:7? Here the reference is to the call that comes at conversion to change one's pattern of life or behavior. God is the one doing the calling, and he calls us not to uncleanness but to holiness. This way of putting it, in the midst of paraenesis and exhortations of various sorts, makes clear that Paul thinks that unclean and immoral behavior is certainly possible, and that to do such a thing is to go against one's calling, against the lifestyle one has been called to live. As Marshall says, this text makes clear that the ethical response to the call is an ongoing matter, and the potential of going against one's calling is an ongoing possibility.[18]

1 Thessalonians 5:24 is of interest in this discussion as well. Here, calling is something God does in the present ("the one who calls you"), and this usage is exceedingly common in Paul's letters (Rom 4:17; 9:11; Gal 1:6, 15; 5:8; 1 Thess 2:12; 2 Tim 1:9). Paul promises that God, for his part, will be faithful and that he is capable of entirely sanctifying a person and keeping a person blameless "at/in the coming of the Lord Jesus" (this is what Paul prays for in 1 Thess 5:23). This seems to refer to something God will do at the eschaton, for notice here the reference to the body as well as the human spirit.

In other words, Paul seems to be referring to what happens at the resurrection, when the believer is glorified and transformed into the likeness of Christ (see 1 Cor 15). This is Paul's prayer that his converts will be in the right condition when Christ comes to judge the world, and so will be found both pure and blameless at that juncture. This then would be similar to the eschatological statement at 1 Thessalonians 2:12. It would not, in short, be about the "perseverance of the saints" before and leading up to the return of Christ but about the condition of the believer on that day or at the time of the parousia of Christ. Had Paul wanted to talk about perseverance, he could have used the preposition *eis* and spoken of being kept blameless "unto/for," or the preposition *achri* and spoken of "until" the coming. He uses neither of these prepositions here.

Gundry Volf takes this text to mean that since God will be faithful to the end, "he will complete the salvation begun in their calling."[19] The problem with this conclusion is that besides missing the point that Paul is talking about God's direct action on behalf of the believer at the eschaton, in which God raises the believer and presents him or her pure and blameless and with a glorified body before Jesus when he sits on the *bema* seat to judge even believers (see 2 Cor 5:10), there is the further problem that when Paul does talk about holiness and progressive sanctification during this lifetime he includes remarks like we find in 1 Thessalonians 4:3–5 where human actions are involved, and not solely divine ones, and we have exhortations such as we find at 1 Thessalonians 5:22 to hold on to the good and avoid evil.

Confirmation that we are right in our eschatological interpretation of 1 Thessalonians 5:23 can be found in 1 Thessalonians 3:13, which refers to the ongoing process of God strengthening hearts so that believers will be blameless, not now, but when Jesus returns with the holy ones. Obviously there is a relationship between progressive sanctification and final glorification, but the former involves both the strengthening and purifying work of God and also the correct responsive behavior of believers, whereas what happens at the eschaton is purely a matter of divine action. It will be too late to change one's behavior at that juncture.

One of the interesting points that Marshall makes most strongly when considering some of the similar texts in 2 Thessalonians (e.g., 2 Thess 1:11–12; 2:13–14) is that there is a paraenetic character or implication to Paul's prayers in two ways: (1) on the one hand, praying that disciples will behave in a certain way is a good indirect way of urging or persuading them that they need to behave that way, and Marshall goes on to rightly point out the paraenetic context of these prayers; (2) he also points out that if one reads these Pauline intercessory prayers carefully, there is in them an element of doubt, which is to say the reason Paul feels he needs to pray for these things is because it is not absolutely certain that his converts will persevere in the faith. Prayer is a vehicle which aids them in the process of doing so, then, in two ways— galvanizing both them and the Almighty to that good end.[20]

Lastly we may consider 2 Thessalonians 3:3. Here we have a pastoral assurance that God will protect these converts under pressure from the Evil One. As Marshall says, this probably means that the Evil One's attacks, though real, will be in vain. As such this is close to the assurance Paul offers in 1 Corinthians 10:13.[21] Gundry Volf takes this to mean that God will not allow the believer to fail the final test of perseverance, even though he allows small stumblings and acts of disobedience along the way.[22]

The problem with this exegesis is that Paul is talking about protection from an external source of trial, tribulation, and temptation. He is not talking about a believer wrestling internally with the possibility of committing apostasy. The text is about protection, not a guarantee of human perseverance come what may. In Romans 8:38–39 we have a similar promise for believers about no external force or factor separating them from the love of God. However, the one thing not listed in that list is, of course, the individual himself. That text does not suggest it is impossible for a called and chosen believing person to commit apostasy, and neither does our text, 2 Thessalonians 3:3.[23]

What this discussion has shown is that Paul's reasoning on these matters is eschatological to the core. He speaks pastorally about what God has already accomplished through Paul's proclamation of the gospel in Thessalonike, what God is doing now with his calling still echoing in the ears of the believer, and what God will do when God raises the dead believers at the eschaton. Protology, or God's decisions before the foundation of the world, is not really a subject of these discussions. In other words, the discussion of calling and election and perseverance comports with the *narration* which begins with the story of the Thessalonians' conversion and then moves forward, pressing on relentlessly to the return of Christ. The narration then prepares admirably in 1 Thessalonians for the exhortations in 1 Thessalonians 4–5 about the parousia and the state of the dead in Christ.

PERSEVERING WITH BEALE

Sometimes one can see that a theological system is causing problems for the exegesis of particular texts when the exegete in question simply refuses to allow that the text is saying what it seems clearly to be saying. Such is the case with G. Beale's handling of some of the perseverance texts in 1 Thessalonians 5 and 2 Thessalonians 1. Beale tries to argue that the use of the aorist participle *endusamenoi* in 1 Thessalonians 5:8 "indicates not that believers make their own efforts to put on armor, but that as 'sons of light' they have already been clothed with the armor. That is, although Christians have been clothed with the armor of faith, love and hope in Christ (as 1:3 affirms) they need to grow in these virtues and in their identification with Christ."[24] But 1 Thessalonians 1:3 says nothing about where the faith, hope, and love have come from; indeed, that verse is focusing on the labor and endurance that comes forth from those virtues. Romans 13:12–13 makes perfectly clear that Paul *does* talk about the efforts Christians make to put on the armor. It says "let us put aside the deeds of darkness and let us put on (*endusametha*) the armor of light." Furthermore, Paul regularly uses the language of "putting on" to refer to human activity (cf. Gal 3:27; Eph 4:24; Col 3:10, 12). Attempts to blunt the hortatory character and force of this verse in 1 Thessalonians and Paul's theological ethics in general should be resisted. As Ephesians 6:11–17 later shows, such texts are all about exhortations to take up and put on and bear witness to and exhibit these qualities of the Christian life, and it is presumed that effort is required by the Christian to accomplish this aim. Here the aorist participle could mean "having put on," referring to an action the converts have taken in the past, or if pure "Aktionsart" is in view, it may be an exhortation to punctiliar action—"put on": either is possible here, but in either case we are talking about human actions.[25]

It is of a piece with the quote cited above from Beale that he goes on to argue, "Why is the apostle persuaded that the majority in the church at Thessalonica will be adequately prepared for Christ's return? Paul is convinced that most of his readers are elect (1:4) and that therefore *God did not appoint them to suffer wrath but to receive salvation*

(5:9)."[26] But the texts cited by Beale say nothing about "the majority" of the audience being elect or "some" of them being destined to obtain salvation. Paul addresses the *entire* Thessalonian audience in this fashion throughout this letter. Why is this? Because Paul believes that God desires that all should be saved, and that God has appointed all believers to avoid wrath and obtain salvation.

Beale goes on to add that the reason things turn out as they do for believers is clear: "God's sovereign determination of someone for his own particular purposes."[27] But unfortunately for Beale's viewpoint, the language of election, appointing, destining is used in a variety of ways in Paul, and indeed in the NT, and in no case is it used in a fashion that suggests that humans are predetermined for salvation or wrath regardless of their own volitions or desires, as if only God's will was involved in such crucial matters, or as if only God's will determines the outcome of these things.

In 1 Thessalonians 5:9 the converts are reassured that God did not appoint them to suffer judgment and wrath in the future, but rather to receive salvation through "our Lord Jesus Christ." Notice that the sentence begins with *hoti*, "because." The converts are to put on the armor *because* God did not appoint them for wrath. Their destiny is different from those referred to as sleeping or drunk in v. 3. But of course, destinies and destinations can change. Those in darkness may finally see the light, and those in the light may make shipwreck of their faith (see 1 Tim 1:19).

One reason Paul insists here on speaking of salvation as something to be obtained[28] in the future is precisely that Christian behavior can affect the outcome until one dies or Jesus returns. Salvation is a gift whether one is talking about initial or final salvation, but when one is referring to the latter it is a gift given to those who have persevered, have put on the armor, have stayed alert, have remained faithful and true, and the like. The word *etheto* here as elsewhere indicates God's soteriological purpose. It is believers whom God appoints or destines for final salvation (cf. 1 Pet 2:8).

This passage in 1 Thessalonians 5:9 is somewhat like Romans 8:28–29, and in both cases the language of destining is used to reassure Christians, those who already love God, about their future. The subject is not about destining or electing some to be believers.[29] Finally notice that salvation is obtained through the Lord Jesus. He is the medium or agent of salvation and if one is not connected to him one cannot obtain final salvation. It is his work on the cross that makes possible the giving of the gift of salvation.

The idea here is that God has provided the believer with the necessary "equipment"—if they will put on the armor, stay awake and alert, and so persevere they may obtain the gift of final salvation. Paul "does not suggest that God's plan is fulfilled independently of the action of [human beings] . . . Paul's exhortations to vigilance would be nonsensical if vigilance was the product of some inward causation in the believer by God or if there was no possibility of disobeying the exhortation."[30]

1 Thessalonians 5:10 flows logically from v. 9 and is important because it shows that Paul already had an understanding of the salvific nature and importance of Jesus' death, and how it was the key to believers being joined together and with Christ at the eschaton. There is dispute as to whether the crucial preposition here was originally *peri* or *huper*. Aleph, B, and MS 33 alone have the former reading, but p30, A, D, and many others have the latter reading. Both the number and the geographical spread and diverse text types represented by the latter reading favor *huper* as being original. The difference of nuance is that *huper* more clearly makes evident the beneficial nature of Christ's death—"he died on behalf of us."[31]

This would surely seem to imply also that he died instead of us— i.e., a vicarious death, though this is not explicit here. In any case this theology is expressed more fully elsewhere (cf. Gal 1:4; Rom 14:9; 2 Cor 5:15, 21). There may be something to the suggestion of M. D. Hooker that Paul has the idea of interchange in mind here—that Christ became what we are and died, so that we might become what he is and live.[32] This idea is certainly in the mind of Irenaeus when he reflects on the meaning of Paul's letters and the Christ event (*Haer.* 5, pref.). That Paul does not have to elaborate on the significance of Jesus' death here suggests that his audience had already been instructed on this matter, which was perhaps the most scandalous part of the Good News— namely, the death on the cross of the Savior.

The *hina* clause describes the purpose of his death—he died *in order that* a people, made up of both deceased and living believers, will one day live with him (see Rom 14:8). Though Paul does not usually use waking and sleeping in tandem as metaphors for being alive and dead, it is fitting that he does so here as he draws the eschatological section of the exhortation to a close.[33] Here Paul touches again, in a reassuring way, on the matter discussed in 1 Thessalonians 4, namely that the deceased believers along with those believers who are alive when Jesus returns will enter into life or begin to live together with the Lord when he returns. "In Paul 'life' means more than 'existence with'; it implies 'resurrection life'; Paul envisages the Christian as entering into the resurrection life which depends on Christ's resurrection, and the Christian's life is transformed when this happens (1 Cor 15; Phil 3:21 . . .)."[34] Beale has rightly noticed the clear parallels between 1 Thessalonians 4:14–18 and 5:10–11, and that both sections conclude with essentially the same remark.[35] This makes quite clear that Paul is not addressing sequential events in 1 Thessalonians 4:14–18 and 5:1–11.[36]

Paul's overall message in this text is much like we find in Philippians. God is working in their midst to will and to do, but they in turn must work out their salvation with fear and trembling (Phil 2:12–13). Initial salvation is by grace through faith; final salvation involves not only grace, and faith, not only progressive sanctification worked inwardly by the Holy Spirit, but also active persevering on the part of the believer. There are three tenses to salvation in the Pauline discussion of the matter: I have been saved, I am being saved, I will be saved or obtain salvation. Until one passes through all three of these tenses of salvation, the situation is still . . . tense. There is still the possibility of apostasy, a willful rejection of the work of God in the believer's life.

It is necessary now to turn to Beale's treatment of 2 Thessalonians 1:3–4. He argues, "That Paul thanks God and not the readers for their faith, love, and endurance shows that they contributed *nothing* to achieving salvation but were the object of God's unconditional, gracious action."[37] Here again we see a theology of perseverance that requires Beale to deny that the text is saying what it is actually saying or implying—that God has enabled and empowered the Thessalonians to endure, be faithful, and persevere. There is more than just the action of God involved here, and the human portion of the action is seen as vital to the outcome, not as an afterthought or inevitable consequence of God's grace and actions. It is of course true that God is thanked here, but it is also true that the Thessalonians are being praised for how they have drawn on the grace and power of God to endure. It is not God who is being said to exercise faith or be faithful here, nor is it God's endurance through much suffering that is being commended in these verses. It is rather the Thessalonians' actions and faith, and Paul will not hesitate to boast to other congregations about the Thessalonians' Christian behavior (see v. 4).

Perseverance of the saints is not a foregone conclusion for Paul, nor merely a matter of God acting and it inevitably happens. This becomes especially clear when one reads Paul's earlier letters not in light of Augustine and Calvin's exegesis but in light of the Pastoral Epistles where Paul talks about the dangers of apostasy on page after page, and even names those who have made shipwreck of their Christian faith (1 Tim 1:20), something you cannot do unless you first have Christian faith.

There is a synergistic nature to perseverance as God works in the person or persons to will and to do, but they also must work out their salvation with fear and trembling. The human part is not optional or otiose, which means that God has chosen to allow us to participate in the process of our own sanctification and final salvation. Once again, Beale fails to take into account that initial and final salvation are not one and the same thing, and while God is involved from start to finish, humans and their responses to God are a necessary part of the process before it is all over. This leads us quite naturally to a discussion of that most controverted of all texts when it comes to these matters—Romans 8.

Knowing Your Pre-destination

Rather than diving right into the exegesis, Romans 8:28ff. is such a crucial text for Evangelicals that we will start with a fresh translation of the relevant section.

> But we know that for those who love God, all things work together[38] for good, for those called according to choice/purpose, for those whom he knew beforehand, he also destined beforehand to share the likeness of the form of his Son, so that he might be the firstborn of many brothers. Those he destined beforehand, he also called, and those he called he also set right, and those he set right he also glorified.

> What then shall we say to all this? If God is for us, is anyone against us? For he who did not spare his own Son but delivered him up for us all, how will he not with him, give us all things? Who will make an accusation against God's chosen? God is the one who sets it right. Who will condemn? Christ is the one who died, rather was raised, who also is at the right hand of God, who also intercedes for us. For what will separate us from the love of Christ? Will suffering or anguish or persecution or famine or nakedness or danger or the sword? Just as it is written "For the sake of you, we die the whole day, we are regarded as lambs for slaughter." But in all these situations we triumph gloriously through the one who loves us. For I am convinced that neither death nor life, nor angels nor rulers, nor things present nor things to come nor powers, nor height, nor depth nor any other part of creation is able to separate us from the love of God which is in Christ Jesus our Lord.

In v. 28 Paul makes a statement that he assumes is common knowledge ("we know," though this could be rhetorical, really meaning "we all ought to know"). This verse is interesting for a variety of reasons, not least of which is we have the rarity of Paul speaking about the believer's love for God. It is crucial, if one is to understand his argument here, to bear in mind that Paul is talking about those who are already Christians. For Christians who are called, all things work together. Paul is not talking about some evolutionary or inevitable process that happens like magic for believers. He is referring to the sovereignty and providence of God over all things and processes. God is the one who works things out, as the alternate textual reading, which inserts the words *ho Theos*, makes even clearer. That God is the subject is made clear by the reference just afterwards to "those whom he called."[39]

Whatever this verse means, it certainly does not mean exemption from the hardships of life, as Paul will go on to suggest when he lists such things later in this chapter. Probably *panta* (all things) here has especially in mind the sufferings of the present age. Paul believes that God can use such events, weaving them into his plan for a person's life, using all things to a good end (cf. 13:4)—namely, to the eventual end of the redemption of believers' bodies. The point is that all things can be made to serve the end of our redemption, not necessarily our earthly comfort or convenience. What this text does not mean is that God destines bad or evil things to happen to God's people to strengthen their character. There is more than one will in operation in the universe. There is God's will and human wills, not to mention the willing of angels and demons and the devil. What this text indicates is that God's will is the most powerful and dominant one, and he is thus capable of working even bad things and events together for good for those who love him. What Satan intends for harm, God can use for good.

The next phrase reads literally "those called according to purpose/choice." The word *his* often found in translations before the word *choice* is not in the Greek text. Some commentators have urged that *prothesis* could refer to human beings here, in which case the text would mean "those called according to (our) choice," or as we would say "by choice," the free act of choice by which those called respond to God's call. This is grammatically perfectly possible and is in fact the interpretation of this verse by Origen, Chrysostom, Theodoret, and other ancient Greek commentators who knew Paul's Greek far better than we do.

Chrysostom for example says in commenting on v. 28: "For if the calling alone were sufficient, how is it that all were not saved? Hence he says it is not the calling alone, but the purpose of those called too, that works the salvation. For the calling was not forced upon them, nor compulsory. All then were called, but all did not obey the call" (*Hom. Rom* 8). Thus the choice or purposing is seen by Chrysostom to be that of the respondent here. That human purpose or choice is in view seems to have been the view of almost all the Greek commentators. In support of the view that God's choice is meant here is probably Romans 9:11 (cf. Eph 1:11; 3:11; 2 Tim 1:9; Philo *Mos.* 3:61),[40] and one may point to the general tenor and drift of the passage, particularly the emphasis on divine action for the believer in 8:29. Since, however, this same verse refers to our love for God, the exegetical decision is not so clear cut and obvious, contrary to the impression left by most translations. Above all, the word "his" should not be inserted here, but rather the matter should be left open. It seems likely that Chrysostom was right.

Romans 8:29 must be read in light of v. 28; the *ous* at the beginning of v. 29 must refer back to "those who love God"—Christians. The discussion that follows is about the future of believers. Paul is not discussing some mass of unredeemed humanity out of which God chose some to be among the elect.[41] But what are we to do with the *hoti* in v. 29? It seems likely that it means "for" or "because" here, and is not merely an unimportant connective. If this is the case, then what follows the *hoti* in vv. 29–30 is going to explain why all things work together for good for believers. This working together for good happens because God has had a plan for believers all along. Verse 29, since it should be connected to v. 28, means "those believers that God knew in advance, he also destined beforehand to share the form of the image of his Son."

Is Paul then talking about a pretemporal election plan of God where the outcome is predetermined because of God's sovereign hand in and on every step of the process? This, of course, is how Augustine and his offspring read this text, but it is *not* how various of the crucial Greek fathers that came before Augustine read it, including most importantly Chrysostom. Paul is speaking about God foreknowing and destining in advance Christians to be fully conformed to the image of Christ.[42] It needs to be borne in mind that Paul's audience for these statements is Roman Christians, a largely Gentile audience, whom Paul apparently felt needed some encouragement due to suffering or persecution or other calamities they might be facing.

It is perfectly feasible in such a situation that Paul would want to tell believers not how they became Christians in the first place, but rather how God always had a plan to get believers to the finish line, working all things together for good, showing them how they will be able to persevere through whatever trials they may face along the way. In Christ they have a glorious destiny, and Paul will go on to stress that no outside power, circumstance, degree of suffering, or temptation can rip them out of the firm grip that God has on their lives. He is working things together for good in every stage of the salvation process.

The end or destiny of believers is to become fully Christlike, even in their bodily form. Paul has just said that the believer's hope is the redemption of their bodies; here he explains how God will be working to get the believer to that goal. P. Achtemeier strikes the right balance:

> As Paul uses [the terms foreknow and predestine], they do not refer in the first instance to some limitation on our freedom, nor do they refer to some arbitrary decision by God that some creatures are to be denied all chance at salvation. They simply point to the fact that God knows the end to which he will bring his creation, namely redemption, and that the destiny is firmly set in his purposes. . . . In that sense Paul can speak of "pre-destination." It means just as the word says, that the destiny has

already been set; and that destiny is the final redemptive transformation of reality.[43]

In short, and particularly in light of vv. 31–39, this comforting text is about the perseverance of the saints, not about the election of some to be saints out of a mass of unredeemed humanity, the choice being determined purely on the basis of God's fiat. That latter notion makes a nonsense of the very concept which is said to be determining this whole matter, namely love—not only God's love for believers, but the believer's love for God. It is "those who love God" who are called according to purpose and whom God foreknew, and that purpose they must embrace freely and fully in love.[44]

Love of God can be commanded, but it can neither be coerced, predetermined, or engineered in advance, or else it loses its character of being love. The proof that this line of thinking, and not that of Augustine, Luther, or Calvin, is on the right track is seen clearly in Romans 11:2 where Paul says plainly that God foreknew his Jewish people, and yet not all of them responded positively to God's call. Indeed, only a minority had when Paul wrote this letter. God's foreknowledge, and even God's plan of destiny for Israel, did not in the end predetermine which particular individual Israelite would respond positively to the gospel call and which would not. Paul will make clear in Romans 10:8–15 that the basis of that response is faith and confession. Just so, God's plan for his Elect One, Jesus, does not inexorably predetermine who will end up being "in Christ." What Paul has done in Romans 8 is reassured believers, saying, God has always known you and planned for your future, even from before the foundations of the universe. Some of the details of v. 29 need to be considered at this juncture.

First notice that Paul distinguishes between what God knows and what God wills or destines in advance. Knowing and willing are not one and the same with God. The proof of this, of course, is that God knows very well about human sin, but he does not will it or destine it to happen. What is implied in this is that God loved believers before they ever responded to the call and loved God. There are various early Jewish texts which speak of God's foreknowledge (cf. 1QH 1:7–8; CD 2:8; Jer 1:5).

The word *summorphous* probably does not have in view the conforming of the believer to the image of Christ that takes place internally and during the process of sanctification, or at least that is not the sole subject here. If it is referred to at all, it is referred to as part of the process that leads to the final act of conforming believers to Christ— namely the resurrection. Notice that Paul goes on to say that Christ becomes the firstborn of many brothers and sisters through this process. In view of 1 Corinthians 15:20–24 this surely refers to Christ's resurrection, his so-called birth (rebirth) being at the resurrection—"first fruits" and "firstborn" being two ways of speaking about the same thing, both of which imply that there would be more to follow. Käsemann is probably right to see the Adam story, grounded in the comparison in Romans 5, behind all of this.[45] Christ is the first of a new race, the race of the resurrected ones, who for now are being conformed internally but not yet externally to Christ's image.

Romans 8:30 then sums this all up, reassuring the Romans that God is in control of all these matters. Those believers whom he foreknew, he also destined in advance; those he destined, he also called; those he called, he also set right; and those he set right, he also glorified. The tenses of the verbs here make clear that we should take them as if Paul were looking at things from the eschatological end of the process with even glorification already having transpired. *Doxa* here refers to the future glory of resurrection as before. Paul's emphasis is on God's hand of involvement in every step of this process, and so he does not choose to mention or discuss in the midst of this verse the human response, positively or negatively. Notice he does not even mention sanctification.

But he has already spoken of believers loving God in v. 28, and that should be kept in view throughout the reading of vv. 29–30. If these latter two verses stood in isolation, and apart from a clear connection with vs. 28, that would be one thing; but they do not, and they must be interpreted in the light of the broader context of Pauline thinking about grace and faith, foreknowing and human purpose and the like. If vv. 29–30 stood alone, then Paul indeed would sound like the most deterministic of early Jews, such as we sometimes find in some of the early Jewish literature at Qumran and elsewhere. But they do not. What the Romans needed to be assured of was God's involvement, not their own, in all of the salvation process and plan. This text admirably stresses the hands-on nature of God and his providential plan. This truth, when it comes to looking at the Christian life as an exercise in persevering, will be even further highlighted in vv. 31–39.

Verse 31 begins in the first-person plural, but Paul becomes more direct and personal as the passage goes along. The *tauta* points back to what Paul has just spoken of, and so we are meant to see these verses as bringing to light certain conclusions that follow in view of the truths already shared. It is right to see these verses as the climax of the entire first part of the letter. Cranfield suggests that the theme here is "if God is for us, who can be against us," and he sees this as a concise summary of 1:16b–8:30.[46] This is correct, and it is no accident that Paul rises to an emotional climax here as well, with vv. 38–39 being in the first person singular. This conclusion is in the rhetorical form of the diatribe, where questions are again asked and then answered by Paul himself.

In order to demonstrate the theme of "if God is for us," Paul lists some of the things which are ranked against believers from time to time. Verse 32 sets forth the opposition, but puts them in perspective and in their place. In effect, the verse says that since God did not spare his own Son, certainly he will take care of the things that are trials for Christians, to make sure of their deliverance. Notice that the conditional statement (introduced by *ei*) in v. 31 introduces a real condition, not merely a probability.

Some commentators have seen in v. 32 an echo of the story of Isaac (Gen 22:12, 16, LXX). The traditions about the binding of Isaac were important in early Judaism, but the dating of various of those traditions, especially the one which suggests that the unconsummated sacrifice of Isaac atoned for Israel's sin, probably postdates the writing of Romans. If there is an allusion to such traditions here, then the point would be that Christ's sacrifice was greater than Isaac's, for it was completed. Romans 3:25 might also be alluding to such a tradition. Rather than sparing his Son, as Isaac was spared, God delivered him up to death "for us all," which at the very least means for all believers. Possibly Isaiah 53:12 (cf. Rom 4:25 for the verb) is alluded to here. If God will give up even his Son to death, how will he not give all things to believers? But what are these "all things"? The context makes clear that Paul is not talking about material wealth and the like. He means all that is necessary for salvation, all that is necessary to protect believers from spiritual danger in all sorts of difficult and dangerous circumstances. Again, this is not a promise of continual good health, or that believers will never suffer or die, but rather that no third party or power or force or circumstance or lesser supernatural being will be able to separate the believer from the love of God in Christ.

As Käsemann says, the Christ event of Jesus' death and resurrection forms the central dominant paradigm and idea out of which Paul interprets all that happens to the believer in the world, and all that is past, present, and future.[47] Not an abstract concept of God, but rather God with flesh on, God in Christ reconciling the world to himself characterizes Paul's understanding of deity. Paul speaks only of him as the God who reveals himself, not as the hidden God whose will and ways are inscrutable, and whose hidden counsels might actually be the opposite of his revealed Word. At the end of v. 32 we have the verbal form of *charis*, which we should translate "give graciously."

Then in v. 33 Paul enumerates the real and probable situations of difficulty and danger that he had had, and that his audience might well face. Verse 33 speaks of accusations against believers, perhaps envisioning a courtroom scene, and Paul asks, Who will make accusations against God's chosen ones? Paul does not answer by informing the listener as to who would make such accusations; rather, he chooses to say why such accusations would be fruitless and pointless and meaningless. God is the one who justifies those accused ones. If God sets them right, who could possibly condemn them (see Rom 8:1)? The highest judge of all has pronounced no condemnation as the verdict. Possibly Paul is drawing on Isaiah 50:7–9 here. There seem to be several probable allusions to the Servant Songs here as Paul concludes his positive arguments. It seems likely to me that Paul would indeed have seen Christ as the Suffering Servant referred to in those passages in Second Isaiah. More specifically, the language about God's Elect comes right from the OT way of talking about the people of God as a group (1 Chr 16:13; Ps 89:3; 105:6; Isa 42:1; 43:20; 45:4; 65:9–22; Sir 46:1; 47:22; Wis 3:9; 4:15; *Jub.* 1:29; 1QS 8:6; CD 4:3–4). What a careful reading of these texts will show is that these do not seem by and large to entail the notion that elect individuals have some sort of advance guarantee of salvation. No, the concept of "the Elect" applies to the group, and individuals within the group can, and indeed often are said to, commit apostasy. This is not because they were not chosen to be Jews, or "true" Jews in the first place. It is because they became unfaithful and chose to wander away.[48]

Even if the accusations were valid, Paul goes on to say that Jesus paid the price. He died for believers and rose again, and furthermore is seated in the seat of honor and influence beside God in heaven where he intercedes for the believer. The thought of Jesus as our intercessor is not uniquely Pauline (see also Heb 7:25; 1 John 2:1). Here we have two relative clauses, the second one being dependent on the first. The first seems to be alluding to Psalm 110. Pelagius in a striking remark says that Christ intercedes for us by constantly showing and offering the Father his perfect human nature. The point would be: "Don't judge them. In view of my work on earth they are redeemable."

The list of difficulties in Romans 8:35–36 has often been related to similar pagan lists, but unlike those lists Paul does not include happier circumstances along with the more difficult ones, and furthermore Paul's list is related to Christ and his sufferings, mentioned twice in the previous verses. All such things are to be viewed in the light of Christ's death, resurrection, and intercession while sitting on the seat of power (a phrase perhaps creedal in origin). As Käsemann says, Paul is not simply listing chance misfortunes but rather the woes that can and do come to those who are witnesses for Christ. In short, the context is the messianic woes in all probability, a special sort of suffering or tribulation.[49] All of the words in this list, except perhaps *stenochoria*, list external experiences, and refer to anguish caused by such experiences. Some of the items here are listed in pairs, and probably then we should see these particular two (*trouble* and *hardship*) as referring to outward suffering and inward pain or anguish. Notice how the same two words are paired in Romans 2:9.

The next word in the list is *persecution*, and could relate to what was just listed. But the following two, *famine* and *nakedness*, go naturally together, as do *danger* and *sword*. Possibly the word *sword* is last here because Paul is thinking of execution. For Roman citizens capital punishment took the form of beheading (cf. Rom 13:4). Obviously execution would be the last woe a Christian would face in this life. None of these things can separate the believer from the love of God received in Christ. Paul then at Romans 8:36 quotes from Psalm 44:22 (LXX 43:23), and the point of this quotation is much the same as the point of one part of 1 Corinthians 10: no danger that overcomes Christians is anything new or unexpected for the people of God. It is interesting that in 2 Maccabees 7 this same text is applied to the martyrdom of a mother and her seven sons. The *hoti* simply functions as a colon here to introduce the quote.

Romans 8:37 makes evident that Paul does expect his listeners to experience many if not all these calamities, but to triumph over and through them: "But in all these circumstances we triumph gloriously through the loving one." Cranfield points out that it is possible that *en toutois pasin* is a Hebraism meaning "in spite of all these things," but more probably it just means "in all these things."[50] In v. 38 Paul states a firm conviction that neither death nor life, nor angels, nor archangels, nor things present, nor things to come, nor powers, neither height nor depth, nor anything in all creation (*ktisis* again, meaning subhuman creatures and nature) is able to separate us from the love of God which is in Christ Jesus our Lord. This stringing together of Jesus' titles and names is also found in Romans 5:1.

The point of what is said at the end is that believers only really know the love of God in Christ Jesus, and experience it in him. There they know and experience it truly. Paul is saying that no natural or supernatural malevolent forces, even if they are capable of taking the believer's very life, are capable of separating the believer from the love of God; indeed, to take a believer's life is to send him directly into the presence of Jesus. Nothing that believers now experience or will experience can separate them from the love of God. The mention of angels and archangels is important as they perhaps represent the cosmic forces ranged against the believer (see Eph 6:12). It is not impossible that the term *powers*, or the term *rulers* refers to earthly authorities before whom the Roman Christians might be brought. The terms *height* and *depth* were traditionally thought to refer to things above the sky and beneath the earth.

Note the hymnic character of this entire passage. Paul has gone into a doxological mode here at the end of his positive arguments. There is, however, one item that Paul does not include in the list of things that cannot separate the believer from God's love, namely the believer himself. His point is to stress that no other forces, powers, experiences, or events external to the believer's own heart or mind can do so. Thus the believer has nothing to fear from the world in this respect. The scope of God's love is greater than the scope of the world's powers and forces, whether natural or supernatural. This is a great reassurance indeed and is meant, as is this whole passage, to bolster the idea of the perseverance of the saints and their salvation so long as they rest in the firm grasp of the hand of the Almighty.

In concluding this section it will be well to offer a quotation from a famous commentary on Romans by another Protestant Reformer, Philip Melancthon. On this passage he says the following:

> The Scholastics dispute whether a righteous person could lose his virtues, since Paul says: "Who shall separate us from the love?" as if he wanted to say: "In what way could we lose our love?" They thought that love should be interpreted of our virtues, that is, the love with which we love God. But this is unsound interpretation and must be rejected. It is certain that saints can fall and lose the Holy Spirit, faith, and love, as the prophet Nathan condemns David on account of adultery.
>
> Why then does he say that the love of God is everlasting? I answer: As the evangelical promise is perpetual and valid, but in such a way that it requires faith, so Paul is here speaking to believers, as if he said: "As long as you believe, as long as you do not fall from faith, it is most certain that the love of God toward you is in force." The meaning is this: Without doubt the love with which God loves us is always valid, firm, and certain for the believer. . . . Others have twisted this to refer to predestination, but there is no need to turn to that in this passage, for he is speaking of our victory. . . . The meaning will be simple and plain if it is understood of believers.[51]

The point of this quotation is not to endorse all that Melancthon says, though he is right that this passage is about those who are already Christians, and he is equally right about Paul believing in the dangers of apostasy. The point is to show that even within the Reformed, in this case the Lutheran tradition of interpretation, there were varying views on controversial texts like those we find in Romans 7 and 8. As it turns out Paul was neither a Lutheran nor a Calvinist before his time.[52] But what of Paul's discussion of election in Romans 9:11, what are we to make of it? As we shall see, it is of a piece with what we have found in Romans 8: election is a corporate concept, and individuals can opt in or out of the elect group. In fact, as we shall see, Paul's views of election have far more in common with early Jewish ones than Augustinian ones.

One more remark is in order in preparing for discussing Paul's controversial metaphor about being broken off or grafted into the people of God in Romans 9–11. Paul, like other early Jews, is fond of calling the Christian life a "walk." It involves certain deliberate and determined behavior by the believers in a certain direction if they are to enter the dominion of God in the future and so receive final salvation. Thus whether in Galatians 5 Paul is urging "walk worthily of your calling" or "walk in the Spirit, and you will not indulge the desires of the flesh," walking is required for reaching one's pre-destination. Christians are to choose the path less traveled and be prepared to enter by the narrow gate, and when in that same Galatians 5 text Paul warns all his Christians in Galatia that if they persist in or have a life characterized by any of the behavior mentioned in his vice list (murder, adultery, theft) they will not enter the dominion of God, he is not making idle threats. Christian behavior affects progressive sanctification (walk in the Spirit . . . and you will not indulge . . .), and progressive sanctification is needed to reach the finish line: the preapproved, previewed, pre-announced destination.

The Election of Jews and Jesus

The discussion of election in Romans 9–11 is a discussion of corporate election, in the midst of which there is individual rejection by some and selection for historical purposes of others. In other words, Paul gives equal emphasis to election and apostasy in his discussion. This is especially clear when Paul starts speaking of "you" singular in Romans 10.

To those Gentile Christians who are already saved he warns sternly in Romans 10–11 that they could be broken off the tree in a heartbeat if they choose to become unfaithful and unbelieving. Neither God's foreknowledge nor corporate election prevents individuals from becoming unfaithful and committing apostasy. Paul says if it happened in Israel, it can happen to Gentile believers as well if they do not watch out. In other words, nothing in this discussion of election suggests that the election results are rigged in advance for particular individuals, or that Paul was an early advocate of "once saved always saved" if by that one means that apostasy is impossible for those truly chosen by God. A close reading especially of Romans 10–11 makes this clear. And there is something else. Paul speaks of non-Christian Jews being broken off and grafted in, *after* in Romans 9 he has already listed all the perks, including their election and the covenants (plural) that Jews have had from God's grace. Obviously none of those benefits prevented one or another Jewish believer from going A.W.O.L.

Paul's views on predestination, election, the remnant, apostasy, and salvation fall within the parameters of such discussions in early Judaism, rather than within the framework of the later Augustinian, Lutheran, and Calvinistic discussions of the matter. Those early Jewish discussions make full allowance for both the notions of corporate election and the meaningful choices of individuals who may commit apostasy and opt out of the people of God.[53]

If we follow the flow of the narrative in Romans 9–11 it becomes clear that Paul does indeed draw on his Jewish heritage in discussing election, rejection, perseverance, and the like. For one thing, it becomes clear that God's foreknowledge is something that can be distinguished from God's destining in advance, which is to say that God's foreknowledge does not predetermine things (see Rom 11:2, where it is said he foreknew his whole Jewish people, but not all were saved). For another thing, Paul is capable of talking about individual Jews or Christians being broken off from the people of God, and even being grafted back in by grace through faith later. Indeed the whole drift of his argument in Romans 9–11 is that God still has a plan for Jews and that a large number will be grafted into the body of Christ by grace through faith when Jesus returns. What then are we meant to think of Paul's view of perseverance? Perhaps a brief parable will make his view clearer.

Picture a father crossing a busy highway with a small boy by his side holding his hand quite firmly. The father has good judgment, and he is capable of shielding the child from any calamity and protecting him from any outside force as they make their way across the highway. The one eventuality the father could not prevent, however, was the child being willful, wrenching himself free from his grasp, and running off and being struck by a vehicle. The child, you see, was old enough and strong enough to do so.

This, it seems to me, is an adequate parable of what Paul means by the last powerful paragraph of the argument in Romans 8, which leads quite naturally to the discussion in Romans 9–11. Paul does mean that God has a firm, loving grip on the believer, and no outside force can separate the believer from God and God's love. A believer cannot lose his salvation, like one might lose one's glasses. But by willful rebellion there is the possibility of apostasy, of making shipwreck of one's faith. The good news, then, is that one cannot lose or misplace one's salvation or simply wander away by accident. Indeed, only by an enormous willful effort could one throw it away. Such is the loving grasp God has on his children. We must now consider one further text of relevance to this discussion: Ephesians 1.

Beginning at Ephesians 1:4, Paul talks about the concept of election. The key phrase to understanding what he means by this concept is *in him* or *in Christ*.[54] When Paul says believers were chosen before the foundation of the world "in him," he does not mean that believers preexisted or even merely that God's salvation plan preexisted, though the latter is true. He means that Christ preexisted the creation of the universe, and by God's choosing of him (who is the Elect One), those who would come to be in him were chosen in the person of their agent or redeemer.

God, because of his great love, destined those who believe for the adoption as sons.[55] This freely given love is stressed in Ephesians 1:5. This happens only through Christ and according to God's good pleasure. Paul says "we were graced with this grace" in the Beloved, Christ, and for the sake of God's praise. The concept of election and destining here is a corporate one. If one is in him, one is elect and destined. Paul is not talking about the pretemporal electing or choosing of individual humans outside of Christ to be in Christ, but rather of the election of Christ and what is destined to happen to those, whoever they may be, who are in Christ.[56] The concept here is not radically different than the concept of the election of Israel in Romans 9–11. During the OT era, if one was in Israel, one was a part of God's chosen people; if one had no such connection, one was not elect. Individual persons within Israel could opt out by means of apostasy, and others could be grafted in (see the story of Ruth).[57] These concepts of election were then applied to Christ, who as a divine person could incorporate into himself various others. Christ becomes the locus of election and salvation because in Paul's thinking the story of the people of God is whittled down to the story of Jesus the Anointed One, and then built back up in the risen Christ thereafter. When Paul speaks of how a lost person gets "into Christ," he speaks on the more mundane level of preaching, hearing, and responding in faith, not of God's prechoosing of our choices for us. This doctrine of corporate election in Christ is meant as a comfort for those who already believe, reassuring them that by God's grace and their perseverance in the faith they can and will make the eschatological goal or finish line.[58]

This approach to the matter also comports with the ecclesiocentric focus of this document. As R. Schnackenburg says, the Christology found in Colossians 1:15–20 is here used in Ephesians' service of an explanation of the benefits believers have in Christ. "The faithful, the members of Christ's body, the Church are included in God's all-embracing plan for and accomplishment of salvation by means of that cosmic christology including Christ's pre-existence."[59] It is possible that Jesus' baptismal scene is in mind at Ephesians 1:6–7, for Christ is called the Beloved Son, and at Christ's baptism there is also the language of washing away of sins. The word *apolutrosis* (cf. Dan 4:34 LXX) can refer to a buying back or ransoming of a slave. Paul says nothing of a ransom paid to Satan, as God owes Satan nothing. Christ is redeeming the lost person from the bondage of sin by paying the price for that sin for them. Redemption is only had "in him." This redemption terminology then is metaphorical, as is shown by the equation with forgiveness of sins.

Forgiveness comes to the believer out of the riches of God's grace, not because she or he merits it. This grace is said to overflow to Gentiles as well as to Jews, and it comes about by the revelation of the secret, the *musterion,*[60] which here refers to God's plan to reconcile all things, all peoples, all worlds in Christ. Paul in this discourse favors the use of the verb *made known,* found here in Ephesians 1:9 but also in 3:3, 5, 10, and 6:19. This comports with the epideictic nature of the discourse which has as one of its main goals making things known, aiding the understanding of fundamental values of the community.

The revelation of the secret comes in preaching, but the preaching only comes about because God has first done something in human history through the death and resurrection of Jesus. It is thus quite unlike other religions that may have had purely otherworldly mysteries in view. This open secret is about what God has accomplished in Christ in space and time. Christ was sent for the administration or ministry[61] in the fullness of time (cf. Gal 4:4–5; an apocalyptic concept see 2 Esd 4:37; 2 *Bar.* 40:3; 1QpHab 7:13–14), summing up under one head, all things in himself. The idea of the fullness of time connotes not merely that the right and ripe time has come, thus bringing a long-awaited event or process. It also conveys the notion of the starting of a whole new set of circumstances at the precise time God chose to begin it. The word *anakephalaiosasthai* can simply mean "summing up," but in view of the way Paul is going to use the term *head* of Christ in v. 22, it is much more likely that he is playing on the literal meaning of the term, "bringing together under or in one head." This bringing together or summing up in Christ involves both things in heaven and on earth. This would be puzzling were there not things in the heavens that needed this unifying work.

Ephesians 1:11 reiterates the theme of v. 4 that believers were chosen in him. The constant refrain of "in him" must be kept steadily in view throughout the eulogy. Christ carries out the intention of God's good will. Verse 12 says that believers as redeemed, are redeemed for the purpose of God's glorious praise. This is the ultimate aim of humanity: to live for the praise of God, to let all we are and all we do be doxology, a giving of glory to God. The Scottish catechism puts it well in saying that the chief end of humankind is to love God and enjoy God forever. It was in Christ that the good news was heard, the word of truth about God's plan, good will, and intention. It was in him that believers believed and thus in him were affixed with the seal—the promised Holy Spirit.

The seal here is not likely baptism, since Paul nowhere mentions baptism in this passage, but rather the Holy Spirit. "The metaphor of a seal does not imply that the Holy Spirit has stamped us with a seal . . . but that he himself is this seal, a sign characterizing our Christian existence."[62] The function of a seal in antiquity was to authenticate a document, but this term here could also refer to the branding of a slave. In that way one would know to whom the servant belonged. In view of the "ownership" or "acquisition" in v. 14 (*peripoineos*), it likely has the latter meaning here. The point is not the protection or eternal security of the person in question, but rather the identification of who belongs to Christ. Notice the change from "we" to "you" in v. 13. As Fee suggests, Paul is here giving a sneak preview of the discussion in 2:11–3:6 where the "we" is clearly Jewish Christians.[63] While it is true that the "you" draws the audience into the praise, it also distinguishes them from the author and his fellow believers who were Jewish Christians.

This Spirit is also the pledge of our inheritance. The term *arrabon* means "down payment" or "first installment" or "deposit." It does not simply mean "guarantee" here, though that idea is not excluded. It is the first installment, and thus surety that God plans to complete his work of salvation in the believer. The Spirit then is foretaste, not mere foreshadowing; down payment, not mere pledge of the eternal inheritance. "Although Ephesians depicts the gifts of salvation as fully present in the lives of believers, the designation 'pledge' suggests a future perfection to this experience."[64] The benefits Christians already enjoy are but a foreshadowing of the blessings yet to come, a fact which should stimulate even more praise to the ultimate benefactor. "Despite their minority status in the world of first century CE Asia Minor, Christians found themselves the center of God's cosmic design because they belonged to the risen Lord, who is exalted over all the heavenly powers. Benefits that humans might expect to receive from 'the heavens' have been conferred by God in Christ."[65]

Yet still all believers await the acquisition of full redemption, or perhaps better said await God's full redemption of his possession, namely the church. Even in Ephesians, there is a not-yet dimension to salvation. A quote from G. B. Caird can help us conclude this section of our discussion: "The salvation of man is not to be conceived as the rescue of favored individuals out of a doomed world to participate in an otherworldly existence totally unrelated to life on earth. Man's personality is so intimately linked with his environment that he must be saved in the context of all the corporate relationships and loyalties, achievements and aspirations, which constitute a genuinely human existence."[66] Just so. We need at this juncture to draw some conclusions for this part of our discussion.

CONCLUSIONS

Though the Reformers were not all equally indebted to Augustine, it seems clear that the indebtedness of Luther and Calvin was considerable, especially when it came to the understanding of issues like predestination, election, salvation, perseverance of the saints, and the nature of the limited atonement of Christ on the cross. Behind all of this was a particular conception of God's sovereignty, a conception which in the case of Augustine owed something to Manicheanism, and fatalism. Unfortunately, when this heritage was brought to bear in interpreting the Scriptures, Paul in particular suffered. It took Paul out of his Jewish context and read him as an exponent of a later and, one might add, a largely non-Jewish theology, which muffled the Jewish focus on orthopraxy, on how the believer should live.

The conclusions that seem warranted from this discussion are various. First, Paul's conception of election is a corporate one, and it does not predetermine which particular individuals can be in or out of the group. Furthermore, Paul does not operate with an "invisible elect" amidst the people of God concept. The Israelites or Christians who are true are all too visible and evident. The tree is known by the fruit it bears. Second, Paul fully affirms that perseverance is necessary to salvation, and that it involves human effort. He also affirms that apostasy is possible for a true believer, something other texts such as Hebrews 6 fully confirm as well. One is not eternally secure until one is securely in eternity.

Third, Paul believes that Christians are under a new covenant, not any administrations of the older ones. He does see the new covenant as the fulfillment of the Abrahamic one. Among other things, this means that Christians, whether Jew or Gentile, are no longer under the Mosaic Law. They are rather under the Law of Christ.

Fourth, it is worth adding, though we have not really discussed this in this chapter,[67] that Paul also does not operate with a concept of imputed righteousness, if by that phrase one means Christ's righteousness is counted in place of ours. A careful reading of Galatians 3 and Romans 4 will show that what Paul says on the basis of Genesis 12–15 is that Abraham's faith was reckoned or counted as righteousness. His faith was reckoned as his righteousness. This is a very different matter than Christ's righteousness counting in the place of that of the believers.

Paul affirms that believers are initially set right with God by grace through faith, but that they must go on with the aid of grace to be righteous, to manifest holiness, indeed even to go on to completion or perfection at least at the point of the resurrection of the believer when in body as well as in spirit they become truly whole.[68] Righteousness needs to be imparted by the Spirit, not merely imputed. God is not deceived, nor does he ignore the Christian's sin. It is not the case that when God looks at the believer he simply sees the righteous Christ. And as 2 Corinthians 5:10 (cf. 1 Cor 3) makes perfectly evident, Christians will be held accountable for their behavior when they appear before the judgment seat of Christ. If they choose to persist in their sin such that they commit moral (or for that matter theological) apostasy, as Paul so clearly warns in Galatians 5:19–21, they will not enter the dominion of God when it comes with Christ in eschatological glory at the end of the age.

Fifth, the Reformation inclination to say the atonement is limited was correct, but as texts like Romans 5:1–11 and 1 Timothy 1:15 make evident, Christ came to die for sinners, not the elect. Indeed, as 1 Timothy 2:4–5 makes perfectly clear, God desires all persons to be saved (so also John 3:16), and Christ gave himself as a ransom for all sinners. This means that it must be human beings in their response to God in Christ, not God through some process of choosing individuals, who limit the atonement.

Sixth, since numerous NT authors, including Paul and the author of Hebrews, not to mention Jesus himself, warn against the problem of apostasy, this in turn must mean that God's saving grace is both resistible at the outset and rejectable later. There may be moments of overwhelming grace in a human life—such as, for example, at the moment of Paul's conversion—but it does not follow from this that grace is always irresistible.

Seventh, the character of God as a God of holy love and also a God of freedom is such that he expects these same qualities to be reflected in his creatures, whom he calls to freely respond to his gift of salvation. Love cannot be coerced, manipulated, or predetermined.

Eighth, in our discussion of Romans 7 we also noted that Luther was wrong to think that Paul was discussing the Christian life in that text. Rather we have a Christian view of a non-Christian condition, perhaps a person on the verge of conversion in Romans 7:14–25, while Romans 7:7–13 retells Adam's tale.

The tension in the Christian life is not between old person and new person, but rather between Holy Spirit and sinful inclinations, on the one hand, and inner self, which is being renewed, in contrast to outer self, which is wasting away. However, as Paul makes very clear in 1 Corinthians 10:13, the believer has sufficient grace available to him or her to resist any temptation, and as Romans 8:1–3 says (cf. Rom 7:4–5) the Christian has been set free from the bondage to sin by the powerful Holy Spirit of life. A Christian should never assume that righteousness only has to do with his or her position in relationship to God, rather than also with his or her condition.

Christians are called to holy living, and they are empowered to carry out such living. This involves realizing that God's grace is greater than fallen human nature, and that God expects obedience and progress toward entire sanctification. We will have much more to say about these things when we turn around and try to come to grips with the exegetical weaknesses in the Arminian way of thinking about these soteriological issues. Now, however, it is time to consider a much more recent theology—Dispensationalism—that has spread like kudzu throughout the conservative Protestant Church and is threatening to overrun and overwhelm traditional Protestant theology of various ilks. As we shall see, it is exegetically by far the weakest of these three theologies we are critiquing.

PART TWO

ON DISPENSING WITH DISPENSATIONALISM

CHAPTER 5

Enraptured but not Uplifted:
The Origins of Dispensationalism
and Prophecy

If the major problem with Calvinism had to do with its Augustinian vision of the way sovereignty is exercised by God, and the scope and nature of the divine plan of salvation, coupled with an Augustinian view of human nature (even redeemed Christian nature falls under the rubric of Romans 7:6–25), the major exegetical problems of Dispensationalism have more to do with eschatology, ecclesiology, and even ecology, not to mention its hermeneutics and understanding of prophecy.[1]

Of the three theological systems we are examining in this book, Dispensationalism is in fact the new kid on the block, only dating back to the nineteenth century, and it is clearly the most exegetically problematic as well. It is necessary to start with a brief survey of the history and nature of Dispensationalism and the Dispensational approach to the Bible and especially biblical prophecy before dealing with the primary texts used to prove things like a rapture, or an actual Armageddon involving human armies, or the existence of two returns of Christ, two peoples of God, and the like.

Unlike the case with Calvinism, the Dispensational approach to the Bible did not arise after profound study of the Hebrew or Greek Scriptures or detailed scholarly exegesis of the text. It was a system that apparently arose in response to a vision and as a result of a pastoral concern about unfulfilled biblical prophecy, and was promulgated by various ministers and evangelists and entrepreneurs in the nineteenth and twentieth centuries. More recently, it has often been wed with the all-too-American gospel of success and wealth, not to mention the belief that America is in some way God's chosen instrument, though of course the Bible says nothing about America. Sometimes, in addition, one is dealing with a double problem because some highly influential Dispensationalists (e.g., Jerry Falwell) are also

Calvinists as well, which makes things even more exegetically problematic. Then too, there is the problem that many if not most Messianic Jews are also Dispensationalists.

Thus when one tries to deconstruct Dispensationlism, one is at the same time deconstructing major building blocks of several forms of Evangelical theology, and one sometimes has to fight on several fronts at once to make clear what the exegetical problems are. Nevertheless, in this section of the book we stick to the texts that have really been distorted in Dispensational schools of thought.[2]

FROM THE PLYMOUTH BRETHREN TO PLYMOUTH ROCK

In 1830 in Glasgow, Scotland, a young girl named Margaret MacDonald attended a healing service. She was said to have received a vision on the occasion of a two-stage return of Christ, though it is not clear whether she envisioned a pre-tribulation or a post-tribulation rapture to coordinate with the first of these comings.[3] The matter might have fallen into obscurity except that a British Evangelical preacher named John Nelson Darby heard the story and spread it far and wide. Darby, who was to become the founder of the Plymouth Brethren denomination, explained more fully and clearly that Christ would definitely come twice, the first in secret to rapture the church out of the world and up to heaven. He would then return after seven years of worldwide tribulation to establish a dominion on earth based in Jerusalem. Darby coordinated this latter event with the discussion of the "glorious appearing" referred to in Titus 2:13 and distinguished it from the discussion of the "parousia" in 1 Thessalonians 4.

The term *rapture*, of course, does not occur anywhere in the New Testament. It comes from the Latin word *raptus/raptio* which in turn is a translation of the Greek word *arpadzo* which means "caught up" (1 Thess 4:17). For both Darby and later Dispensationalists the most important Scriptural basis for the notion of a rapture was 1 Thessalonians 4. We will say much more about this and related texts shortly.

The teaching of the rapture might have remained a relatively obscure matter confined to one small Protestant group in the British Isles except for the fact that Darby made numerous evangelistic trips to America between 1859 and 1877 and won many American converts to the rapture theology. Note carefully the dates of these trips. Darby showed up on the brink of the Civil War, during the war, and after the war, right when many Americans were quite vulnerable to an escapist theology that promised they would not have to go through the great tribulation. The timing could not have been better for promulgating such a theology.

To his credit Darby refrained from going for the eschatological jackpot of predicting specific dates for the end of the world or the rapture, or the visible second coming of Christ. What he did instead was to invent "dispensations," by which was meant intervals of time in God's timetable of eschatological events, with various texts and prophecies coordinated with and applicable to different dispensations. Darby concluded that God had divided all of history into seven distinct Dispensations or ages. In each of these Dispensations God dealt with people differently, and according to differing rules.[4]

Again, the matter might have been a flash in the pan, except for two further developments. Dwight L. Moody became enamored with this theology and began promulgating it on both sides of the Atlantic, furthered by the founding of the Moody Bible Institute, and eventually by Moody Press and by a radio network. But by far the single most enduring tool for spreading this theology was a reference Bible, put together by one Cyrus I. Scofield and first published in 1909.

The Scofield Reference Bible had both the King James Version as text and extensive notes throughout, coupled with maps, charts, and Dispensational headings. Most of the major prophetic texts were commented on and coordinated with one or another of the Dispensations according to Darby's teachings. The headings and notes were woven in with the text itself, which made it appear as if this teaching was self-evident and indeed arose directly from the text. With the publication of this Bible, Scofield hit the jackpot, selling millions. What few know about him today is that he was an embezzler and forger who abandoned his wife and children and did time in jail even after his conversion to Christianity. Never mind all this; his Bible had a life of its own, due in large part to the promotion of the Moody Bible Institute and a very wealthy Chicago businessman named William E. Blackstone, who himself had already cashed in on the rapture theology by writing the book *Jesus Is Coming* in 1878 (veiling his identity by simply having the initials W. E. B. appended to the book and its title page). Blackstone was an avid Zionist, and his book helped further the fervor for studying scriptural theology in light of this sort of prophetic schema.

There was, however, a major problem that needed to be addressed. Despite the ever-growing popularity of this theology with laypeople, frightened by one war or another that America was embroiled in, this theology did not have any scholarly grounding or basis. It did not arise out of detailed exegetical study of the biblical text in its original languages, unlike Calvinism and Lutheranism, and Arminianism. Indeed it was dependent in many ways on the King James translation of the Bible. This was a lay theology formed and promulgated by preachers and laypersons.[5]

It is certainly not surprising then that someone like Lewis Chafer, a Presbyterian, would come along feeling the need to establish a Dispensational training center, in part to shore up the exegetical and theological liabilities of Dispensational theology. The result was Dallas Theological Seminary founded in 1924, which has produced the likes of John Walvoord (who was president of the institution between 1952 and 1986), Charles Ryrie, Hal Lindsey, and many names familiar to Evangelicals who have been readers of popular Evangelical theology. These leaders and their writings have impacted Jerry Falwell, Pat Robertson, Timothy and Beverley LaHaye, and a host of Dispensational televangelists who will remain nameless.

In the wake of the enormous success of the Left Behind series, selling in the millions, and in view of how biblically illiterate our culture and even the church has become, it is not surprising this theology has continued to be popular, especially when America continues to get itself involved in stressful wars in Kuwait or Iraq or Afghanistan and elsewhere. American Christians are looking for the theological equivalent of comfort food and escapist entertainment, and Dispensational theology is readily meeting these needs. But it needs to be asked: is this a true version or a perversion of what the Bible actually teaches? Only detailed attention to the biblical text can answer such questions.

A word of caution: one will need to drive slowly through the following material and study carefully the detailed road signs along the way. Biblical prophecy is complex and cannot be figured out by a sorting system, multicolored charts, or a string of chain references, or even by a few detailed word studies. Instead one has to ask about the very nature of biblical prophecy and of apocalyptic and figure out how such material was meant to function and what truths it is trying to tell believers in every age of church history, not just late Western Christians.

THE CONTEXT AND CHARACTER OF BIBLICAL PROPHECY

Dispensationalism arose in part due to a concern about apparently unfulfilled biblical prophecies. To their credit, Dispensationalists recognized rightly that the NT has a profoundly eschatological orientation and much to say about the future, and indeed even a good deal of OT prophecy seems to have not yet been fulfilled. The problem in part with Dispensationalism was not only that it did not recognize that a good deal of biblical prophecy either actually has been fulfilled (though sometimes in a less than absolutely literal manner), but also that a good deal of biblical prophecy was conditional in nature to begin with (and thus when the conditions were not met, the fulfillment never came). When a prophecy begins, "If my people who are called by my name will repent and turn to me," and then goes on to make predictions or promises, it was not always realized that if God's people did not repent, one should not expect the fulfillment of the conditional prophecy or promise of God. Lurking behind the Dispensational approach was perhaps also the worry that unfulfilled prophecy might be seen as false prophecy, or worse, that unfulfilled prophecy might make God appear to not be a keeper of his word. Unfortunately these sorts of anxieties were answered by coming up with a view of prophecy and its character that largely ignored the original historical context and nature of such prophecy. So let us consider the matter directly.

"In the beginning was the Word." It is a familiar and seemingly simple assertion, and yet its profundity in a largely oral cultural environment can be overlooked. In an ancient culture the living Word, the living voice, always had a certain precedence over a written word. And of all the wordsmiths of antiquity, none had more power or authority than those who could speak for God, or in a pagan culture, for the gods. Indeed, those who could proffer a late word from God might well be the most important members of an ancient society.

It is not at all surprising that a study of prophecy in antiquity reveals that apparently almost all such cultures had some persons who exercised roles we would call prophetic. I have undertaken such a detailed study of prophecy elsewhere, and can here only summarize some of the salient points of relevance for our discussion of Dispensationalism.[6] Prophecy did not begin with the period of the Israelite monarchy nor did it end when that monarchy was eclipsed, for even in Israel prophecy in some forms carried on beyond that period of time. Nor were the prophets of Israel, any more than the NT prophets, operating in a cultural vacuum. It was possible for a Balaam or a Jonah or a Paul to cross cultural boundaries and still be recognized as some sort of prophetic figure. This is because the social functions and roles and to some degree even the forms and contents of the messages of prophets were the same throughout antiquity in the eastern end of the Mediterranean.

Whether we are talking about the period of the Babylonian Empire or the Roman Empire, certain traits marked out prophetic figures such that they could be recognized throughout the region as some sort of spokesmen or spokeswomen for the divine, and could cross cultural and ethnic boundaries and still function. Indeed prophecy was such a cross-cultural phenomenon that Babylonian kings might well have Jewish prophets serving in their court, and Roman emperors might well listen to the word of an eastern and Jewish prophet before making a major decision. If one wants to understand biblical prophecy, one necessarily must be prepared to fish with a large net.

It is worth pondering why such a large proportion of the Hebrew Scriptures involves prophetic books, while the NT, unless one counts the apocalyptic revelation that concludes that corpus, contains no books which could be called prophetic as a whole or even any that in the main involve collections of oracles. Could it be because the NT writers believed that they already lived in an age when these prophecies, through and as a result of the Christ event, were rapidly being fulfilled? Yes, this is indeed part of the truth, but there are also many clues about Hebrew prophecy, being a part of the larger ancient Near Eastern (ANE) phenomenon, that were missed by the Dispensationalists.

While there was a range of things that prophets might do and say in the ancient world, nonetheless their activity, the form of their discourse, and the social purposes and effects of this discourse were similar in all these Mediterranean cultures, so much so that a person traveling from, say, Rome to the extremes of the eastern end of the empire in the first century A.D. could speak about prophets and prophecy and expect most any audience to have a reasonably clear notion of the subject matter of his discourse. Similarly, during the time of Jeremiah one could travel from Babylon to Jerusalem and expect the social phenomenon of prophecy to be in many, though not all, ways the same in a variety of these ANE cultures. The story of Jonah, like the story of Balaam, encourages us to look at prophecy as a cross-cultural phenomenon, with influence moving in various directions and development happening through the course of time.

I have discovered in my odyssey through the prophetic material that a great deal of loose talk has been allowed to pass for critical thinking about who were prophets and what the nature of their utterances was. For example, in my discipline, but also in OT studies, prophecy is often simply lumped together with preaching or with the creative handling and interpreting of earlier sacred texts. Part of this lack of clarity may be put down to confusion on the difference between prophetic utterances and the literary residue of such utterances, namely books of prophetic material, collected and edited by scribes over the course of time. I have found it important to distinguish between the prophetic experience, the prophetic expression, the prophetic tradition, and the prophetic corpus, all of which are part of the social phenomenon that falls under the heading of prophecy.

I have been struck over and over again how across a variety of cultural lines and over the course of an enormous amount of time Jews, pagans, and Christians who lived in the eastern end of the Mediterranean crescent all seem to have reasonably clear and reasonably similar ideas about what constituted a prophet and what constituted prophecy. To share a few of the conclusions of my earlier study, a prophet was an oracle, a mouthpiece for some divine being, and as such he or she did not speak for himself but for another. A prophet might also be many other things (teacher, priest, sage), but the role of prophet could be distinguished from these other roles and functions.

Prophecy, whether from Mari or Jerusalem or Delphi or Rome, was spoken in known languages, usually in poetic form, and so was an intelligible, even if often puzzling, kind of discourse. It might involve spontaneous utterances or a reading of omens or signs of various sorts, but in either case it was not a matter of deciphering ancient texts, which was the task of scribes and sages and exegetes of various sorts. Furthermore, consulting a prophet was an attempt to obtain a late word from one or another deity about some pressing or impending matter. In sociological terms the prophet must be seen as a mediatory figure, which therefore makes him very important but also subjects him to being pushed to the margins of society if the divine words involve curse rather than blessing, judgment rather than redemption.

At least in the setting of Israel and early Christianity the prophet also is one who deliberately stands at the boundary of the community— the boundary between God and the community, but also the boundary between the community and those outside it. It is the task of the prophet to call God's people to account and to reinforce the prescribed boundaries of the community while reestablishing or reinforcing the divine-human relationship.

This takes us to another factor which has too often been underplayed in the scholarly discourse (perhaps in order to avoid the embarrassment of having to say that a particular favorite prophet might be wrong). I am referring to the fact that prophecy was more often than not predictive in character, though most often its subject matter dealt with something thought to be on the *near* horizon, not something decades, much less centuries, in the future. And even when the more remote future was the subject of prophecy, the subject was raised because it was thought to have a rather direct bearing on the present. In short, ancient prophets and prophetesses were not by and large armchair speculators about remote subjects. Nostradamus (if even he was such a speculator) would not have felt comfortable in this company.

What is also interesting, as a close reading of Isaiah 40–66 will show, is that prophecy about the more distant horizon was deliberately less specific and more universal or multivalent in character, dealing with ideas and themes that the immediate audience could understand, but also themes that could transcend the immediate and particular circumstances of those listening to the prophet. I should also stress the imagaic character of prophecy dealing with the more distant horizon. Almost all oracles have something of a poetic form, but prophecy about the more remote future tends to involve even more metaphor, simile, and poetic devices like hyperbole to make its point.

Thus when the prophet talks about Eden renewed, with lions lying down with lambs, and swords being beaten into plowshares, not only are such images not code terms for the cessation of the stockpiling of nuclear weapons in the modern era, they are also not about building factories in antiquity where swords would literally be beaten into plowshares. They are rather metaphorical ways of speaking about the cessation of hostilities. It is especially interesting that when the OT prophets, including the apocalyptic ones (Ezekiel, Daniel, Zechariah), thought about the more distant horizon, they did not dwell on impending doom or Armageddon, but rather eventual redemption and restoration of God's people and Eden-like conditions.

These predictive prophecies were indeed meant to be taken seriously, as they are referential, but they were inherently figurative in character, and so were not intended to be taken literally. One of the main ways that Dispensationalism repeatedly has violated the character of biblical prophecy is by taking poetry as prose, figurative as literal. There is in addition the problem of mistaking material that was fulfilled long ago in Israel or in general in biblical times as material awaiting a literal fulfillment as the Christian era nears an end. However, Jesus was not joking when he said that the events leading up to the destruction of the temple would all occur within a generation (see Mark 13). Only a minority of what is said in Matthew 24–25 or Mark 13 has any bearing on current or future events as we view them in the beginning of the twenty-first century. We will say more about this shortly. Especially problematic is the way apocalyptic literature has been treated in Dispensationalism—and when I refer to apocalyptic literature, I am referring to those texts that are the heart and guts of the Dispensational schema: Daniel, Ezekiel, Zechariah, and Revelation. But what is apocalyptic literature? Here is a definition that begins to help us decipher such material, followed by an orienting discussion.

The Society of Biblical Literature definition, arising out of its seminar on apocalyptic literature, is as good a starting point as any. It says that an apocalypse is "a genre of revelatory literature with a narrative framework, in which a revelation is mediated by an otherworldly being to a human recipient, disclosing a transcendent reality which is both temporal, insofar as it envisages eschatological salvation, and spatial, insofar as it involves another, supernatural world."[7] To this definition is sometimes added the statement that this literature is minority literature written in coded language to comfort a group of believers undergoing some sort of crisis.

The essence of the definition is that present, mundane reality is interpreted in light of both the supernatural world and the future. For the book of Revelation this entails beginning with the present experiences of the churches and trying to help them interpret and endure those experiences in the light of the larger perspective that John's visions of what is above and beyond give them. This book at least is clearly minority literature written in a somewhat coded way for persons enduring some sort of crisis.

Eschatological ideas are not necessarily the heart of what apocalyptic is all about, for such ideas are found in many types of early Jewish and Christian literature, and for that matter there are apocalypses that do not really focus on the final form the future will take. Apocalyptic then is primarily a matter of the use of a distinctive form—visions with often bizarre and hyperbolic metaphors and images. Some apocalypses focus almost entirely on otherworldly journeys without saying much about the end of human history. In other words, historical apocalypses are not the pattern for the whole genre.

The very heart of apocalyptic is the unveiling of secrets and truths about God's perspective on a variety of subjects, including justice and the problem of evil, and what God proposes to do about such matters. This literature is the dominant form of prophecy in Jewish contexts from the second century B.C. to the second century A.D., and it reflects the fact that its authors believed they lived in the age when earlier prophecies were being fulfilled, and, therefore, it was right to contemplate what God's final answer and solution would be to the human dilemma. This dominance of apocalyptic also reflects the deeply held conviction that God's people lived in dark times when God's hand in matters and God's will for believers were not perfectly evident. God's plan had to be revealed like a secret, for matters in human history were mysterious and complex.

My view is that the major cause of the shift from traditional prophecy to apocalyptic during the era mentioned above was not the fact that there were not still traditional-style oracular and sign prophets abroad (e.g., John the Baptist), but because of the conviction that God's people were living at the dawn of or actually in the eschatological age. The final things had already been set in motion, and under such circumstances it was appropriate to talk about the end of the end times.

It is no accident that the historical apocalypses begin to disappear from Jewish literature after A.D. 70 and from Christian literature in the second and third centuries A.D. Otherworldly journeys, such as we find in Dante's *Divine Comedy*, take their place. Future eschatology came largely to be replaced by otherworldly eschatology and mysticism the closer one got to the Middle Ages. The grip of imminentist eschatology on believers gradually loosened after the first century A.D. This is as true of Jewish as of Christian literature. A futurist eschatological outlook explains much about Jesus, about the earliest Christians' belief system, and about the belief system of the author of Revelation.[8]

What is completely lost in the shuffle in the Dispensational discussion of such material is not merely literary sensitivity to the sort of material one is dealing with, but the recognition that these prophecies were the Word of God for Jews and Christians many centuries ago, and they had meaning for those audiences. Indeed, they were written for those audiences in the first place, not for us. What the text meant then is still what the text means today, and what it could not possibly have meant in the first century A.D. or before, it does not mean now. These texts were not written to scare the living daylights out of late Western Christians now living at the dawn of the twenty-first century. The Christian authors of the oracles in the NT believed that their own immediate audiences already lived in the age of fulfillment, already lived in the end times.

When one delves into Greek and Roman literature, one quickly learns that there was a widespread belief in the pagan world that dreams and visions were real means by which gods and demigods could reveal truths to and instruct human beings.[9] But it is not just dreams and visions that are pertinent to the discussion of how John's audience would hear Revelation. There is also the oracular tradition in the Greco-Roman world about the succession of emperors and empires. We find this sort of material in the Sybilline Oracles. One example will have to suffice from the eighth Sibylline Oracle, which seems to see the terminus of things in the reign of Hadrian and so comes from within twenty years of the date of Revelation:

> When the sixth generation of Latin kings will complete its last life and leave its scepter, another king of this race will reign, who will rule over the entire earth, and hold power over the scepter; and he will rule well in accord with the command of the great god; the children and generation of children of this man will be safe from violation according to the prophecy of the cyclic time of years.
>
> When there will have been fifteen kings of Egypt, then, when the phoenix of the fifth span of years will have come . . . there will arise a race of destructive people, a race without laws, the race of the Hebrews. Then Ares will plunder Ares, and he will destroy the insolent boast of the Romans, for at that time the luxuriant rule of the Romans will be destroyed, ancient queen over conquered cities. The plain of fertile Rome will no longer be victorious when rising to power from Asia, together with Ares, he comes. He will arise arranging all these things in the city from top to bottom. You will fill out three times three hundreds and forty and eight cycling years when an evil, violent fate will come upon you, filling out your name. (*Sib. Or.* 8:131–50; trans. D. Potter)[10]

The sixth generation of Latin kings in all likelihood refers to the Flavians, with Nero being the sixth Caesar, who is in turn a part of the sixth generation (cf. the number 666 of the Neronian antichrist figure in Revelation). My point in referring to this example is to show that the character of Revelation would not necessarily have seemed so foreign to the Gentile mind, which was well familiar with the notions of revelatory dreams, visions, and oracles about human history. A detailed knowledge of the Jewish practice of gematria or the use of symbolic numbers would not be required to realize that various of the numbers in Revelation had symbolic significance. Jewish apocalyptic imagery offered a new twist, but the story was still about political matters and the rise and fall of rulers and realms, and their times and seasons. This larger Greco-Roman context also makes clear that it would be unlikely for John's audience to see his work as *not* historically referential. Rather, it would be viewed as some sort of symbolic but nonetheless real prophetic material involving the history of the period leading into the final future of humankind, unveiling the overarching and underlying supernatural forces involved in the human drama.

One of the major points I made in my earlier study of prophecy is that it is important to distinguish between prophetic experience, prophetic expression, and the prophetic tradition. The book of Revelation is certainly not simply a transcript of a prophetic experience, as its epistolary framework makes clear. Rather the seer has incorporated into a complex literary whole a report of his vision or visions reflected upon in light of the Hebrew Scriptures and a variety of other sources. John had visions, and then fashioned an apocalyptic prophetic work to express not merely what he had seen, but what bearing that vision had on his audiences. This means we might well not have an apocalypse at all had John not been some distance from his audiences. Rather he might have just shared most of the visions orally with his churches as they came, without resorting to a literary creation.

We probably should not imagine John on Patmos poring over Hebrew Scripture scrolls and then creating a literary patchwork quilt. The visions that came to John came to a Scripture-saturated mind, but also to a mind well acquainted with popular and mythical images of the larger Greco-Roman world. What John heard he may well have transcribed almost verbatim, but what he saw he had to describe, and thus he drew on his existing mental resources to do so. When what one sees is images and symbols in odd combinations, one must grope for analogies to describe the experience (hence the repeated use of the phrase *it was like*). One must resort to aspective, metaphorical, mythological, and some times multivalent language. One must resort to somewhat universal symbols, which explains why such works have been able to communicate across time, which in itself also helps explain why these works were preserved. But paradoxically, it is also true that apocalyptic prophecy always requires interpretation or explanation. It is indeed a somewhat coded form of language, and those not knowing the universe of discourse will be in the dark.

While it is certainly true that there are various examples of otherworldly visions in Revelation, it is crucial to bear in mind that this work is not just about what is transpiring in heaven. The seer is not simply a mystic, like other early Jewish or Christian mystics. There is a historical and eschatological dimension to this book not only in the opening letters but also in the descriptions of destruction followed by a new earth as well as a new heaven. The seer is concerned not just about a heaven that is spatially near, but events that are thought to be at least possibly temporally near. His focus is not just up there, but also out there. It is perhaps a product of modern tendencies to separate the social and the spiritual, or the mundane and the supernatural, that one finds the notions of traffic between heaven and earth, or of an open heaven and an influenced earth, or indeed of a merger between heaven and earth (Rev 21–22) somewhat off-putting. John has not substituted an otherworldly view of eternity for an earlier, more temporal, historical, eschatological one. Rather, the two are intertwined here. A quick comparison with the Shepherd of Hermas or, even better, Dante's *Divine Comedy* will show just how eschatological John's Revelation actually is.[11]

On the other hand, it also will not do to assume that John himself believed he was simply using mythical images to describe all-too-mundane realities. John really believed not merely in God and the Christ and angels but in their regular interaction with humankind in the earthly sphere. The angels, for instance, are not symbols or figures of human beings. One should not be misled by the hyperbolic nature and rhetorical dimensions of various of the apocalyptic images into thinking that this material is not intended to be referential. Indeed it is, but the references are sometimes to human figures and sometimes to superhuman ones.

That this material uses universal metaphorical symbols and is not literally descriptive should not lead one to assume that it is not referring to some reality John believed existed. John's focus, like most biblical writers, is on the redemption and judgments of God in space and time. As such, he shares an essential kinship with other prophets and seers in the Jewish and Christian tradition who are concerned about the future of God's people not merely in heaven but on earth. This is one of the things that distinguishes John from those who simply have mystical visions of heaven or go on ecstatic otherworldly tours of heaven and its occupants and activities. Indeed, it could be disputed that John even had an otherworldly tour in the Spirit. It appears more likely that John's experience was simply a matter of receiving certain revelations seriatim. His account does not read like Enoch's tour of heaven.

E. Schüssler Fiorenza's conclusion is worth pondering at this point: "Early Christian prophecy is expressed in apocalyptic form and early Christian apocalyptic is carried on by early Christian prophets. Early Christian prophecy is an ecstatic experience in the Spirit and the revelation of divine mysteries."[12] What is not so apt about this is the assumption that all early Christian prophecy took this form or was an expression of apocalyptic, or that apocalyptic is the mother genre and prophecy a subset under it. But this much is absolutely correct: apocalypses like that of John are not purely literary products of tradents. They are generated by prophets and grounded in prophetic experience of an apocalyptic sort. Schüssler Fiorenza is also quite right that Revelation shares with early Christian prophecy the following: it is an eschatological revelation of or about Jesus Christ which has as a main purpose exhortation and strengthening of communities and is meant to be read aloud or performed in Christian worship, for unlike much of Greco-Roman prophecy, it is not individual but rather communal in nature. Christian prophecy and apocalyptic were not, in general, matters or products of private consultation.

It cannot be stressed enough that one of the rhetorical functions of a work like Revelation is to give early Christians perspective, especially in regard to the matters of good and evil, redemption and judgment. Revelation seeks to peel back the veil and reveal to the audience the underlying supernatural forces at work behind the scenes that are affecting what is going on at the human level. In short a certain limited dualism is evident in this literature. The message is often: "though it appears that evil is triumphing, God is still in his heaven and all in due course will be right with the world." It is stressed that the goal of life is ultimately beyond death in either the afterlife or the afterworld on earth or both. There is also usually a strong sense of alienation and loss of power in these documents, and thus a major stress on God's sovereignty and divine intervention in human affairs. The stress is on transcendent solutions to human dilemmas, though human efforts have not been rendered either meaningless or pointless.

Here is a good place to say a bit more about the use of multivalent symbols in Revelation. It is true that the wounded beast in Revelation 13 and 17 probably does allude to Nero, but with the help of mythological imagery Nero is portrayed as but a representative example of a higher supernatural evil—the antichrist figure. The author knows that Nero does not exhaust the meaning of the figure, but he certainly exemplifies it well. There could be other such figures as well, for the author is dealing with types. These symbols are plastic and flexible, and on the order of character analysis rather than literal descriptions. Christ can be depicted in Revelation as the blood-drenched warrior or a lamb who was slain, or a lion, or an old man with snow-white hair. All these descriptions are meant to reveal some aspect of his character and activity. In this respect, these symbols are very much like some modern political cartoons.

Apocalyptic literature is basically minority literature, and often even sectarian literature, the product of a subset of a subculture in the Greco-Roman world. While it is not always true that such literature is written in a time of crisis or for a people experiencing crisis or persecution at that specific point, it is certainly written for people who feel vulnerable in a world that largely does not concur with their own worldview. In the case of Revelation, there is probably enough internal evidence to suggest that there had been some persecution and even martyrdom and that more was expected.

It is not surprising then that apocalyptic prophecy often has a political dimension, dealing with the dominant human powers that appear to be shaping the destiny of God's people. Whether it is Revelation portraying Rome as a modern-day Babylon or Daniel portraying a succession of beastly empires, there is frequent discussion of these matters in such literature but always under the veil of apocalyptic symbols and images. One must be an insider to really sense the referents and the drift of the polemic and promises. This aspect of apocalyptic literature grows directly out of the classical Jewish prophetic material where nations and rulers including Israel's are critiqued, but here this is carried out by "outsiders" (those who do not have controlling access to the political process) using insiders' language.

There is such a strong stress on God's control over the final eschatological situation in apocalyptic literature that when in fact one gets to the final showdown, it turns out not to be a battle between human forces, which we might call Armageddon, but rather a divine execution. Consider, for example, 2 Thessalonians 2:8. At v. 8 we arrive at the same juncture in time as in 2 Thessalonians 2:3, with vv. 6–7 dealing with the prelude to the final acts in the eschatological scenario. It is not made clear how long the Lawless One will operate unhindered before Christ returns. The issue is to make clear his ultimate downfall.[13] One of the most interesting features of this verse is that it makes clear that the final judgment of the Lawless One will be accomplished by word rather than by war, indeed by the breath of Jesus' mouth. Compare how in Revelation 19:21 the Rider on the White Horse (aka Christ) executes the kings of the earth and their armies by the sword of the word coming out of Messiah's mouth. We may compare how in Revelation 20:7–10 the final judgment of Gog and Magog transpires also by direct divine action, in this case fire from heaven. There will be no final great battle between human forces called Armageddon, only a final divine execution as is described in various ways in these texts. This makes all speculation about some great Middle Eastern war between human combatants not only otiose, but odious, since in fact the NT suggests a different end-game scenario involving direct divine intervention.

But perhaps we should ask, what caused the change from ordinary prophecy to apocalyptic in Israel? Why did prophets like Ezekiel turn to this remarkably imagaic and visually stimulating form of poetic expression? It was not just the loss of the monarchy that changed Jewish prophecy and prophets, but its replacement by a not infrequently hostile and anti-Semitic foreign power. All Jewish or Christian prophets in such a situation are peripheral prophets and often must resort to coded language to express their message. From a psychological point of view, one might wish to consider the suggestion that having been cut off from their spiritual center in Jerusalem (or in John's case in the Christian communities in western Asia Minor), revelation was expected to come to God's people in less clear and more enigmatic ways, for they were further from the perceived central locale of the divine presence. There was also the important matter that God's justice seemed to be delayed or deferred. When would it come to pass? Would the saints get their just deserts in this life, or perhaps would it be in another world or a later time? These are the things that Jewish prophets began to reflect on, and surprisingly enough what developed was an expanded view and understanding of both the afterlife and the otherworld, the supernatural realm of heaven and hell.

THE GEMATRIA GAME AND HOW NUMBERS COUNT

There is certainly a great fascination in apocalyptic literature with symbolic numbers, and so something more must be said about gematria. There are, of course, some oft-repeated numbers: four, seven, ten, twelve, and their multiples. Knowing that seven means completion or perfection helps one to understand not only why there are the number of seals that one has in Revelation (a complete and comprehensive set of judgments), but also why the antichrist figure is numbered 666, which signifies chaos and incompletion. There is also a tendency in this literature to speak of time elusively or elliptically—such as Daniel's "a time, a time and a half, and a time" or his famous interpretation of Jeremiah's seventy weeks. Yet, it is surprisingly rare to find in either Jewish or Christian apocalypses any sort of precise calculations about how many days or years are left before the end.

Scholars have often puzzled over the two different numbers, apparently referring to the same time period in Daniel 12:11–12, but it need not be a case of recalculation or later editorial emendation. If the numbers are symbolic in nature (e.g., multiples of seven, or one half of seven), they should probably not be taken as attempts, much less failed attempts, at precise calculation. What such numbers do suggest when they describe periods of time is that matters are determined or fixed already by God, and thus God is still in control so that evil and suffering will at some point in time cease. The message of such numbers is "this too will pass," or "this too will come to pass." They were not meant to encourage ancient or modern chronological forecasting.

But what if justice is indeed deferred, or not seen to be done in a reasonably short period of time? Certainly one of the major impetuses producing apocalyptic literature is this sense of justice deferred for the minority group, which has led to a robust emphasis on vindication both in the afterlife, and more importantly in the end times. It is not an accident that apocalypses often manifest interest in justice and political issues on the one hand, and the otherworld and the afterlife on the other. There is a relationship between these two things; if there is no life to come, then many of the wrongs done in this life will never be rectified, and God's justice will be called into question.

Apocalyptic literature and especially apocalyptic prophecy are often attempts to deal with the issue of theodicy. For instance Revelation reassures the saints not only about personal vindication in the afterlife, but justice for God's people in the end times. Indeed it is at the point where cosmology and history meet, when heaven comes down to earth in the form of the messiah and the new Jerusalem, that there is finally both resolution and reward for the saints, and a solution to the human dilemma caused by suffering and evil. Suffering and death are overcome by resurrection and everlasting life, and evil is overcome by the last judgment. Obviously, the persuasiveness of this schema depends entirely on the audience's belief in not only a transcendent world but also a God who actually cares enough to intervene in human history and set things right once and for all.

But the very fact that this sort of information is only conveyed through visions and dreams and oracles makes clear that without revelation, without the unveiling of divine secrets and mysteries, humans would be in the dark about such matters. It is the message of apocalyptic literature that the meaning and purpose of human history cannot finally be discovered simply by an empirical study or analysis of that history. This does not mean that the author has given up on history, as is sometimes asserted, but rather that he is placing his trust in what God can finally make of history, rather than what humans can accomplish in history.

What is the upshot of this discussion for Dispensational theology? Several points need to be stressed:

(1) To take apocalyptic prophecy literally is to *violate* the character of such prophecy which, while referential, is also highly metaphorical and imagaic.

(2) To strip either regular oracles or apocalyptic prophecies out of their historical contexts and to fail to realize that much of this material has already been fulfilled in generations gone by is a major mistake.

(3) Even when one is dealing with prophetic material in Revelation that focuses on events which are still outstanding, such as the second coming of Christ, it is critical to bear in mind that OT and NT writers were not writing with late Western Christians in mind. We must enter their world. They are not speaking directly in our language.

(4) Careful exegesis will show that even in Revelation judgment is not ever exercised by anyone other than divine agents— Jesus or his angels or those who come with him from heaven. There will be no Armageddon between human armies. There will be no rebuilding of the temple in Jerusalem by human forces; all divine solutions to the human dilemma descend from above. They do not have to do with human machinations, invasions, and plans. Neither America nor any other nation is depicted as dealing with the antichrist. Only the Rider on the White Horse can do that. One should not look to the modern secular state of Israel as some sort of fulfillment of biblical Israel. Not even orthodox Jews in Israel see the current government in Israel as biblical!

(5) At no point in biblical prophecy, either Jewish or Christian, are there envisioned two separate peoples of God to whom differing groups of prophecy apply. Always the people of God is either Jews with Gentile adherents united in Israel or, in the later Christian schema, Jew and Gentile united in Christ.

(6) From a Christian point of view, all OT promises and prophecies are to be fulfilled in or by Christ, not apart from Christ and/or the church.

(7) In terms of what Dispensationalism gets right, it is true that some of this biblical prophecy is predictive, and some of it is eschatological in character and has not yet come to pass. It is often, however, not as particularistic in character as Dispensational interpreters might like. Perhaps this is because God only reveals enough of the future to give us hope, but not so much that we no longer need to exercise faith!

We will give a more detailed sample of how Revelation ought to be read in a later chapter, but in the next chapter we must turn to the issue of the rapture itself.

CHAPTER 6

What Goes Up, Must Come Down: The Problem with Rapture Theology

Every theological system has certain key ideas that are essential to the system, so essential that without them the system would collapse. In the case of Dispensationalism that idea is the rapture of the faithful. But this idea about the fate of the faithful was not an idea in play in early Christianity; indeed, as we have seen already, it does not seem to have arisen before the nineteenth century. What is the textual warrant for this idea, and how should we view those texts? This is the subject we must address in detail at this juncture.

VISION QUEST

It is easy enough to show the problems in Dispensational theology when it comes to a text like Revelations 4:1—"After this I looked and there before me was a door standing open in heaven. And the voice I had first heard speaking to me like a trumpet said 'Come up here, and I will show you what must take place after this.' And at once I was in the Spirit, and there before me was a throne." This is not a description of a magic carpet ride to heaven taken by John of Patmos. It is a description of a visionary experience, as is true of the whole rest of the book of Revelation. John "in the Spirit" is enabled to see into heaven, to take a tour of what is happening there, and to see into the future. This description is much like that which we find in other apocalyptic literature that uses this sort of metaphorical language. Notice, for example, Revelation 17:3—"then the angel carried me away in the Spirit into the desert." Once again John has not left the rock pile known as Patmos. It is "in the Spirit" that he is transported and in which he sees a desert scene. This is a way of talking about a visionary experience.

Another of the favorite texts to prove that the rapture is biblical is, of course, Matthew 24:36–41. The context of the discussion is in fact the events that surround the coming of the Son of Man from heaven, which will include cosmic signs of distress (24:29), making far-fetched the idea of this coming being secret or clandestine. Indeed we are told that once the sign of the Son of Man appears in the heavens, all the nations of the earth will see it and mourn (v. 30). He will come on the clouds with power, glory, and angels (v. 31). Verse 37 makes perfectly clear that the very same second coming is in view in vv. 37–41. The discussion is still about the coming of the Son of Man, and the material in vv. 29–31 refers to the same event described in vv. 37–41.

An analogy is drawn between the days of Noah and the days of the end. The issue has to do with what is meant by "one is taken, and the other left." Two things need to be said: those who are "taken away" in the days of Noah are swept away by the flood, and so are judged. Second, in terms of the oppressive situation during Jesus' own day, when someone is "taken," they are indeed being taken away by the authorities for judgment. It is the ones left behind who are fortunate, which in fact is what vv. 40–41 means in its original context. Being "taken," whether in Noah's day or in Jesus', was not a favorable outcome; it meant judgment. Notice as well that there is no reference to the person taken being "taken up" or being "taken to heaven." This text has nothing to do with such an idea. But the heart and soul of the case for the rapture, whether pre-trib, mid-trib, or post-trib, is of course 1 Thessalonians 4–5 and to a lesser degree 2 Thessalonians 2, and so we must deal in depth with those texts now.

1 Thessalonians 4:13–18 and 5:1–11 are of course eschatological texts, but we need to stress that their focus is on the current state of the dead and the bearing of the future on the present behavior of the living. That is, Paul is not discussing the afterlife or the end of history for its own sake, but in service of the exhortation he is giving his converts in Thessalonike. This shapes the character of his rhetoric here, which is about his converts being people of faith, hope, love, self-control, and alertness. A fresh translation of the whole section is in order.

> But I do not want you to be ignorant, brothers, concerning those who have fallen asleep,[1] in order that you may cease grieving/being sad as the rest having no hope. For if we believe that Jesus died and arose, so also God will bring with him those who have fallen asleep through/in Jesus. For this I say to you in/on the word of the Lord that we the living, those who are left around until the parousia of the Lord will not forestall those who have fallen asleep, for the Lord himself with a summons, with the voice of the archangel, and with the trumpet of God will come down from heaven, and the dead in Christ will rise first, then we the living,

those left around, together with them shall be caught up in the clouds unto the public welcoming of the Lord in the air, and so we will always be with the Lord. So console one another with these words. (1 Thess 4:13–18).

But concerning the times and seasons, brothers, you have no need for me to write to you, for you yourselves know accurately that the Day of the Lord as a thief in the night, thus it shall come. When they are saying "peace and security," then suddenly destruction will come upon them just as the birth pangs of a woman having a baby in the womb, and there will be no escape. But you brothers, you are not in the dark, in order that the day, like a thief,[2] overtake you, for all of you are sons of light, you are also sons of the day. You are neither night nor darkness. So then you should not sleep like the rest, but keep awake and be sober. For those sleeping sleep at night, and those getting drunk, get drunk at night. But we being of the day, are sober, having put on the breastplate of faith and love, and the helmet of salvation, for God has not appointed/destined us unto wrath but unto the acquisition of salvation through our Lord Jesus Christ who died for us in order that whether we are awake or asleep together we shall enter into life/begin to live with him. Therefore encourage one another and build up one on one, just as also you are doing. (1 Thess 5:1–11)

Though Paul will speak to his audience using Jewish concepts of death and resurrection, and more specifically Christian concepts about the return of Christ, it is impossible to miss how he uses the language of empire so familiar to his audience here to speak about the coming of Christ in a variety of ways, ranging from the quotation of the slogan "peace and security" to the language of the royal visit to a city with the greeting committee going out to meet the ruler. Why does Paul feel it necessary to make these sorts of remarks? Notice that while he believes his audience is familiar with the issue of the unknown timing of the second coming, he assumes that they do not know much about the fate of the Christian dead.

In 1 Thessalonians 4:13 Paul introduces a new subject using a phrase he was to employ more than once to start a new topic: not wishing his audience to be ignorant (cf. 1 Cor 10:1, 12:1; Rom 11:25). It is the equivalent of saying he wishes them to know (cf. 1 Cor 10:1; 2 Cor 1:8; Rom 1:13, 11:25; Col 2:1). The subject is of course related to what has already been said or suggested about the parousia in 1 Thessalonians 1:10, 2:13, and 3:13.

It is interesting that the use of the term *sleep* as a euphemism for death can be found in both Jewish and Greco-Roman sources (cf. Gen 47:30; Deut 31:16; 1 Kgs 2:10; Job 14:12–13; Ps 13:3; Jer 51:39–40;

2 Macc 12:45; John 11:11–13; Acts 13:36; 1 Cor 11:30; Homer, *Iliad* 11.241; Sophocles, *El.* 509). We may compare *Psalms of Solomon* 17:50 and *4 Ezra* 13:24, where a distinction is made between the living who manage to experience the coming glory and the dead who will miss out because they died before it came. In the non-Christian examples among those cited above, the term does not really tell us anything in particular about the condition or fate of the dead. It is more a comment on how they appear to the living after they die—namely motionless and quiet, like one sleeping.

What we find beginning in Daniel 12:2 and continuing in *Testament of Judah* 25:4 and *Testament of Issachar* 7:9, 2 Maccabees 12:44–45 and *1 Enoch* 91:10 and 92:3, however, is a connection between sleeping and being awakened by the resurrection, an idea Paul further develops here and at 1 Corinthians 15:20–21. We may perhaps make something of the use of the present participle here in 4:13— "those who are falling sleep." This may well imply Paul is envisioning and commenting on not only the Thessalonians who have already died, but all those who will die prior to the parousia.[3]

We may also think of certain Gospel stories with sayings such as Mark 6:39: "she is not dead but rather sleeping." Perhaps it was primarily the teaching of Jesus which led to the notion in early Christianity that death is like sleep in this respect; its effects are no more lasting or harmful than sleep if it is followed by being raised from the dead.[4] Notice it is also the case in the teaching of Jesus that using the metaphor of sleep for death is not meant to be a comment on what the dead are currently experiencing (cf. the parable in Luke 16:19–31).

Notice also the connection in 1 Thessalonians 4:13 between grieving and being like the remainder of humanity that has no hope. The use of the present subjunctive verb here implies the cessation of the continuation of something. The Thessalonians are grieving for those Christians they have already lost, and Paul wants them to stop grieving.

Grieving is for those without hope, and indeed it is the natural reaction for those who have no positive view of the afterlife. Notice as well the implication of the phrase "the rest of humanity who have no hope." Paul is suggesting that outside of Christ there is no hope of life beyond death. Paul was certainly no universalist or pluralist when it came to the matter of salvation, but it was not just that pagans had no hope of a positive afterlife. According to 1 Thessalonians 1:10 and 5:9 (cf. Rom 1:18–32, 11:7; Eph 2:3) they faced the judgment of God both in the present and in the future. Things look bleak for pagans from Paul's viewpoint.[5] On the opposite end of the spectrum, Paul is assuming that for Christians, an increase in hope will cause an increase in holiness in the lives of the believers. They will be in earnest about Christian behavior because they know what is coming. He is also assuming that a proper knowledge of the fate of the Christian dead should put a stop to hopeless grieving. The *kathos kai . . .* really cannot be translated "to the same extent as the pagans." Paul is here urging a cessation of grieving which was already ongoing.

A primitive Christian confession may be included in 1 Thessalonians 4:14 even though it is cast in the form of a conditional statement. What suggests this is the use of the proper name Jesus and *aneste*, which is not usually the verb Paul prefers (cf. 1 Cor 15:3–4). The verb, however, is in the present tense, indicating a real condition.[6] It is, however, interesting that Paul says "we believe" rather than "we know," suggesting that what Paul has in mind is more than just the facts that Jesus died and rose from the dead. At least in the case of his death, faith was not required to affirm that Jesus had died. Usually Paul speaks of Jesus being raised from the dead (by God—cf. 1 Thess 1:10; Gal 1:1; 1 Cor 15:15; 2 Cor 4:14; Rom 4:24, 8:11, 10:9; Col 2:12), but this is surely implied here in view of the second half of the sentence.

What Paul is then doing in the second half of the verse, which is grammatically awkward, is showing what follows from believing Jesus died and rose. This belief has a consequence for what we should believe about the fate of the Christian dead. The structure of the Greek as we have it favors linking the phrase "through Jesus" with "those who have fallen asleep."[7] But what does it mean to have fallen asleep through Jesus? Does it mean what Acts 7:29 suggests, namely that Jesus will receive the spirit of the Christian when she dies? Possibly.

It is also possible that *dia* has the force of *en* here, in which case Paul is speaking about dying in the Lord—that is, dying as a Christian (1 Cor 15:18). In fact the aorist participle here, *koimethentas*, favors this interpretation since it refers to the moment, not the condition of death—they died in the Lord. It is only deceased Christians whom Jesus will bring with him or bring back from the dead when he returns at the parousia.[8] This may mean they will be brought with Jesus from heaven, but it may simply mean they will be brought back from the dead, and so raised when Jesus returns as texts like 1 Corinthians 6:14 and 2 Corinthians 4:14 suggest. Paul seems to assume that the concern in Thessalonike was not about resurrection per se but about the relationship of the Christian dead to the parousia and whether they would participate in the greeting party in the air when Jesus returned and they would be with him forever.

1 Thessalonians 4:15 has been a flashpoint in the discussion of Pauline eschatology at least since the time of A. Schweitzer. Here, it is said, we have proof positive that Paul believed that he would definitely live to see the parousia of Jesus. Unfortunately these sorts of discussions have tended to overlook at least a couple of key factors: (1) Paul did not know in advance when he would die;[9] (2) he argues that the second

coming will happen at an unexpected time, like a thief in the night. It could be soon, it could be later, and in either case the indeterminacy of the timing is what fuels exhortations that one must always be prepared and alert. It needs to be stressed that since Paul did not know the specific timing of either his death or the return of Christ, and does not claim to know such things, he could not have said here, "We who are dead and not left around to see the parousia of the Lord."

In short, Paul does not know that he will *not* be alive when Jesus returns, and so the only category he can logically place himself and others of his contemporary Christians in is the "living" category when it comes to discussing this matter.[10] What these verses surely do imply is that Paul thought it *possible* that he might be alive when Jesus returned. Paul, until he was much older and near death, always had both possibilities before him, both the possibility of living until the parousia and the possibility of dying first and rising at the parousia when Jesus returned.[11] The reason we do not hear the language of possible survival until the parousia in the later Pauline letters is because one of the two unknown factors, the timing of Paul's death, was becoming more likely to precede the parousia. We should not speak of Paul's changing his view about the second coming or his considering it delayed in the later Paulines for the very good reason that the term *delay* implies that one knows with some precision when it was supposed to happen, and when it does not happen then, one could speak of it as being "late." But Paul's imagery of the thief implies a denial of knowing with that sort of precision.[12] We need to consider the particulars of this verse at this juncture.

The meaning of the phrase *in the word of the Lord* has been debated. Some scholars have argued that it refers to a saying of the historical Jesus, and should be seen on a par with other Pauline texts such as 1 Corinthians 7:10, 9:14, or 11:23. Unlike at least the first of those suggested parallels, we do not have here a direct quotation of a saying of Jesus. Various possible sources of this verse in the Jesus tradition have been suggested, but with the possible exception of Matthew 24:30, the parallels are at the level of ideas not actual wording (cf. Matt 10:39; 16:25, 28; 20:1–2; 24:31, 34; 25:6; 26:64; Luke 13:30; John 5:25; 6:39–40; 11:25–26).[13]

Another form of this same suggestion is the view that Paul is citing an otherwise unknown saying of Jesus, one not found in the canonical Gospels. This is certainly possible and has been argued, but it is a conjecture that cannot be verified.[14] What we *can* say about the echoes and allusions to the Jesus tradition in Paul, with some assurance, is that he almost always feels free to paraphrase that tradition or put it in more Pauline wording, rarely quoting it verbatim. Here it could be argued that Paul combines a saying of Jesus with his own reflections on Daniel

7:13–14 and 12:2–3. This lack of direct quotation makes it difficult to know when Paul has and when he has not drawn on a saying of Jesus.

A different line of approach has suggested that "in the word of the Lord" refers to a prophetic word revealed to Paul himself, coming from the risen Lord. This is certainly possible and has in its favor the fact that the very same phrase *legomen en logo kuriou* appears in the Septuagint to indicate when someone speaks for God (cf. 1 Kgs 21:35; 13:1–5, 32; Hos 1:1; Ezek 34:1; 35:1). This suggestion, however, hardly explains the echoes from the synoptic material that we do find here. 1 Corinthians 15:51–52 can be pointed to as a close parallel to v. 16, but not v. 15, and there Paul refers to a "mystery" which would seem to mean a revelation Paul received directly from God.

Perhaps the least problematic solution to this conundrum is to recognize that Paul saw himself as both a prophetic interpreter of the sayings of the historical Jesus and of the OT and also as someone who received direct messages from the risen Lord himself. In 1 Thessalonians 4:15–5:7 Paul does draw on the Jesus tradition found in Matthew 24, but in 4:16–17 he also draws on both his own reading of Daniel and prophetic insight that he himself had been given by the risen Lord. The following chart shows the various parallels:

	1 Thessalonians	Matthew
Christ returns	4:16	24:30
from heaven	4:16	24:30
accompanied by angels	4:16	24:31
with a trumpet of God	4:16	24:31
believers gathered to Christ	4:17	24:31, 40–41
in clouds	4:17	24:30
time unknown	5:1–2	24:36
coming like a thief	5:2, 4	24:43
unbelievers unaware of coming judgment	5:3	24:37–39
judgment like a mother's birth pangs	5:3	24:8
believers not deceived	5:4–5	24:43
believers to be watchful	5:6	24:37–39
warning v. drunkenness	5:7	24:49[15]

These parallels should not be minimized, and they make it likely that Paul is drawing on the general sense and trajectory and imagery of some of that synoptic material. They also make clear an important point. Paul does not think there is some difference between the parousia and the second coming (or glorious appearing). Indeed, as in Matthew 24, all of this material is referring to one event: the coming of the Son of Man on the clouds. Notice that the parallels with Matthew 24 continue on into 1 Thessalonians 5:1–11. This is because Paul does not think he is describing some different event in 1 Thessalonians 5:1–11 than he was in 1 Thessalonians 4:13–18. We can say with even more assurance that the rhetorical function of citing a "word of the Lord" here is to console and reassure the audience about the fate of their deceased Thessalonian brothers and sisters and their equal participation in the parousia event.[16] Something needs to be said about the Danielic material as background at this juncture.

Echoes of Daniel and the Emperor's Visit

Daniel 7:13–14 is of course part of the famous oracle about "the one like a son of man" (*bar enasha*). Though it has been debated as to whether this figure goes up into the clouds and heaven to meet the Ancient of Days, or comes with the clouds to meet the Almighty on earth for the day of judgment, in view of v. 14 it must surely be the latter. It is the kingdoms "under heaven" that are handed over to the Son of Man figure and to the saints, and we are told all rulers will worship and obey this figure. It is surely not envisioned that these non-Jewish kingdoms and rulers are in heaven or are ruled from heaven. The rule, like the final judgment, takes place on earth. Notice as well the statement that the Son of Man figure comes with the clouds of heaven, an image of clouds coming down from above, not clouds rising up from the earth with someone ascending with them. This background material is important for another reason. Daniel 7 is about a ruling on earth of this Son of Man figure, ruling over those who had oppressed God's people. It is not about rescuing God's people out of this world into heaven for an interim period of time. The Son of Man language and imagery taken over from Daniel 7 in the sayings of Jesus in Matthew 24 and here by Paul in 1 Thessalonians provide further proof that 1 Thessalonians 4:13–20 is not about a rapture.

Daniel 12:1 speaks of a major distress "at that time" from which God's people will be delivered. This is followed in v. 2 by the promise that multitudes who sleep in the dust will awake, some to everlasting life, others to everlasting shame. It seems very likely that Paul has some of this material in mind in 1 Thessalonians 4:15–17 as well—though typically, as he does with the Jesus tradition, Paul has made the material his own, using his own way of phrasing things.

The phrase *we the living, those who are left around/remain* is important, for it means Paul envisions that Christians will still be living on planet Earth when Jesus returns. It also may suggest that he thinks the majority of Christians will be dead when Christ returns.[17] But what sort of return is Paul envisioning here; could it be said to be a secret or invisible one? Do we have some sort of theology of a pre-tribulation rapture here with Jesus not actually coming to earth? The details of the text as well as the use of the language of the royal visit to a city surely rule out such a view.

It has been rightly stressed by G. Beale that we should probably take vv. 14–15 together, with v. 15 providing the reason that believers can be confident about the resurrection of the deceased Christians, namely that Jesus himself spoke of this matter and affirmed this truth.[18] We should also not neglect what Paul says in v. 15b, namely that the living shall not have precedence or any advantage over those who have fallen asleep when it comes to participating in the parousia event. All believers will be on the same footing, or one might say, on the same cloud, when Jesus returns.

As v. 16 makes quite clear, Paul connects the resurrection of believers who are dead with the parousia and with the meeting of Christ in the air. Clearly enough it is the parousia which precipitates these other two events. Notice that there is no mention of the resurrection of unbelievers at this juncture. Paul takes that to be a separate event and one that occurs on a different occasion (contrast *4 Ezra* 4:1–5). 1 Thessalonians 4:16 makes it clear as one could want that we are dealing with a public event—announced not only by a loud command as on a battlefield,[19] and the voice of the archangel (see Jude 9; *1 En.* 20:1–7; *4 Ezra* 4:36), but also by the trumpet call of God, though these may be three ways of referring to the same thing.

The images conjured up are martial, as if Jesus were summoning his army. Notice that in 2 Thessalonians 1:7 we also hear about angels playing a role in the second coming (cf. Mark 13:24–27). Only audible rather than visible factors are mentioned first. The meeting place is said to take place in the clouds or in the air, not in heaven. Notice that Paul considers the dead in Christ to be persons who can be "awakened" or "addressed." It is quite likely that Paul is drawing on the Yom Yahweh (Day of the Lord) traditions here, which refer to a trumpet blast announcing the event (cf. Isa 27:13; Joel 2:1; Zech 9:14; 2 Esd 6:23; *Sib. Or.* 4.174; 1 Cor 15:52).

But it was also the case that when there was a royal visit to a city, it would be announced by a herald (see Ps 24:7–10) and might well also be announced by a trumpet blast meant to alert those in the city that the king was coming. This imagery is pursued further in 1 Thessalonians 4:17 with the use of the term *apantesin*. Notice, for example, what Cicero says of Julius Caesar's victory tour through Italy in 49 B.C.: "Just imagine what a meeting/royal welcome (*apanteseis*) he is receiving from the towns, what honors are paid to him" (*Att.* 8.16.2 and cf. 16.11.6 of Augustus—"the municipalities are showing the boy remarkable favor . . . Wonderful *apantesis* and encouragement"). This word then refers to the action of the greeting committee who goes forth from the city to meet the royal person or dignitary before he arrives at the city gate to pay an official visit. The greeting committee will then escort the dignitary back into town on the final part of his journey. "These analogies (especially in association with the term *parousia*) suggest the possibility that the Lord is pictured here as escorted on the remainder of the journey to earth by his people—both those newly raised from the dead and those remaining alive."[20]

Chrysostom picked up these nuances quite clearly. He says, "For when a king drives into a city, those who are honorable go out to meet him; but the condemned await the judge within. And upon the coming of an affectionate father, his children indeed, and those who are worthy to be his children, are taken out in a chariot, that they may see him and kiss him; but the housekeepers who have offended him remain within" (*Hom. 1 Thess.* 8).[21] Paul's Thessalonian audience may have missed some of the allusions to the OT, but they would not have missed the language used here about a royal visit, indeed an imperial visit (cf. also Acts 28:15). They would remember the visit of Pompey and later Octavian and others in the days when Thessalonike could even be talked about by Pompey as the capital in exile. But there is more to be said along these lines as Paul keeps using such loaded language in 1 Thessalonians 5. K. P. Donfried sums things up nicely:

> If 1 Thessalonians is at all representative of his original preaching then we certainly do find elements which could be understood or misunderstood in a distinctly political sense. In 2.12 God, according to the Apostle, calls the Thessalonian Christians "into his own kingdom"; in 5.3 there is a frontal attack on the *Pax et Securitas* program of the early Principate; and in the verses just preceding this attack one finds three heavily loaded political terms: *parousia*, *apantesis*, and *kyrios*. *Parousia* is related to "the 'visit' of the king, or some other official." When used as court language *parousia* refers to the arrival of Caesar, a king or an official. *Apantesis* refers to the citizens meeting a dignitary who is about to visit the city. These two terms are used in this way by Josephus (*Ant.* XI.327ff.) and also similarly referred to by such Greek writers as Chrysostom. The term *kyrios* especially when used in the same context as the two preceding terms, also has a definite political sense. People in the eastern Mediterranean applied the term *kyrios* to the Roman emperors from Augustus on. . . . All of this, coupled with the use of *euaggelion* and its possible association with the eastern ruler cult suggests that Paul and his associates could easily be understood as violating "the decrees of Caesar" in the most blatant manner.[22]

Donfried then goes on to suggest that the dead in Christ in Thessalonike were victims of the persecutions elsewhere alluded to in this letter, which is certainly possible. In Acts 7:60 Stephen is stoned and then "he fell asleep" (*ekoimethe*). This language in the context of persecution could refer to one who suffered death through persecution. We may need to take seriously that when it was suggested that Paul and his coworkers had violated the decrees of Caesar (see Acts 17:7), this had severe repercussions not only for Paul and his coworkers but also for his converts. Some lost their lives. No wonder Paul was so concerned about them.

But it must be noted that Paul in 1 Thessalonians is not backing down from his anti-imperial rhetoric, or better said his coopting of imperial rhetoric and applying it to Jesus. It cannot be an accident that the word *parousia* shows up four times in 1 Thessalonians (2:19; 3:13; 4:15; 5:23), twice in 2 Thessalonians (2:1, 8), and only once elsewhere in Paul (1 Cor 15:23). The borrowing of imperial rhetoric is especially apparent in the Thessalonian correspondence.[23] H. Koester has helpfully pointed out that the problem in Thessalonike is certainly not the delay of the parousia, but rather concern about the fate of the Thessalonian Christian dead, concern exacerbated by persecution and possibly even martyrdom. Will the dead Christians join the living in the great welcoming of the return of their Lord?[24] Paul's answer is an emphatic yes. But in the course of giving that assurance and making some remarkable christological and eschatological assertions, Paul is also busily deconstructing the extant pagan value system so his converts will not lapse back into allegiance to it. N. T. Wright puts it this way:

> Paul's opposition to Caesar and adherence to a very high, very Jewish Christology were part of the same thing. Jesus was Lord—*kyrios*, with all its Septuagintal overtones—and Caesar was not . . . neither the recognition that Paul's main target was paganism, and the Caesar-cult in particular, nor the equal recognition that he remained a thoroughly Jewish thinker, should blind us for a moment to the fact that Paul still held a thorough and stern critique of non-messianic Judaism. . . . If Paul's answer to Caesar's empire is the empire of Jesus, what does this say about this new empire, living under the rule of its new Lord? . . . This counterempire can never be merely critical, never merely subversive. It claims to be the reality of which Caesar's empire is the parody. It claims to be modeling the genuine humanness, not least the justice and peace, and the unity across traditional racial and cultural barriers, of which Caesar's empire boasted.[25]

Notice that it is particularly in Paul's more eschatological sections of his letters that the imperial cult language shows up. This is because the imperial cult was an eschatological institution itself, suggesting that a human being, namely the emperor, was divine and was walking around on the earth bringing the final form of peace and security to earth (see Virgil's *Aeneid*), a thought fully embraced in the eastern part of the empire. Along came Paul into the same segment of the empire suggesting there was another God walking on the earth offering kingdom, and this one had even come back from the dead. In such an environment this was an explosive message with considerable political implications. This message qualified as a subversive one, violating Caesar's decrees.[26]

It should be clear from the beginning of 1 Thessalonians 4:16 that Christ is said to come *down* out of heaven and meet his followers somewhere else, in this case in the atmosphere where there are clouds. There is likely an echo of Micah 1:3 here—"For behold the Lord is coming forth out of his place, and will come down and tread upon the high places of the earth." Clouds are regularly said to accompany a theophany, when God comes down to the human level, not when humans are taken up into the presence of God in heaven (see Exod 19:16; 40:34; 1 Kgs 8:10–11; Ps 97:2). Trumpet blasts also accompany theophanies (Exod 19:16; Isa 27:13; Joel 2:1; Zech 9:14).[27] The meeting does not take place in heaven, so there is no discussion of rapture into heaven even here.[28]

Paul then adds, as the ultimate reassurance about the dead in Christ, that they will rise first, after which according to 1 Thessalonians 4:17 the living Christians will be snatched up in a bodily condition (cf. Rev 12:5; Acts 8:39; Wis 4:11)[29] together with them in the clouds to meet the Lord in the air and be with the Lord forever.[30] Far from the deceased Christians being left out of the parousia party, they will be first to be involved. It will be the ultimate family reunion with the King. There may be echoes here of the promises made sometimes in Greco-Roman contexts and epitaphs that the deceased would be with the "heroes," perhaps even in the Elysian fields. How much better to be with the Lord himself than just the heroes.

Paul does not tell us here what he thinks happens next after the reunion in the air. That information Paul conveys in 1 Corinthians 15, and in both these texts nothing is said or suggested about nonbelievers participating in this resurrection. Paul separates what will happen to believers and what will happen to nonbelievers when Christ returns. Note the reference to future wrath in 1 Thessalonians 5:9. What Paul most wants to convey about what happens at the parousia is that the dead will not only not be left out or be disadvantaged, they will in fact take precedence. In a culture where pecking order was important, it would have reversed normal expectations to suggest that the dead had an advantage over the living.

1 Thessalonians 4:18 involves an exhortation to encourage and comfort each other with these eschatological promises, the very sort of rhetoric that would be appropriate in an epideictic attempt to help the

bereaved (cf. 1 Thess 5:11). With hope in the parousia and coming resurrection "not only could they expect to see their loved ones again but
also they could expect a grand and permanent reunion for all the believers" and with Jesus.[31] Notice finally that the Thessalonians were to
actively convey this consolation to each other (cf. P.Oxy. 115—*pare-
goreite oun eautous*); it was not just a matter of hearing and heeding
what Paul said. They were to participate in their own healing.

IT TAKES A THIEF

The second division of the eschatological paraenesis in 1 Thessalonians
4–5 begins at 5:1. The use of *peri de* as well as the use of the term
brothers makes evident that Paul sees this as a new topic or a new angle
on a previously discussed topic, and here it is clearly one which is
related to what has just been said about the parousia. In 1
Thessalonians 5, the rhetorical function of the eschatological material
is a bit different. Rather than consolation through new information,
this segment is more about exhortation based on the eschatological
knowledge the audience already has. This section seems to have three
divisions, and the markers of each involve the word *de* ("but"): (1) "but
concerning"—5:1; (2) "but you"—5:4; (3) "but we"—5:8. Paul will
deal in turn with three related topics in these sections—the sudden, and
for some, unexpected coming of the Day of the Lord when unbelievers
will be judged (5:1–3), the preparation of believers for that day (5:4–7),
and the necessary faithfulness of God's people, all of which are the basis
for encouraging one another (5:8–11). The structure of this material is
carefully wrought, with the section ending with an inference to be
drawn in v. 11 from what has just been said.

It is a helpful exercise to compare what is said in this whole passage
with Romans 13:11–14. There are obvious similarities in the use of the
language about waking and sleeping and sobriety. If there is debate
about which of these passages conveys more of a sense that the eschatological clock is ticking and the end may be nearer than one thinks, it
is surely the Romans passage, which just goes to show that no easy evolutionary schema of development will work when analyzing Pauline
eschatology. Romans was surely written after 2 Corinthians, and yet
Paul is still talking about the return of Christ, and how the Day of the
Lord is possibly imminent.

The attempt to take 1 Thessalonians 5:1–11 as if it were referring
to events after the catching up of believers into the air—rather than seeing 1 Thessalonians 4:13–18 and 5:1–11 as both talking about the
parousia, though in two different ways (parousia = Day of the Lord)—
must be said to be special pleading. Both of these passages deal with the
one and only parousia/return of Christ from slightly different angles

and with differing rhetorical functions, both commending the same sort of behavior of Christians in light of the eschatological events. The exhortations in 1 Thessalonians 5:1–11 would be pointless if in fact believers were not envisioned as still on earth until the Day of the Lord. Notice the repetition of the phrase *with the Lord* in 4:17 and 5:10, and the similar endings directed toward the immediate audience in 4:18 and 5:11. Both the context and the content of these passages indicate that Paul is speaking in them both of the one and only second coming.[32] What is not usually appreciated is that while the former passage examines the second coming from the angle of the coming rescue of believers, the latter passage examines the same event from the perspective of judgment on unbelievers.[33]

The phrase *chronoi kai kairoi* is an important one found elsewhere in early Jewish and early Christian literature (Acts 1:7; 1 Peter 1:11; Ignatius, *Poly.* 3; cf. Neh 10:34; 13:31; Dan 2:21; Wis 8:8; Eccl 3:1 and Demosthenes, *3 Olynth.* para. 32). It is too simple to say that *chronos* refers to a longer period of time, and *kairos* a shorter one. *Chronos* is the general term for time whether a long or short period is involved, and refers to the date of something if a particular event is in mind. *Kairos* can refer to place or time and has the sense of the fit measure, the appropriate or propitious moment or the right place. In reference to time it surely refers to the right moment. In short, *chronos* refers more to the quantity of time, while *kairos* refers to the quality of time, or of other things, and since the propitious moment is usually a brief one, it often does refer to a short length of time, though this is incidental to its real thrust. The gist of the phrase here, then, is that the audience has no need to be informed about how much time must elapse before the big event happens, or what significant occurrences will mark or punctuate that crucial occasion.[34] Paul refuses to set up timetables for this event because he cannot do so.[35] The timing has not been revealed. Indeed what had been revealed is that no one knows the timing of this event, not even Jesus during his ministry (Mark 13:32). All the pointless speculation about the timing of the rapture or the return of Christ is an exercise in futility because the former event is not going to happen, and we are told that the latter event will happen at a hitherto undisclosed time.

1 Thessalonians 5:2 then tells us nothing about when Jesus will come, but rather how—in a sudden and unexpected manner.[36] Paul is describing here a sudden intrusion into human history, catching many unawares and unprepared. The controlling metaphor, "thief in the night," goes back to the Jesus tradition (cf. Matt 24:43; Luke 12:38–39; 1 Thess 5:2; 2 Pet 3:10; Rev 3:3; 16:15) and stresses both the suddenness and unexpectedness of the event, but also its unknown timing. It also has an aura of threat or unwelcomeness to it, at least for the unpre-

pared.[37] Notice that strictly speaking it is the Day of the Lord, rather than Jesus, that is said to come like a thief, except in the epistles, but it is Jesus elsewhere.

Paul uses several related phrases to refer to this coming event—*the Day* (1 Thess 5:4; 1 Cor 3:13; Rom 2:5; cf. 13:12), *that Day* (2 Thess 1:10), *the Day of the Lord* (1 Thess 5:2; 2 Thess 2:2; 1 Cor 5:5), *the Day of our Lord Jesus Christ* (1 Cor 1:8), *the Day of the Lord Jesus* (2 Cor 1:14), *the Day of Christ Jesus* (Phil 1:6), or simply *the Day of Christ* (Phil 1:10; 2:16). Paul has adopted and adapted the Yom Yahweh traditions from the OT and applied them to Christ, for now it is Christ who will bring the final redemption and judgment to earth.[38] If one compares 1 Thessalonians 4:14–17 and 1 Thessalonians 5:2 it becomes clear that "the Day" is the same as "the Day of the Lord" which in turn is the same as the parousia. It is in no way surprising that when the phrase *Day of the Lord* is used by Paul, judgment is most frequently spoken of since it is this phrase which in the Hebrew Scriptures and Septuagint was used most often to speak of coming judgment (cf. Rom 2:5).[39] Zephaniah 1:15–18; 2:2–3, and 3:8 (cf. Amos 5:18–20; Obad 15; Joel 1:15; 2:1–2, 31–32; Zech 14:1–21) stress the idea that the Day of the Lord is a day of God's judgment, though in Obadiah and Zechariah it is also a day of deliverance. Paul says that his audience knows very well (the phrase is emphatic, *you yourselves know very well*) about this matter.[40] There is a note of irony here. The audience knows very well that the timing of the parousia has not been revealed and so is unknown and unpredictable.[41] In addition, Paul says that this day will come like an event at night![42] If this is not a use of metaphor and simile, nothing is.

1 Thessalonians 5:3 begins with the phrase *when they say peace and security*. It has sometimes been conjectured that Paul is drawing on an OT phrase here, perhaps Jeremiah 6:14 or Ezekiel 13:10.[43] The latter text condemns false prophets for crying "peace" when there is no peace, but says nothing about security specifically, though the comments about the whitewashed wall may imply such a concern. Jeremiah 6:14 is of the very same ilk, criticizing false prophets for crying "peace, peace" when there is no peace. Clearly Paul's phrase is not a direct quote of an OT phrase, and if his audience is mainly former pagans, they could not be expected to recognize such an allusion anyway. "When they say . . ." is also a very odd way to refer to the OT prophets, but it makes perfect sense if Paul is quoting here a cliché or proverb familiar in his audience's world. The diction here is not Pauline; Paul does not use either *legosin* or *eirene* (here in the political sense of cessation of hostility and violence) in quite this sense elsewhere, and he does not use *asphaleia* at all elsewhere.[44] There is some likelihood that at least the second half of this sentence is echoing the Jesus tradition,

specifically material found in Luke 21:34–36, but again that material does not account for the combined "peace and security" phrase, and Paul would hardly introduce a word of Jesus by "when *they* say." The "they" suggests outsiders, not insiders.

Here is where we note that there were inscriptions up all over the empire attributing to Rome and to its army the bringing of peace and security to one region after another. For example, in Syria we have the inscription which reads, "The Lord Marcus Flavius Bonus, the most illustrious Comes and Dux of the first legion, has ruled over us in peace and given constant 'peace and security' to travelers and to the people" (OGIS 613). Velleius Paterculus says, "On that day there sprang up once more in parents the assurance of safety of their property, and in all men the assurance of safety, order, peace, and tranquility" (II.103.5). It is added that "The Pax Augusta which has spread to the regions of the east and of the west, and to the bounds of the north and the south, preserves every corner of the world safe/secure from the fear of banditry" (II.126.3). Tacitus speaks of the time after the year of the three emperors as a time when security was restored, and then he adds that the "security of peace" includes work without anxiety in the fields and in the homes (*Hist.* 2.21.2; 2.12.1). Not to be plundered by robbers either at home or on journeys is "peace and security" (Josephus, *Ant.* 14.158–60, 247).

A variant of this "peace and security" slogan was the "peace and concord" slogan. We find this in inscriptions dating back to 139 B.C., referring to a pact between Rome and the cities of Asia "preserving mutual goodwill with peace and all concord and friendship" (SIG 685.14–15).[45] Paul must have thought, "What foolish slogans and vain hopes when the Day of the Lord is coming." Paul then is critiquing the slogans and propaganda about the Pax Romana. It is on those who offer this rhetoric that destruction will come, which may suggest that Paul foresaw the same future for Rome and its empire and those who cooperated with it as John of Patmos did in Revelation 6–19.[46] Paul does not want his audience to be beguiled by such rhetoric, especially after Paul has been expelled and they have suffered persecution from those who are supposedly the bringers of peace and security. It is the imperial propaganda and prophecies that Paul is offering a rebuttal to here.

What is predicted for those who offer this slogan is sudden destruction, which comes upon them much like a birth pang seizes a pregnant woman unexpectedly (cf. Ps 48:6; Isa 26:17, 66:8; Jer 30:6–7; Mic 4:9; 4 *Ezra* 16:35–39; *1 En.* 62:1–6). The wording here is closely parallel to Luke 21:34–36.[47] Paul stresses the fact that there can be no escape from this coming destruction for "them." Paul is not a crusader against the empire in the sense of someone leading a social movement for reform.

Rather he is a believer that God in Christ will intervene once and for all and right the wrongs that Paul and his audience have been experiencing because of their witness. God in Christ is the one who will bring justice and peace and security once and for all, not the emperor with his slogans. Paul says more on this theme in 2 Thessalonians 2. The rhetorical effect of what Paul has done is to create a sense of urgency in regard to heeding the exhortations here. "Paul in no way seeks to decrease, let alone defuse, the eschatological pressure felt by the Thessalonians."[48] The "they" of v. 3 will now be contrasted with "but you brothers" in v. 4.

Notice in 1 Thessalonians 5:4–5 we have a clear contrast between believers and unbelievers. Using the darkness and light metaphors, Paul in essence says that his converts are neither in the state of darkness nor that darkness is the source of their existence. They should not be surprised by the coming of the Day of the Lord even if it arrives at an unexpected time. "Unpredictable events have different effects on those who are unprepared for them and those who are ready for them."[49] Believers are children of the day, sons of light (cf. Luke 16:8; John 12:38; Eph 5:8). The self-descriptive language of the in-group here is much like that we find at Qumran (1QS 3:13–4:26; 1QM 1:1–3). A saying of Euripides helps us understand the force of the imagery here: "Night is the time for thieves, daylight is the time for truth" (*Iph. taur.* 1025–26).[50] Verse 5 is interesting because it calls the audience both sons of light and sons of the day. Here we see the two poles of Paul's eschatology. The light had already dawned in Christ, and his converts were already children of light, transformed into new creatures.[51] But they awaited the day. Provisionally they are also called here sons of the day, reassuring them they will be participants when Jesus returns.[52] Notice that Paul says that "all" his audience are sons of light and sons of the day. Paul does not hold to a concept of an invisible elect amidst the church. He assumes his whole audience believes in Jesus and so is among the elect and will be sons of the day.[53] But before they arrive at that day there is much to prepare for, and much to persevere through. They must remember that they are no longer of the night nor of darkness. They are not in a benighted condition, and so they should not be caught out by the coming of the day.

Knowledge is power, but it can also be used for motivation, and in 1 Thessalonians 5:6 Paul turns to his exhortation based on what the Thessalonians know about the eschatological situation. With *ara oun* ("so then") as a marker that he is turning to a logical conclusion or a moral consequence of what he has just said, Paul draws an ethical conclusion about how Christian behavior should differ from that of "the rest." Lightfoot distinguishes between sleepers and drunkards. The former, he says, refers to the careless and indifferent, the latter to the profligate and reckless.[54] It is interesting that Paul uses the metaphor not only of being awake and sober but of wearing certain clothes, or as we might say, keeping our day clothes on, to describe the state of preparedness of Christians for the parousia.[55] Paul in vv. 6–8 uses the hortatory subjunctive form of verbs four times to bring home his application.[56] Notice as well that he uses the terminology for sleep in three different ways; in v. 6 it is metaphorical, in v. 7 it is literal, and in v. 10 it is a euphemism for death, as before in 1 Thessalonians 4.[57]

The exhortation here probably owes something to Mark 13:34–37 (cf. also Matt 24:42–43), and in any case Paul is not saying what Clement of Alexandria later said, namely "we should sleep half-awake" (*Paed.* 2.9.79). No, Paul is calling for his converts to remain awake and alert, and to remain sober (cf. Eph 5:14). Malherbe insightfully notes that while in those synoptic texts alertness is mainly grounded in the fact that there is ignorance of the timing of the second coming, here it is mainly grounded in one's Christian identity—a Christian is of the light and enlightened and as such should always remain morally and spiritually alert.[58] *Nepein* occurs only here and at 2 Timothy 4:5 in the Pauline corpus, and it means literally to be sober, though it could be translated to be self-controlled. It is no good being awake but drunk. One will still not be prepared for the "thief" in that condition. So Paul is urging both intellectual and moral preparation and readiness for the parousia. The opposite of this is being morally and spiritually asleep or unconscious. It is interesting that Plutarch the moralist also urges his audience to be awake and sober and contrasts this with being asleep or drunk using these same terms (*Prin. iner.* 781D).

1 Thessalonians 5:7 is a sort of gloss on, or illustration from ordinary life of what has just been said, explaining that sleepers and those who get drunk generally do so at night.[59] The implication is that Christians are not of the night, nor should they be given to these sorts of "night moves." "What is true at the level of everyday human experience applies on the religious and ethical plane."[60] Christians are held to God's twenty-four hours of daytime standard.

Verse 8 states the consequences of being daytime people. We must be awake, sober, and put on the appropriate clothing to deal with the "slings and arrows of outrageous fortune." Notice the reference here to the famous triad—faith, hope, and love (cf. 1 Thess 1:3; 1 Cor 13). Here we have the breastplate of faith and love, and the helmet is said to be the hope of salvation, seen as something to be experienced in the future, an imagery further developed in Ephesians 6:14–17. In both texts there is an indebtedness to Isaiah 59:17 where God wears the helmet of salvation on his head.

The terminology is probably chosen carefully. The most vulnerable part of a person in a life-threatening situation is the head. One can survive wounds to almost any other part of the body, but a deep wound to the head of any kind is usually mortal. The Scriptures therefore speak of the helmet of *soteria,* a term that can mean rescue, help, heal, or save in a mundane or profound sense. But in this case it is the helmet of the *hope* of salvation. What protects the believer against a mortal blow to his faith is to some degree the hope of salvation. If one has no hope or trust that God will one day make things right, then one's faith is fragile and can be overwhelmed by the problems and the injustices of the present.[61] But this hope not only protects the person in the present, it gives them courage in the face of the coming judgment of God, knowing that one will be saved or rescued from that maelstrom.[62]

One of the real weaknesses in the Dispensational approach to texts such as 1 Thessalonians 4–5 is that on the one hand they want parousia to refer to the secret rapture of the church here and in 2 Thessalonians 2:1, while on the other hand they tend to concede that parousia refers to the second coming in this very same argument at 2 Thessalonians 2:8. But Paul everywhere always uses this term consistently when speaking of Jesus to refer to the second coming, an all too visible event. The further proof of this comes not only because of the general use of this term to refer to a public event, but also because in this very context in vv. 8–9 we can note how parousia is used in parallel with the verb *revealed* to refer to the very public coming of the Lawless One. Let us consider 2 Thessalonians 2:1–2 in just a little more detail.

Notice that right off the bat Paul reminds his audience about something he has clearly spoken to them about before—the parousia and the gathering of the believers to him at his coming. These subjects, of course, were addressed in 1 Thessalonians 5 and 1 Thessalonians 4, respectively. We should compare the use of the term *episunagogos* ("gathering") to the use of the verbal form of the word in Mark 13:27 and Matthew 24:31, where it refers to the gathering together of the believers at the coming of the Son of Man. Notice the parallel usage in 2 Maccabees 2:7, where it refers to the regathering of Jews into the temporal kingdom after the Babylonian exile.[63] Paul is here alluding to 1 Thessalonians 4:17 in the use of this term and so is speaking of the same event as he spoke of there—the second coming.

It is truly remarkable that it was 2 Thessalonians 2:1–2 that caused J. N. Darby to become convinced about a rapture of the saints before the Day of the Lord, which in turn led to the attempt to distinguish what is referred to here from the discussions in 1 Thessalonians 5 about the return of Christ. But alas for this sort of logic, the subject of 1 Thessalonians 5 is said to be the Day of the Lord, and that very same subject is discussed in 2 Thessalonians 2:1–2, as the second of these verses makes perfectly evident.[64]

What is the upshot of this reading of 1 Thessalonians 4–5, 2 Thessalonians 2, and the other related texts sometimes thought to refer to a rapture? Unless by rapture one merely means being taken up into the air to welcome Christ and return with him to earth, there is no theology of the rapture to be found in the New Testament anywhere, never mind the term itself. But if this is so, what then are the implications? Well, if there is no rapture, much of the Dispensational system falls down like a house of cards.

For one thing it means that the church of the last generation will go through the fire, just as every other generation of Christians has had to do. This is why Jesus' word of comfort in Mark 13 is not that we will be spared the tribulation, but that God has shortened the time of it for the sake of the elect people of God, which clearly refers to the followers of Jesus (Mark 13:20). Notice for example what Revelation 12:1–6 in fact promises. The woman who represents the people of God in this chapter is not raptured out of the world when the Devil pursues her; rather she is protected from any spiritual harm while remaining in the world. Such is the lot of the people of God in every generation until the Lord returns.

There will be no "beam me up Scotty" effect for the last generation of Christians. Rather there will be suffering and martyrdom, just as there was in the time when John wrote Revelation. What was true then will also be true in the end. Perhaps it will be worthwhile to spend a bit more time on the term and idea of parousia, since it figures so prominently in Dispensational discourse.

What Exactly Is the Parousia?

And why was this term chosen to refer to the return of Christ? What difference if any does the literal meaning of this word make? As it turns out, it makes a considerable difference to the interpretation of this event.

It has been argued, for instance, that parousia refers merely to "presence" in 1 Thessalonians, and that what is envisioned is not a descent but rather an unveiling, with a removal of the barrier between earth and heaven, like the raising of a curtain.[65] The Greek text of 1 Thessalonians 4:16, however, speaks of Jesus coming down from heaven. As for the meaning of *parousia*, Paul can use the term to mean "presence" in a noneschatological context (2 Cor 10:10; Phil 2:12), but he can also use it to mean "coming" in a noneschatological context (1 Cor 16:17; 2 Cor 7:6–7). The question is, how is he using it in an eschatological context like this one in 1 Thessalonians 4?[66]

We must bear in mind that the word had come to have special association with the arrival of significant persons already in the Hellenistic period, and when coupled here with the language of coming down it is hardly likely to mean anything else. In fact most commentators say that every time this word appears in an eschatological context it means coming or arrival, and they have the majority of the evidence on their side. As Best says, the word in its primary meaning has a sense of movement anyway.[67] A good example of the usage in a Hellenistic context in connection with an arrival and a greeting of a royal figure can be found in Josephus, *Jewish Antiquities* 11.26–28, where a priest is awaiting the parousia of Alexander in order to go out and meet (*hypantesis*) him.

We must also keep in view that everywhere else in the NT, the term is used in the eschatological sense of the coming or arrival of the Lord/Son of Man (Matt 24:27–39; Jas 5:7; 2 Pet 1:16; 3:4; 1 John 2:28). Best concludes, "The secular significance of parousia reinforces the conception of a coming of Christ which is a public event, in which he returns from 'outside' history to end history and which therefore eliminates any idea of a gradual development of events within history which themselves share the End."[68]

It is also true to say that no one spoke of a second coming before Justin Martyr (*Dial.* 14.8; 40.4; 118.4) in the second century A.D., and it is well to remember that the word *parousia* just means "arrival" or "coming" it also does not carry the connotation of "return," and it is never used of the incarnation before Ignatius, *To the Philadelphians* 9.2.

Lastly, it seems clear that the concept enshrined in this term is found in the Aramaic prayer *marana tha* ("come O Lord"; 1 Cor 16:22). We must conclude then that the translation "presence" here in 1 Thessalonians 4–5 or elsewhere suits neither the eschatological context nor the history of the use of the term when speaking of "lords" or royal figures, and Paul always uses the term parousia in 1 Thessalonians in connection with the term *lord* (2:19; 3:13; 4:14; 5:23).[69]

Here is where I say that we must be thankful to Dispensationalists for putting eschatology and especially the return of Christ back on the front burner in the last century and a half, and for arguing long, and correctly, that Revelation 20 is after all about a millennial reign of Christ on earth. The early church prior to Augustine knew this. It just will not involve a pre-tribulation or mid-tribulation rapture. It also will not involve a separate but equal status for ethnic Israel now or later. We need to spend some time in the next chapter trying to understand what Paul says about the people of God, for one of the linchpins of Dispensationalism is that some future prophecies are about Israel and others about the church because there are two peoples of God. But this was clearly not Paul's view. To sum up in advance, it is Jew and Gentile united in Christ, both now and later. Furthermore, the promises and prophecies are viewed by Paul as all fulfilled by Christ or in the context of his followers. We must discuss this further at some length in the next chapter.

CHAPTER 7

Will the Real Israel of God
Please Stand Up?

Who are the people of God? Is ethnic Israel still God's chosen people?
Does Paul think God has abandoned non-Christian Israel? These are
important questions, and they are addressed in Paul's lengthy rebuttal
argument in Romans 9–11. Romans 9–11 is all of a piece, being one
continuous argument. It will be good then to hear a fresh translation of
the whole discourse and allow Paul to have his say first.[1]

> Romans 9: I speak the truth in Christ, I am not lying, my conscience
> bears witness with me in the Holy Spirit, that it is a great sorrow to me,
> and a continual pain in my heart. For I could pray to be "anathema," I
> myself [separated] from Christ for my brothers and kinsmen according
> to the flesh. Who are Israelites, whose are the sonship, and the glory, and
> the covenants,[2] and the legislation of the Law, and the worship, and the
> promises, whose are the fathers, and from whom came the Christ,
> according to the flesh, [but] above all who is God, blessed unto all eter-
> nity, amen.
>
> But, it is not, of course, that the Word of God has failed, for not all
> of those who are from Israel are Israel. Nor is it that the seed of Abraham
> are all children, but "In Isaac, will be acknowledged [those] who are your
> seed." That is, it is not the children of the flesh that are the children of
> God, but the children of promise are reckoned as seed. For the word of
> promise is thus: "According to this time I will come, and there will be a
> son for Sarah." But not only so, but also Rebecca from one of our fathers
> had on a marriage bed Isaac. For not yet bearing children, nor do they
> do what is good or bad, in order that the plan/purpose of God be pre-
> served/remain according to free choice, not from works but from the call-
> ing told to her that "the older will be slave to the younger," just as it is
> written "Jacob I loved, but Esau I hated."

What then shall we say? Is there not injustice with God? Absolutely
not! For to Moses he says, "I will have mercy on whom I will have mercy,
and I will pity whom I will pity." So then it is not the one who wills, nor
the one who runs, but it is of the mercy of God. For the Scripture says to
Pharaoh: "Unto this same thing I raised you up, thus to show in you my
power, and thus proclaim my name in all the earth." So then whoever he
wills, he has mercy on, but whoever he wills he hardens. You will say to
me then "Why then is there any blame? For can anyone resist his will?"
"O mere human being, who are you to answer back to God?" Does the
molded one/creature say to the Molder/Creator "Why have you made me
thus?" Does not the potter of the clay have power/authority to make
from his lump on the one hand the vessel unto honor, and on the other
hand one unto dishonor? But if God wishing to show wrath and make
known his power endures with much patience the vessels of wrath who
have been preparing themselves for destruction, and in order that he
might make known the wealth of his glory upon the vessels of mercy who
are prepared before hand unto glory, even us who also he called, not only
from the Jews, but also from the Gentiles/nations, as it even says in
Hosea: "I shall call those not my people, my people, and she who is not
my beloved, beloved. And it will be in the place where it was said, 'You
are not my people,' there you will be called children of the living God."
But Isaiah cries out for Israel: "But even if the number of the sons of
Israel be as sand of the sea, those left behind/ the remnant will be saved.[3]
For the Lord will make upon the earth the Word of accomplishment and
of limitations," and just as Isaiah foretold, "Unless the Lord Sabaoth
left to us seed, we would become as Sodom and become like unto
Gomorrah."

What then shall we say? That Gentiles who did not pursue righteousness attained righteousness, but righteousness that comes from
faith? But Israel pursuing a law of righteousness in the Law did not attain
it? Why is this? Because [it was pursued] not from faith but as from
works? They struck the stone of stumbling just as it is written "Behold,
I put a stone of stumbling in Zion and a rock of scandal/offense, and the
one believing in him will not be put to shame."

Romans 10: Brothers, the deep desire of my heart, and my petition
to God for them is for salvation. For I bear witness about them, that they
have a zeal for God, but it is not according to knowledge. For failing to
recognize the righteousness of God, and seeking to establish the same,
they did not submit to the righteousness of God. For Christ is the end of
the Law for righteousness, unto all those believing. For Moses writes
about the righteousness from the Law, that "The person doing it shall
live in it." But the righteousness from faith speaks thus: Do not say in
your heart, "Which one will ascend into heaven?" (that is, to bring
Christ down) or "Who will descend into the abyss?" (that is, to bring

Christ up from the dead). But what does it say: "The word is near to you, in your mouth and in your heart." This is, the word of faith which we preach, for if you confess with your mouth the Lord Jesus, and believe in your heart God raised him from the dead, you will be saved. For you believe in your heart unto righteousness, but you confess with your lips unto salvation. For the Scripture says: "All those believing in him shall not be put to shame." For there is no distinction of Jews and Gentiles, for the same [is] Lord of all, of riches unto all who call upon him, for "all whoever call upon the name of the Lord, shall be saved."

How then shall they call unto one in whom they have not believed? But how shall they believe in whom they have not heard? And how shall they hear without preaching? But how can they preach unless they have been sent? Just as it is written: "How beautiful the feet of those proclaiming the good." But not all obey the proclamation. For Isaiah says "Lord, who has believed our oral report?" For faith [comes] from hearing, but hearing through the word of Christ. But I say, "Have they not heard?" Certainly they did. "Unto all the earth, the voice of them has gone out, and unto the limits of the inhabited world the word of them." But I say, "Did Israel not understand?" First of all, Moses says: "I myself will make you jealous of those not a people. A people without understanding will excite your anger." But Isaiah shows greater daring and says: "I was found among those who did not seek me, and I became visible to those who did not inquire after me." But to Israel he says: "The whole day I stretched out my hand to a disobedient and resistant people."

Romans 11: God has not pushed away/rejected his people, has he? Absolutely not! For I also am an Israelite, from the seed of Abraham, the tribe of Benjamin. God has not rejected his people whom he foreknew. Or do you not know in Elijah what the Scripture says, how he pleaded to God against Israel: "Lord, they have killed your prophets, they have dug up your altars, and I alone am left remaining, and they seek my life." And what does the oracle say to him? "I have left behind/remaining for myself 7000 men who have not bent the knee to Baal." So then in the present time there is a remainder according to the free choice of grace. But if it is from grace, then it is no longer from works since grace is no longer grace [under those circumstances]. What then? Israel sought it, but did not attain it, but the chosen attained it. But the rest were hardened, just as it is written: "God gave them a spirit of torpor, eyes of those not to see, and ears of those not to hear, until the present day." And David says: "May their table turn into a snare and a trap, and into a scandal and a requital to them, may their eyes be darkened so as not to see, and their backs always be bent over."

I say then, have they stumbled so as to fall? Absolutely not! But their false step/trespass was the salvation of the Gentiles, unto the making of them jealous. But if their misstep meant riches for the world, and their failure riches for the Gentiles, how much more will the full number of them mean?

But to you Gentiles I am speaking. I so far as I myself am apostle of the Gentiles, I am honoring my ministry, so somehow I might make jealous the flesh [kin] of mine and might save some from among them. For if their rejection [means] the reconciliation of the world, what will their acceptance [mean] if not life from the dead? But if the firstfruits are holy, then also the mass of them, and if the root is holy, so also the branches.

But if some of the branches were broken off, but you a wild olive branch were grafted on in them and are fellow sharers in the root, of its sap of the olive tree, do not exult over the branches. But if you individually exult, bear in mind that you do not carry the root, but the root carries you. You will say then, "Branches were broken off in order that I might be grafted in." Very well, they were broken off for unbelief, but you remain standing by faith. Do not preoccupy yourself with thoughts of grandeur, but rather be afraid. For if God did not spare the natural branches, is it likely he will spare you? Behold then both the kindness and the severity of God. Upon the falling on the one hand severity, but upon you on the other hand kindness, if you individually persevere in the kindness, otherwise you individually will also be cut off. And those others, if they do not persevere in unbelief they will be grafted back in. For God is able to graft them back in again. For if you from the against-nature wild olive tree were cut out and might be grafted into the cultivated olive tree, how much more those who are according to nature might be re-engrafted by the same mercy.

For I do not wish you to be ignorant brothers of this mystery, in order that you might not be wise in yourselves because a hardening in part has happened to Israel, until the fullness of the Gentiles comes in, and thus, in the same manner all Israel will be saved as it is written: "The Deliverer will come from Zion. He will turn away the ungodliness from Jacob, and this to them shall be my covenant, when I take away their sins." On the one hand they are enemies according to the gospel because of you, but on the other hand according to the election they are beloved because of the fathers. For the grace gift and the call of God are irrevocable. For in the same way once you were disobedient to God, but now you have found mercy because of their disobedience. Thus also those now have disobeyed on account of mercy shown to you in order also that they might receive mercy. For God shut up all of those unto disobedience in order that he might have mercy on all. Oh the depths of the riches and wisdom and knowledge of God, how inscrutable his judgments and untraceable his ways. For "who has known the mind of the Lord? Or who has been his adviser? Or who gave to him beforehand, so as even to have it repaid to him?" Because from him, and through him and unto him are all things. Glory to him unto eternity. Amen.

CRY FOR THE BELOVED PEOPLE

Though it was not the intended effect of Paul's discourse up to this juncture, nonetheless, most everything that Paul has said up to now in Romans in one way or another raises questions about the status of Israel, especially if righteousness or being set right is obtained through faith in Christ, and Israel by and large has rejected Christ. It is understandable how Gentiles might conclude that God had forsaken his first chosen people for another one, or at the least, Jews no longer had any privileged status since God was impartial and the people of God were to be defined as Jew and Gentile united in Christ, and furthermore all come to God on the basis of grace and faith.

Paul then writes Romans 9–11 to refute certain wrong deductions about the status of Jews, and God's relationship to them, and also about whether God might renege on his promises to them, which would mean that the Word of God had failed or was unreliable. There are profound issues of theodicy, the character of God, ecclesiology, election, prophecy, and the truthfulness and trustworthiness of Scripture involved in this discussion. This section is the climax of Paul's theological discussion, not a mere appendix to that discussion. Indeed, this section builds on what was said in Romans 1–3 about God's impartiality and faithfulness, in Romans 4 about Abraham, and in Romans 8 about predestination and the final goal and outcome of God's salvation plan. Failure to see the eschatological drift of this discussion has often led to misunderstanding about the future of Israel and the nature of election.

Another of the major issues this section of Romans raises is: Who is Paul discussing in this section? All Jews? All Jews who have rejected Christ? All Jews who have accepted Christ? That Jews are the focus of the discussion is not really a matter of scholarly debate. That is accepted almost without question. But once one begins to think about salvation by grace through faith, and the majority of Jews who do not believe in Jesus, one has a theological problem.[4] If it is true that God has abandoned his plan for Israel, what sure and certain hope can Gentiles have in regard to the future? If God's love for Israel has ceased, is it really true that nothing can separate the believer from the love of God? There are various pitfalls that need to be avoided in the interpretation of this section of Romans, and some of them have been ably summed up by N. T. Wright:

> The controversial revolution in Pauline studies that produced the so-called new perspective of the 1970s shifted attention away from late-medieval soul-searchings and anxieties about salvation, and placed it instead on (in Sanders's phrase) the comparison of patterns of religion. It was a self-consciously post-Holocaust project, aimed not least at remind-

ing Paul's readers of his essential Jewishness. But this should not blind us
to the fact that, precisely as a Jewish person, Paul begins this section with
grief and sorrow—because he sees his fellow Jews rejecting the Gospel of
their own Messiah. Paul is not writing a post-Enlightenment treatise
about how all religions are basically the same; nor is he writing an essay
on a modified version of the same project: namely how the one God has
made two equally valid covenants, one with Jews and the other with
Christians. Nor is he writing a postmodern tract about how everyone
must tell their own story and find their own way.[5] . . . These chapters
remain profoundly Christian—that is, centered on Jesus as Messiah and
Lord. Paul does not accommodate himself to our agendas and expectations any more than he did to those of his contemporaries.[6]

We are confronted with the issue of God's righteousness, just as at
the outset of Paul's discourse in Romans 1, and by "righteousness" Paul
means a variety of things, here especially God's being true to his Word,
and so God's faithfulness, even in spite of his people's unfaithfulness
and rejection of Jesus as Messiah. Vindication is at issue here, God vin-
dicating his own Word, as well as delivering or saving his own people.
Their rejection of Jesus has prompted something of a crisis of hope, if
not a crisis of faith in someone like Paul, and so he must wrestle
through it to an answer about God, about his salvation plan, and about
the future of his own kin according to the flesh, his fellow Jews. But on
top of all that, he has to deal with Gentiles in Rome who apparently
believe that God is indeed a supersessionist, having by and large
replaced his first chosen people with another one. Paul will and must
deny what appears to be the case, and he must undercut Gentile hubris,
and make clear their indebtedness to the "root" and their status as
grafted-in "wild olive branches."

It is important to recognize that Paul is not introducing the "Israel"
question now for the first time out of the blue in Romans 9–11. He has
already had a dialogue with a Jewish teacher in Romans 2–3, and
already in 2:28–29 he has raised the question of who is a true Jew. He
has already made clear he operates with a remnant theology. Wright
stresses that what actually happens in Romans 9:6–10:21 with its
plethora of OT references is a retelling of Israel's story from the time of
Abraham until Paul's own day.[7] But it is more than that. Paul is using
the Scriptural references and stories to refute a bad theology held, even
if not openly espoused, by the majority of his audience, who are
Gentiles. The Scriptural references prove two things: (1) that God is
faithful to his Word; and (2) that God has historical purposes that have
always taken into account Israel's faith and unfaithfulness, and taken
into account promises made to Israel and also Israel's apostasy. God
was not taken by surprise when most Jews rejected Jesus. The discus-

sion of election in Romans 9–11 is a discussion of corporate election, in the midst of which there is individual rejection by some and selection for historical purposes of others. In other words, Paul will give equal emphasis to election and apostasy in his discussion. This is especially clear when Paul starts speaking of "you" singular in Romans 10.

To those Gentile Christians who are already saved he warns sternly that they could be broken off from the tree in a heartbeat if they choose to become unfaithful and unbelieving. Neither God's foreknowledge nor corporate election prevents individuals from becoming unfaithful and committing apostasy. Paul says if it happened in Israel, it can happen to Gentile believers as well if they do not watch out. In other words, there is nothing in this discussion of election that suggests that the election results are rigged in advance for particular individuals, or that Paul was an early advocate of "once saved always saved," if by that one means that apostasy is impossible for those truly chosen by God. Rather, Paul's views on predestination, election, the remnant, apostasy, and salvation fall within the parameters of such discussions in early Judaism, rather than within the framework of the later Augustinian, Lutheran, and Calvinistic discussions of the matter.[8] Those early Jewish discussions make full allowance for both the notions of corporate election and the meaningful choices of individuals who may commit apostasy and opt out of the people of God, as we have already pointed out.

The tour de force argument in Romans 9–11 begins abruptly by Paul swearing an oath. The rhetorically astute audience would recognize this as a prelude to a specific kind of argument, namely one having to do with a testimony of witnesses—Paul as witness and the Scripture as witness—as well as God himself speaking through the divine Word. Paul must rebut the notions that God has forsaken his first chosen people, or that the Word of God has failed, or that Israel has stumbled so as to be permanently lost. Underlying these rebuttals is the refutation of the assumption of Gentile superiority in the Roman church. Here as elsewhere Paul is seeking to level the playing field so as to make clear all are "in" the people of God by God's mercy and grace, and no one has a right to boast in their own accomplishments. He also wants to make clear that the salvation of Israel is still part of God's game plan despite how things now appear.

There may be another and even more subtle sort of rebuttal going on as well. Wright argues:

> From this perspective we may suggest that the retelling of Israel's story in 9.6–10.21 is itself designed not only to suggest a new way of reading Israel's own history but also quietly to undermine the pretensions of Rome itself. Rome, too, told stories of its own history, going back to the

brothers Romulus and Remus a thousand years earlier, coming through
the long story of the republic and finally arriving at the emperor who was
now enthroned as lord of the world. Paul, having declared in 9.5 that
Jesus, the Messiah, is "God over all, blessed forever," . . . returns to the
point in 10.12: Jesus is Lord of all, Jew and Gentile alike. Israel's history,
climaxing in Jesus, is designed to upstage Roman history, climaxing in
Augustus.[9]

Paul asserts right from the beginning at 9:1 that he is absolutely
telling the truth, and he seems to be suggesting that the rule of the testimony of two witnesses has been met, because both he and his conscience attest that he is telling the truth; but he also affirms that the
Holy Spirit is involved, so that what he says are Spirit-inspired words.
Notice how in Romans 2:15 conscience is seen as a cowitness as well.[10]
He explains his continual heartache and sorrow for his Jewish kin, by
which here he must mean non-Christian Jews. Paul even goes so far as
to say that he could wish himself accursed (anathema) by Christ for
the sake of these fellow Jews. Here the notion of anathema seems
to mean something like separated, for he speaks of being anathema
from Christ.[11]

It is interesting that Paul calls his fellow Jews his brothers as well
as his kin according to the flesh in 9:3. Here the term *brother* is used
not in the spiritual sense of fellow Christian, nor in the literal sense of
a member of Paul's own physical or extended family, unless one
includes all Jews as his extended family. Paul describes them as
"Israelites" in 9:4, indicating something of their spiritual nature as
God's chosen people. Paul is probably already setting up the argument
which is to follow, because he wants to maintain that God has not
rejected non-Christian Jews as part of Israel. Indeed, the term *Israel* is
going to be used in 11:26 to refer quite specifically to non-Christian
Jews. But Paul goes on to say in 9:6 that not all those who are from
Israel, are Israel. He does not use the qualifier "true" Israel here, and it
is probably not appropriate to bring it into the discussion. Paul is saying that the term Israel does not apply to some Jews. He will use the
righteous-remnant concept in his discussion, as we shall see.

Paul goes on in 9:4 to provide a list of spiritual credits or benefits
of Israel, trying to build up their honor rating in the eyes of the largely
Gentile audience. Yet, of course, in fact it is precisely these benefits that
make it all the more puzzling that the majority of Jews have rejected
their own messiah. Here he is building on what he said in Romans
3:1–8. He mentions sonship being theirs first of all. This is simply
another way of saying they have a family relationship with God, with
all the benefits that pertain thereto. Paul next mentions the glory, which
here surely means the divine presence dwelling in the midst of God's

people, or less likely the hope of eschatological glory at the resurrection. But Paul is not talking about hope here; he is talking about what they have. Theirs are also the covenants, by which Paul means at least the Abrahamic, Mosaic, and new covenants. This is why Paul says "to the Jew first" in his thesis statement in Romans 1:16–17. The promise of eschatological redemption and renewal was for them first. Next is mentioned *latreia* which in a pre-A.D. 70 context would likely mean the worship that goes on in the temple in Jerusalem. This is likely how the largely Gentile Roman audience would have understood it as well, for pagans associated worship with temples, not with meetings in synagogues or homes, for example. To them was also given the rule of law, or as the phrase means literally, the legislation of law, probably referring in particular to the Mosaic Law.[12]

Paul is building up the impression that Israel is a duly and indeed divinely constituted people with many gifts from God. He then adds that to Israel are also given the promises (such as those to Abraham). Now we have gotten beyond heritage or history to something that has to do with the future, a benefit that is still outstanding. Paul then lists the "fathers," by which he means the great patriarchs of the faith: Abraham, Isaac, Jacob, Joseph, and so on. Then finally Paul lists what is in his mind their greatest asset and gift to humankind: the Messiah. Paul says that *kata sarka*, "according to physical descent," the Messiah came from the Jewish race. Paul elsewhere indicates that on the basis of other criteria, or in other ways, he came from God.[13]

Romans 9:5b is one of the most debated verses in all of Pauline literature. Is Paul actually calling Christ God here? The question here hinges on the matter of punctuation. There is no question but that it is better Greek if one considers the *ho hon* which follows the words "the Christ" as referring back to Christ rather than forward to the term *theos*.[14] Furthermore, whenever we find a doxology elsewhere, including in Paul, it begins with the word *blessed* or some similar term, not with *ho hon*. Those who want to find an independent doxology to God here are hard-pressed to explain why it does not follow the normal pattern for such doxologies. In fact, the one real objection to Christ being called God here is that supposedly Paul does not do so elsewhere. But this is not true. Paul does do so in equivalent terms in Philippians 2:5–11; furthermore when he calls Christ "Lord," he is predicating of Jesus the divine name used for God over and over in the Septuagint. In this very argument we find Jesus called "divine Lord," indeed confessed as such in Romans 10:9, and then an OT passage (Joel 3:5 LXX) where God is called Lord is applied to Jesus at 10:13.

Paul has christologically redefined how he understands monotheism, and this text is just further evidence of the fact. There are, however, still two ways one could translate the text recognizing that Christ is called God here: either "Christ according to the flesh, who is God over all blessed forever amen" or "Christ according to the flesh who is over all, God blessed forever amen."[15] As Wright points out, Paul in Romans 1:3–4 is perfectly capable of talking about the Messiah in both his human and his divine dimensions in the same breath.[16] But this Christ is not through with Israel yet, and precisely because he is also the God of mercy he will return to turn Jacob back to his God, as the end of this entire argument will urge.

NOTIONS ON REMNANTS

The preamble now being over the argument proper begins at Romans 9:6. Paul immediately gets to the point: it is not like the Word of God to Israel has failed. Rather one must understand the concept of the remnant. The remnant proves that the Word of God to Jews has not failed. But who is this remnant? Paul apparently is referring to persons like himself, Jews who are followers of Jesus.[17] And furthermore, Paul will go on to argue that God is not finished with non-Christian Jews either.[18] Indeed we will learn in the third part of his argument that God temporarily hardened some Jews so that the Gentiles could be grafted into the people of God, and so in fact the other Jews could be regrafted into the people of God on the basis of grace and faith in Jesus. Then all will have been saved on the basis of faith in the promises.

This leads to an important point. When Paul is referring to the hardening of some, he is not talking about their eternal damnation. He is talking about a process in history that is temporal and temporary. In other words we are going to see that what Paul is talking about in vv. 22–23 is not those saved or damned from before the foundation of the world, but rather as Cranfield says, those vessels that are currently positively related to God, and those vessels which currently are not.[19]

In Romans 8:7–10, Paul provides some Scriptural backing for what he has just asserted. The examples are meant to show that not all Israel turns out to be children of the promise, even though they are all children of Abraham. The most telling example of course is Jacob and Esau, who, before they had done anything, were given certain lots in life. They were the product of one act of intercourse (which is probably what the euphemistic reference to the marriage bed is meant to convey here). The elder would serve the younger, not because the younger deserved better or had done better deeds, but because God in his unmerited favor decided to do it that way, showing mercy on Jacob more than Esau. Esau's historical role, however determined by God, does not mean that God had cursed Esau and damned him for eternity. As the OT context of the saying "Jacob I loved and Esau I hated" (Mal 1:2–3) shows, in fact, the subject there is two nations, not two individuals, and as we have said, even when individuals are in the picture, it is not their eternal destiny that is being spoken of.

The quoted verse then may speak of God's elective purposes, but the discussion is about a role these people were to play in history, not their personal eternal destiny.[20] This brings us to a second and crucial point. When Paul discusses Israel, he is discussing the history of God's choices and historical purposes, not the history of a race.[21] The story being told here is the story of God's dealing with Israel to illustrate his righteous character and plan. Paul does also want to squelch the notion that physical descent determines the elect, and he does this by carrying his argument through more than one generation of patriarchs. There is nothing here about the replacement of one Israel by another, or about a true Israel. The discussion is about how the one people of God have developed through time.

Paul's use of the Scripture is trying to demonstrate that God has always done things a certain way, namely that there has always been selection for special purposes within election, and there has always been a remnant concept operating as well. These two ideas are juxtaposed, but they are not identical. Paul explains that though the large majority of Jews have currently rejected Christ, this should not be taken as a sign that God has rejected them, not least because there have been various times in Israel's history (e.g., the wilderness-wandering period) when the majority of Jews rejected God's plans and purposes for them. In fact, Paul will argue that God knew they were going to reject him, and so he planned for, and made room for, the acceptance of Gentiles in large numbers, and the acceptance of all on the basis of grace and faith and God's mercy toward all, not on the basis of some obligation. Thus, as Cranfield states, this separation process is not an illustration of God's inscrutable judgment but ultimately an illustration of his mercy over all, though of course God does not cease to be just.[22]

But it is too seldom noticed that the concept of the righteous remnant is used to further the discussion about God's historical purposes, and in particular his purposes to produce a Jewish messianic figure to save the world. The discussion is not about a saved group of Israelites as opposed to a permanently non-elect group of Israelites, for Paul goes on to say that even those Jews temporarily and temporally broken off from the chosen people can and will be regrafted in. The description of the remnant process is also meant to make clear how God works to create a people for his purposes. Israel was chosen or created not primarily for their own benefit, but to be a light to the nations.

Paul is describing that process of election and selection for such purposes. Israel's or anyone else's salvation is not finally completed until the eschaton. Until then, there can be assurance of what is hoped for, but this assurance always stands under the proviso that one must persevere until the end of life, something that is only possible by God's grace and through faith, working out one's salvation with fear and trembling, as Paul puts it in Philippians. Unless we see salvation from the end of the process we will not understand this discussion. Salvation does not happen in full, or to its completion, before Christ returns and the dead are raised. This is not only because salvation in its final form means a resurrected person who even in the flesh is conformed to the image of the resurrected Jesus. It is also because Paul believes that even for the saved person, there is always danger of unfaithfulness and apostasy in this life. One is not eternally secure until one is securely in eternity.

Paul also believes, since all have sinned and fallen short of God's glory, God owes salvation to no one, and none can merit it. It is all a matter of mercy and grace. Thus God is free to choose and use whoever he wills for the divine purposes, without injustice. One can be chosen for God's purposes, like a Cyrus or a Pharaoh, and not be saved. Being chosen for historical purposes and being saved are not one and the same thing. Salvation for individuals is by grace and through faith. Election, insofar as the creation of a people is involved, is largely a corporate thing; it is "in Israel," or it is "in Christ," but the means of getting in is by faith.[23] Israel as a nation was chosen to be a light to other nations. This is election for a historical purpose, and it says nothing about the eternal salvation of individual Jews.

In regard to the corporate notion of election so far as the issue of God having a Christian people, Barrett is right on target: "election does not take place . . . arbitrarily or fortuitously; it takes place always and only *in Christ*. They are elect who are in him . . . (cf. Gal 3:29). It is failure to remember this that causes confusion over Paul's doctrine of election and predestination."[24]

At Romans 9:14 Paul asks the rhetorical question, "So then, is there injustice with God?" This suggestion Paul roundly repudiates. It should be noted that the quote in v. 15 from Exodus 33:19 says nothing about "I will judge those whom I will judge." Both phrases speak of mercy. That word *mercy* could be said to be the theme of this and the following two chapters. The word for mercy occurs seven times in some form in these three chapters, and only five times in the whole rest of Paul's letters. This must be kept constantly in view when we consider what follows.

Verse 16 draws a conclusion from the Scripture citation: it is not to those who will or run, but to God who has mercy.[25] It is God's mercy which explains this separation and temporary hardening process. This is about the character of God, not the worthiness or unworthiness of this or that vessel. God's elective purposes should never be taken outside the context of God's mercy and his revelatory and salvific work in

Christ. Election is in Israel in the first instance, and then in Christ. It is not some abstract or inscrutable will of God that lurks behind the revealed will of God, for God's will and heart are truly revealed in Christ. Whatever is not known about God must comport with what God has revealed to the world in Christ. Thus it is not helpful to talk about pretemporal eternal decrees by God, unless one is talking about what God decreed about and for his Son, the chosen and destined One.

Verse 17 offers another illustration. In this case Pharaoh is used as an illustration. He is said to be raised up for the purpose of showing God's power in him and so as to proclaim the glory of God throughout the earth. The text in question here is Exodus 9:16, though Paul's version differs from the Septuagint at various points. Pharaoh is used to demonstrate God's awesome saving power as applied to his people. That Pharaoh is judged or hardened is a byproduct of this, but God acted to redeem his people. It is, however, a regular feature of God's work that what is redemption for one person may require or involve judgment on another one. When you liberate the oppressed you judge the oppressor at the same time. The focus is on what happens to Israel. Nothing is said about Pharaoh's eternal state, but rather how he was used by God during the exodus. The verb *raise up* does not likely refer to resurrection here, but rather that God brought him on the stage of history and hardened him, to reveal his mercy and power to save Israel.[26]

Verse 18 speaks of this dual process. God has mercy on whom he wills, and he hardens whom he wills. This remark must not be isolated from the rest of what Paul is saying here. If Israel is any analogy, then *hardening* does not mean damning. It involves a temporal action of limited duration. The point of this discussion in any case is to deal with the fate and condition of Israel, not Pharaoh. How does one explain their rejection of their Messiah? What hope do they still have?

Thus far, in Romans 8–9 Paul has talked about predestination of two groups: Christians in Romans 8, and Israel in Romans 9. Israel was destined to stumble so Gentiles might rise, but also so that all might rise up by the grace of God. This destining is not to heaven or hell, but for God's historical purposes, as was the case with Pharaoh.[27] "Reading this part of Romans is like riding a bicycle: if you stand still for more than a moment, forgetting the onward movement both of the story of 9:6–10:21 and of the letter as a whole, you are liable to lose your balance—or, perhaps, to accuse Paul of losing his."[28] It is also true that proof-texting, or taking certain verses of this section out of the flow and context and trajectory of this rhetorical argument, has led to all sorts of bad theology. When the effect of an argument is intended to be cumulative, and there is deliberately an ebb and flow, assertions and then qualifications involved in it, it is a major mistake to focus on one or another verse to get at Paul's "theology" of election and the like. In any case, what we have here is Paul's active theologizing into a specific situation, not Paul's theology as we often speak of it today.

The Potter and the Clay

Romans 9:22–23 belong together and may seem particularly harsh. Paul is in the middle of using Jeremiah's metaphor (Jer 18:6) about the potter and the clay to discuss the relationship of God to his creatures. That it is a metaphor must be stressed again and again. Verse 22 is problematic because it involves a conditional sentence without an apodosis, so we must supply the first part of the sentence to make it work. In view of vv. 14–18 it is clear enough that Paul is dealing with what he believes to be a real condition here, not merely a possible or probable one. The real question about v. 22 is whether it should have a causal or concessive clause beginning with the word *thelon*. If it is causal then the meaning is, "But what if God endured vessels of wrath, prepared for destruction with much long suffering here, *because* he willed to show forth his wrath and to make known his power, and in order to make known the riches of his glory upon vessels of mercy?" If we have a concessive clause then the sentence will read, "What if God, *although* he willed to show forth his wrath, . . . nevertheless endured vessels of wrath, with much long suffering in order to make known the riches of his glory upon the vessels of mercy?"

On the one hand, it is understandable that Paul might be saying that though God would show forth his wrath against the vessels of wrath, nonetheless he had patience with them for an extended period of time. It is difficult to imagine Paul saying that God endured the vessels of wrath because he wanted to show forth his wrath. It is clear enough that Paul does believe there will be a wrath to come (see 2 Thess 2), though in Romans 1 he could also talk about a wrath in the midst of time being exercised by God. Thus it seems clear that the concessive clause view of this sentence makes the most sense. God's endurance of the vessels of wrath shows God's patience and mercy, giving time for amendment of life.

What is often overlooked is that Paul is also drawing on the sapiential reading of the story of Israel found in Wisdom of Solomon 12:3–18. The passage emphasizes: (1) God's forbearance of the wicked; (2) the inappropriateness of the created and fallen person to challenge God's right to judge; (3) God's righteousness, which includes the notion of God's justice, and not just his mercy or faithfulness; (4) God's right to judge mercifully if he so chooses (12:13–18). Later in this book at 15:7 we read about the potter who forms from the same clay "both the vessels that serve clean uses and those for contrary uses, making all alike." Both Paul and the author of Wisdom of Solomon assert that "God has the right both to remake nations and peoples in a new way and to withhold judgment for a while in order that salvation may spread to the rest of the world"[29] Furthermore, Paul seems to be aware of the discussion in Sirach 33:12–13 where it talks about God distinguishing between persons.

It is necessary now to deal with the difficult phrases about the vessels of mercy and the vessels of wrath. It is important to note that Paul uses two different verbs when talking about these different vessels. The vessels of wrath are framed/prepared/fit/put together for wrath while the vessels of mercy are prepared beforehand for glory.[30] The former verb (*katertismena*) is a perfect passive participle. The latter verb (*proetoimasen*) is an aorist active indicative. This change in verbs cannot be accidental, and it suggests that Paul means that the vessels of wrath are ripe or fit for destruction.[31] Indeed one could follow the translation of John Chrysostom here and render it as a middle verb "have made themselves fit for" destruction.

If this is the case, this verse certainly does not support the notion of double predestination. Rather the verse refers to the fact that these vessels are worthy of destruction, though God has endured them for a long time.[32] Notice, second, that the discussion about the vessels of mercy is not about what they are destined to be beforehand, but what they are being *prepared* to be beforehand. This suggests that the subject is not some pretemporal determination, but rather what Romans 8 refers to— namely, that God did always plan for believers to be conformed to the image of God's son, and during their Christian lives, through the process of being set right and being sanctified, they were being prepared for such a glorious destiny. Thus, Paul would be alluding to the process of sanctification here, though it has a pretemporal plan behind it. Furthermore, as Ephesians 2:3–4 makes quite evident, someone can start out as a vessel of wrath and later become a child of God by grace through faith. The issue is where one is in the story of a particular vessel, not some act of divine predetermination of some to wrath.

In Romans 9:30–33 Paul sums up some of the implications of what he has just said. Gentiles who did not pursue righteousness attained it, but it was a form of righteousness that came through faith. On the other hand, Israel pursued the law of righteousness, yet did not attain it. The Israelites were pursuing a ruling principle of righteousness in their lives, by means of the Law. The Law then did bear witness to righteousness. It was a law about that. The problem was not that Israel realized God required obedience. The problem is that they pursued righteousness by works of the Law, not by faith in Christ, and therefore did not attain it. This is precisely what Paul says in verse 32: "Because not by faith, but as from works they pursued it, they did not attain it."

The fault was not that Israel used the Law in a legalistic way or was glorying in works of righteousness. The problem in part was with the Law itself. It could not empower a person to obey or keep it (cf. Gal 3–4; Rom 6–7). Nor could the Law create or give the faith or righteousness it spoke of. These only came from Christ and through the Holy Spirit. The Law is not evil. Indeed it is holy, just, and good. But it is impotent and inadequate to help fallen persons keep it.[33]

Beginning at vv. 32b–33 Paul seems to be drawing on a traditional catena of Scriptures from Isaiah 28:16 and 8:14 in the Septuagint. They stumbled or struck their foot on the stone of stumbling. It is God who raised up that stone of stumbling, according to the quote in v. 33a. But v. 33b adds those believing upon him shall not be put to shame (or we might translate "shall not be disappointed"). The shame in view here is the eschatological shame of appearing at final judgment naked—i.e., in the wrong condition. Thus clearly, Paul has had a future wrath in mind in this discussion, not merely a present one (cf. Rom 5:5). Käsemann says: "Judaism must take offense at Christ to the degree that the requirement of faith enforces a break with its religious past. It cannot see that precisely in this way it is summoned back to the promise it has been given. The continuity of the fleshly conceals the continuity of the divine word maintained in Scripture. It thus conceals the eschatological goal."[34] The problem with this assessment is that it seems to assume that faith was not a requirement before Christ, which is not so.

The End of the Law and the Beginning
of Righteousness

Romans 10:1 begins something like 9:1 did, expressing Paul's heartache about his fellow Jews, whom, it will be noted, are seen as lost and in need of salvation. This is Paul's heart's desire and what he prays for repeatedly. Paul is thinking, as Romans 11:26 will show, of future salvation on the last day, otherwise he would speak not only of prayer but of proclaiming. At v. 2 he speaks of having a zeal for God that was not according to knowledge. Too often people mistake earnestness for truth. One can be zealous for the wrong cause, and it may well be that Paul has put it this way precisely because he was Exhibit A of such zeal when he was wrongly persecuting the followers of Jesus as a Pharisee. What Paul believes then is that non-Christian Jews lack understanding, and in some cases they have been rebellious and rejected God's Word to them.

The matter of righteousness, both divine and human righteousness, comes up again at this juncture. Paul says that non-Christian Jews, despite their zeal, are ignorant of the righteousness that comes from

God, not least because they have been seeking to "stand" by their own righteousness. Notice the language Paul chooses here. He is not talking about "getting in" but rather "staying in" to use Sanders's terminology. He is saying that Jews seek to stand on the basis of their own righteousness, having already been granted the gracious privilege of being part of God's people. It may be doubted Paul would call this covenantal nomism, for he speaks of "their own" righteousness, and not the righteousness of the Law per se. There is an issue of their not submitting to the righteousness of God. Here in this discussion "righteousness" certainly does not mean "right-standing with God," for they already had that. The issue lies elsewhere. As those who were already God's people, they were standing in the wrong place, and not submitting to the right righteousness.

Verse 4 then reads literally, "for end/termination/purpose/goal of the Law [is] Christ for righteousness to all those believing." This is one of the most debated verses in the entire Pauline corpus. It is of course true that Paul believes that no longer being under the Law does not mean no longer being required to behave in a righteous manner. On the other end of the spectrum, it is not true that Paul is simply talking about the badges, or marks of righteousness, such as sabbath keeping and circumcision here, when he says that Christ is the end or termination of the Law. Something more profound is going on.

The term *telos* can indeed have several possible meanings.[35] The sense of end as completion or termination does not exclude the notion of end as goal.[36] However, in Paul's writings the term *telos* seems always to include the notion of termination, whatever other nuances it may have (cf. 1 Cor 1:8; 10:11; 15:24; 2 Cor 11:15; Phil 3:19).[37] As Barrett remarks, when something has reached its goal or termination, then "when an object has served its purpose, it may be discarded."[38] It is a mistake then to try and translate *telos* as "aim" here, as though he merely meant that the Law points to Christ.[39] This is because Paul will go on to say that righteousness for those who believe is available now through *another* means—not through the Law but through faith. Now if this is the contrast in mind, then righteousness should logically mean the same thing in both cases. Righteousness is not attained nor maintained by this means but rather by this other one.[40] Christ has put an end to the Law as a way of pursuing righteousness.[41]

It needs to be stressed that v. 4 is used as an explanation for what has been said in v. 3. The righteousness that comes from God is very different from "their own righteousness" (i.e., from the pursuit of righteousness, from the pursuit of right standing before God by keeping the Law). Refusing to submit to God's righteousness is a mistake *because* Christ has put an end to any other means of righteousness. Christ, not the Law, is now the means of righteousness for believers, whether we mean by that either right standing, sanctification, moral behavior, or final righteousness. Paul will speak about the Law of Christ when he wants to talk about a code or standard of righteousness for Christians, not Torah.[42] The argument here is salvation-historical, not merely Christological. He is not trying to argue that Christ embodies the Law's righteousness or is the aim of the Law, though he might well agree with those ideas. The sense here is close to 2 Corinthians 2:13–14, where the point is the end of the Mosaic covenant, spoken of metaphorically as the end of the glory of Moses' face, which was being annulled.

Moses is the one who said about the righteousness that is from the Law, that the one doing it shall live in it. Paul in v. 5 is quoting Leviticus 18:5, which is the same text he uses in Galatians 3:12. It is interesting that the quote from Deuteronomy 30:12 which follows in v. 6 is applied to personified Wisdom in Baruch 3:29–30 but here to Christ. Paul juxtaposes a different voice to that of Moses at v. 6: the voice of a concept personified—"The Righteousness from Faith says." The citation is of Deuteronomy 9:4 and Deuteronomy 30:12–14, and so we have in a sense Moses pitted over against himself here! The point of this citation is that it is not a matter of human searching and striving. The righteousness from faith makes house calls! One does not need to have a vision that takes one up into heaven to find Christ, or make a subterranean journey, as is sometimes described in apocalyptic literature, to bring him up from the dead. No, the Word, both written and incarnate, is near at hand, as the quote from Deuteronomy 30:12–14 shows.[43] Paul is talking about something that can both be embodied and confessed. He means the word of faith about Jesus and the righteousness from faith that comes from having a relationship with him. He may also be calling Jesus the Righteousness from Faith, which might explain the personification. Paul says in v. 8 that it is *this* righteousness that he has been preaching. It is interesting that Paul follows the same kind of commentating techniques, citing a verse, and then interspersing a comment introduced by "that is" (vv. 6–8) that we find at Qumran (see 1QpHab 2:10–11 quoting Hab 1:6). It is also important, however, to note that he uses these texts in a way similar to what one finds in earlier Jewish sapiential literature (Sir 24:5; Bar 3:29–30) where Wisdom is the assumed subject that is sought for in the abyss and in the heavens, only Christ now replaces Wisdom as the one sought after in such out-of-the-way places.[44] Paul appears to have been a trained exegete well before he became a Christian, but then too he seems here and elsewhere to function as something of a sapiential prophet as well.

In Romans 10, vv. 9–10 should be dealt with together. The issue here is salvation. A true confession coupled with true believing leads to salvation. The confession that we find here is parallel to what one finds at 1 Corinthians 12:3, which suggests Paul is using a set formula his audience would recognize. Notice how the mention of Jesus as Lord is immediately followed by reference to God raising him from the dead. Both things are to be confessed together precisely because Jesus is the risen Lord. In Jesus, God has inaugurated the eschaton, and as Barrett says, this last clause would clearly distinguish confession of Jesus as Lord from other such confessions in the Greco-Roman world.[45] Jesus, unlike these other so-called lords, had died and been raised from the dead, and only fully assumed the role of Lord at and by means of the resurrection.

Verse 10 is especially crucial for our purposes. Notice how righteousness and salvation are in parallel object clauses here. The important thing to be said about this is that just as salvation has an experiential dimension here, it is likely that Paul means righteousness does as well. Thus Barrett's translation, "faith works in the heart to produce righteousness," is correct.[46] After all, believing in the heart is an internal matter, not merely a matter of some objective status or standing. Righteousness then would perhaps here refer not only to being set right by God, but also to the beginnings of being made righteous, what is normally called sanctification. What is certainly nowhere on the horizon here is the notion of Christ's alien righteousness being predicated of the believer in lieu of his or her own personal righteousness.

Verse 11 provides us with another Scripture quotation, this time from Isaiah 28:16. Here the matter of honor is raised. A person who believes in Jesus will not be put to shame (at the eschaton, when all is revealed and all are evaluated). In fact Paul has modified the quote by adding the word *all* up front to stress the intended universal scope of God's salvation plan. In v. 12 we have reiterated God's impartiality, a theme we heard enunciated much earlier in the letter. The reason there is no distinction between Jews and Gentiles is that there is one Lord over all, and this Lord is prepared to bestow blessings on one and all who call upon him.[47] In Romans 3:22 the absence of distinction between Jew and Gentile had to do with all being sinners, here with all being under the same Lord who wishes to bless all. Again in Romans 10:13 we have the verb *saved* in the future tense. Here Joel 2:32 is quoted. The emphasis is on the word *all*. All who call upon this Lord will be saved. Paul here is countering any notions that God has plans to save only a few, or only desires to bless a few. On the contrary, anyone who responds to the gospel, and calls upon and confesses the name of the Lord, will be saved. Paul's stress is on the wideness of God's mercy, not the narrowness of the size of the remnant or elect group.

Beginning at v. 14 we have a chain or sequence of events required for someone to be saved. What is interesting is that there is nothing in this chain about God's predetermined decrees of election. Salvation happens because: (1) someone has been sent; (2) the someone who was sent has preached; (3) someone has heard; (4) someone who has heard has believed; (5) someone who has believed has called upon the Lord, and so been saved. The emphasis is placed here on the necessity of preaching and responding to it.

Verse 15 involves a quote of Isaiah 52:7—how beautiful are the feet of those preaching the good (news). Paul is nearer to the Hebrew rather than the Septuagint version of the verse, and it may be suggested that Paul knew both, and like other early Jewish exegetes would go with the version that best illustrated his point. But then Paul gets to the heart of the problem—not all respond to the gospel positively, or as Paul puts it, not all "obey" the preaching. He amplifies on this problem in Romans 10:18–19. It is clear enough that Paul is still concerned with the issue of non-Christian Israel, which is referred to in v. 19 again. Israel has heard and does know about the gospel. It is interesting that Paul seems to assume that the gospel has already in the 50s gone out to a large portion of the empire (cf. 15:19, 23; and Mark 13:10 and 14:9). This is of a piece with Paul's assertion that he had completed his work in the eastern half of the empire and wishes to move on to Rome and further west. He seems to assume that Diaspora Jews, at least in the eastern half of the empire, have heard, or at least have heard about the gospel.

But the quotes from Deuteronomy 32:21 in v. 19, and from Isaiah 65:1 in Romans 10:20, however, provide the basis for Paul's analysis in Romans 11 of what is happening with Israel. God is making non-Christian Jews envious by bringing in Gentiles into the people of God, who are characterized as not a nation, and as lacking understanding. God in fact is said to have revealed himself to those who were not seeking him. Paul thus has a rationale for what has happened with Israel, as well as for why so many Gentiles are responding to the gospel when so many Jews are not. It is a story with many twists in it, and it is interesting that Paul relies mainly on Isaiah and the Pentateuch to provide the story line and the explanations as well. Verse 21 is plaintive. Isaiah 65:2 is cited, and God is presented as a parent or suitor stretching out his arms toward a child all day long, but the child is obstinate and wayward.

THE HOPE OF ISRAEL—WHEN THE REDEEMER COMES FORTH FROM ZION

Romans 11:1 brings us to the third major part of Paul's argument, and reflects Paul's major concern. He does not want the audience in Rome to think God has rejected Israel.[48] He emphatically rejects such a notion. The proof he gives immediately is himself: he is an Israelite, from the seed of Abraham and from the tribe of Benjamin.[49] God has certainly not rejected his people whom he foreknew. Foreknowledge here is predicated of a whole group of people, ethnic Israel, many of whom are not, in Paul's view, currently saved. Foreknowledge does not mean foreordination unto salvation here, clearly enough, unless one assumes that in v. 26 Paul is predicting the salvation of every single Jew who ever existed.[50] At 11:2, then, we also have a nonrestrictive use of the term *foreknew* applied to God. Here the term clearly does not mean something like God's prior choice.[51]

Paul in vv. 2–3 paraphrases the story from 1 Kings 19:10–14 about Elijah.[52] Paul was not the first to complain and worry about Israel's unfaithfulness. Elijah did so as well, and was told that there were in fact many who were not worshiping the gods of this world—seven thousand, in this case. There was a leftover. Romans 11:5 speaks of a remnant or remainder or a leftover "according to the free choice of grace." The term *ekloge* could be translated "election," but that would not really convey the essence of what Paul is getting at. Notice that this "free choice" probably refers to God's choice of a group—the remainder. Again election or selection is corporate in sense here.

Verse 6 once again states the fundamental contrast between the free choice based on grace, and a choice based on works, in this case works of the Law. The point is that God's free choice was not based on the remnant's works of the Law. This is not a contrast between libertinism and legalism. Paul's critique of the Mosaic Law is based on the assumption that it is obsolescent, for Christ is the end of the Law as a way of righteousness. It had no power to enable a fallen person to keep it. His is a salvation-historical argument with the Christ event being the crucial turning point.

C. H. Talbert seeks to argue that Paul is opposing legalism, by which he means Paul is opposing "doing works of the Law" as a means of striving to stay in the people of God and then obtain final or eschatological salvation.[53] But this hardly plumbs the radical nature of Paul's argument. Paul is not merely opposing a legalistic way of approaching the Mosaic Law or the Mosaic covenant. And in any case, Paul is all for his converts keeping the Law of Christ, and tells them they must avoid the deeds of the flesh and do the Law of Christ if they want to enter the kingdom (Gal 5–6). In other words, Paul is an advocate of just what Talbert thinks Paul is critiquing. Paul affirms a sort of covenantal nomism, though it is grace empowered and Spirit driven. It is just not the Mosaic covenant he wants Gentiles to keep. It is a mistake to call any demand or requirement to obey a law "legalism" within a context where salvation is by grace and faith. The obedience which necessarily must follow from and depends on living faith is not legalism. Paul's problem is not with obedience or good works, or laws per se. Those are all seen as good things by him. Paul's problem is with anachronism in a fallen world where the Mosaic Law cannot empower fallen persons to keep it, and it has been brought to an end as a way of righteousness by Christ, especially when Christ and the Spirit *can* empower obedient living.

Paul then will contrast in v. 7 the "remainder" or "elect" within Israel who obtained what all of Israel sought. Not all who are from Israel are Israel, as Paul has earlier said in this argument. Election of Israel as God's chosen people was no automatic guarantee of salvation. It is interesting that Paul then applies the "hardening" principle to the rest of Israel, and cites two sets of Scriptures to back up the claim— Deuteronomy 29:4 and Isaiah 29:10 first, and then Psalm 69:22–23 and 35:8. In both sets of texts hardening is described as being plagued with spiritual darkness or blindness or imperceptiveness. They were made impervious to hearing or seeing the Word. Paul in fact has sharpened the quotation of Deuteronomy 29:4 by placing the word *not* with the infinitives *to see* and *to hear* rather than with the verb *gave*.

In Romans 11:11–25 we have the conclusion of Paul's major argument in Romans 9–11 about God, the Jews, and their future. Once again we must keep steadily in mind that Paul is not talking about Jews who are followers of Christ in this segment, any more than he was in the previous two parts of this argument. Paul says that he is going to reveal an apocalyptic *musterion* ("a mystery") something which a person only knows because God has revealed it to him or her. It is indeed possible that Paul is describing some of a vision that he had, for Paul was indeed a visionary (see 2 Cor 12:2–10).

What Paul said in Romans 9:6–11:10 could have easily led to the conclusion that the unbelieving Jews were lost altogether, God having rejected them in favor of the Gentiles. Thus once again, Paul begins a segment of his argument with a rhetorical question: have they stumbled so as to fall (permanently)? Here *hina* must surely mean "in order to" or possibly "so as to." The former would be an example of a final *hina*, the point being that God made them stumble so as to fall. But here the discussion is not focused on divine determination, but rather on the outcome for the Jews. Thus the translation, "so as to" is to be preferred. Fall here then would mean fall into ruin, into irrevocable disfavor with God. Paul's response is: absolutely not! Paul is surely not dealing here with a purely hypothetical question. It must have occurred to some Gentiles at some juncture.

Paul says that, in fact, as a result of their stumbling/trespass (*paraptoma*),[54] salvation has come to the Gentiles.[55] Part of the reason it has come to the Gentiles at this juncture is said to be to make non-Christian Jews jealous. Paul at Romans 10:19 had already quoted Deuteronomy 32:21 about making Israel jealous. Now we get a hint that Paul hopes for and indeed sees his mission to the Gentiles as an indirect way to bring into the Christian faith some Jews as well. Furthermore, this is not mere wishful thinking on the part of Paul; rather he sees it as God's mysterious plan revealed unto him.[56]

We have a specific sort of argument in v. 12, from the lesser to the greater. If it is true that the temporary lapse of some Jews from their place in the people of God means riches for the Gentile world,[57] what will their reinclusion mean? The word *pleroma*, fullness or full number,[58] appears here and is going to reappear later in this argument as well. As E. E. Johnson has pointed out, in other early Jewish apocalyptic texts there is talk about the "full number" of the elect being collected, brought in, reunited before the eschaton (see *4 Ezra* 6:25; *2 Bar.* 81:4).[59] Paul inverts such discussions which have the order: (1) full number of Jews reunited, saved; (2) Gentiles stream to Zion, or become part of God's people. Paul instead has the order: (1) full number of Gentiles are saved; (2) then all Israel will be saved.

The emphasis in the term *pleroma*, which can simply be translated "fullness," is probably not on a set number of the elect, but rather on a full or large number, a great multitude. Paul's vision of salvation is grand. He does not believe only a tiny remnant of Jews and Gentiles will be saved. Käsemann suggests that what is in view is the filling up of remnant, so that eventually "all Israel" is saved.[60] It is true that some have interpreted *pleroma* to mean something like the full restoration or conversion, but this is unlikely. Here Paul is making a quantitative comparison between a small remnant and a fullness of the saved. The only question is whether Paul sees this as the adding of the unbelieving majority to the believing minority of Jews, which then amounts to "all Israel." Or is he talking about adding the unbelieving majority of Jews to the whole people of God, and so the whole people are brought up to "fullness," both Jew and Gentile united in Christ? But if in v. 26 Paul means by *pleroma* those Gentiles now converted plus those yet to be converted, the parallel would then suggest that the "fullness" in mind here and by the phrase *all Israel* in v. 26 is the adding of the now-unbelieving Jews to the believing ones to make a full complement.

In v. 13 Paul emphatically and directly addresses the Gentile majority of his audience. He has a right to single them out and address them, not least because he is the apostle to the Gentiles (*ephoson* means "in so far as"). Paul says he honors his ministry. *Diakonian* has the more specific sense of ministry, not just any service in general here. Paul honors and glories in this ministry because it is an honor to lead people to Christ, and Paul hopes it will even have some good effect on his Jewish kin. Paul sees his mission to Gentiles as indirectly a mission to Jews as well. To judge from a reference like 2 Corinthians 12:24–25, Paul did indeed evangelize in synagogues, as Acts confirms, and he paid a price for it. It appears that even the apostle to the Gentiles took seriously the gospel priority of "for the Jew first, and also for the Gentiles," though his focus was on Gentiles.

Verse 14 brings a note of realism. Paul hopes to make his fellow Jews jealous and so save some from among them (tinas ek auton). Paul does not expect by himself to bring the fullness of Israel into the Christian faith. Käsemann is surely wrong that Paul thought his own mission would result in "all Israel being saved."[61] 1 Corinthians 9:22 illuminates what Paul is talking about here, which is that there will be an eschatological miracle at the return of Christ.[62] "Evidently, though Paul can hope for the final salvation of all Israel (v. 26), he does not hope for it in terms of the actual conversion of all individual Israelites; salvation of them all is a mysterious eschatological event, which is only prefigured in occasional personal conversions."[63] It is the latter Paul refers to when he says "some" here.

Romans 11:15 makes clear that Paul sees these unbelieving Jews as temporarily rejected or pushed away (apobole), which comports with his later metaphor that they have been broken off from the tree of God's people, by God temporarily. This verse provides yet another from the lesser-to-greater kind of argument. The rejection of the Jews could refer to either their rejection of Jesus or God's rejection of them, or the latter based on the former, and so both. Since the focus here seems to be on God's role, the stress would seem to be on the latter. On the word katallage we should compare Romans 5:10–11. Cranfield urges that the word "reconciliation" here refers specifically to Christ's death.[64] If so, then what might be in view here is that the rejection of Jesus that led to his death and the world's reconciliation was at the same time God's rejection of such Jews. Verse 15b must be taken seriously and probably literally. The acceptance by these Jews of Christ, or their reacceptance by God, will mean resurrection of the dead. If, as I think, we should take this as a literal reference to the resurrection at the end of human history, then Paul is admitting that he does not envision a gradual progressive conversion of the Jews, but a large or mass change at the end of history which will usher in the resurrection of the dead and the messianic or millennial age.[65]

In short, Paul has no delusions that he will participate in "the end" during his lifetime. Ei me in 15b must mean "except," though the literal rendering would be "if not." The phrase life from the dead is similar to John 5:24 and indicates that Paul sees the conversion of the Jews in an eschatological light. On the one hand, it will not transpire until God's timing for it (i.e., until the full number of Gentiles come in). On the other hand, God, not Paul, will bring about this result at the end of things. What Paul envisions is the unifying of the people of God, Jew and Gentile in Christ at the end of things.

Verses 16–17 begin to illustrate by metaphor some of what Paul has in mind. I take the reference to "firstfruits" here to mean the first fruits of conversion to Christ among Jews. Paul's point, contrary to what Cranfield suggests,[66] is not that a few Jewish Christians sanctify the mass of non-Christian Jews. Paul is not using the holiness language here in that way. His argument is rather that if the first few Jewish converts are set apart to God, and are in truth a sort of first fruits and so a harbinger of things to come, then the mass of Jews is still ultimately "set apart" or "holy" unto God, and set apart for salvation. God has not finally rejected them.

Many have been misled by dwelling too much on Paul's use of Numbers 15:20–21, but I think Paul is simply drawing on OT language and ideas here to make his point. Cranfield rightly notes that though early Jewish teachers did talk about the firstfruits sanctifying the rest, neither Paul nor the OT says anything to this effect elsewhere.[67] A closer parallel than the later Jewish discussion would be 1 Corinthians 15, where Christ is called "firstfruits from the dead," which implies more will be coming in similar fashion and condition. That is also the point here.

There has also been endless debate about what the word "root" refers to here. Notice that this second analogy is not about root and tree, but about root and branches, probably because it allows Paul to go on and talk about branches broken off. The root, of course, gives nourishment to the tree and so to the branches. In view of v. 28, what root likely means here is the patriarchs, though it could be a reference to Jewish Christians. The point then would be, if it refers to the patriarchs, that the mass of Israel, even unbelieving branches, have a special place in God's plan as a result of the faith of the patriarchs, or better said, as a result of the promises made to them. I agree with Cranfield that root and firstfruits need not refer to the same thing in this discussion.[68] Rather we have two different illustrations of the same point that Paul wants to make.

At v. 17 Paul takes up another metaphor, that of the olive tree, which is of course a symbol for the people of God (cf. Jer 11:16; Hos 14:6).[69] Why has Paul chosen this metaphor rather than the more normal vine metaphor for the people of God? If one looks at the context of Jeremiah 11:16 and Hosea 14:6 in both texts, the discussion is about God's judgment, about broken branches, and in Hosea about restoration to a beautiful condition beyond judgment. It is the broken condition of Israel that has led to the use of the metaphor of the olive tree. Some have faulted Paul for being horticulturally challenged in what he says here, and others have defended him, saying that the grafting of a wild olive branch into a domesticated olive tree was not unknown in antiquity. But clearly, Paul is not trying to give a lesson in horticulture here, as is made perfectly clear by the fact that Paul will go on to speak of the regrafting in of natural branches, which was never practiced in antiquity. Strict verisimilitude should not be expected.[70]

A figure of thought is being used to talk about the relationship of Jews and Gentiles in the people of God. While we do not have a full-blown allegory here as in Galatians 4, nonetheless the discussion about root and branches and about pruning, grafting, and regrafting falls under the heading of such a figure of thought. Paul begins with the assertion that some of the branches were broken off (the passive suggests this was done by God). Notice that he says *some*.

Had God totally rejected his people once and for all, we would have expected Paul to say "all," and we would have expected there to be no Jewish Christians like Paul. But this was certainly not God's plan. Paul addresses the Gentiles in his audience directly, using *su*, which suggests he has individual Gentiles in mind. They are all called wild olive branches which have been grafted "into them." This phrase *en autois* must mean "in among them," not "in place of them." This strongly suggests that for Paul the continuity with the OT people of God is in Jewish Christians, and before them, in Christ, and before him, in the patriarchs. His view that the gospel has gone out into the Diaspora also supports the conclusion that the "remnant" in his day is viewed as Jewish Christians, rather than just any pious Jews.[71] He is also not suggesting that mysteriously these Christian Gentiles had secretly been grafted into non-Christian Israel of his own day. The remnant for Paul is not pious Jews in general, but rather Jewish Christians like Paul himself, who have the job of mediating the Jewish heritage to Gentiles.[72]

Thus, Paul reminds the Gentiles: you were grafted into them, and became fellow sharers in the fatness (i.e., sap) of the root of the olive tree. This is presumably a symbol of the blessings of that religious heritage, and the promises that go with it. How this works is made abundantly clear in Galatians 3–4. It is interesting that wild olive trees never produced useful oil. Since Paul clearly identifies the Gentiles with wild olive branches that have been grafted in, he is seeking to put overweening Gentile Christians in their place in two ways. He makes it clear that Jewish Christians, and before them the patriarchs, are the natural part of the tree, thus giving Jews precedence in the people of God, and that as wild olive branches they bring nothing into the union. God simply grafts them in by pure grace.[73] Paul counters the problem of Gentiles in Rome disparaging or even writing off Jews and perhaps even Jewish Christians.

Thus Gentiles should not exult over the broken-off branches or even over the Jewish Christians, for the Gentiles do not carry the Jewish heritage, rather "the root carries you." On the basis of *1 Enoch* 93:5, 8; Philo, *Who is the Heir* 279; and *Jubilees* 21:24, probably "root" refers to the patriarchs, perhaps in particular to Abraham. This conclusion may be supported by Romans 4:1–2, where Abraham is called "our" Father according to the flesh. Paul's observation as to why what has happened has transpired begins to become apparent in Romans 11:19. Here we have the diatribe and the interlocutor is a Gentile advocate of a different theology who says, "the branches have been broken off so I myself may be grafted in." The *hina* clause here surely indicates purpose. Paul actually agrees with this argument so far as it goes, but the problem is it does not go far enough.

At v. 20 we find that Paul agrees. He says "good" or "very well." Here Paul makes clear that this breaking off and grafting in is not some arbitrary process. Those whom God broke off were unbelieving, and those he grafted in, he grafted in by faith, and they only stand by faith. The dative with *pistis* and *apistis* here is causal in both cases. The breaking off was because of unfaith (it was not arbitrarily decided and done by God), and the standing was because of faith. The corollary of this should be clear: if the Gentiles also manifest unfaith, they too may be broken off. They no more have an arbitrary or irrevocable privileged status than unfaithful Jewish individuals. This being the case, Gentiles should not get high-minded; rather they should fear God, and realize that they are not beyond apostasy and unfaith and therefore not immune to the wrath of God should they behave in such fashion.

The logic of v. 21 should be clear. If God did not spare the natural branches from such a breaking off, from such a judgment (which nonetheless was not final), why should he spare the Gentiles from it? Thus there is absolutely no basis for Gentile boasting. Verse 22 points out that God has more than one attribute; kindness and severity are mentioned. Thus God must not only be loved, but honored and obeyed. The Jews who fell away received severity, but the Gentiles kindness. It is necessary to persevere in that kindness; otherwise even Gentiles may be cut off. But if anyone does not remain or persevere in their unbelief, God has the power to graft them (i.e., unbelieving Jews) in again. Verse 24 brings the analogy to a close. If a wild olive branch received mercy and was grafted into the natural olive tree, how much more should God have mercy on the natural branches temporarily broken off.

Paul makes a new beginning at v. 25, and he explains he does not want the Gentiles in the audience to be ignorant of the "mystery" of God's future plan of salvation for both Gentile and Jew, and how it will work. Kasemann thinks that the mystery is the future salvation event itself for the Jews.[74] Some have suggested that Mark 13:10 might stand in the background here, and this is possible. The fact that Paul reveals this mystery as something new may well suggest it was a special revelation Paul himself received, and like a prophet or seer he is here proclaiming it. Notice how at 1 Corinthians 13:2 mysteries are closely grouped with prophecies. Paul is talking about insight into the eschatological reality God will bring about. Paul seems to see salvation happening in three stages: (1) the rejection by the Jews; (2) acceptance by the full number of the Gentiles; (3) then all Israel will be saved. This is certainly different from the notion found in numerous OT and Jewish texts (Ps 22:27; Isa 2:2–3; 56:6–8; Mic 4:2; Zech 2:11; 14:16; Tob 13:11; 14:6–7; *Pss. Sol.* 17:34; *T. Zeb.* 9:8; *T. Benj.* 9:2) where the Gentiles will flow into Zion after Israel has first been restored to its intended glory.

Paul's use of the language of hardening is interesting. In Romans 9:16–18 Paul uses the verb *skleryno*, which normally has the sense of "harden" or "stiffen." The verb we find in 11:25 however is *poroo* which has the basic sense of petrify, and in the passive it has the metaphorical sense of deadened or insensible (cf. Mark 6:52; 8:17; John 12:40; 2 Cor 3:14). The OT sources of such an idea include Deuteronomy 29:4 and Isaiah 29:10, which are indeed cited at 11:8. For Paul, when such a judgment falls on Israel it is temporal and not final judgment, as becomes clear in 11:25. This hardening happens "until" (*achris*) a particular point in time.

Romans 11:25 says explicitly that the hardening came *apo merous* of Israel. Should this phrase be taken as adjectival or adverbial? In view of vv. 5, 7, and 17, Paul could not affirm that hardening had come upon all of Israel. Käsemann rightly points to the contrast with the *pleroma*, which is mentioned just afterwards.[75] Thus I must disagree with Käsemann's conclusion that what is meant is that all Israel experienced a partial hardening. This is not true of Paul and other Jewish Christians. Rather what must be meant is that a part of Israel, a large part, was hardened, but this condition was of a limited duration. *Achris* here must mean "until"—until the full number of the Gentiles enter into the kingdom. *Pleroma* must mean here what it meant earlier in this argument. It thus refers either to all the Gentiles who will be saved, or all the additional number of Gentiles yet to be saved after the time Paul was speaking. It does not mean the Gentile world as a whole. The implications of this verse must be allowed to have their full force—temporarily some Jews, but not all, are not part of the people of God because they have rejected Jesus' messiahship. Paul nowhere in Romans 9–11 suggests there are two peoples of God.

Verse 26 is one of the most controversial verses in all of Romans 9–11.[76] The quandary is over who "all Israel" refers to. Is it: (1) Jews and Gentiles who are in Christ? (2) All the elect of Israel? (3) The whole nation of Israel including every individual? (4) The nation of Israel with certain exceptions?[77] It is extremely problematic to try and understand Israel in v. 26 to mean something different than it means in v. 25, where it surely does not refer to any Gentiles, especially when v. 26 is linked to v. 25 by *kai houtos*. Paul gives no hints or qualifiers to lead the listener to think that Israel means something different here in v. 26 than it meant in v. 25.

Since Jews and Gentiles are contrasted throughout vv. 11–32, one would expect that to be true in v. 26 as well. *Houtos* in itself normally has the meaning "so" or "in this manner," but when combined with *kai* it could refer to a temporal rather than just a logical sequence, with the sense "and then," or "and thus." The discussion of P. W. van der Horst needs to be fully considered at this juncture.[78] Van der Horst is able to produce various examples where *kai houtos* has the temporal sense of "thereafter," or "and then." For example, in Theophrastus's *Characters* 18, where after checking to make sure all of the house is locked up, "only then" (*kai houtos*) is the owner able to go to sleep. Or again in Plato, *Protagoras* 314c we have a clear instance where Socrates and Hippocrates are said to first finish their discussion, and "thereafter" or "only then" (*houtos*) go into the house. Various other clear examples are produced (Plato, *Gorg.* 457d; Xenophon, *Anab.* 7.1.4; *Cyr.* 2.1.1; Aristotle, *Poet.* 1455b1). Especially clear is Epictetus, *Diatr.* 2.15.8, where we have *kai houtos* with the temporal sense. There are also examples from Jewish literature of the period as well (cf., e.g., *T. Ab.* 7:11). Van der Horst can also produce some very likely examples within the NT, for example, Acts 7:8, where the sense is surely that "God gave Abraham the covenant of circumcision and thereafter (*kai houtos*) Abraham begot Isaac." "Luke does not want to inform his readers about the physical condition in which Abraham begot the son that would be the heir of the covenant, but about the fact that this happened only after he had received the sign of this covenant!"[79]

Acts 20:11 seems an even clearer text where the temporal sense must be present. If we wish to see an example from Paul, we may turn to 1 Thessalonians 4:16–17 where a temporal sequence is clearly in view, as is made evident by the use of the term *epeita* in v. 16. In this sequence where *kai houtos* follows *epeita* it is surely most natural to take it to mean "and thereafter" or "and then"—so we translate "the dead in Christ will rise first; *thereafter* we who are alive, who are left, will be caught up in the clouds together with them to meet the Lord in the air, and then we will be with the Lord forever."[80] One may also compare 1 Corinthians 14:25: "the secrets of his heart become evident *and then* (*kai houtos*) falling on his knees he worships God." "Quite apart from the grammatical and lexical possibilities that the word *houtos* had, it is also the context of Romans 11 that makes it very probable that it was the temporal meaning of *houtos* that the author had in mind here."[81]

Even if, less probably, *houtos* does mean "in this manner,"[82] then the combination of vv. 25–26 should probably be read to mean: "some

Jews have been hardened until the full number of Gentiles are brought in (by grace through faith), and in the same manner all Israel will be saved." The discussion then of this verse should also not be isolated from what Paul has already said in 11:15: first the reconciliation of the Gentile world while Jews are temporarily rejected, then these Jews will be accepted, which will be the signal for the resurrection. Dunn in his treatment of the verse, while recognizing a reference to the parousia in the Scripture quote which follows, seems to think that in this verse Paul is talking about the effect of the full number of Gentiles coming in, provoking Israel to jealousy and so to conversion.[83] But Paul could just as well be paralleling the way Israel will finally be brought back in to the way Gentiles were brought in by mercy and grace and faith, without linking the two events. The grammatical and lexical evidence produced above in any case favors the temporal sense of *kai houtos* here, as does the context of Paul's discussion.[84]

Against view (3) above, elsewhere in this chapter Paul has made very clear that he believes apostasy happens. Persons do not remain saved unless they remain or stand in and on their faith. We cannot assume that Paul would say anything here in v. 26 to vitiate his previous argument about salvation being by grace and through faith. Thus, it would appear that either (2) or (4) above are the only really viable views.

The problem with arguing that all the elect from Israel are meant is that such a view would be self-evident, even absurdly so in light of what he has previously said. More importantly, Paul is speaking about something that transpires at the eschaton. Furthermore, if we look at passages like 1 Samuel 7:5, 25; 1 Kings 12:1; 2 Chronicles 12:1; Daniel 9:11; *Jubilees* 50:9; *Testament of Levi* 17:5; and *M. Sanhedrin* 10:1, in all these cases the phrase "all Israel" does not mean literally every single Israelite (cf. also 1 Sam 18:16; 2 Sam 2:9; 3:21; Deut 31:11; Judg 8:27). There are some exceptions. *M. Sanhedrin* 10:1 deserves to be quoted: "All Israel have a share in the world to come . . . except he that says that the Law is not from heaven . . . and he that reads heretical books, or that utters charms over a wound. . . . Also he that pronounces the Name with its proper letters." The idea then is that the great mass of them, or a very large number, are saved.[85]

We must remember that Paul has been discussing non-Christian Jews. Paul already knew of many saved Jewish Christians, and it is hardly likely he has them in view here. Rather, he says this "all Israel" group will be saved after the full numbers of Gentiles have come in. Thus, I conclude he is talking about a mass conversion of non-Christian Jews at the end of salvation history. The word *houtos* which introduces the key clause is emphatic. It could mean "thus" or "in this way" or "in this (same) manner," but most likely it means "and then." Sometimes some commentators have made the mistake, on the basis of this word alone, that what Paul had just said was the end of the process—namely when the fullness of the Gentiles comes in, this constitutes all Israel being saved. However, v. 15 is definitely against such a view.[86] And it was Israel which was hardened in v. 25, unlike the Gentiles, and in v. 26 it is this same Israel that is then said to be saved.

It is interesting that in texts like *Testament of Daniel* 6:4; *Testament of Judah* 23:5; *4 Ezra* 4:38–43, there is a pattern which indicates that Israel has missed the mark and needs to repent, and that before the end she will do so, and when she does so the end will come, and then salvation will come to the Gentiles. Paul has just inverted the order of this sequence. This is followed by a quote from Isaiah 59:20–21a as a sort of proof text. Paul means to show that this truth he is conveying about Israel was already mentioned in the OT, where it says: "The Deliverer will come from Zion, he will turn away ungodliness from Jacob, and this is the covenant I will make with them, and I will take away (or forgive) their sins." Paul has altered the quote which speaks of a deliverer coming "to" Zion (MT), or "on behalf of" Zion (LXX), to "from" Zion. In this case the new Jerusalem is in view (see Gal 4:26). This quote must surely be taken to refer to what will happen to non-Christian Jews when the Deliverer comes, namely at the parousia.[87] There is some evidence from later Jewish discussions that this verse was referred to Messiah rather than God, and Paul may be following a tradition of that sort of exegesis of this text. Cranfield suggests that we compare 1 Thessalonians 1:10 at this juncture.[88] Thus, when Christ comes again he will turn back unbelief amongst his Jewish kin. Then indeed he will come for the lost sheep of Israel, and they will finally hear. But this quote also clearly implies that only the Deliverer will accomplish this, not some present plan to evangelize Jews.

Thus, Romans 11:28 contrasts the present status of Jews in two different ways. According to the gospel they are enemies (or one might translate this "hated"), for the Gentile's sake. But according to the election they are beloved, for the sake of the fathers. The free gift and call to Israel is irrevocable, even if individual Jews choose to opt out of God's salvation plan for them. For in the same way that Gentiles were once disobedient to God, but now in the eschatological age have been ushered in and have found mercy through Christ and through the Jews' disobedience, so also the Jews have been disobedient, so they too may find mercy.

Verse 32 sums this all up nicely—for God shut up all to disobedience in order that he might have mercy on all. This means quite clearly that: (1) all Paul had previously said about hardening and Israel being vessels of wrath was a *temporary* condition, and its ultimate purpose anyway was so God could have mercy on all;[89] or (2) to put it another way, God did this so all would have to relate to him on the basis of grace and faith, so none would think they had God in their debt, or that he owed them something; and (3) God did it this way so all would recognize that God only sets right sinners, the ungodly, and that includes all the human race, even pious humans of all sorts.[90]

This was a very scandalous and unconventional gospel that Paul preached, and it is clear that Paul sees all things in light of his understanding of God's righteousness, which involves both wrath and salvation. Käsemann says: "The whole epistle stands under the sign that no person [not even a Jew] is justified by works and that even the pious do not enter the kingdom of God on the basis of their piety. . . . Paul is bold enough to view both each individual and world history from the standpoint of the doctrine of justification. The end of the old world and the beginning of the new world can be thought of only as justification of the ungodly. Logically then the problem of Israel can only be solved under the same theme."[91] While the use of the forensic way of putting this does not capture the scope of what Paul means by *diakaiosune*, Käsemann is basically correct, and as the doxology which follows will show, all humans are indebted to the riches of God's mercy.

And it is precisely the contemplation of the mercy of God that leads Paul into an outburst of doxological praise in vv. 33–36, which concludes this magisterial argument. Paul first extols the infinite resources of God. The juxtaposition of depths and riches suggests a bottomless treasury of mercy.[92] God understands all, and wishes to have mercy on all, and God has the wisdom to work out a plan where even those temporarily left out can be grafted back in, for God is a God of second chances and forgiveness. The means God devised to have mercy on all was not something one could figure out, even from close study of the OT. This doxology, like a good deal of the discussion in Romans 1–11 is rooted in the Jewish Wisdom tradition (cf. *2 Bar.* 14:8, 9; 20:4; 1QH 7:26–33; 10:3–7). It is the longest of all of Paul's doxologies. God's judgments, and his decisions about the world and about human matters cannot be figured out by human beings.

At v. 34 Paul quotes Isaiah 40:13 (LXX). A full 40 percent of Paul's OT quotations in this section, and for that matter in Romans, are from Isaiah. God's mind is unknowable unless he reveals it, hence the need for the revelation of his apocalyptic secret of a salvation plan. Furthermore, God is in no one's debt. Paul in v. 35 quotes Job 41:11 from some source other than the Septuagint. "With God, man never earns a recompense; he can only be loved and treated with mercy."[93] It is striking that in his concluding words of this last of the theological arguments, Paul speaks of God in what seem to be Stoic, but also biblical terms. M. Aurelius, *Meditation* 4.23 says: "From thee are all things, in thee are all things, unto thee are all things" (cf. Seneca, *Ep.* 65.8). God is the source, the means, and the goal of all things, all historical purposes, all salvific events. Paul's largely Gentile audience may well have known this familiar saying, and Paul may have used it here precisely because, rhetorically speaking, it would help him to win over his audience to his remarkable view of Jews and Gentiles in God's plan of salvation.

The God Gentiles had known only vaguely, and through sources like nature (Rom 1) and Stoic thought, Paul is now glorifying because he is the God of all peoples in all ages, and God's plan is for Jews and Gentiles to be saved in and by Jesus Christ, and to be united in him. It may be that this doxology is theologically rather than christologically focused precisely because Paul is speaking for the Jews he has just said are yet to be saved, the "all Israel" who could speak this doxology but not one focused on Jesus. The God of the Bible then, as described in this climactic argument, is the God to whom all praise and glory should be given forever, for this God alone is the one who could judge all, and still extend mercy to all. When Paul turns to the parenesis in Romans 12, it will be building precisely on the lessons learned in Romans 9–11 about the saving mercy and great righteousness of God which believers appropriate the benefits of, and try to live on the basis of, through faith in Jesus Christ.

CONCLUSIONS

What may we learn from this lengthy discussion of Romans 9–11? First, election does not work as Calvin thought it did. Second, Paul consistently affirms that there is only one people of God at any one juncture in human history. It would be a very odd thing to argue that God was busily fulfilling promises and prophecies to non-Christian Israel in the present when he had in fact broken them off from the people of God temporarily during this same period of time! The fulfilling of promises to Israel in this text is said to happen when Christ comes back, and Israel is grafted back into the people of God. The two-track system of Dispensationalism, with some promises being fulfilled in Israel and some in the church, simply will not work in the Pauline scheme of things, when one examines the details of Romans 9–11. Paul also in this section of Romans stresses that in the end all are saved on the same basis, by the grace and mercy of God, and through faith, not by some predetermination from before the beginning of time. Paul's conception of the people of God is Jew and Gentile united in Christ as Galatians 3:28 says, and the old categories no longer count in the body of Christ.

We have learned something else in this chapter as well: Paul was not an early example of a Dispensationalist in the mold of Darby or Scofield. He believed, for example, that the teaching Jesus gave to his original disciples was applicable to his own converts. Thus he draws not only on Matthew 24 but also the Sermon on the Mount at various points to teach his converts how to live the Christian life. He also believed any number of OT prophecies had already come to pass in Christ, were coming to pass in the body of Christ, and would continue to come to pass precisely in that context.

There is in addition a hermeneutical issue that needs to be stressed. As we saw in our discussion of prophecy, including apocalyptic prophecy, this was not material meant only for late western Christians. It was intended to be revelation for the first-century Christians, and every generation thereafter. It had meaning for those first Christians, and both John of Patmos and Paul would be very surprised to hear many of the correlations that are being made today by Dispensationalists with what they said, not least because they were not making specific comments about figures in American history, or in twenty-first-century struggles.

John and Paul were talking about their own era leading up to the destruction of the temple in A.D. 70 and its aftermath, and they were talking in general terms about the consummation of human history which would indeed be brought about not by the plans and schemes of humans but by the one and only visible return of Christ who would judge the nations and silence the armies of the world with fire coming down from heaven (see Rev 20:8–9). There will be no final battle, only a conflagration. The armies are assembled only to be dismissed when they are "fired" from above.

But there is more. According to the book of Revelation only God is the proper executor of justice and final judgment on the world, not human beings. Revelation is about the most antimilitaristic book in the Bible as it never once encourages any humans, never mind Christians, to take up arms. Rather it encourages them to pray and be spiritually prepared to suffer for their faith. A theology of suffering and becoming victors through martyrdom, not through killing, is enunciated in this work. The author would find shameful the way this book has been used in the *Left Behind* series and by many of the televangelists.

And there is yet more. Both Paul and John in the book of Revelation call believers to live their lives and make their major decisions on the basis of faith, not fear. The called-for response to persecutors and tormentors is not to respond in kind at all, but rather to be examples of suffering love just as Jesus was when he died on the cross. It calls for trust that history is in Jesus' hands, and vengeance or, better said, justice is his, not ours. Paul's and John's words were meant as words of comfort for a persecuted minority, which was even enduring martyrdom in some cases, not words encouraging triumphalism by those with nuclear weapons.

As C. Hill stresses in his critique of Dispensationalism and especially the theology of the rapture:

> Ideas have consequences. . . . At worst, such a belief is a form of escapism. The hope of impending departure can lead believers to abandon interest in the world and its problems. The expectation of deteriorating conditions prior to the soon-approaching rapture is morally corrosive, encouraging pessimism, fatalism, and the forsaking of political responsibility. Disengagement from the problems of the world is ethically indefensible, but it is all too common among today's prophecy elite. Their books tell us that nuclear war is inevitable, that the pursuit of peace is pointless, that the planet's environmental woes are unstoppable, and so on.[94]

In fact we even have Dispensationalists opposing the Middle East peace efforts and the like because it impedes the progress of the prophecy timetables, and the desire is for an acceleration of ruin so that the rapture will hurry up and arrive. There is nothing in this outlook compatible with Jesus' blessing of peacemakers! But alas, this characteristic pessimism and fatalism and escapism is an endemic part of the Dispensational system, and has been since day one. It was Darby himself who wrote, "I believe from Scripture that ruin is without remedy," and he goes on to stress that Christians should all expect nothing but "a progress of evil."[95] How very odd it is to read these words in the twenty-first century after so much remarkable progress in various positive ways in the world of medicine, technology, education, and other fields since 1750. Darby obviously was not only a prophet of doom; he was also a false prophet in various respects.

As we conclude this section of our discussion of the problems with Evangelical theology, one thing has come to light that we have not properly stressed thus far and wish to highlight now. It would appear that it is precisely in the ways that Dispensational and Calvinist interpretations deviate from various forms of early Christian interpretations of the NT (by early, I mean pre-Augustinian) that these systems go wrong. Put another way, it is in the distinctives of these systems that they deviate from the scriptural teaching on a variety of subjects.

For example, Dispensationalists are right that Revelation 20 talks about a millennial reign of Christ on the earth. This is very much how Christian interpreters understood that text before the time of Augustine. Where they go wrong is in adding their distinctive and unbiblical idea about the rapture as a prelude to that reign.

Similarly, it is not in their high Christology, or their Trinitarian emphasis, or in their belief in the atoning death of Jesus or in the fact that God is omnipotent that Calvinists go wrong. It is rather in the distinctive way the T.U.L.I.P. theological system (Total depravity,

Unconditional Elect, Limited atonement, Irresistible grace, Perseverance of the saints) causes them to interpret the death of Jesus or the sovereignty of God that causes divergences both from the historic way the relevant NT texts were understood by exegetes ranging from Ignatius of Antioch to Chrysostom, and from the most probable reading of a whole host of NT texts, especially Pauline and Johannine ones.

The antidote to such misreadings is: (1) a better and more open-minded reading of these texts without imposing later theological systems on the text, and (2) a reading with an open exploration as to what could have been meant by authors of a Jewish background, such as all NT writers were (with the possible exception of Luke), who brought Jewish ideas of election and apostasy and the coming of the Messiah into their Christian ways of thinking. Notice the discussion above about early Jewish ideas about apostasy and election.[96] There is much more to be said along these lines, but now we must turn to yet another popular Evangelical school of thought that has its own distinctive way of looking at the NT in light of concepts of prevenient grace, perfection or entire sanctification, and even eradication of the sin nature. I am referring to Arminianism, more commonly called Wesleyanism, to which we now devote our attention.

PART THREE

MR. WESLEY HEADING WEST

CHAPTER 8

Jesus, Paul, and John:
Keeping Company in the Kingdom

I was always taught that it is not polite to sass your mother. Well, I am a cradle Methodist. Rumor has it that my first two words were "John Wesley." It is always awkward and difficult to criticize one's own theological parent when one loves him so much. I have, however, spent too much time exegeting the NT as a whole not to realize that there are exegetical weaknesses in the Wesleyan way of reading the NT. These weaknesses are the focus of this section of the book. They simply prove that when it comes to Evangelical theology, there are better and there are worse theological systems, but none are perfect, all having exegetical weaknesses, particularly when they veer off into distinctive territory. I have to say, however, that there appear to me to be fewer weaknesses in the Arminian approach to biblical texts than in various other systems of approach.

The problem is, Evangelical Wesleyans tend to be even less biblically grounded or knowledgeable about their own tradition and more experiential in their orientation than other Evangelicals, and in an affective, experientially oriented culture, that can cause serious difficulties. When James once said "it seemed good to us and the Holy Spirit" (Acts 15) he was not suggesting that experience trumped the Scriptures—indeed he had just based his whole argument about the inclusion of the Gentiles on the exegesis of OT texts. Not even the book of Acts suggests that experience should be the final litmus test of truth or norm for Christian living. We must bear these things in mind as we work through the materials in this chapter.

ARMED BY ARMINIUS, BUT DRINKING AMERICAN WATER

As has long been noted, Jacob Arminius, from whom the word "Arminian" comes, started out as a Calvinist and then had increasing problems swallowing the whole Augustinian/Calvinistic pill. His revisions were done with one eye on the Calvinistic system. This conversation between orthodox Protestants continued in the eighteenth-century revival in England, and can be seen in living color in the various salvos between John Wesley and his fellow Methodist George Whitefield (who was indebted to the greatest of American theologians, Jonathan Edwards), among other sparring partners, such as the composer of "Rock of Ages," one A. Toplady. It is important to say from the outset, then, that Wesley's approach to the Bible, profoundly indebted as it was to the Puritans and to various Anglican forebears, was rather different from various modern Arminian or Wesleyan ways of dealing with theology and the Bible. One can also note that Wesley was far more indebted to the church fathers who preceded Augustine than were Luther or Calvin, and like many early Catholic theologians got much of his ethics from the Gospels, especially from Matthew's Sermon on the Mount. It has even been said that he wed a Protestant theology of justification with a Catholic theology of sanctification and ethics. There is some truth in this claim.

As for how Wesley would have reacted to modern Arminianism in America, he would have been equally appalled by modern American voluntarism (i.e., the "free will" assumption) and by modern advocacy of open theism. Wesley did not doubt that original sin was real, and that Paul was correct in saying that all have sinned and fallen short of God's glory. Nor would he have agreed with the notion that there are things that God either does not know or learns as time goes by. The critique I am about to offer has more to do with modern Arminianism than with John Wesley's own theology.

A second point that needs to be stressed at this juncture, since it is sometimes questioned, is that John Wesley certainly was a scholar of the same caliber as John Calvin, and an equally keen exegete. He taught at Oxford University. The problem has not been primarily with Wesley, or his immediate theological successor in the early nineteenth century, Richard Watson. The problem has been with their successors, very few of whom were experts in the Bible and many of whom cut their theological teeth on non-Wesleyan teething rings, for example, on German idealism (which led to the school of Boston personalism). As was carefully chronicled long ago by R. E. Chiles, there was also a transition in American Methodist theological thinking in the nineteenth century, such that an optimism about what God's grace could accomplish with human nature was exchanged for a truly Pelagian optimism about human nature.[1] Methodism more reflects the character of American democratic, libertarian-inspired culture than Calvinism, except perhaps the culture that grew in and out of New England, spawning

Harvard, Yale, and then Princeton (of which Jonathan Edwards was once president), not to mention Red Sox fatalism (until 2004!).

Partly because the Methodist movement in America was led by circuit riders, and certainly not by scholars, Methodist theology absorbed various populist notions from the culture, and then when it finally got around to theological training of its scholars, it sent them to Germany and other places that left them with a non-Wesleyan theology in the main. Even today, some Wesleyan scholars and exegetes owe more to Karl Barth than to Wesley, and some of our leading ethicists owe far more to Anabaptist ways of thinking (i.e., cf. Stanley Hauerwas, John Howard Yoder) than to Puritanism or Anglicanism.

In truth, it has only been since the pioneering work of Frank Baker and Albert Outler and their successors in the last thirty years that we have begun to have a critical edition of Wesley's works that is comparable to the critical editions of Calvin's or Luther's works, and these volumes are still in the process of emerging. What I am telling you is that we are only now beginning to be able to fully assess the powerful theological legacy of Wesley. Calvinism has had a huge head start, and Calvinists may be forgiven for thinking Wesley was no theologian when Methodists themselves did not care enough until recently to keep his works in print in a good critical edition.

This section of our study is not going to focus at all on the varieties of things said by modern Methodist theologians, but seeks to deal with Arminianism in its neoclassical Wesleyan form, which is the form embraced by Evangelicals of an Arminian bent. What we will discover is that, as with the case of Calvinism and Dispensationalism, the real exegetical weaknesses in the system come in its attempt at distinctives—the distinctive theology of prevenient grace, and the theology of perfection.

Wesley was in many ways an interesting and synthetic thinker, combining insights from deep study of the church fathers with indebtedness to Luther and other Protestants. His favorite texts to preach on were from John's gospel and from Paul. There was not much difference between what Wesley said about justification by grace through faith, and what Luther said in these matters. Where they disagreed was in regard to the more Augustinian portions of Luther's theology. Or again, there does not seem to be much difference between what Wesley says on progressive sanctification by means of the Holy Spirit and what Calvin says on this subject. Calvin's *Institutes* reflect a far more robust theology of the Spirit and the Spirit's effects on believers than Luther's works do.[2]

My concern here, however, is not with these similarities but with the Wesleyan distinctives, and perhaps the best way to deal with this is to consider certain texts once more. Unlike in the previous sections, I am going to take the time to actually cite and interact with the critical editions of Wesley's works and with various of his favorite texts because they are not widely known even in Evangelical circles (and shamefully even in some Methodist ones). We begin with the topic of the kingdom of God, which provides us with a difference especially from Dispensational Evangelical theology.

Jesus, Paul, and the Dominion of God

Perhaps the first thing to be said about the dominion of God is that the phrase *basileia tou theou* is not best rendered "kingdom of God," for the very good reason that the phrase often does not refer to a place, but rather to an event or the result of an event, or to a state of being. It is true enough that both Jesus and Paul do sometimes refer to the dominion as something that exists in the future and can be inherited, entered, or obtained, but just as often they refer to the dominion already existing in some sense in the present. There is then an already and not-yet quality to the dominion of God in both the teaching of Jesus and Paul. This must be kept steadily in mind as we consider this topic.[3]

I have chosen the phrase "dominion of God" to translate the underlying Greek concept, for the very good reason that it can convey both a verbal and a noun sense. One can have dominion over something or someone, but a dominion can also be a place one enters. The phrase has different nuances in different contexts in the teaching of Jesus and of Paul, sometimes referring to God's present saving activity breaking into human history, sometimes referring to a future realm that one may enter or inherit. While it is true that in some early Jewish literature the phrase "dominion of God" could refer to God's ongoing sovereign rule of all things or his rule in heaven (consider the phrase "thy kingdom come, . . . on earth as in heaven"), by and large it does not have that sense in the NT. One could certainly point to an exceptional text like Luke 23:42, where the request by the thief to be remembered when Jesus comes into his dominion is answered by the response that they are both about to enter Paradise. On this showing, the dominion of God is the dominion of heaven, a common enough concept in early Judaism. But far more often in the teaching of Jesus it refers to something in the present and on earth, for the phrase has a dynamic sense referring to God's divine saving activity. Presumably, Jesus did not think that God needed to exercise his salvific efforts in heaven.

Let us consider two key texts where Jesus indicates that the dominion of God is breaking into history in his own time and through his own ministry. The first of these is the saying found in Luke 11:20/Matthew 12:28. Here Jesus interprets his exorcisms as not merely evidence that the dominion of God has broken into their midst, but as instances of this happening. The dynamic saving activity of God which rescues lives is seen as God's reclaiming the victims of evil and darkness. In other words, it is seen as God exercising his divine Lordship in a human life. This inbreaking of God's dynamic saving power and rule can and does affect the whole person.

Another significant text is Luke 17:20–21. While this text has been sometimes been translated "the dominion is within you," this is probably a misleading rendering. Jesus could hardly be suggesting that God's dominion was already to be found within the hostile Pharisees who were then confronting him. More probable is the rendering "the dominion is in your midst." This, however, makes quite clear that Jesus believed that his own time was a time when one would not merely look for harbingers or signs of the dominion's coming, but would actually experience it breaking into their midst in overwhelming force and power. The same sort of concept of a present dominion is suggested by a saying like Mark 12:34, which suggests that a person living in Jesus' era was not far from the dominion of God.

There are, of course, also numerous texts where Jesus refers to the dominion as a future entity. Obviously the petition in the Lord's Prayer (Matt 6:10 and par.) speaks of a dominion that must still be prayed for, as something that will come in the future. Mark 10:5 is also an important text that seems to have a partial parallel in John 3:3, 5. In the Markan saying we hear about receiving the dominion freely like a child would a gift, but then Jesus speaks of entering the dominion. Here the idea of a future realm comes to prominence. The cadre of related sayings in Mark 9:42–50 also refer to entering the dominion as something that happens in the future.

One of the more important future dominion sayings is found in Matthew 7:21. Here the proper confession of Jesus is linked to the future entering of God's dominion. There are various sayings which suggest there are ethical prerequisites to entering the dominion (cf. Mark 9:42–50), but here theological prerequisites seem to be in view. Of just as much interest is a saying like Matthew 8:11–12/Luke 13:28–29, which speaks of dining in the dominion with a wide variety of interesting dinner guests. Clearly a meal after the resurrection is in view since Abraham and others will be attending. This brings up an interesting point. The future dominion of God that one participates in after the resurrection is certainly much like the extant practices of Jesus' own ministry, for he dined with all sorts of unexpected folk, including the least, the last, and the lost. The dominion that is yet to come is not an entirely alien realm unlike this life at its highest and best. To the contrary, the dominion that has already been coming is a foretaste of glory divine, according to Jesus' teaching. We may helpfully compare

Matthew 8:11–12 with Mark 14:25 where Jesus speaks of his looking forward to drinking the fruit of the vine anew in the dominion of God, after his impending demise. The notes of celebration and *koinonia* are hard to miss in these sorts of sayings. The dominion's coming is something to celebrate, and it is also the place where the celebrating will transpire.

At this juncture it will serve us well to consider various of the dominion sayings which appear in our earliest NT sources: the letters of Paul. In at least eight instances Paul uses the phrase *dominion of God* to say something about God's salvific work. The complete list is as follows: 1 Thessalonians 2:11–12; 2 Thessalonians 1:5–12; Galatians 5:21; 1 Corinthians 4:20–21; 6:9–10; 15:50; Romans 14:17, and Colossians 4:10–11. In regard to the first of these sayings, which speaks of God's glorious *basileia*, it appears that Paul is suggesting that while the call to enter it comes in the here and now, the actual entering comes later. It is in fact a repeated theme in Paul's use of the term that whenever he speaks of entering or inheriting the dominion he is referring to something that will transpire in the future.

In 2 Thessalonians 1:5–12 Paul speaks of being counted worthy of the dominion. He then suggests that this dominion will show up when Christ returns with his angels. He further describes the dominion as the place where Christ will be glorified by and marveled at amongst the people of God. It is useful to mention 1 Corinthians 15:24 at this juncture, for here Paul speaks of Christ delivering up the dominion to God *after* he returns to earth and after the resurrection of believers. This is clearly associated with "the End." The connection of the future dominion with the active reigning of Christ is clear.

1 Corinthians 15:50–52 adds a bit more to the discussion. Here Paul discusses inheriting the dominion, and he states flatly that in the present state of flesh and blood, no one can enter the dominion. This is not because Paul envisions the dominion as a place filled with disembodied spirits. Rather, he has in mind the fact that only a permanent body, no longer subject to disease, decay, and death, will do in the eternal dominion of God. The perishable cannot inherit the imperishable.

Inheriting the dominion is also the theme of Galatians 5:21, and 1 Corinthians 6:9–10 as well. Just as 1 Thessalonians 2:10–11 and 2 Thessalonians 1:8 suggest that one must be righteous and holy and blameless to enter the dominion in the future, so also Galatians 5:21 suggests there are ethical prerequisites for doing so. Those who engage in any of the vices listed in Galatians 5:21 will not enter that domain. In 1 Corinthians 6:9–10 as well we have a brief vice catalog, or catalog of the excluded, coupled with the very specific reminder that the wicked will not inherit the *basileia*.

Even though Paul certainly believes that salvation is by grace through faith, he is also quite clear that certain forms of behavior by believers can make one unworthy of God's dominion. This is an important point often overlooked in the study of the Pauline corpus, but it has not been overlooked in Wesley's treatment of this matter. It was, of course, Wesley's view that initial justification was by grace through faith, but final justification and entrance into God's dominion was on the basis of faith plus deeds of piety and charity. Texts such as those just listed were important for Wesley when he wanted to stress that the conduct of Christians could affect their final destiny. Of course, a text such as Matthew 5:20 would also be cited by Wesley where Jesus suggests the same thing. Unless one's righteousness exceeds that of the scribes and Pharisees, the dominion cannot be entered. Nor would Wesley put up with either quietism (one need do nothing, God will simply do it all through the internal workings of the Spirit) or with the notion that while one must do good works to please God, for the good tree will bear such fruit, in the end such works are either incidental or superfluous to one's being saved. Wesley took seriously the three different ways salvation is spoken of in the NT (I have been saved, I am being saved, I shall be saved to the uttermost), and he believed that our behavior, at least in a negative way, could affect the final outcome if we are talking about final justification, final sanctification, final entrance into the dominion.

It seems clear enough from the above texts that Paul sees the future dominion as a place which one enters or inherits as a realm, and that one can only do so after Christ returns and the dead in Christ are raised. In fact, Paul believes that there are both physical and moral prerequisites to entering God's dominion. But Paul, like Jesus, also has something to say about the dominion in the present. Some of his thoughts on this subject are revealed in 1 Corinthians 4:20–21 and Romans 14:17.

In view of the reference to God's power in 1 Corinthians 2:5, and to the power of the cross in 1 Corinthians 1:17, and to the Spirit's power which is active when Paul preaches (2:4), when Paul in 1 Corinthians 4:20–21 says the dominion does not consist in talk but in power, it seems clear that he is talking about a power presently active in the world. The term then seems to connote for Paul the present dynamic saving activity of God. This sort of suggestion is also helpful when we come to a text like Romans 14:17. Here, again using a "not . . . but" construction to contrast what is and is not the case with the dominion, Paul says the dominion does not consist in food and drink, but rather in righteousness, peace, and joy in the Holy Spirit. This seems to be a definition of what characterizes the effects of the dominion in the present. The focus here, then, is not on the dynamic saving activity itself, but on its results within a human life.

This particular text, Romans 14:17, was one of John Wesley's most frequently referred-to dominion texts, not surprisingly because, during the eighteenth-century revival which he helped lead, he was most concerned with soteriology, the effects of God's saving activity on human lives. It is intriguing that in both 1 Corinthians 4:20–21 and in Romans 14:17 the context seems to be polemical, with Paul correcting misconceptions about the dominion.

Colossians 4:11 refers to Paul having coworkers for the dominion of God. This suggests that the dominion already exists and can be worked for by Paul and others. But in none of the present dominion sayings does Paul suggest that anyone enters or inherits the dominion in the present. That activity is always seen as happening in the future. This in turn means that dominion as a realm is for Paul, as for Jesus, only a future entity. To put it another way, for both Paul and Jesus the dominion in the present is seen in a primarily spiritual way, focusing on the way it changes human lives, rather than in a material or physical way. By contrast, when they refer to the dominion in the future, various material aspects of it come to light: it involves eating and drinking, it involves resurrection, it is a place where one can go, and so on. Indeed, at the eschaton it involves the meek inheriting the land or the earth, depending on how one views the sense of that beatitude. Just as a purely material view of the present dominion of God will not do, so a purely spiritual one of the future dominion will not do for Jesus or Paul. What neither Jesus nor Paul promises is that Israelites will get back all their land before the return of the Son of Man. This is not in the offing. Indeed, ominously, both Jesus and Paul talk about a coming destruction of the Jerusalem temple, and the only sequel of consequence to that event they discuss is the coming of Christ accompanied by cosmic signs (cf. Mark 13 and 2 Thessalonians 2).

It should also be clear from the above discussion that neither Jesus nor Paul equates the dominion of God with the church. The church indeed is something one can enter or become a part of here and now. The church is the people of God gathered for worship and fellowship. The dominion, however, is God's saving activity which redeems people and then reigns in their lives. Thus, the church is certainly a place where one sees the dominion of God happening, but the two cannot be equated. Indeed, one may also see the dominion happening outside the church, when someone is rescued, saved, or exorcised by the power of God.

It is also quite clear that neither Jesus nor Paul equates the dominion of God with the world as it now is. Had they done so, the prayer "thy kingdom come . . . on earth" would have made no sense. The dominion at present is on the earth, or in the earth, but the kingdoms

of this world have not yet completely become "the kingdoms of our
Lord and of his Christ." This is why mission work is crucial—taking
the divine saving activity to places where God does not yet presently
reign on earth. Yet clearly from a text like 1 Corinthians 15, or from
Jesus' vision about the messianic banquet, it seems clear that both Jesus
and Paul believed the future would see a day when Christ has put all
things on earth under the dominion of God.

JOHN WESLEY AND THE DOMINION OF GOD

I have had occasion to discourse elsewhere at some length on Wesley's
eschatology, but here I only wish to make a few points of relevance on
the general topic before turning to the specific issue of Wesley's treatment of the dominion theme.[4] A careful study of Wesley's eschatology
shows an increasing interest in future eschatology the further one goes
in Wesley's life. More specifically, it is in the last thirty-five or so years
of Wesley's life that he began to preach regularly on things like the coming final judgment, the messianic woes and the iniquity now at work in
the world, and the general spread of the gospel. Wesley's "optimism of
grace" propelled him to a kind of postmillennial theology in his sermon
"On the General Spread of the Gospel" (1783), where he envisions the
current revival continuing and thriving and leading to a worldwide
revival approaching the end of all things. In other words, in this sermon
he envisions the general spread of God's reign throughout the earth as
a result of the general spread of the gospel. On this view, Christ will
return after a golden age in church history to conclude all things. The
conclusion of that sermon is as follows:

> All unprejudiced persons may see with their eyes that he is already
> renewing the face of the earth. And we have strong reason to hope that
> the work he hath begun he will carry on unto the day of the Lord Jesus;
> that he will never intermit this blessed work of his Spirit until he has ful-
> filled all his promises; until he has put a period to sin and misery, and
> infirmity and death; and reestablished universal holiness and happiness,
> and caused all the inhabitants of the earth to sing together "Hallelujah."[5]

We may say then with some assurance of being correct that Wesley
had an increasing interest in the future of God's dominion on earth the
longer his life lasted.[6] This is the context in which one must exegete his
remarks about the dominion in the present, which proliferate in his earlier and standard sermons. There is a danger of assuming, when one
reads these earlier sermons, that Wesley was almost entirely interested
in realized eschatology. This would be a false assumption, but that is
where the emphasis lies in the earlier sermons. A glance, however, at the

last portion of Wesley's *Notes on the New Testament,* where he comments on Revelation—something even Calvin the great Protestant commentator refrained from doing—should have warned us against such a conclusion. Here, Wesley writing in mid-career does indeed tackle the issues of future eschatology. Thus, as we turn now to some of the discussion of the dominion in the earlier sermons, we must not forget the larger eschatological context of Wesley's thought.

The second sermon that Wesley ever wrote or preached was on Matthew 6:33 with the title "Seek First the Kingdom."[7] This sermon begins much like the later sermon on Romans 14:17, "The Way to the Kingdom."[8] Wesley contrasts worldly concerns about eating and drinking with seeking the dominion. The difference in this sermon is that it suggests that the earthly things will be added after one gets one's kingdom priorities straight, whereas the later sermon simply focuses on matters spiritual.

Wesley explains that the dominion that Christ bids his audience to seek is "not of this world."[9] Wesley argues that this kingdom he refers to can be equated with the heavenly mansions that await the believer beyond the grave. In other words, in this sermon he is associating the kingdom with the dwelling place of God and true believers, namely with heaven. He then stresses that Christ not merely commands us to seek the dominion of God first, but also God's righteousness. This same sort of emphasis is found in Wesley's *Notes on the New Testament* when he comments on Matthew 6:10 and says that we pray for the heavenly kingdom to come, but if it tarries we look forward to entering it, the kingdom of glory, at death.[10]

Here as in the later dominion sermon, "The Way to the Kingdom," righteousness is explained to mean the love of God and neighbor or the whole of our duty to both God and neighbor. The importance of this association of righteousness with kingdom is that works of piety and charity are seen as part of the seeking of or preparation for the dominion. Seeking the dominion then is not a mere theological or inward quest. It involves ethics, and especially the keeping of the greatest commandment about loving God and loving one's neighbor.

It is fair to say that Romans 14:17 was one of the major texts for Wesley during the earliest part of the revival. He preached on this text some seventeen times between 1739 and 1743, but the evidence suggests he proclaimed this text only twelve times thereafter between 1744 and 1791. In the Standard Sermon, "The Way to the Kingdom," he couples this text with a treatment of Mark 1:15, which was in fact one of Wesley's great favorite texts for oral preaching. Wesley defines the dominion of God at the very outset of this sermon as "the nature of true religion."

Like Paul in Romans 14:17, Wesley begins to explain what he means by the dominion of God by explaining what it is not. It is not "meat and drink," which Wesley interprets to refer to all the food laws and related matters in the OT, or more broadly as "any ritual observances."[11] Wesley stresses that the kingdom does not consist in "any outward thing whatever, in anything exterior to the heart; the whole substance thereof lying in 'righteousness, peace, and joy in the Holy Ghost.'"[12] Wesley, like many of his religious contemporaries, distinguishes between the heart and the mind, and so he goes on to say that true religion (kingdom) also does not consist in correct opinions or orthodox thoughts. Rather it has to do with qualities in and of the heart: righteousness, peace, and joy. By righteousness, Wesley says, what is meant is love of God from the heart and love of neighbor as self. Doing this, says Wesley, is the fulfilling of the Law. It is clear from this discussion that Wesley's focus is on the effects of God's divine saving activity in the human being, not on the activity itself. This reflects his soteriological and practical focus on heart religion. It is interesting that only a minority of biblical texts relate the dominion to its internal salvific effects, but Wesley saw this as the heart of the matter.

Next he speaks about peace as the effect of the dominion in the heart of the person. He does not mean the mere absence of activity. He means the presence of God, which brings happiness and contentment. "It is a peace that banishes all doubt, all painful uncertainty, the Spirit of God 'bearing witness with the spirit' of a Christian that he is 'a child of God.'"[13] The Spirit banishes even the fear of death and the devil. It is interesting that Wesley relates the dominion closely to the presence of the Spirit within the believer's life. The reign of God within the believer is exercised or carried out by the Spirit, who produces the aforementioned effects by the Spirit's presence. Finally, Wesley refers to the joy that the Spirit produces, by which he means a rejoicing in the Lord, and a happiness or contentment that the Spirit gives to the believer, caused by the knowledge that his or her sins are forgiven and he or she is a child of God. He sums up this part of his sermon by saying,

> This holiness and happiness, joined in one, are sometimes styled in the inspired writings "the kingdom of God" . . . and sometimes "the kingdom of heaven." It is termed the "kingdom of God" because it is the immediate fruit of God's reigning in the soul. So soon as ever he takes unto himself his mighty power, and sets up his throne in our hearts, they are instantly filled with this "righteousness, and peace, and joy in the Holy Ghost." It is called the "kingdom of heaven" because it is (in a degree) heaven opened in the soul.[14]

Wesley then goes on to stress that Jesus said the dominion was at hand because he was God manifest in the flesh and he was setting up his kingdom among humans, reigning in the hearts of the people. Again the interior nature of the dominion is stressed. Wesley goes on to stress that the way the dominion of God enters a human life is by means of repentance and believing the gospel. "Believe this and the kingdom of God is thine. By faith thou attainest the promise . . ."[15] "Now cast thyself on the Lamb of God, with all thy sins, how many soever they be"; and "an entrance shall *now* be ministered unto thee into the kingdom of our Lord and Savior Jesus Christ."[16]

We have said enough to show that the focus of Wesley's early theologizing about the dominion was on the present dominion and its internal effects on the believer. We see this same emphasis in his *Notes on the New Testament* on Luke 17:20–21, where he says that the phrase "within you" or "among you" in fact means that the dominion is now in our midst. "It is now in the midst of you: it is come: it is present in the soul of every true believer: it is a spiritual kingdom, an internal principle. Wherever it exists, it exists in the heart."[17] Yet we must not forget that in later years Wesley turns more and more to a focus on the future dominion of God, which will visibly appear on earth when Christ returns and the dead are raised. And finally we may note that Wesley did not entirely neglect the dominion to come even in his earlier period. Consider what he says in his *Notes* on 1 Corinthians 15:24: "For the divine reign both of the Father and the Son is from everlasting to everlasting. But this is spoken of the Son's mediatorial kingdom, which will then be delivered up, and of the immediate kingdom or reign of the Father which will then commence."[18]

THE DOMINION OF GOD IN THE WESLEYAN TRADITION

In this all too cursory survey of the dominion theme in the NT and in the teachings of Wesley, we have noticed certain themes in regard to the present and future dominion. The already and not-yet character of the dominion is noted in both sets of sources. We noted that the dominion could not be equated with the church, and now we may add that the NT authors also do not equate it with Israel, any more than John Wesley did. But in this segment of our discussion we want to consider some of the implications of the teachings of Jesus, Paul, and John Wesley on the dominion for a Wesleyan theology about the future, and God's will for that future.[19]

Though it could be said from a Wesleyan point of view that in the present the dominion of God exists on earth only in the lives of those who acknowledge its saving reign in their lives, yet the dominion is regularly described in the NT as a place which can be entered, obtained, inherited, and the like in the future. The vision of the future includes a time when God's saving reign will spread throughout the earth, when the "kingdoms of this world become the kingdoms of our God and of his Christ." But if the dominion of God is going to be on earth and God is going to dwell here below, then necessarily there will have to be some changes in the world we live in. God in Christ is light and in him there is no darkness at all. God in Christ is life, and in him there is no disease or decay or death at all. God in Christ is holy and in him there is no impurity at all. If God is going to dwell with us, not only must we be totally transformed into a truly holy people full of the likeness of Christ, but our surrounding supporting environment will likewise need to change. God is a God who is pleased when the creation he made is as it was created to be and is intended to be. We must explore now the dimension of the dominion that involves the renewal of the earth in the end times.

The OT prophets often conjured up images of the end times as being like the beginning of time in the garden of Eden. Consider the following extended quote from Isaiah 65:17-25:

> For I am about to create a new heavens and a new earth; the former things shall not be remembered or come to mind. But be glad and rejoice forever in what I am creating; for I am about to create Jerusalem as a joy, and its people as a delight. I will rejoice in Jerusalem, and delight in my people; no more shall the sound of weeping be heard in it, or the cry of distress. No more shall there be in it an infant that lives but a few days, or an old person who does not live out a lifetime; for one who dies at a hundred years will be considered a youth, and one who falls short of a hundred will be considered accursed. They shall build houses and inhabit them; they shall plant vineyards and eat their fruit. They shall not build and another inhabit; they shall not plant and another eat; for like the days of a tree shall the days of my people be, and my chosen shall long enjoy the work of their hands. They shall not labor in vain, or bear children for calamity; for they shall be offspring blessed by the Lord—and their descendents as well. Before they call I will answer, while they are yet speaking I will hear. The wolf and the lamb shall feed together, the lion shall eat straw like the ox; but the serpent, its food shall be dust! They shall not hurt or destroy on all my holy mountain, says the Lord.

To this we could add the familiar testimony of Isaiah 2:4 which speaks of the time of final judgment upon the earth when God will judge between the nations and "they shall beat their swords into plowshares, and their spears into pruning hooks, nation shall not lift up sword against nation, neither shall they learn war any more." What is striking about both these poetic passages is that they envision a perfectly good but also perfectly natural new heaven and new earth. Eden, not eternal life, is the benchmark or desideratum here. The first passage speaks of people living out a lengthy blessed life and then dying. Though there is no premature death of young or old, nothing is said about living forever. What is suggested, however, is that the surrounding animal and human world will be at peace, which will facilitate normal, lengthy, healthy human life. No more human strife is to transpire, no more predatory behavior by animals will transpire. "Shalom," or peace and wholeness in its full sense, will have descended upon the world. As beautiful as this picture is, the descriptions in the NT go even further, suggesting not merely the elimination of human strife and other causes of premature death, but the elimination of death altogether by means of resurrection (cf. 1 Cor 15). Furthermore, the NT passages I have in mind suggest the renewal of the earth, so the raised may live in an environment suitable to their new holy and blessed condition. For example, consider the testimony of Romans 8:19–24:

> For the creation waits with eager longing for the revealing of the children of God; for the creation was subject to futility, not of its own will but by the will of the one who subjected it, in hope that the creation itself will be set free from the bondage to decay and will obtain the freedom of the glory of the children of God. We know that the whole of creation has been groaning in labor pains until now; and not only the creation but we ourselves, who have the first fruits of the Spirit, groan inwardly while we await the adoption, the redemption of our bodies. For in hope we were saved.

The fate of creation and of creatures is bound up together. The effects of the fall on the world were extensive, and thus we would expect the effects of redemption to be equally extensive. Paul is talking about a promise that the creation will one day be set free from its bondage to decay and will obtain the same sort of freedom as God's children will at the resurrection. New persons, made like the risen Christ, will live in a brand new world. And it will not be just a matter of Eden revisited. It will be Eden as it should have become if Adam and Eve had eaten of the tree of eternal life, not the tree of the experience of both evil and good, including the evils of disease, decay, and death.

So often at funerals we have heard the stirring words of Revelation 21 about the descent of the new Jerusalem and then the voice from the throne saying: "Behold, the dwelling of God is among mortals. God will dwell with them as their God; they will be his peoples, and God himself will be with them; he will wipe away every tear from their eyes. Death will be no more; mourning and crying and pain will be no more, for the first things have passed away" (vv. 3–4). If this promise were to come true it would necessitate not just new persons but a new environment, one free from disease and decay, one free from struggle and strife.

Of course, God's permanent residence with his people would also necessitate such changes, for God is holy and purely good.

If we ask why and how this transformation will transpire, the short answer is because of and by means of God's very presence. Notice for example how in Revelation 22:1–5 the water of life flows directly from the presence of God, alluded to by reference to the throne, and this river enlivens and heals all that it touches. It is like the opposite effect of a polluted and disease-filled river which defiles all that it touches and all that touch it. The upshot of all this is that God is the ultimate conservationist or ecologist. This should not surprise us since the God of the Bible is a God who made all of creation, and then, when that work was finished, reveled in what had been made, pronouncing it very good. It is also worth reminding ourselves that when the Bible refers to redemption it is creation that is being redeemed, and this entails not just human beings but all of creation. The visions of Revelation 21–22 are not just about a new humanity, but about a new creation, a new world.

A moment's reflection will show the wisdom of God's plan. Imagine perfected human beings with eternal life and resurrection bodies who live in a world full of imperfections and disease and decay. Imagine perfected human beings who would have to spend eternity watching all things bright and beautiful and all other creatures great and small continuing to decay and die. This scenario would only lead to eternal frustration and sorrow. It would be only somewhat more preferable to the condition of the man in the story by Jonathan Swift who asked for eternal life, but failed to ask for eternal youth, thereby condemning himself to getting older and older and more feeble, and yet being unable to die. There is good reason that the new creation is depicted in the Bible as one where God will be wiping away the tears from every eye, and there will be no more sorrow or suffering. Eternal life without eternal joy and love and peace would not be the best of all possible worlds. Eternal life without the companionship of the rest of God's creation would not be life in its fullest form. The Bible does not encourage us to have an egocentric view of salvation, as if it were all or only about saving human souls and letting the material world go to blazes. To the contrary, God has much bigger things in mind for all of creation. These texts about "heaven on earth" are important and must be taken seriously.

Such texts make as much of a mockery of a theology that says Jews living in war-torn Israel today are a fulfillment of eschatological prophecy as they do of a theology that says the church age prior to the return of Christ is the millennium or messianic age upon the earth. How anyone could believe that Satan and the powers of darkness have not run rampant through church history boggles the imagination. Even more incredible is the idea that Satan has been put in his place during church history and not been allowed to deceive the nations (see Rev 20:1–3). And yet this is what one must say if one treats Revelation 20 as about the church age. The more one studies the present and the future of the dominion of God upon the earth, the more one realizes that neither Dispensationalism nor amillennial Calvinism does any real justice to the future-kingdom texts. The reason all this needs to be stressed is that Wesleyans today typically do not know Wesley's views on the dominion and are more likely to be affected by the sort of views one finds in popular Evangelical literature—perhaps especially in the novels of LaHaye and Jenkins, unfortunately.

The transcending beauty of this whole biblical vision of the future can also be seen in some of Jesus' brief remarks about the ultimate fellowship meal: the messianic banquet in the dominion of God when it is fully established on earth. Notice that Jesus speaks of his disciples sitting down with the OT saints such as Abraham or the prophets, at table in the dominion of God (Matt 8:11–12; Luke 13:28–29). This gathering (presumably in Israel) does not take place before Jesus returns. In fact, Jesus himself said he was looking very much forward to the day after his death when he would once again drink the fruit of the vine anew in the dominion of God (Mark 14:25). The parable of the wedding feast involving the wise and foolish virgins (Matt 25) or the parable of the king's wedding feast (Matt 22; cf. Luke 14:16–24) could also be pointed to, but the images are those of celebration at the consummation of the ultimate union—namely the marriage of God to the people of God. Now if there are to be such fellowship gatherings there must also be food, which, unless the menu always involved manna from heaven, requires the good earth which supplies such food. All things considered, most of the descriptions of the afterlife in both the OT and the NT strongly favor a less ethereal, more concrete vision of what the final future will be for the world and its inhabitants than we sometimes hear about from our pulpits. It is not pie in the sky by and by that Jesus or Paul have in mind, but rather bread and wine on the veranda in the new earth.[20]

Of course it is right to observe that much of what I have been dealing with above comes in parables or apocalyptic literature. It is more a form of poetry than prose. Thus the temptation is to not take these images very seriously. This would be a significant mistake, for as we have seen above in Romans 8 and in our study of apocalyptic literature,[21] we find the very same sort of ideas about the renewal of creation and creature in prose passages. I take it then that we are meant to think that God does indeed have a plan for the future of this material world as well as for his people, even if some of the images used to convey this fact are poetic and not meant to be taken literally. The fact remains that all of this material is meant to describe a hoped-for and believed-in future reality that appears when Christ returns and the dominion of God comes in full on earth.

What then are the implications of such a worldview or, better said, dominion view? For one thing it suggests that if we wish to be harbingers for the world of what the afterlife will be like, we would do well to tend and care for the garden God has given us, which we call the earth. It could be said that the doctrine of the resurrection is the ultimate statement indicating God's concern for the conservation of matter and energy. "Nothing wasted, nothing for nought" would seem to be God's motto. All of creation has a purpose, and all of it has a future. We thus must treat that creation with care and respect.

Caring for the earth is not merely sensible for the short term, so our children and grandchildren will have a decent place to live as they grow up. It is also a good witness that we understand that the earth and all that is in it belongs to God (see Ps 8). We are not owners of this world; we are only stewards and caretakers of it, for God's sake. The Bible does not support either a godless communistic philosophy of property and use of the world's resources, nor does it support a godless capitalistic vision of the same. The Bible suggests there is neither private nor public property, only God's property, of which we are all stewards. The whole modern theory of ownership is faulty, for we brought nothing with us into this world, and we will take none of it with us. It also follows from this theology of stewardship that since it belongs to God, we have an obligation to use and dispose of it all in a way that glorifies God and helps humankind. The theory of charity too often has as its essential premise "what's mine is mine, but I may choose to share it with you." The problem with this thesis is that the earth is the Lord's and all that is therein. We have simply been entrusted with a small portion of it to tend and use for the good of God's dominion while we are here. This sort of theology of good stewardship of our earthly resources in preparation for the coming of the kingdom on earth is Wesleyan to the core, and is one of the ways Wesleyanism is far more biblical in its approach to the future than either Dispensationalism or otherworldly forms of Calvinism. God is not finished with us, or with the earth just yet.

This theological perspective is part of what it means to take seriously the future reign of God upon the earth, because most assuredly God will hold us accountable for our stewardship of things. This may not prove a very pleasurable experience for those of us who are terribly wasteful. What shall we answer when God asks why Americans throw away enough food every day to feed the world's starving and still have leftovers? What shall we say when God asks why we support industries that heedlessly pollute our rivers and destroy our air, simply in the name of profits? How shall we answer when God asks us why we persist in mistreating our bodies by repeatedly eating things that hasten disease, decay, and death in our bodies? If we are supposed to treat our bodies like a temple where God dwells, many of us need some reconstructing of our bodies and our chosen lifestyles.

The function of this discussion is not merely theological (to heighten our awareness of what the Bible says about the future of God's dominion) but also ethical (to heighten our sense of responsibility as those who are to mirror the values of God on a variety of subjects). It was John Wesley who suggested a threefold dictum about the matter of good stewardship of the earth and its resources: (1) make all you can by working hard at an honest and honorable trade; (2) save all you can, never squandering money; (3) give all you can while supporting first your own immediate family, then the household of faith, and then one should do good to all. Wesley in his usual memorable fashion says all this in the sermon "The Use of Money," a sermon which he preached more frequently than all his other sermons except "Justification by Faith." He adds that if you make all you can and save all you can, but do not give all you can, you may be a living person but you will be a dead Christian. Lest we arrive at the door of God's dominion spiritually D.O.A., it would be wise of us to reflect here and now, long and hard on our spending habits, and our stewardship of the resources we have in this world. The parable of the talents should not be overspiritualized. God wants an accounting of what we do with what he has bestowed, involving both spiritual and material resources.

One of the upshots of the whole line of thinking introduced in this discussion is that we seem too often, especially in the West, to settle for a purely spiritual gospel, a purely spiritual dominion of God so we do not have to deal with the implications of God's Word for our material realities. But if in fact God's reign is a reign over both body and human spirit, a reign over both the invisible and visible realms, over both heaven and earth, then the spiritual/material division of things is unjustified. It is a cop-out, meant to help us justify our irresponsibility in the way we handle the material world. The later reflections of Wesley on the future dominion are especially helpful in prodding us in the right direction on this matter.

If we examine the gospel closely, the gospel is about the salvation of the whole person, both body (at the resurrection) and spirit, heart, mind, and will (beginning here and now). Furthermore, there are even incursions of miraculous healing in the here and now where God makes plain that he has not given up on embodied existence either. If the dominion of God is indeed coming to earth in the future, and there will be an accounting for what we have done on this planet, it behooves us to recognize the implications of the whole gospel for every aspect of life here and now. The dominion has a claim on it all.

This in essence is what both the biblical and Wesleyan witness insist on in various ways. We would do well to recover such an emphasis in our teaching and preaching today. A church without a vision of the eschatological future of God's divine saving activity is indeed a church which itself is without a future. Whatever exegetical weaknesses there were in Wesley's early emphasis on the interiority of the dominion, these were more than compensated for by his later focus on the future eschatology of the NT, and his continual stress—for example, in his thirteen Standard Sermons on the Sermon on the Mount—that working out one's salvation and the reign of God in one's life involved deeds of piety and charity. These were not optional for entering the dominion in the future, but rather obligatory.

Wesley never did emphasize future eschatology to the degree the NT does, and this is a weakness in Wesleyan theology then and now, for which Dispensationalism more than overcompensates. Dying and going to be with the Lord was Wesley's primary focus in his discussions of the afterlife and the need for salvation, whereas resurrection and the life on earth after Christ's return is the focus of the NT. Still, Wesley was not in error in what he affirmed about the present dominion, and except for a brief flirtation with post-millennialism in the sermon "On the General Spread of the Gospel," he was by and large right in his analysis of the future eschatology of the NT. He stuck to the creedal elements: Christ would return, the dead would be raised, the new heaven and new earth would arrive, and Christ would reign forever. But something more needs to be said at this juncture about Wesley's treatment of Johannine and Pauline literature, as we turn to our next chapter.

CHAPTER 9

New Birth or New Creatures?

Though it is certainly possible to talk about interpreting the Bible in a Wesleyan or Calvinistic manner, and it is of course true that no one comes to the text of the Bible without a point of view, when one speaks about interpreting the biblical text according to a certain tradition, one has already made certain assumptions about what should have priority in interpretation—namely the tradition rather than the Scripture itself.[1] In his preface to the *Standard Sermons*, John Wesley professed to be a true son of the Reformation when he called himself *homo unius libri*. He, at least in principle, endorsed the hermeneutical approach of allowing the Scripture to have its own say—have the first, and indeed the last word—and if that word is at odds with one's church tradition, so much the worse for that tradition. The Scripture was seen as the ultimate authority and the final arbiter of the truth about any given tradition, experience, or rational claim.[2]

NICK AT NIGHT—JESUS AND JOHN ON SPIRITUAL BIRTH

"Are you a born again Christian?" Evangelicals and especially Wesleyans are the products of revivalism and camp meetings going all the way back to the early nineteenth century, and this question has always been on their lips. I have one good friend who grew up in the Wesleyan holiness tradition and says he went to the altar so many times at those meetings and was "born again" so many times he now has stretch marks on his soul! It behooves us then to say something about the foundational texts that generated the born again theology.

Though this point is often overlooked, it is only in the Fourth Gospel that we actually have any discussion about being "born again" or "born from above," and that language is actually only featured in one passage: John 3. It is, of course, true that one cannot determine the theological importance of an idea by the frequency with which it is mentioned in the New Testament. Nonetheless, it needs to be said from the start that the concept of "being born again" is not frequently mentioned even in the Johannine corpus. In the heat of a revival, like the eighteenth-century Wesleyan revival, a few texts were used with great frequency because of the need for renewal. It is this urgency that makes a text like John 3 especially important to someone who stands in the Wesleyan tradition. What then does Jesus' dialogue with Nicodemus actually suggest?

First, it is extremely important not to be anachronistic in one's reading of this much-used text. The discussion here is not about baptism or baptismal regeneration, but indeed about a spiritual transformation or about-face which we usually call conversion. Here we have a presentation of a discussion between two adult Jews, and one of them is saying to the other that a radical transformation of oneself is required in order to see the dominion of God. Such a conversation was not unknown amongst early Jews, but there is an unexpected element in the conversation here. Jesus is suggesting that those who are Jews, indeed even leading teachers among the Jews, must experience this transformation in order to see the dominion of God. Early Jews might discuss such a matter when the subject was what Gentiles or proselytes might need to do to join the people of God, or perhaps even if the subject turned to bad or apostate Jews, but Nicodemus fits neither of these categories. In this regard, Jesus' behavior may be compared to that of John the Baptist as he is portrayed in Matthew 3:1–12 (contrast Luke 3:7–17, where it is the crowd, tax collectors, and soldiers rather than Pharisees and Sadducees who are addressed by John). The upshot of Jesus' dialogue with Nicodemus is surely that everyone needs to be born again, or born from above, even Jesus' fellow Jews, even his fellow Jewish teachers. It is not surprising that such a teaching produced a response of shock and bewilderment on the part of Nicodemus. Was God then treating his chosen people like pagans or proselytes as the eschatological reign of God broke in? Some of the details of the text need to be attended to at this juncture.

John 3:5 speaks of a birth "out of" or "from" water. As I have shown elsewhere water was the normal Jewish metaphor for various parts of the procreating process—insemination (with a drop of water), the water surrounding the child in the womb, the childbearing, and the actual birthing process (coming forth from water—cf. Prov 3:15–18; Song 4:12–15; m. 'Abot 3:1; 3 En. 6:3; 1QH 3:9–10).[3] The phrase *born out of water* in such an environment would normally be taken to refer to physical or natural human birth. Our text couples the reference to that sort of birth with a reference to birth out of or from Spirit. Water and Spirit are seen as the mediums or agencies through which birth happens. It is possible—since we have but one preposition before the phrase *water and Spirit*, and neither of these nouns have the definite article—that the Evangelist is referring to one birth, not two. But grammatically this conclusion is not required, and in John 3:6 we hear, "flesh gives birth to flesh, and Spirit gives birth to Spirit," suggesting two births are meant—hence, the phrase *born again*. The gospel of John is, of course, laden with irony, and so Nicodemus assumes that Jesus is somehow referring to a second physical birth. Thus Jesus must distinguish the two births here, not identify them.

In the parallel text in 1 John 5:6–8 we have articleless references to water and blood, preceded by one preposition, and there it is rather clear that we are dealing with metaphors for two different events—namely the birth and death of Jesus, by which means he comes to us. Thus neither the gospel context nor the larger Johannine corpus favors the view that water and Spirit refer to the same event, much less that the author means that one gets the Spirit through water baptism. The issue here is spiritual regeneration, not sacramental theology. Here Wesley made the same mistake as his Anglican forebears in referring the water reference in this text to Christian baptism and assuming that the Spirit reference refers to receiving grace through water baptism, even infant baptism.

But behind the discussion here lies also a robust theology of creation; both being physically born and spiritually reborn are required if one is to see the dominion of God or enter it. John 3:7 indicates that Nicodemus is astounded by Jesus' teaching. The following verse draws an analogy between the wind and its work and that of the Spirit. The analogy is especially apt because in this gospel *hearing*, not seeing, the Word is the necessary prerequisite to new birth and entering the dominion of God.

It may be said that John Wesley's instincts, in the way he chose to preach on this particular text, were generally consonant with the thrust of the passage itself, though Wesley offers a notional assent to his Anglican tradition affirming baptismal regeneration in his sermon on "The Marks of the New Birth." He says: "That these privileges . . . are *ordinarily* annexed to baptism (which is thence termed by our Lord in a preceding verse, "the being born of water and of the Spirit") we know . . .,"[4] but he then immediately goes on to say that the first mark of the new birth is faith, by which he means true living faith, not mere notional assent to various propositions.

Indeed, drawing on John 1:12–13 he stresses that the new birth comes by no natural means, but rather only from God. That text does indeed contrast birth from God with physical human birth, and human decisions and activities that lead to it.[5] Will Wesley then go on to repudiate his Anglican baptismal teaching? No, but he does say clearly enough that though a person may have been baptized, may have been made a child of God by that means, in terms of actual spiritual experience, "how many are the baptized gluttons and drunkards, the baptized liars and common swearers, . . . the baptized whoremongers, thieves, extortioners?" He stresses that one can and must be born again outside of baptism if one does not manifest the marks of the new birth subsequent to baptism.[6]

He adds, "Lean no more on that staff of that broken reed, that you *were* born again in baptism. Who denies that ye were then made children of God, and heirs of the kingdom of heaven? But notwithstanding this, ye are now children of the devil? Therefore you must be born again."[7] Thus, while on exegetical grounds, one might fault Wesley for trying to have it both ways (baptismal regeneration and the new birth subsequent thereto in the case of most persons), his instincts throughout the revival to placing the emphasis on the *marks* of the new birth as proof of the condition, with the primary mark being living faith, were surely correct. Wesley chose wisely when he picked this text to preach on the marks of the new birth, to focus on spiritual experience gained through faith rather than on sacramental theology.[8]

Conversion, then, from a Johannine perspective, is something brought about by the Holy Spirit and involving a real spiritual experience which in some ways is analogous to birth, an experience that results in a change in human character and behavior. It should be noted that the analogy with childbirth clearly places the emphasis not on the action of the one being born, but on the action or influence of outside forces. The unborn does not make a decision to be born, or call for womb service! Notice that in John 1:12–13 the author specifically denies that human will is what *causes* or produces the new birth. Rather it is a divine action and initiative of God that creates this condition. This is not to deny that such actions of God require that one respond in faith, but the emphasis in John is placed squarely on the divine side of the equation, not on the voluntarist side of the ledger, as is so often the case in Wesleyan and Arminian discussions of conversion.

Privileges of the Newly Reborn

It will be in order to consider briefly another Johannine text, 1 John 3:9, which also was the theme verse for a Standard Sermon of Wesley entitled "The Great Privilege of Those that are Born of God." As is well known, the Elder (or "old man") who wrote these epistles makes a distinction between sin as a condition and sins as activities. The verse in question would seem to be referring to activities in view of the verb *to do*, which here is in the present tense. Some have attempted to argue that we should translate this "does not continue to/in sin" or even "does not continually sin" on the basis that this verb is seen as in the present continual tense. This is probably overpressing the grammar at this point, for the author of this material is not famous for his nuanced use of the language's capacity. Is then our author an early advocate of the Wesleyan view that if one defines sin as a willful violation of a known law a person who is born again can avoid such an act?

Some consideration must be given to the possibility that the biblical author is deliberately putting things dramatically or with use of rhetorical hyperbole, a point supported by the observation of many scholars that 1 John is more of a homily than a letter. What we know is that because the Elder is operating in a situation that is spiritually dangerous for his converts, he feels a need to use stark and strong language involving polar opposites in order to persuasively warn his converts not to sin. I. H. Marshall puts the matter succinctly: "John makes his statements in absolute terms: the way in which he can interchange subjects and predicates indicates that there is a one-to-one correspondence between those who are born of God and those who do what is right, love one another, believe in Jesus, overcome the world, and refrain from sin. There are no shades of grey here: it is a case of belonging to the light or the darkness, to God or to the devil, to righteousness and love or to sin."[9]

When one is faced with real spiritual danger, even the prospect of apostasy, strong and polemical language is in order. Such language is meant to be taken seriously, but it is usually not intended absolutely literally. What then should one conclude from 1 John 3:9 when considered in its own original literary and rhetorical context? It is probably *not* true that the Elder defines sin so narrowly that it only refers to willful acts, for when he speaks about "having sin" in 1 John 1:8 this appears not to be the same thing as "doing sin," and when he speaks of the blood of Jesus cleansing one from all sin in 1:7, he is speaking not of deeds but of cleansing from the inward effects of sin such as guilt, yet this can be called sin as well. It is, however, true that our author believes Christ's blood will cleanse the believer from all the effects of sin, and it is also true that he believes that a person born of God need not "do sin" (i.e., willfully and willingly commit sinful acts). The bottom line is that our author believes wholeheartedly in the theology of the new birth enunciated in texts like John 3; it involves a radical transformation of the individual which cleanses their hearts and empowers them to walk in light and so avoid conscious acts of darkness.

It would be hard to overplay the importance for Wesley of the insights about sin and human nature, including the Christian's nature, found in 1 John. In his sermon on 1 John 3:9 he stresses several points which were crucial for his own theology of conversion:

(1)   He did not concur with those of the Reformed faith who tended to equate justification by faith with the new birth. Justification has to do with one's position in relationship to God; the new birth has to do with one's actual spiritual condition. "The former changes our outward relation to God so that . . . we become children; by the latter our inmost souls are changed, so that . . . we become saint";[10]

(2)   "The being born of God . . . implies not barely the being baptized, or any outward change whatever; but a vast inward change, a change wrought in the soul by the Holy Ghost";[11]

(3)   If one abides in God, in love, and faith, in the spirit of prayer and thanksgiving, in such a state and in such a condition of relationship with God focusing wholeheartedly on God, one does not commit, indeed cannot commit sin—one is too busy doing other godly things;[12]

(4)   But so dependent is the believer on God in this matter that he requires the continual spiritual respiration of God into his soul so that he may keep his soul from sin. The believer must fight an ongoing battle with temptation, and if he remains in living dependency on God, reliant on God's daily supply of aid and grace, he or she can overcome temptation and avoid conscious sin.[13]

These are the sort of conclusions Wesley draws from the material in 1 John. He welds together a Pauline conception of justification with a Johannine conception of sin and the new birth or what it means to be born of God.

Yet it must be said that even for the author of 1 John the definition of sin as "a willful violation of a known law" is surely too narrow. As Marshall says, the issue of law does not come up in 1 John, and accordingly there is not a focus in 1 John on sin being a matter of violating or breaking a known law.[14] There is more to be said for the view that the Elder is focusing on rebellion against God (and so apostasy) as the essence of what is meant by sin. And such rebellion involves both a condition and the actions that manifest that condition. It is a violation of a relationship, not a violation of code or a commandment that the Elder is chiefly thinking of when he speaks of sin. The Elder, however, would have agreed with Wesley that victory over willful sin is possible if one abides in God. What then of Wesley's handling of Paul on this matter?

MR. WESLEY'S HANDLING OF PAUL

One cannot help but be struck by how very dependent Wesley was on Paul for the essence of his message about justification, salvation by faith, and the work of the Spirit in the believer's life. Of the first seventeen of the Standard Sermons, no less than twelve of them have as their theme text some passage from either Romans, Ephesians, or 2 Corinthians. It follows, of course, that—as with the case of the Johannine corpus—if Wesley badly misunderstood the thrust of the apostle to the Gentiles, this must mean he badly misunderstood matters at the heart of the *ordo salutis*. We must consider now several Pauline texts in their original context, and afterward ask how Wesley's understanding of them fares by comparison. Since we have already dealt with the exegesis of Romans 7 earlier in this study,[15] we must ask how Wesley handled Romans at this point. Is *simul justus et peccator* really the most Wesley thought Paul wanted to say about the state of the converted person?

How then did John Wesley view Romans 7?[16] First, Wesley rightly stresses that Romans 7 is a continuation of Romans 6, and the subject is the comparison between the former and present state of a person who has become a Christian. He adds that Paul is trying also to wean Jewish believers from their fondness for the Mosaic Law. Of Romans 7:5 he says Paul speaks of the state of nature, before a person believed in Christ. It is interesting that from a rhetorical point of view, Wesley takes vv. 7–25 of Romans 7 as a digression. Here is how he describes Paul's rhetorical tactics in these verses: "the apostle, in order to show in the most lively manner the weakness and inefficacy of the Law, changes the person and speaks as of himself, concerning the misery of one under the Law. This St. Paul frequently does, when he is not speaking of his own person, but only assuming another character, Romans 3:5, 1 Corinthians 10:30, 4:6. The character here assumed is that of a man, first ignorant of the Law, then under it and sincerely, but ineffectually, striving to serve God. *To have spoken this of himself, or any true believer, would have been foreign to the whole scope of his discourse; nay utterly contrary thereto, as well as to what is expressly asserted in Romans 8.2.*"[17] At the end of this exposition Wesley reminds the reader that Paul was not referring to himself or Christians but "that I, the person whom I am personating, till this deliverance is wrought" and when Wesley comes to Romans 8:1 he says that Paul picks up again the thread of his discourse, which he had interrupted at 7:7.

What can be said about Wesley's exegesis of this difficult text? First, it will be noted how he insists on reading the text in its larger literary context, and thus avoiding a certain kind of proof-texting. Second, Wesley rightly attributes to Paul a certain degree of rhetorical finesse and flexibility, all the while avoiding an Augustinian reading of this text. He believes that Paul not infrequently uses the device of impersonation—taking the point of view or playing the role of someone other than himself. Wesley had been trained in rhetoric at Oxford, and it is not a surprise that he would pick up the rhetorical signals in Paul's discourse. He profitably points to Romans 3:5 as another example of this practice, and he refers to 1 Corinthians 4:6 as demonstrating that Paul is perfectly capable of using rhetorical figures of various sorts.

There are, however, some difficulties with Wesley's general assumptions in dealing with Romans 7. He rightly recognizes that Paul believes in the bondage to sin of those outside of Christ, but this admission sits somewhat awkwardly with Wesley's theology of prevenient grace. Furthermore the person in Romans 7:14–25 is specifically denying he has the power of contrary choice to avoid sin. He would like to do so, but he is unable to do so, for there is a power at work in him so great that the will of his mind is constantly overcome by the rule of sin and death in members. Yet perhaps one could argue that prevenient grace does not give one the power of contrary choice, but rather does something less than that for the nonbeliever (illuminate him about the will of God and about his own spiritual condition so he will seek God?).

Thus, while Wesley's instincts are right on target in regard to seeing Romans 7 as a description of those outside of Christ, as seen from a Christian point of view, his theology of prevenient grace seems to cause him to somewhat underplay the radical nature of conversion. In fact, he uses a threefold paradigm of natural man, legal man (man under the Law), and evangelical man, and sees Romans 7:14–25 as describing a conversion from the second to the third of these states. But Paul knows no such threefold paradigm, and Wesley to his credit was later to realize this and abandon the threefold paradigm. All those who are in Adam are already in one sense under the Law, whether that Law is only written on their hearts or known through study of Torah (see Rom 2:14–15). The Law was first given to Adam, and it was part of the Mosaic Law. Thus, while Wesley is quite right that Paul is offering an anatomy or story of conversion in Romans 7–8, it does not have quite the nuances Wesley wishes to find there in regard to particulars such as prevenient grace or the distinction between natural and legal "man."

SALVATION THROUGH FAITH, AND SIN BY CHOICE

At this juncture we wish to turn to a few of the Pauline texts Wesley used repeatedly during the revival to speak about the nature of conversion, asking first what Paul meant in these verses. The first of these texts is Ephesians 2:8, which speaks about salvation by grace through faith. The first thing to be said about the larger context of this verse is that the subject under discussion in the main is Gentiles. There is in this entire epideictic homily, which we call the Letter to the Ephesians, a toggling back and forth between what Paul wants to say is true about

Jews, and in particular Jews in Christ, and what he wants to say about Gentiles both outside and within Christ.

Careful attention must be paid to the personal pronouns in this sermon, whether the term is *we* or *you* (most often used to refer specifically to Gentile converts [cf. 2:11 and 4:17]), or *I* to refer to the apostle himself. A case can be made that in Ephesians 1 for example, the discussion is entirely about Jewish Christians in 1:3–12 who are called the saints in 1:1, while at 1:13–14 Paul is referring to Gentiles, those who are called the faithful in 1:1.[18] Again we may notice how in 2:1–2 Paul refers specifically to the case of Gentiles, though he goes on to add that their condition outside Christ is not greatly different from anyone else who is also a child of Adam (see 2:3). The emphasis, however, at 2:8 is that the Gentiles he is addressing have been saved by grace through faith, not by works, a point especially needing to be emphasized since the heart of Greco-Roman religion was works of piety such as prayers and sacrifices. Paul stresses that the Gentiles were those who were far off (2:13), as opposed to God's first chosen people, the Jews, who were near (2:17).

Notice the language in 2:19, especially addressed to Gentile converts: "but you are no longer foreigners and aliens but fellow citizens with God's people and so members of God's household." The statement stresses that the Jews have always been God's people, and it is a matter of including Gentiles into that fold. But more particularly Paul means that God has made one new humanity of first Jews in Christ, to which has been added Gentiles in Christ, not only reconciling both to God but to each other as well (2:15–17). This is the one body referred to in 2:16. The argument then recognizes the priority of Jews and of Israel, but sees the current people of God as Jew and Gentile united in Christ. This is even more apparent in Ephesians 3:6, where the distinction between the Gentiles and Israel, the former becoming heirs of God with the latter, is stressed. Again at 3:18 the distinction is made between "you" and all the saints, with the latter appearing to be a reference to the Jewish Christians with whom the Gentiles have been joined together in Christ.

Paul is the apostle to the Gentiles, and the latter is the "you" he addresses in this homily. He must exhort them to turn their backs on the way they lived as pagans (4:17–20), turn their backs on darkness and embrace the light (5:8–13). The language used throughout this letter is typical Jewish language used when speaking about non-Jews who need to be converted. This is the especial topic of this letter, but Paul also admits that Jews who are now in Christ were in need of redemption as well (see 2:3).

How does Wesley use Ephesians 2:8? There is, first of all, the strong emphasis that salvation is not a matter of human works of any kind. Wesley does not appear to be cognizant that the discussion is particularly about the works, in particular the religious works, of Gentiles, as he is thinking more broadly of human efforts in general. Rather, Wesley stresses that salvation is a matter of mere grace, an undeserved benefit from God. It is in order to point out that while the argument in Ephesians stresses that Gentiles have been included by grace through faith in the body of Christ, the language of predestination is used in Ephesians 1 of God's dealings with Christ and with the saints (i.e., the Jews, and more particularly the Jewish Christians). A distinction is made between those who are far off and are simply brought in by faith, and those who are near who are said to have been "chosen in Christ," destined in advance and finally said to have been the first to hope in Christ (see Eph 1:11–12). What we have said before in this study about corporate election in Christ applies here, but we are now able to refine that point a bit further by noticing that Paul is referring in these phrases to Jewish Christians who are in Christ.[19] Paul speaks of the burden of his own gospel to the Gentiles being a mystery, an apocalyptic revelation that was given to him. This mystery is that God had decided as his purpose to bring together in Christ all things on heaven and earth and indeed all peoples both Jew and Gentile (1:9–10). It is in particular the inclusion of Gentiles into the fellowship with the saints that is said to be the mystery revealed to Paul and proclaimed by him as the apostle to the Gentiles (3:3–8).

Of these nuances in the Pauline argument, Wesley seems to be ignorant. He studiously avoids the subject of election broached in Ephesians 1 and sticks with what Paul says is true about Gentiles. He concentrates instead on the discussion of the sort of faith that could be called saving faith, by which he means a true and sincere faith and trust in Christ for salvation, not a mere notional assent to a list of religious propositions or dogmas. He goes on to stress that the salvation referred to in the text of Ephesians is a present salvation, not merely a promise of salvation. Emphasis is placed on the particular grammar: "you have been saved." Wesley then expands and expounds on this to stress that this means salvation from all guilt and fear for past sin, indeed salvation from all original and actual, past and present sin. Notice that nothing is said about salvation from sin committed in the future by the Christian.[20] What Wesley also says is that this means salvation from habitual sin and from willful sin. The point is that sin no longer reigns in the believer's life.

It should be clear that Wesley goes well beyond what Paul says in the text, though one could argue that the pith or essence of Wesley's case is indeed grounded in the text here. But while going beyond the text, does Wesley go against it? Paul is indeed talking about real present salvation that changes a person's life, affecting their will, emotions, mind, and heart, but he is addressing his particular audience, the

Gentiles, when he does so. Paul does not make the distinctions Wesley would between habitual and occasional sin, or between willful or accidental sin, at least in this text. Elsewhere Paul will distinguish between sin and transgression, the latter being a willful violation of a known law—see Romans 3–4—but the former still definitely viewed as a violation against God.

It must be admitted that the tendency to limit sin to willful sin is one of the major difficulties in dealing with Wesley. If one defines sin narrowly enough, then of course one can talk about Christians being entirely sanctified and so avoiding sin, or not sinning and having clean hearts, but it would appear that Paul has a broader and more comprehensive concept of sin, even though it is true to say that the emphasis in Ephesians is placed on willful trespass, on sinful deeds.

It will be possible to deal with Romans 4:5 and 8:1 together since Wesley uses these texts to preach on the nature of justification by grace through faith, and the first fruits of that faith. It is fair to say that for the Wesleyan revival, like the Lutheran and Swiss revivals before it, justification by grace through faith was the theological dynamite that produced the most noise and effect throughout the church and the culture when the notion was promulgated. The first question, however, must be: What is the Pauline thrust in these Romans texts which were so crucial to the Wesleyan revival?

We must begin with the observation that the term *dikaiosune* is used outside the NT mainly in forensic contexts and sense. Aristotle, for instance, says *dikaiosune* is that moral disposition which renders people apt to do just things and act justly, by which is meant to do things that are legal (*Eth. nic.* 5.1129[a]). *Dikaiosune* involves doing what is due, what is owed. While in the OT there is a regular distinction made between the righteous and the wicked, with God being on the side of the former (see Gen 18:25; Ps 24:5), Paul stresses that there are none righteous, all have sinned and fallen short of God's glory (Rom 3). This means that for Paul, God counts or reckons as "righteous" those who are not in fact intrinsically righteous. It is true to say that Paul emphasizes salvation by grace more than is done in early Judaism, and of course he stresses that Christ is the agent and means of this salvation, something with which non-Christian Jews would not agree. The classic question of how God can be both just and the justifier of sinful persons was a live issue for Paul.

Often salvation and righteousness were linked in the OT as they are in Paul's letters (cf. Isa 46:13; Ps 98:2; 103:6), which explains in part why some Judaizing Jewish Christians were incensed over Paul's idea of justifying the sinner by or through faith. But Paul's point is that God relates to sinners on a different basis and in a different manner than he did in the Mosaic era. God now pardons the wicked or the sinner. Since all receive salvation while still sinners, this shows that God justifies the ungodly. It would appear that Paul believes that there are two standards of righteousness: one which the Law demands, about which Paul says he was blameless in regard to violations (Phil 3:4–9), and then there is the righteousness of God himself, by which standard no one is righteous, for here the standard is not just a matter of avoiding illegal behavior but of being positively just and righteous. Yet when Paul uses the phrase the "righteousness of God" in Romans 1:17, he appears to mean by it the same thing as what he means by the phrase *righteousness of faith* (see Phil 3:9). In other words, Paul is talking about God's eschatological redemptive activity.[21] Yet at Romans 3:25–26 it seems clear that the phrase refers to God's character rather than his saving activity. Christ's death proves that God is indeed righteous and could not overlook sin forever. His justice had to be served at some point.

When righteousness is predicated of God, it refers in part to God's activity at the final judgment when he will play the role of the just judge. However, Paul believes that God was manifesting that judgment already on the cross, with Christ bearing the brunt of it. Divine righteousness was firmly vindicated at Calvary, and it is vindicated again when God only accepts those who have faith in the Christ who atoned for sins on the cross. In what sense then are believers righteous through faith?

Is righteousness through faith a position or a condition, a status before God or a standing? Is this righteousness a legal fiction? Is God deceived about believers, so that when God looks on them he only sees the perfectly righteous Christ? No, rather what the term means is that such people are acquitted in God's court, justified, reconciled to God, in right standing with him. This means that God has pardoned their offenses, but not without those offenses being atoned for first by Christ. Notice that in 2 Corinthians 5:17 the new creation and righteousness are not synonymous. It is the right standing with God that is the basis of the transformation of the person and his or her moral life.

In a key text, Romans 4:3ff., Paul uses the ledger language "to reckon." Abraham is seen as the prototype of Christian faith. Yet notice that Abraham's faith in God was not righteousness in itself but was counted as righteousness. The same is said to be true of Christians in Romans 4:3; faith in Christ's death is credited or reckoned to believers as acquittal, leaving them in right standing with God. This is not merely a legal fiction because someone has actually already paid the price for the sin that separates the believing person from God. Notice, however, that Paul goes beyond a forensic sense in Romans 5:9–10 where we are told that the believer is righted or made righteous by the blood of Christ, which is seen as involving the believer being reconciled to God. Not merely are negative obstacles removed from the divine-human encounter, but there is the positive reestablishing of a living relationship and fellowship between the two parties. Being reckoned as righteous means also in part being saved from the wrath to come on judgment day. It has an eschatological reference. Christ makes things right between the sinner and his God.

The conclusion of this discussion must be that when Paul uses the *dikaiosune* language of human beings, he is referring primarily to the status or standing they have before a righteous God, though sometimes there are ethical nuances to the discussion as well. What Paul does not say is that Christ's righteousness is imputed to believers. It is the believer's faith which is credited as righteousness, just as in the case of Abraham. When Paul wants to speak of moral purification and sanctification, Paul uses an entirely different set of terms. Paul neither fuses nor confuses the ideas of justification or objective righteousness, and sanctification or subjective righteousness. As Romans 8:33–34 says, to make righteous is the opposite of to condemn (see Rom 8:1). 2 Corinthians 5:19 means that Jesus was reckoned to be a sinner, so that we might be reckoned to be in right standing. *Dikaiosune* here has to do with one's legal guilt and position as a result. Thus, while it is true that Paul primarily uses this language in Romans and Galatians, one cannot determine the importance of the idea by mere word count. This is the language Paul chooses to refer to how one gets into Christ, or how right relationship with God is reestablished.

One of the two sermons Wesley most preached during the revival was "Justification by Faith," based on Romans 4:5. In this sermon Wesley stresses that actual righteousness is not what is meant by this language. It is not a matter of being made just; that is what is meant by sanctification. Justification is the clearing of sinners from the accusations against them, the pardoning of their offenses.[22] God's Son has made propitiation and expiation on the cross, and the result is reconciliation of the ungodly with God. Wesley insists that, of course, it is the ungodly that God justifies, for if there were those who were perfectly righteous they would not need to be justified by God. Christ was not in a condition that he required to be justified before God. The sinner was in a condition where he had to be justified by God, and the objective means of that justification was the death of Christ, while the subjective means was by faith alone. In this presentation Wesley does not differ significantly from the classical presentation of Luther or Calvin, though he disagreed with both about the scope of the atonement (e.g., Christ died for all sinners, not just the elect). The fruit or results of justification are discussed in a sermon entitled "The First Fruits of the Spirit." When one is justified through faith, one has right standing with God, and on the negative side is no longer condemned by God. To put this in a positive manner, one is at peace with God and is capable of walking in or by the Spirit.

While Wesley puts more emphasis on the concept of justification than does Paul, it does not appear that Wesley deviates in any serious way from the Pauline sense of the concept. He clearly sees the forensic thrust of the language and does not confuse justification with sanctification, or even justification with the new creation. The language of legal reckoning or crediting is familiar to Wesley, and he understands the point of the Pauline analogy between Abraham and the believer in regard to the matter of faith. One could, however, perhaps quarrel with Wesley about the lack of clarity about the issue of final justification and its basis on judgment day. Wesley in other contexts insisted that final justification is based on faith plus works, if there is time and opportunity to perform them. It is not clear that this is wholly congenial to what Paul says about justification, but the matter could be debated.

The author of the Johannine literature presents conversion and salvation from a divine point of view, from the top down (born from above, born of God, born again). Paul, on the other hand, presents conversion from a more mundane and human point of view, from the bottom up (new creature, new creation; formerly in Adam, now in Christ). Both use dramatic metaphors to describe a dynamic event, an event like a human birth, an event like the beginning of the human race. Both sense the drama and the necessity of human conversion if persons are to cease being sinners and become saints, move from darkness to light, abandon Adam for Christ (the eschatological Adam). Both believe that conversion results in a change not just of opinions or orientation, or even of relationship with God and humans, but a real inward change, a change of heart and will and mind and emotions, though the new creature/newly born still awaits a new body. It is this reality that involves both a relational and a real change that these writers use a variety of metaphors to describe.

What makes this especially amazing is that in the Greco-Roman world of the first century, not many believed that human character could be changed. Most felt that character was determined at birth by generation, gender, or geography, and only revealed, not developed or changed, over time. Against this flow of widespread cultural assumptions comes the Jewish and Christian theology of conversion. As it turns out, early Jews and Christians were saying, you can teach old dogs new tricks, as Nicodemus learned to his surprise from Jesus.

CONCLUSIONS

All interpreters of the Bible have their own urgencies when they approach the text, and John Wesley was certainly no different. Some of the concerns and emphases of the Elder or of Paul are absent in Wesley, and sometimes Wesley overlooks or distorts the real thrust of a biblical text, but on the whole his exegetical instincts and his concern for context are commendable. On the central question being addressed in this chapter on conversion, Wesley was surely on target to conclude that conversion is a major thrust of both the Johannine and Pauline literature. But as for the nature of conversion, there are issues that the Johannine and Pauline texts raise that Wesley does not address, and on the other hand there are concepts that Wesley adds or brings to the text which are probably not part of the original author's intended meaning. A few examples will suffice.

On the one hand, Wesley's handling of Romans 7 is remarkably deft and nuanced. Wesley recognizes that Paul is involved in rhetorical role-playing by his use of the first-person singular in this text. He rightly stresses that the earlier portion of Romans 7 and the material which follows in Romans 8 must rule against identifying the "I" with a Christian. Yet he also brings his tripartite schema of natural, legal, and evangelical man to the text, which is foreign to Paul who knows only two categories—those in Adam or those in Christ, those freed from the Law or those in its thrall, a fault Wesley was later to admit. Nor does Wesley really grapple with the issue of "I" exclaiming that he is unable to do what his mind wishes to do. This surely has implications for one's theology of prevenient grace. Still, his overall handling of this crucial text is consonant with Paul's theology of lostness and of salvation.

Again, Wesley's instincts in his treatment of John 3 are good. The real thrust of the material has to do with spiritual experience, not sacramental practice. He is right that Jesus is suggesting that all persons must be born again in order to see the dominion of God. Wesley does not recognize that the word *water* in this text is a metaphor for natural birth, as it is in 1 John 5 as well, but still he understands the essence of the dialogue with Nicodemus. While not denying his Anglican heritage of baptismal regeneration, he minimizes its importance by saying that the vast majority of people can and do need to be born again after infant baptism, having sinned away the blessing of baptism by their adult years.

The discussion of the material in 1 John led to the conclusion that a definition of sin as lawlessness or lawbreaking was inadequate. Though it would appear the Elder would agree that a Christian can avoid a willful violation of a known law, he would not agree that this is the full scope of sin which he is discussing. He speaks of both having and doing sin, of both sin as condition and sin as behavior. Wesley seems to understand some of this complexity, but he wishes to place the emphasis on the real positive change that happens in conversion, enabling a Christian to have victory over temptation and sin.

There is not a great deal to quibble with when it comes to Wesley's handling of justification in Romans, although he places more stress on

the idea than does Paul. This is perhaps because Paul is largely addressing those who are already Christians. More exception can be taken to
Wesley's treatment of Ephesians 2 in this respect—he fails to read the
signals in the text which suggest that Paul is discussing almost entirely
the plight of the Gentiles, and on the other hand he generalizes the text
to make it refer to all sorts of human works. Yet Wesley is surely right
that Paul wanted to stress the present nature of salvation and that it is
experienced through or by means of saving faith. The relationship of
Jews and Gentiles in Christ falls outside Wesley's purview because it is
not a burning issue he must address as was the case with Paul.

In regard to the major concern of this segment of our discussion, it
must be said that clearly the texts which Wesley regularly used in the
revival do deal with the matter of conversion and salvation. The Pauline
and Johannine writers placed great stress on the need for the new birth
or the new creation, and indeed stressed that all need to experience it.
The issue is not just one's position before God or God's declaration
about a person (no condemnation) but one's actual spiritual condition.
Salvation amounts to more than justification, even for Paul. The difficulties cited above in the way that Wesley handles some of these texts
should not be allowed to deflect us from the conclusion that essentially
he was well grounded in the Word when it came to his theology of conversion. Indeed, one could only wish that his progeny of today were
equally well-grounded in such texts. We have hinted at answers in the
discussion above, but now it is time in the next chapter to take head on
the issues of prevenient grace and perfection by dealing with the texts
Wesley usually trotted out.

CHAPTER 10

Amazing Prevenient Grace
and Entire Sanctification

One of the key principles of critical study of the Bible is that one needs to avoid reading too much into silences. Absence of evidence is not necessarily evidence of absence. By this I mean that theology always involves the filling in of some gaps on the basis of the implications of biblical texts. For example, the NT says little or nothing about the inspiration of itself, but it speaks about the God-breathed character of the Hebrew Scriptures (2 Tim 3:16). This sort of statement is applied then by logical extension to the books we call the New Testament. It is thus not enough to say that the phrase *prevenient grace* does not occur in the NT. Neither does Calvin's phrase *common grace*. The question is whether the idea is present in the NT or is a logical extension of ideas that are in the NT.

PREVIEWING PREVENIENT GRACE

Wesley's concept of prevenient grace is frankly weakly grounded if we are talking about proof texts from the Bible. Sometimes Wesley would refer to a text like Matthew 5:44–45, which urges the loving of enemies because God makes his sun to rise on the evil and the good, and makes his rain to fall on the just and the unjust. This is certainly a good text from which to draw conclusions about the way God is gracious in a general way even to the lost. God's general blessings that come through the created order can and do benefit all, regardless of their relationship to God. While this may be said to tell us something about God's character, and the fact that God even blesses those who are at odds with his will and ways, can one then conclude from such a text that God bestows his prevenient grace—not just a general blessing but something that enables the will of all persons so that they can respond positively to the gospel if they have an opportunity to do so? This, it must be admitted, is a stretch.

Wesley to his credit does not limit prevenient grace to sacramental means of receiving grace such as baptism. He thinks that texts like Matthew 5:44–45 show that there is a more general dispensing of such grace by God. Yet if this is so, how then do we account for texts like Romans 7:14–25, written by a Christian, which says that the person in that pre-Christian condition knows the will of God but is unable to do it? In other words, what do we make of various texts which suggest that non-Christians, at least, find sinning inevitable? They really are in the condition of being "not able not to sin." They really are in the bondage to sin. This is, of course, a theme we find quite clearly in the OT as well in the Psalms and in Ecclesiastes. Human wickedness is profound and universal, and even human thoughts are said to be regularly if not continually evil (Ps 5:9; 7:9; 12; Ps 14:3—"there is none who do good, not even one"). While human fallenness is not such that human beings are unredeemable, or as bad as they possibly could be, nevertheless the fall's effect has been extensive; human minds, hearts, wills, bodies, relationships, and even nature itself is subject to such futility (see Rom 8:19–20).

Anyone who has read Wesley's longest single treatise, a treatment on original sin, will know that Wesley did not think like modern Pelagian Arminians who often talk rather blithely about free will. For Wesley, there was such a thing as fallen human will enabled by grace to respond to the gospel. This is a very different matter from a belief in free will. But can we really say, even from inferences based on texts like Matthew 5:44–45, that there is such a thing as universal prevenient grace? This would certainly comport with John 3:16, which tells us that God loves everyone and desires that none should perish but all obtain everlasting life. But it then becomes difficult to understand various texts in the Bible about the depths of human depravity and fallenness.

Perhaps, then, one could argue that God gives prevenient grace or enabling grace to those he knows will respond positively to the gospel? Or again one could argue, God gives prevenient grace at a specific time in a person's life, namely when they are at the point of conversion and are truly considering responding positively to the gospel. The person described in Romans 7:14–25 is at the point of conversion, but apparently he is still crying out for grace and help. Yet if bondage to sin is the general condition of all persons outside of Christ and not at the point of conversion, what do we make of Philippians 3:6, where Paul says that he was faultless in his keeping of the Mosaic Law? That text can be explained presumably by the distinction between sinlessness and being a lawbreaker. Paul does not claim he was sinless when he was a

Pharisaic Jew. Faultlessness under the Mosaic Law is not equivalent to being guiltless in the sight of God.

Perhaps we need to admit that there is some mystery about all this, and neither the concept of universal prevenient grace nor the concept of common grace and particularistic election adequately explains the biblical data. In my view, some sort of concept of God's graciousness to fallen human beings outside of Christ is required to explain how anyone overcomes the bondage to sin, much less keeps God's Law faultlessly for any particular period of time, never mind always. But precisely how that grace works and when someone gets it, is not revealed in the NT. And, of course, here is one of the major problems with doing theology without being constantly tethered to sound exegesis. You start filling in gaps that the Bible does not speak to, and before long you distort what it does say about correlative matters. This is as much of a problem in popular theologizing as it is in the scholarly enterprise of systematic theology.

Prevenient grace certainly comports with the character of a gracious God and his desire that none should perish, but one should not hang one's entire theology about what sinners can do by free choice on such an exegetically weakly supported notion. I would prefer to say that sinners are enabled by grace, in the moment of crisis and crying out, to respond to the gospel. It seems unbiblical and going against human experience to suggest that fallen persons who are not on the doorstep of conversion are not in the bondage to sin. Sin is indeed inevitable for the lost and fallen person. They have inherited this itch, and they inevitably must scratch it from time to time—some more so than others, it appears.

ENCOUNTERING ENTIRE SANCTIFICATION

If the concept of prevenient grace has a weak exegetical foundation, what then can one say about the concept of perfection? In the first place, unlike prevenient grace the term *perfection* does show up in the NT in various contexts. Second, it would appear that how one views the issue of sin will determine how one views the concept of perfection. These ideas seem to be reciprocals of one another. By this I mean that if one defines sin narrowly enough, then it is possible to talk about Christian perfection. For example, if one defines sin as "a willful violation of a known law" then it would appear that perfection is attainable.

Consider for a minute what Paul says in 1 Corinthians 10:13. Here Paul says that when the Christian is tempted, God is faithful and will not allow one to be tested or tempted (the Greek word can mean either thing) past one's ability to bear it. Rather God will provide an adequate means of escape. Here we begin to get a glimpse of a larger picture of things. In Paul's view, it is not about humans having some innate ability to resist temptation or to please God, or to respond to the gospel call. It is about day-by-day, hour-by-hour dependence on God and God's grace. If a Christian will do that, then giving in to temptation need not be inevitable. This comports with Matthew 5:11, which suggests that if a believer will just ask, God can give good gifts, even the ability to avoid sinning. Paul and Jesus are, however, talking about avoiding conscious willful sin. They are not talking, for example, about sins of omission, such as failing to love God with all one's heart, or failing to love one's enemies.

Here is where we must note that Paul uses several terms for sin. *Hamartia* is the most common one, and probably the broadest as well. This seems to encompass both active and passive sin, both sinful actions and sinful thoughts, both attitudes and activities. There is another word Paul uses, *paraptoma* (see, e.g., Rom 5:20). This word has a narrow range of meaning and seems in fact to refer to willful violations of known laws or principles or objective standards. But that is only a portion of the wider concept of sin found in the NT in general and Paul in particular. If one wants to say *paraptoma* can be avoided, one can rightly point to 1 Corinthians 10 (see above) for support. Willful sin of this sort is not viewed as inevitable for the Christian. This is why one of Wesley's more memorable phrases was *while sin remains, it no longer reigns* in the life of the believer. This phrase is true, if the subject is willful sin, and Wesley is right that the Christian is a person who should live without excuses, calling on God's mercies and graces each day to win the battle against willful sin. Victory over such sin is possible by the grace of God.

Wesley did not agree with Luther at this juncture, and on this point Wesley's optimism about what grace could accomplish in the life of the believer seems to be supported by various NT texts. The Christian life is to be a life lived without excuses, with the avoiding of conscious sin, and the pursuing of works of charity and piety. The discussion of sin in 1 John 1:8–10 required some explanation from Wesley's point of view, but the fact that the discussion there has to do with the broader concept of *hamartia* ultimately helped explain what was going on in that text.

In the broad sense, every believer "has sin" and "has sinned" but they also have choice in regard to conscious willful acts of sinning. But this same text says that if one confesses one's sin, God will cleanse one from all unrighteousness. Later in 1 John 3:6, it will be added that no one who dwells in God keeps on sinning (again the chosen activity), and then in 3:9 it says that those who are born of God do not continue sinning. Wesley took these promises quite seriously and literally. Here we are drawing near to the concept of experiential holiness and entire sanctification.

Wesley often returned to 1 John, one of his favorite texts for discussing sin and holiness in the life of a believer, not least because he could point to 1 John 2:2, which says quite plainly that Christ is the atoning sacrifice not only for believers or the elect, "but also for the sins of the world." For Wesley, here was a text that made quite apparent that it was not God who limited the scope of the atonement. Christ's death on the cross was sufficient to atone for the sins of the world, but only efficient or effective for those who responded in faith to Christ and him crucified. And, of course, Wesley did not believe that God rigged the election results in advance.

But Wesley was not happy with the idea that perfection or "entire" sanctification simply involved avoiding temptation and willful sin, though it included that notion. For Wesley it had most of all to do with having a heart full of love for God and neighbor. Here, two texts were important for Wesley: 1 John 4:12, 17–18, and Matthew 5:48. The former Johannine text is especially interesting because of its use of the language of perfection. The *teleia/telio* word group and its cognates can be translated "perfect/complete/mature" depending on the context.

It will be seen that we have the perfect form of a verb in vv. 12 and 17, and so the translation must be "made perfect" / "made complete." In the latter verse it is love which is said to be made perfect or complete, not the believer, and in v. 18 the author goes on to speak of the perfect love of God dwelling in the believer and casting out fear of coming judgment. But one can have a true and genuine and profound experience of the perfect love of God, taking away fear, without becoming perfect in the full and normal sense in which we use that term in the modern world. What of 1 John 4:12? Again it is God's love which is said to be made perfect or made complete in the believer if we love one another and God lives in us. The subject is God's love, not the believer, when perfection is discussed here. Wesley knew this, and it is one of the reasons that he did not insist on using the terminology "sinless perfection" when referring to these profound experiences of God's love after conversion.

If we look at Matthew 5:48 however, here the believer is urged to be perfect or complete as God is perfect, and here the focus is on the follower of Jesus and his behavior. In its immediate context, what is referred to, however, is not an *experience* of perfect love, unlike in 1 John, but rather loving conduct, which is analogous to God's own perfectly loving conduct—which includes loving one's enemies. What is interesting in this text as in the Johannine ones previously discussed is how both love and perfection are brought up in the same breath.

Obviously perfection has something to do with fulfilling the great commandment to love God with all one's self and love neighbor as oneself. In other words it has to do with both experiencing God's perfect love and expressing it. Wesley was bold enough to believe that neither the Elder nor Jesus were urging followers merely to strive in this direction. He believed that every commandment of Jesus was a covered promise, and that as Augustine himself had suggested, God will give whatsoever he commands, or enable one to obey them; otherwise the exhortations are exercises in futility.

But the discussion of perfection in the NT does not limit itself to either experiences of the perfect love of God, or expressions of that love in the way we treat neighbors and even enemies. Like the term *sin* there is a use of the term *perfection* that goes beyond inward holiness and outward Christlike behavior. We get a glimpse of this in Paul's powerful and self-effacing discussion in Philippians 3:10–15.

Paul has been talking about the advantages and honors he had when he was a Jew, but he stresses that all those things pale in comparison to what he has obtained and hopes to obtain in Christ. What he has already obtained is right standing with God through the faithfulness of Christ (3:9), an indirect reference to Christ's atoning death on the cross. Paul then goes on to say in v. 10 that it is his desire "to know Christ and the power of his resurrection and the sharing in common of his sufferings, becoming like him in his death, and so somehow to attain the resurrection from the dead. Not that I have already obtained all this or already have been made perfect (*teteleiomai*) but I press on to take hold of that . . ." It seems clear that Paul here associates being made perfect with obtaining the resurrection from the dead. This he will go on to call the prize (v. 14).

Perfection then, in a Pauline sense, comes when there is full conformity to the image of Jesus, not merely inwardly, or even outwardly in suffering like Christ suffered, or even in dying for the good news as Jesus did. No, full conformity to the image of Christ comes when one receives a resurrection body like Christ's. In regard to this measure or standard of perfection, Paul himself says that he has not yet attained it, but he presses on to the goal. It would be interesting to have heard a conversation between the Apostle Paul and John Wesley about perfection. What then is meant by the *teleioi* in v. 15, which Paul assumes at least some of his converts are? It would appear that Paul, as is his wont, is playing on words. Here the *teleios* root refers to being "mature." It certainly cannot mean being complete or perfect in the sense Paul has just enunciated in the preceding verses, namely full conformity in body as well as in spirit to the image of Jesus. But then, if all one means by *teleios* is mature, certainly many Christians become mature believers in this lifetime. But they do not become "perfect" in this lifetime in that fuller eschatological sense Paul has been discussing.

One of the dilemmas Wesley regularly wrestled with is how one could go into the presence of God at death if one was in a less than perfect and truly holy state. He thus sometimes talks about being perfected in the "article" of death, though it is only the human spirit that is being perfected in that case, not the body. He has a point here. Presumably we do not enter heaven wearing dirty linens.

Wesley used Hebrews 2:10 and related texts to reflect on the purgative work of death, though that text is a two-edged sword since it is talking about what happened to Jesus through suffering and death. Wesley did not want to suggest Jesus was less than perfect while on earth, but Hebrews 2:10 says he was "perfected" through his final suffering. Here "perfected" has nothing to do with moral perfecting because the author will go on to say plainly in Hebrews 3:15 that Jesus was without sin during his earthly life. It has to do with being made complete when he was taken into the presence of God and was finally able to assume the role of the perfect high priest in heaven. This text then does not really help the Wesleyan logic much.

Wesley then argues by extension that if God can perfect a person at death, why not sooner? This is, of course, an attempt to think logically and systematically through a problem, but it extends the logic in such a way that it not only goes beyond the biblical text; it seems to go against it, unless by "perfect" one just means able to avoid conscious sin and be a mature Christian. The problem with such a limited definition of sin and perfection is not only that it does not match up with the fuller, more robust definition of perfection in Paul, but also that the word *perfect* today conveys far more than the limited sense Wesley gave it. So, of course, Wesley was right to say in his classic tract *A Plain Account of Christian Perfection* that he does not insist on sinless perfection; but most moderns will ask, "What sense is there in talking about imperfect perfection? Isn't that an oxymoron? Better to just talk about true holiness and perhaps full sanctification." I think Wesley would agree, but it is a credit to his optimism about the effective power of God's grace that Wesley was loath to place limits on what it could do in this lifetime. Perhaps there is more danger in assuming too little about what God's grace can accomplish in this lifetime than in assuming too much. Wasn't it Jesus who suggested that if a person really had faith (a gift of God's grace), he could move mountains?

We have now worked through the texts usually discussed when perfection in the NT is the subject matter. What we have discovered is several-fold. God's love is called "perfect" in more than one place, and it is implied that one's experience of this love can not only cast out all fear, but even cleanse one of all unrighteousness. Of course, one may go on to sin again, as the Elder warns against in 1 John, but nevertheless he has in mind an experience of the perfect love of God, which has a profound effect on the believer. The author of 1 John also envisions not only the need but the possibility of the believer ceasing from conscious willful sinning, though he recognizes this does not mean that the person has not sinned, nor does it mean that he ceases to be in a condition where sin characterizes the ethos in which he lives, and indeed it can be said the believer "has sin," speaking of sin in a broader sense than just willful acts.

Does the experience of the perfect love of God make the individual perfect in the full sense of the term? The biblical author does not say or suggest this is the case. Certainly, neither this author nor Paul suggests that full perfection, full conformity to the image of Christ in body and in spirit, is possible in this lifetime. But we must not neglect the exhortation in Matthew 5. Jesus indicates that believers can and should exhibit the same kind of unconditional love that God exhibited toward them, a love even for one's enemies. Jesus suggests that God can enable them to do this if they will but seek and ask. In the sense of giving unconditional love, followers of Jesus can "be perfect" just as God acts in a perfect way. This latter Matthean text is not about an experience of perfection, but rather about an expression of perfection in the form of unconditional love.

In none of these texts is perfection limited to a few, nor is it clearly linked to some sort of definitive second work of grace, whether one calls it the second blessing or something else. The author links the experience of love perfected "in us" to the coming day of judgment and having no fear in the face of that day. He does not link it backwards with conversion or with some postconversion experience. What is clear is that love, divine love, is to characterize the Christian life from start to finish and in every aspect and respect. One cannot, for example, say they love God and hate their brother or sister.

There are, of course, a whole series of passages in the Fourth Gospel where the language of *telos* and *teleioso* can be found (John 4:34; 5:36; 13:1; 17:4; 19:28, 30). In each case the best translation is "finish" or "complete" or in the case of John 13:1, "to the end/finish." The idea is performing a task to its completion or until it is finished. This really does not have to do with an experience of perfect love subsequent to conversion. One could perhaps meaningfully talk about what is going on in the footwashing story in John 13 with the language of cleansing. This would seem to refer to some kind of sanctification subsequent to conversion. But if they are "all clean," why then the need for subsequent cleansing symbolized by footwashing? Presumably because there is an ongoing issue of needing to be cleansed from time to time, even with the loyal and longtime disciples of Jesus.

ON REACHING IMPERFECT CONCLUSIONS

What can we deduce from this discussion? Was Wesley on the right track when he talked about entire sanctification and prevenient grace? I think in a general way we can say he was. Perfection in the full Pauline sense of the term was, of course, not attainable until Jesus returned and transformed the believers into his likeness. But it was possible to experience the perfect love of God here and now, and so no longer live in fear, and indeed to be cleansed of all unrighteousness. The problem with Wesley's analysis is that sometimes he defined sin too narrowly, as simply a willful violation of a known law, and thus saw perfection as the avoidance of that coupled with the experience and expression of holy love. But this definition of perfection does not include being conformed to Christ in his sufferings and death, much less being made like Christ in his resurrection. But that is what Paul says real perfection—full perfection—amounts to.

In Wesley's defense, however, it can be said that he was right to be optimistic about what God's grace could accomplish in the believer. Whether we think of 1 John 1 or 1 Corinthians 10, or the many morally rigorous exhortations in the NT that its authors expected to be obeyed in faith and by grace, it is clear enough that the writers of the NT thought that conversion and sanctification could and would make a difference when it came to one's experience of God and one's behavior.

It was foolishness to talk about believers still being in bondage to sin, unless, of course, by way of apostasy they chose to go back down that road. Wesley was not naïve about human nature, and he fully accepted the concept of original sin. He even said at one point that what infant baptism accomplished was removing the guilt, *but not the taint*, of original sin. Conversion and sanctification were still required. Though it is not highlighted in the texts we have discussed in this section, there is nothing preventing the conclusion that sanctification could be both progressive and also have crisis moments along the way, where there was sudden and dramatic improvement in one's Christlikeness by the grace of God. But even this does not amount to perfection in the full Pauline sense of the term.

Thus, one must be wary of defining sin too narrowly, not least because even Christians have an infinite capacity for self-justification and rationalization of their sin. One must also be wary of defining perfection too narrowly. But what one must not hesitate to do is say that the NT suggests that the love and grace of God are powerful enough to transform human beings and set them on a journey toward perfection, by which I mean full conformity to the image of the Son. What is certainly also consonant with the NT is saying that temptation and sinning can be resisted or escaped with the help of God. Furthermore, one can become "mature" in Christ in this lifetime, and may look forward to being "perfected" in the article of death so as to enter heaven in a holy state.

Closer attention to the exegetical particulars discussed here might have prevented later Wesleyan discussion about the eradication of the sin nature, or the defining of holiness chiefly by what we avoid doing (e.g., "we don't smoke and we don't chew and we don't go with the girls that do . . ."). Holiness in the NT certainly involves moral integrity and avoiding conscious sin by the aid of grace, but its main focus is on holy love and the expression of that love in one's relationship with God and fellow human beings.

Close attention to a text like Romans 7:14–25 and others might have forestalled some of the more Pelagian remarks about human nature and about free will that sometimes circulate in Methodist communities. Wesley understood quite well the depth of sin, and its extensive effect on human nature, and we should not minimize what the Bible says about such things. It just means that grace is all that more amazing when one realizes the depth of human degradation.

On the whole the Wesleyan Arminian approach to the relevant NT texts is closer than other systems to giving a fair representation of what they reveal about God's character, the nature of salvation, the scope of the atonement, the effect of grace on human nature, and the like. But as we have seen, even this system has its definite weaknesses and limitations and is too often in danger of becoming Pelagian, if not fully voluntarist, in character, especially when it comes to human willing and salvation. Evangelical Wesleyans, in fact, are still in the process of recovering and learning their heritage; and so, perhaps, some patience is in order until they get beyond the period of amnesia when it comes to the Wesleyan and biblical tradition they have inherited. We may be thankful that things like Disciple Bible Study and Alpha have led so many Wesleyans to take a more serious approach to the study of the Bible and their faith. And we have not even considered all of the larger Wesleyan family in this discussion so far. There is another branch or offshoot from Wesleyanism that we need to focus on now, whose theology presents us with its own set of exegetical problems. I am referring to the Pentecostal/Holiness/Charismatic wing of the Evangelical Church.

THE PEOPLE OF PENTECOST

While it is not widely recognized or known, the Pentecostal movement that caught fire in the Azuza Street revivals on the West Coast at the beginning of the twentieth century had its predecessors and parents. This whole movement was an offshoot of the holiness movement of the post–Civil War era; in fact, had it known its theological forebears it could have pointed to the man John Wesley handpicked to be his successor in the Methodist revival: John Fletcher, who unfortunately died prematurely and before John Wesley. Fletcher's theology of the Holy Spirit was a vibrant one, almost a dispensational one, in that he saw the Spirit as that which most characterized and distinguished the church age from previous eras in the history of God's people. He was at the other end of the spectrum from the cessationists who tried to argue that the "charismatic" gifts ceased to function at the end of the Apostolic Era.

Pneumatology, then, is the theological area in which this wing of the conservative Protestant (and Arminian) church found its somewhat distinctive calling card, and it needs to be noted that as with Dispensationalism, this movement was led by and large by laypeople, not by scholars or those well grounded in the Greek New Testament. Not surprisingly, this led to some aberrations in the more distinctive aspects of their theologizing. But first, the good news.

Do Not Quench the Spirit

If one has been a student of church history, one knows from the outset that it is simply historically false to say that the spiritual gifts of prophecy or speaking in tongues or healing ceased when the apostles died out. Whether one thinks of the Montanists in the era of Tertullian, or visionaries like Hildegard of Bingen, or the faith healers of our own era like Kathleen Kuhlman, it is simply false to say that these gifts ceased to exist or be exercised within the church. It is also false to say that these gifts were suddenly revived in the twentieth century. There was, rather, a new appreciation and spread of these gifts in the twentieth century, which affected many Protestant denominations and still is doing so, to the benefit of all. But the careful student of church history knows that these gifts have been alive and well in every age of church history.

It is a strange thing, but about the only exegetical argument that is generally put forward in favor of cessationism has oddly enough to do with 1 Corinthians 13:10—"but when perfection comes, the imperfect disappears." The word perfection (*teleion*) here is taken, in such an interpretation, to mean either the end of the apostolic era (but in what sense was it a good thing or perfection for the apostles to all die out?) or more commonly the coming of the canon of the NT. In our discussion of perfection above,[1] we saw, however, a far more likely interpretation.

Paul is not here prophetically foreseeing the end of the canonizing process in the fourth century A.D. He is rather speaking eschatologically. He is speaking about when we will all see Jesus face to face, and we truly will not need things like prophecy any longer. In other words, Paul is speaking about the eschaton, when Jesus returns, and we will all be fully conformed to his likeness. At that juncture, spiritual gifts which have helped guide and sustain us in the interim before the parousia will no longer be necessary. But short of the eschaton, we need them badly, and Paul exhorts us to seek them, particularly the gift of prophecy (see 1 Cor 14:1). There is no viable argument either exegetically or experientially for these gifts ceasing to exist before the eschaton.

Problems with Experiential Exegesis

What then are the exegetical problems with Pentecostal theology as it has evolved in the last century? One of the problems has to do with the whole concept of subsequence, by which I mean that whether you speak of the baptism of the Holy Spirit (a noun phrase that never appears in the NT), or the second blessing, or entire sanctification as a second definitive work of grace on a par with the new birth, you are saying a mouthful. I do not have, in general, a philosophical problem with the idea of a second definitive work of grace in the life of the believer, but the usual exegetical evidence trotted out to support this notion is not only weak; in some cases it involves the distortion of biblical texts.

Take, for example, the typical argument that goes like this: (1) the original disciples received the Holy Spirit in the upper room (see John 20), and then (2) later at Pentecost they had a Pentecostal experience, a second blessing, which made them "bonafide," full-fledged, Spirit-filled Christians. Several problems accompany this argument, and they involve not only misinterpretations of these two biblical texts, but other texts in Acts as well.

Let us consider John 20 first. As even a cursory examination of John 20 will show, there are two upper-room stories, and unless we are prepared to argue that somehow Thomas was "late for the Holy Spirit," it does not seem likely that the Holy Spirit was dispensed in *any* measure when Jesus first appeared in the upper room. Why not? Precisely for the very reason Pentecostals insist on. They argue long and well that when the Holy Spirit comes into someone's life there is evidence; there are gifts and fruit bestowed. This is, in fact, good theology. The Holy Spirit always leaves its mark in the life of the believer.

But is there any immediate evidence whatsoever that the Ten are any different after Jesus breathes on them and says "receive the Holy Spirit"? The answer is no. They are still huddled in the upper room afraid, hiding from the Jewish officials, a week later when Jesus shows up again. Furthermore, in the Johannine epilogue in John 21 which is surely considerably later, we still do not find the disciples out converting the world, speaking in tongues, prophesying, or manifesting the fruit of the Spirit. What we find them doing is fishing in Galilee!

They have gone backward, not forward into the new age; and notice that Peter has to be restored, and still manifests the same lack of spiritual perceptivity in this story. In short, there is no evidence whatsoever that the Spirit was actually received in the upper room at Easter. The proper way to read that story is that Jesus is performing a prophetic sign act, promising and reassuring that the Paraclete will come when he goes back to heaven. This comports nicely with John 14–17, where we were told that it was necessary for Jesus to go back to the Father *before* the Spirit could and would be sent. What then of Acts 2?

Here is not the place to try and present Luke's theology of the Spirit at length, but suffice it to say that Luke portrays the event recorded in Acts 2 as the birthday of the church, not merely its empowering. Furthermore, Luke does not think a person can be a full-fledged Christian without the Holy Spirit, and it is only *at and after* Pentecost that the Spirit is bestowed as a possession on any disciple.[2] Notice the emphasis in Acts 2:1–4 on the tongues of fire falling on each of the disciples in the upper room, which according to Acts 1:14 includes not only the Twelve but also the female disciples and Mary and the brothers of Jesus! They are all empowered to bear witness to the Jews in Jerusalem.[3]

This leads to a further point. The experience of the disciples on Pentecost did not involve speaking in angelic tongues or some sort of spiritual prayer language. It involved them being given for an instant the miraculous gift of speaking in all sorts of foreign languages, so that the crowd could proclaim: "We heard them speaking in our own native tongues."

Here is a point where Greek grammar is important. One could in theory argue the disciples spoke in angelic tongues, but there was also a miracle of hearing amongst the audience such that they understood it in their native languages. We would then have two Pentecost miracles involving both speaking and hearing. This, however, is not what the grammar suggests. The text literally says: "each one heard them speaking in his own language" (Acts 2:6). The word *speaking* is the word that is nearest to and which qualifies the phrase *in his own language*, not the word *heard*.

About Acts 2:4 then one must ask: When the text says they began to speak in *other tongues/languages*, what is meant? What is the point of comparison—other than human tongues, or other than their native tongue? The answer must surely be the latter in light of the way the story develops in vv. 5ff. Thus we have a story here about what my Greek students regularly pray for: the miraculous gift of knowing and speaking a foreign language without the necessity of studying! In a sense, this is a story about the Tower of Babel in reverse (see Gen 11). The Pentecostal reading of this story, like the one in John 20, involves reading into the text more than the grammar and syntax and story line will bear.

But there is another factor at play, and it has to do with the personal nature of the Holy Spirit. The Spirit is not an "it," not a power, or essence, or something like water, or a mere force ("may the force be with you"). The Spirit is a person, the third person of the Trinity. This is fundamental to NT theology and Evangelical theology. It follows logically from this fact that when the Spirit is bestowed on someone and takes up residence within a believer, it is the whole Spirit who comes, not merely a part of the Spirit. You can no more have a little bit of the Spirit than you can be a little bit pregnant. The Spirit comes as a person and dwells within the believer. The Spirit is the secret agent, the Counselor and Comforter sent by Jesus as his personal emissary. Thus, it makes no sense to talk about getting the Spirit in doses or stages. You either have the Spirit in your life or you do not. Every true Christian is a Spirit-filled Christian, and this does not happen subsequent to conversion; it happens at conversion.

This concept is made clear in 1 Corinthians 12:13: "for we were all baptized by/with the one Spirit into one body." Notice that here we have a clear connection between the word *baptize* and the Holy Spirit. But it is the Spirit, not us, who is doing the baptizing into the one body of Christ, and when Paul talks about entering the body of Christ, he is talking about what happens when one becomes a Christian. This is also made clear from 1 Corinthians 12:3 where he says that no one can even truly confess Jesus is Lord unless they are prompted by the indwelling Holy Spirit. Confession, baptism, gifts, fruit all come from that close encounter of the first kind with the Spirit, and it all begins at conversion, not at some time subsequent to when one enters or is spiritually joined to the body of Christ.

Now it is, of course, true that the Holy Spirit can progressively get hold of more aspects of the believer's life. It is also true that the Spirit can and does subsequent to conversion give more and different gifts and graces. Notice that in 1 Corinthians 12:7–11 it is the Spirit who decides who gets which spiritual gift, and the Spirit dispenses them in such a fashion that it will work to the common good. This is just another way of saying that the gifts are not given primarily for our own personal benefit, but rather to benefit others in the body of Christ. As a by-product these gifts also bless and benefit the believer in question. But is there any one particular spiritual gift that any and all Christians must manifest to demonstrate they are true Spirit-filled Christians? The answer to this question is absolutely not, unless one is talking about the gift of the Holy Spirit himself.

Here again is where a knowledge of Greek grammar is critical. In 1 Corinthians 12:29–30 Paul asks a series of rhetorical questions. The Greek reads literally, "Not all have the gifts of healing do they? Not all speak in tongues do they?" and so on. The questions all begin with a negative particle, *not*, and the only possible intended answer to such a rhetorical question is no.[4] It is thus not the case that Paul, or for that matter any other NT writer, suggests that speaking in tongues is the litmus test everyone must pass to bear witness that he or she really has the Spirit and is a Spirit-filled Christian. This does not diminish in any way the blessing of having this gift, or its validity. It just means that the Spirit does not give every Christian this gift, any more than the Spirit gives every Christian the gift of healing or prophecy. But there is more to be said.

One of the truly difficult things about Evangelical theology is that it sometimes manifests a real naïvete when it comes to the hermeneutics of historical narratives. It needs to be stressed that just because something is reported in Acts does not mean that it is something that is normative for the church or a pattern for its universal experience. Take, for example, the issue of water baptism for a moment. In Acts we have the following three patterns: (1) baptism followed by the reception of the Holy Spirit (Acts 8); (2) baptism apparently simultaneous with the reception of the Spirit (also Acts 8, the Ethiopian eunuch); and (3) baptism following the evident reception of the Spirit (Acts 10, Cornelius and family). When we have multiple patterns in a historical narrative, the only appropriate conclusion is that God can do it however God wants to; he is not mandating a particular order of events. Many Protestant battles over water baptism could have been avoided if this had been realized. But if we find a positive repeated pattern in Acts, then a good case can be made for saying that Luke at least sees this as normal, if not normative.

For example, if we compare the summary passages in Acts 2:42–47 and 4:32–35, we should note that sharing material things in common and making sure that no one in the body of believers was in want characterized the early church. Luke probably is suggesting that the church should go on doing so. What, then, about speaking in tongues in Acts?

Certainly it would appear that in the case of Cornelius in Acts 10 speaking in tongues is indeed the initial evidence that the Spirit has been received, and possibly this was the case with the Samaritans as well in Acts 8, though that text is not clear. But there are numerous other conversion stories in Acts, not the least of which is Paul's, told three times (Acts 9, 22, 26), which have no mention of glossolalia, and we cannot just assume it was manifested on these occasions. Furthermore, it needs to be stressed that the disciples in Acts 19:1–7 are disciples of John, having experienced his baptism. They are not disciples of Jesus. They have not even heard of the Holy Spirit at all! This is why Paul starts over from scratch with them and baptizes them with water into the name of Jesus, after which there is laying on of hands and the reception of the Spirit, though we should definitely see this as all part of one occasion and event. In other words, there is no support whatsoever in Acts 19 for a doctrine of subsequence, or the receiving of the Spirit or becoming Spirit-filled subsequent to conversion.

Again I would stress that none of this minimizes the importance of spiritual gifts, something that every Christian is given at least one of, if not more. I would add too that we now have detailed, soundly exegetical studies done from within the Pentecostal or Charismatic tradition which recognize these exegetical realities and still offer a robust theology of the Holy Spirit.[5]

Evangelical theology needs to include a robust dose of pneumatology, and while there has been some bad exegesis and some excesses that have come from the Charismatic wing of the Evangelical world, there has also been some bad exegesis and some quenching and grieving of the Spirit coming from other wings of the Evangelical community.

It is no fun growing up in the first church of the Frigidaire where spontaneity and the Holy Spirit are not allowed to get a word in edgewise, lest we fail to finish the service at the prescribed time! It would be good to come to a place where we no longer have allergic reactions to each other's theologies just because we can perhaps see the flaws in others more easily than can those who embrace a particular form of Evangelical theology. What was it that Jesus said about splinters in the other person's eye, and logs in our own? We have thus come now to the point where we can ask: how then can we avoid the pitfalls of reading the NT with the liabilities of one or another system or form of Evangelical theology? In the next section we address this issue as we discuss the way forward beyond theological distortions of the NT text.

Part Four

The Long Journey Home—Where Do We Go from Here?

CHAPTER 11

Reimagining the Mystery

We have now come to the end of our rather detailed look at the exegetical problems with various forms of Evangelical theology and theologizing. In a nutshell, we may sum things up as follows:

(1) For the legacy of Luther the problematic issue is dealing with both Augustine's understanding of the sovereignty and character of God, but also Augustine's anthropology, particularly his understanding of human nature, both of those outside and inside Christ. Luther did not handle well the idea that more than one will was truly in play in the universe, or the idea that God's will could actually be frustrated by sin and sinning. If human bondage is absolute, then of course God's election must be equally absolute if anyone is going to be saved. The human response is not merely enabled but rather determined by irresistible grace.

(2) For more Reformed or Calvinistic theology, the issue also has to do with Augustine's doctrine of God and God's sovereignty, and particularly with the ways God exercises that sovereignty. Calvin, however, was more of a careful exegete; Luther more of a dogmatician. Calvin accordingly does more justice to the variety and emphases in the biblical text than does Luther. For example, Calvin has more of a concept of secondary causes than Luther seems to in his famous treatise "The Bondage of the Will," and Calvin also has a far less truncated theology of sanctification. In both the cases of Luther and Calvin, however, the real problems are deeply rooted in some misunderstandings of Paul's thought, particularly in regard to how God's sovereignty and election actually operate.

(3) The problems with Dispensational theology have to do with issues of eschatology and prophecy. Not only is there a fundamental problem with the way prophecy, especially predictive prophecy about the more distant future, is approached (which is as much an issue of hermeneutics as it is exegesis), but by importing into various NT texts a theology of an eschatological rapture—and thereby enabling a theology of two peoples of God, two second comings, two categories of people in which we have the fulfillment of prophecy—the text is fragmented into a more diverse and compartmentalized schema.

(4) The problematic exegetical issues for Wesleyan theology arise out of the distinctive interpretations of texts that have to do with the nature and power of grace, and the doctrine of sanctification. The handling of texts from the Sermon on the Mount, the Fourth Gospel, and the Johannine Epistles are problematic in various regards, and sometimes grace-enabled will is trivialized into a concept of free will, which is not biblical. The optimism of grace is replaced by an optimism about human nature. Sin is too narrowly defined, which in turn allows for talking about perfection in this lifetime in ways the biblical text does not suggest.

(5) The Pentecostal and Holiness legacy also is problematic when it comes to pneumatology and sanctification, especially when we are dealing with issues about the character of the Spirit, the gifting of the Holy Spirit (with tongues as a litmus test of being full of the Spirit), and the inclination to emphasize the concept of subsequence, a second and/or third definitive crisis experience beyond conversion which presumably counteracts backsliding and catapults one more nearly into the category of entirely sanctified. Progressive sanctification is not the issue here. Calvin also talks about such a thing. Nor even is the issue that people have dramatic, cleansing experiences in the Spirit subsequent to conversion or that the spiritual gifts are still alive and well today. The problem comes with the exegetical handles used to interpret such experiences in the Spirit. Especially problematic is the attempt to read two- and three-stage theologies into some combination of John 20, Acts 2, and sometimes other texts as well.

As it turns out, the legacy of experience can be just as much a cause of tendentious exegesis as the legacy of Augustine or Darby and Scofield. Both the more experientially based and the more cognitively based forms of Evangelical theology have exegetical weaknesses in their theology, particularly in regard to the distinctive ideas in each system that are read out of or, better said, into the text.

6) I want to stress that I am primarily talking here about the de facto and existing ways these various theologies are handled today in an Evangelical culture which is far too biblically illiterate. Biblical illiteracy cannot be predicated of Luther, Calvin, or Wesley, who were all able interpreters of the Bible in its original languages. Nevertheless, their theologies already had their exegetical weaknesses, and now in the hands of less able, less biblically informed modern practitioners there are dangers of even worse misuses of the Lutheran or Reformed or Dispensational or Wesleyan or Pentecostal legacies, especially when it comes to the distinctives in each system. What then are our alternatives to such misuse of the Scriptures? Is there a different way we could approach Evangelical theology and theologizing?

If I have not thoroughly confused or alienated my whole Evangelical audience by now, perhaps there can be patience for going one more furlong along the road that we are walking. If all three major Evangelical theological systems have their exegetical weaknesses, and in some cases even involve real distortions of various biblical texts and spiritual realities—including misrepresenting the nature of God and his salvation plan in the past and the future—shall we just throw up our hands and say "a plague on all your houses"? Or is there in fact a way forward besides just saying "let's do more in depth and better exegesis and let each text have its own say"? Yes, I think there is.

All of these Protestant systems are to one degree or another products of Western and Enlightenment ways of reading the New Testament. But the authors of the New Testament were not late Western Christians. They did not live in an almost exclusively Gentile world, nor did they labor in the shadow of Augustine, Aquinas, Luther, Calvin, or even Wesley. They were Jews, and they thought like first-century Jews. The way forward is in part the way backward—to earlier exegetes, more Jewish contexts, a better understanding of the biblical world into which NT words were spoken. It is a daunting task, but it is not impossible to do a better job of understanding the original contexts in which the NT was given, remembering that a text without a context is just a pretext for various sorts of anachronistic readings into the text.

So, for one thing, in an age of biblical illiteracy we must have a renewal of the commitment to contextual study of the NT, including original language exegesis. We must stop watering down our Christian college and seminary curriculums so that students can escape without a hint of understanding the original languages and contexts in which the

Bible was written. But there is much more we must do as well. We must begin to reconceptualize what theology is, and how we may recognize its nature and character. I wish to say more about this at length at this juncture.

EPIPHANIES BY THE SEA

I was in Australia in the summer of 2004 giving some lectures at the Baptist and Anglican theological colleges on the east coast of that wonderful continent, when it hit me. I was at Morling College in Sydney, and the faculty at that institution pride themselves on doing cutting-edge teaching in a postmodern situation, preparing ministers for their largely non-churchgoing audience. The class I was invited to was analyzing films as a tool for ministry; in this particular case we were analyzing the *Matrix* trilogy, which was filmed in Sydney.[1] There have hardly been more brooding and evocative postmodern films than these three, synthesizing as they do many ideas and cultural concepts, including Christian concepts, into one compelling mixture in a story about saving humanity from technology run amuck.

I was busily making the point that in a postmodern and largely biblically illiterate situation the power of one's rhetoric counts far more than the power of one's logic. Persuasion is far more likely to happen by means of powerful and evocative images than by syllogisms. The appeal to the imagination in the postmodern situation time and again trumps the appeal to reason. Yet the church and the academy continue to do theology by and large using an analytical paradigm. Perhaps it is time to ask: what is wrong with this picture, or better said, what is wrong with this sort of theologizing, which does not even involve story and pictures?

As I was puzzling this out, it also dawned on me that we live in an age in which our audiences are primarily and increasingly attuned to visual rather than auditory learning. Hours spent staring at TVs, computer screens, and movies have conditioned us this way. Yet both in our educational institutions and in our churches we continue to plow the old furrow of worship and classes that primarily amount to an oral delivery of words to listeners. Whereas Jesus' audience might well respond to the exhortation, "Let those who have ears, hear," our audience is more likely to respond to the exhortation, "Let those who have eyes, see." Jesus' culture was oral and aural, with only 10 percent or so of the population able to read and write. Our culture, at least nominally, is literate, and frankly prefers seeing to hearing, watching to listening. How many people still listen to baseball games on the radio when they can watch them on TV? How many people would rather see a concert, rather than merely hearing tunes playing on the radio?

If we are going to do the heavy lifting called hermeneutics in our own cultural situation, it will be well to know what sort of learners we are dealing with, and then try and figure out how to reach them. Clearly, simply using more colorful PowerPoints of words and more words projected up on a screen, while helpful, will not be adequate to reach our postmodern world. Something more all-encompassing—appealing to the emotions as well as the mind, the will as well as the intellect, the desire to see, as well as the need to hear—is required.

But hear the good news: the NT writers largely do theology out of a paradigm that appeals to the imagination, including the visual imagination, and so in various ways it is not that hard to translate into a postmodern situation. As it turns out, premodernity and postmodernity have many things in common, and it is not syllogistic or analytical teaching, preaching, or witnessing. It has far more to do with story, as we shall see.

Put bluntly, we do not have "theology" in the New Testament; we have what may be called theologizing—indeed theologizing into specific cultural settings, whether we are talking about Jesus' parables, Paul's rhetoric, or John's apocalyptic salvos. Traditional Western training has prompted us to think in categories like NT theology, historical theology, systematic theology, and so on. The fundamental assumption when it comes to the Bible is that the Bible, including the New Testament, is some sort of compendium of theology. Now if one means no more than that we have plenty of God-talk in the Bible ("theology" deriving from the Greek words *theos* and *logos*), of course that is true.

What is not true is that the Bible is some sort of manual that synthesizes key ideas and then slots them into categories like eschatology, pneumatology, ecclesiology, theology, Christology, anthropology, and so on. To treat the theologizing in the New Testament that way is in some respects just another approach rather like Dispensationalism took with prophecy, slotting things into one box or another. What scholarly treatment of the Bible has done is seek to divide up its material into isolated concepts that can be analyzed, processed, controlled, and then disseminated. It hardly requires much reflection to realize that this involves stripping these ideas of their contexts, particularly their narrative contexts. Perhaps we should have remembered the mantra, "a text without a context is just a pretext for whatever you want it to mean," before we disembodied and disemboweled God-talk from its storied world. But there is a further problem.

The Enlightenment attempt to treat the Bible in a history-of-ideas kind of way—looking for sources of ideas and then tracing their development (e.g., the concept of Satan is said to come from the intellectual attempt to explain where evil came from, if God is all powerful and all good)—needs to be seen as an attempt to foist a way of thinking, which the biblical text does not very readily submit or yield to.

Even before the Enlightenment, the attempt to read the New Testament through the lens of Greek, and particularly Platonic, philosophy led to a skewing of a good deal of the material, and a misuse of the data (e.g., the attempt to find an impassable God in the Bible, or to find the Greek notion of the soul). The Bible was not written by Greek philosophers, much less by later Christian ones ranging from Augustine to Aquinas to Pascal. It has long been time to change the paradigm when it comes to thinking theologically about the New Testament, and part of this change requires that we recognize the serious flaws in the paradigms we have inherited from the postbiblical era, both ancient and modern. This particular study has focused on the flaws in three forms of Protestant theology known as Evangelical theology.

The Bible was written entirely, or almost entirely, by Jews (the author of Luke–Acts may have been a Gentile, but if so, he was a Gentile who had had close contact with the synagogue and knew the Septuagint). Jews told and then wrote down stories; spoke in sapiential ways using poetry, proverbs, aphorisms, riddles, and parables; and were given to prophetic and apocalyptic oracles. Nothing they wrote, at least of the materials that made the canon of Scripture, reads like a lab manual or a philosophical textbook or a scientific treatise. In other words, the sort of speech we find today in the arts rather than in the sciences is far closer to the kind of discourse that early Jews used when they did their God-talk. The good news is that most postmoderns these days are more attuned to hearing and heeding this sort of more right-brained discourse.

I would suggest that the new paradigm for doing theology involves recognizing the following points: (1) theologizing was done by the biblical writers out of a storied world, and into specific situations, using a variety of literary types, as mentioned above; (2) the storied world sometimes lies on the surface of the discourse (e.g., in parables), but sometimes it lies beneath the surface and is only alluded to or partially quoted (e.g., in Paul's letters); (3) what we would call concepts or abstract ideas are configured in the storied world, not in some other sort of reasoning. By this I mean, for example, that when Paul thinks of sin, he thinks of the story of Adam; when he thinks of Law, he thinks of the story of Moses; when he thinks of faith, he thinks of the story of Abraham, and so on. Even Paul's letters are not compendiums of abstract ideas, laid out in syllogisms. This leads to the paradigm: symbolic universe of ideas configured in stories, with the stories then becoming the fodder and framework for theologizing into specific situations. It will be useful at this juncture to give some NT core samples of what I am referring to, and then draw some conclusions.

JESUS THE SAGE AND STORYTELLER

Everyone seems to love Jesus' parables, but unfortunately all too few of us have learned how to properly use them. They are not and were not early examples of sermon illustrations. Rather, they were themselves, whether short or long, the public preaching tools of Jesus. Like much sapiential or Wisdom literature, they were intended to be imagaic and a bit complex, and they were meant to tease the mind into active thought. Jesus did not believe in the philosophy so often heard today about keeping things at a lowest-common-denominator, dumbed-down, simple level. He believed in appealing to the imagination and teasing even the dullest of minds into active thought. His modus operandi was to boil up the people and engage them in lively discourse, not water down the gospel. He accomplished this by using parables.

But lest we think parables are self-contained, stand-alone units that we can then abstract from their historical matrix and use however we please, it needs to be seen that Jesus operated in a specific context where parables were not unusual, and people picked up the genre signals and could understand the sort of contextualizing Jesus was doing. Take, for example, the all too famous parable of the Good Samaritan found in Luke 10. This parable is, in fact, an example of a powerful social critique, because the antipathy between Jews and Samaritans was considerable in Jesus' day. Samaritans were viewed as half-breeds, heretics, outcasts, and the like, and Jews were counseled to avoid them and their country. Jesus' fellow Galileans, when they went on pilgrimage to Jerusalem, regularly crossed the Jordan and skirted Samaria, so that they would not become ritually unclean on the way to Jerusalem. Jesus, by contrast (see John 4), chose to go right through Samaria and reach out to Samaritans.

This particular parable gains force when one realizes: (1) the Samaritan is operating in hostile territory, namely Judea; (2) the lawyer who asked Jesus about neighbors would have identified with the priests and Levites, for whom experts in the Law regularly worked; (3) the priest and Levite probably would have seen the man left for dead on the side of the road as potentially a source of uncleanness, and contracting corpus uncleanness would have meant they could not go to work for a week. They are thus likely being portrayed in a self-serving mode, when they pass by on the other side of the road; and (4) the man lying on the side of the road was surely a Jew, and so it was not the Samaritan but the priest and the Levite who primarily had a duty of neighborliness to him.

In addition, we may note that Jesus really skewers the lawyer by telling him to go act like the Samaritan. Jesus was seeking to break down social barriers, as part of the divine saving activity known as the kingdom or dominion of God that he was inaugurating. He refused to address the limiting question, "Who is my neighbor," which has as its subtext, "Who do I not need to treat as neighbor?" Instead he provided an example of how we are to be neighbors to one and all. Note that the term *good samaritan* would have been seen as an oxymoron in first-century Judea, unlike the way we use the phrase today.

What we should learn from the above is that even though these parables are somewhat self-contained stories, they cannot be properly used without understanding their original context. The context of origin must be allowed to condition how we read them, and thus how we use and contextualize these parables today. In other words, in our biblically illiterate culture, we must ourselves do our homework to make sure we are not misusing these stories. They were never intended as tools intent on teaching general ethical maxims. They are stories about what happens when God's saving activity breaks into our midst.

One more example from the parables of Jesus must suffice. Consider now the parable of the Sower found in Mark 4. This popular parable has sometimes come under scholarly suspicion because it seems too much like a Christian allegory. The different soils represent different people and their levels of receptivity to the gospel, and the Sower is obviously Jesus or his disciples, with the seed being the Word. The truth is, however, that ancient Jewish parables frequently had allegorical elements in them. They did not necessarily seek to make only one point. Indeed they might make several points, though all of Jesus' parables are about the dawning dominion of God.

To understand Mark 4, several things need to be borne in mind. Parables were not intended to be literal descriptions of first-century practices. They were often lifelike, but not literal transcripts of reality. Indeed, it is often the case in Jesus' parables that you can tell when Jesus is making a kingdom point when the story veers off from reality into hyperbole. The yields of grain spoken of at the end of this parable are in fact astronomical, and the point is not verisimilitude, but rather that kingdom work despite many failures can also yield successes out of all proportion to the work done on producing the crop.

In other words, the outcome has to do with God's lavish grace, not merely human effort. What is especially interesting and telling about this story is that if indeed it is a comment by Jesus on his own ministry, it speaks of many failures, but also some outstanding successes. The Word often fell on either deaf ears, or into the lives of distracted persons, or into the lives of persons only partially willing to allow the kingdom message to take root within them.

At the same time, Jesus does realistically speak of certain kinds of agricultural practices of his day. We must think of a tenant farmer who is trying so desperately to produce a crop that he is using every inch of soil at his disposal, whatever its caliber or character. The Word should be spread abroad profligately, without picking in advance a target audience! Notice that what makes the difference between acceptance and rejection of the Word is the soil it lodges in. The Sower, the Word, the nurture of sun and rain are the same in all cases, but it is the difference in the soil that makes the difference in receptivity. This is hardly a predestinarian parable. The soil decides the issue, not the Sower.

What do we learn from these wonderful stories? We learn that context matters, and we also learn that there is a complexity rather than opacity to these stories. They have a variety of points, and they require of us a variety of sensitivities if we are to understand them and properly apply the truths they convey.

One more thing. It is not enough to tell or retell the story. Notice how at the end of both of these parables, Jesus seeks to apply or explain them. Telling the story is not enough. Placing one's audience within the story requires more than that. In regard to the one who wishes to sow these parables today, a detailed knowledge of both the ancient and modern horizons or contexts is needed.[2]

PAUL THE RHETORICIAN AND HIS STORIED WORLD

We have already alluded to the fact that Paul thinks out of biblical stories and into his church situations. The failure to recognize this truth has led to all sorts of misinterpretations of Paul's letters, including the most used and abused of all those letters: Romans. My concern here is to point out that this letter is a word on target for Paul's audience in Rome in the late 50s and is not a compendium of Paul's greatest theological and ethical hits. Notice that such important Pauline topics as resurrection or the Lord's Supper hardly come up for discussion in Romans. Romans must not be seen as an introduction to Pauline theology. It will be useful at this juncture to demonstrate how Paul's rhetoric and storied world affects what he is saying, and how we need to know those things if we are to make sense of his discourse.

Consider, for example, the comparison of the first and last Adams in Romans 5:12-21. Here Paul's storied world comes to the surface of the discourse, and as we have already pointed out, when Paul thinks about sin, he thinks of the story of Adam. He does not think of sin in an abstract way, but rather in a personal way, especially when the issue is where sin came from. In this lively comparison and contrast between Jesus and Adam, Paul assumes that both are progenitors of a whole race of people, and as progenitors they affect all those who are in them. In Paul's storied world you are either in Adam or in Christ, but you cannot be in both at once.

It is in part because of the failure to pick up the narrative signals that there has been so much confusion when it comes to interpreting Romans 7:7-13 and 7:14-25. Part of the confusion comes from failing to realize that the story of Adam and Christ is still in play in Romans 7, and presupposed, and the rest of the confusion comes from lack of recognition of rhetorical signals. Paul is using in this chapter the rhetorical device known as speech in character.

Revisiting what we have said in an earlier chapter, Romans 7:7-13 is the story of Adam retold, and Romans 7:14-25 is the story of all those who are "in Adam" and outside of Christ. In other words, Christian psychologists need to stop reading Romans 7 as if it were a transcript telling us about the psychological dilemmas of Christians caught between a rock and a hard place.[3] On the contrary, here we have a discussion of those lost in the bondage of sin and outside of Christ. If one wants to hear the story about the tensions in the Christian life and the issue of sin for the Christian, one must look elsewhere—Galatians 5 for example. In Romans 7 the use of "I" is a typical rhetorical device to make the story come to life, and make vivid the points Paul is making. The "I" is not Paul, but rather Adam in the first passage and those "in Adam" in 7:14-25.

Notice several contextual factors that are crucial for understanding Romans 7:

(1)   Romans 7:5-6 and Romans 8:1–2 say as clearly as one could imagine that Christians are no longer in the flesh, no longer subject to the bondage of the rule of sin and death in their lives. On the contrary, they have been set free by the Spirit ruling in their lives. Believers are dead to that which once held them captive.

(2)   Notice how the "I" in Romans 7:7–13 was once alive apart from and before the Law. But in Paul's storied world this only describes one person: Adam. Only he existed before any law or commandment was given.

(3)   Notice as well that 7:7–13 only speaks of one commandment that this person is beholden to. Again, this only describes Adam, the man who was given but one commandment.

(4)   Notice the clear connection here between sin and death, in the same way we heard of it in Romans 5:12–21.

(5)   Notice the total absence of reference to the Holy Spirit in both Romans 7:7–13 and 7:14–25. This "I," unlike Paul and other Christians, does not have the Holy Spirit in his life—he can only cry out "who will deliver me from this body of death?"

(6) Romans 7:14–25 has been prepared for earlier in Romans 2–3 where Paul told us that even Gentiles in some fashion had the law of God written on their hearts or minds. Thus, 7:14–25 need not be about Jews specifically who have the Law in their minds, but it could be either Jew or Gentile or both; but in any case it is those who are outside of Christ.

(7) Thinking narratively about Romans 7–8 and noticing the progression of the discourse, it is logical to conclude that in Romans 7:14–25 we have a vivid description of someone outside of Christ—but at the point of conviction and conversion—crying out for deliverance. This person realizes that he must do better, knows something of what God requires, but is unable to do it. Romans 7:25a and then Romans 8:1ff. provide the panacea and the answer the lost person requires: it can be found in Jesus Christ. Unfortunately, we have too often read this narrative anachronistically in light of the much later anguished narratives of Augustine and Luther, which has led to a distortion in our understanding of who Paul is describing.

Herein lies a further lesson. It is not enough to read the text narratologically; it all depends on whose story you are reading in or into this text. The answer needs to be plausible in terms of the storied world of Paul, and texts like Philippians 3:6 make perfectly clear that Romans 7 cannot be said to be a personal transcript of Paul's own Jewish or Christian experience. No, Paul is speaking more generically of all those who are in Adam and outside of Christ, crying out for redemption. We must not merely recognize a story, but recognize whose story it is, before we start preaching and teaching texts like this one.

THE APOCALYPTIC IMAGINATION OF JOHN

In this discussion I have deliberately chosen three very different sorts of texts, reflecting three different genres of literature: parable, rhetorical discourse in a letter, and apocalyptic prophecy. I have chosen three different genres to help make the point that story is fundamental to and undergirds them all. Story is the constant in the theologizing of these different NT figures. Here I must turn to the apocalypse to give one further example.

It is, of course, true that most readers of Revelation, at least intuitively, realize that this material, while it must be taken seriously, nevertheless cannot be taken literally. John is not really envisioning multiheaded beasts roaming the earth. These are ciphers and symbols for all too human, and in other cases, divine beings. Yet even this portion of Scripture has sometimes been wrongly read literally. What is interesting about Revelation is that it alludes to all kinds of stories both biblical and extrabiblical (including ancient combat myths), and yet it seldom quotes the OT. It has more echoes and allusions to the OT than any other book, and yet has almost no quotes from the OT. What are we to make of this?

Our author must assume his audience already knows the stories of Adam and Elijah and Moses and the exodus and many others, so that he feels free to draw on them tangentially and reconfigure them in his telling of what "was, and is, and is to come," focusing the story in light of the Christ story and the story of his converts, partially retold in Revelation 2–3. Story functions in Revelation as both subtext and text, being behind and also part of the ongoing narrative told in Revelation 6–22. This brings up the very good point that the NT writers and speakers all tend to reconfigure their OT stories in light of more recent developments, in particular developments that involve Jesus and the dominion. What is even more interesting is that apocalyptic prophecy becomes the vehicle allowing for the telling of the future story of God's people. John does not just serve up enigmatic oracles about the future; he serves up oracles that tell a tale about the future.[4]

What is also seldom realized about apocalyptic prophecy is that it is often deliberately multivalent: Mr. 666 is Nero, Domitian, or any megalomaniac ruler who is lusting after worship and world domination. The beast in the first place was the Roman Empire, but it could be any evil empire. When it comes to the future, God reveals enough about its character so that we may have hope, but not so much about its details, lest we no longer feel the need to exercise faith.

Just because these prophecies are referential does not mean one is meant to pin them down to one set of referents. That is hardly how apocalyptic works. It deliberately uses generic and universal symbols when speaking of the future. It is crucial, then, neither to dismiss these stories as fractured fairy tales, nor to try and pin them down to one late-twentieth- or early-twenty-first-century set of referents. Indeed, I would stress that John was speaking in the first instance to his own century and people, who certainly had no knowledge of or interest in figures that would only arise two-thousand years later. No, Revelation is a word on target for the seven churches in Asia at the end of the first century A.D. precisely because the battle between good and evil transpires in every generation, and often takes similar forms along the way. The devil, as it turns out, is not very original and creative, and so he keeps playing out his tale and spinning his stories the same way over and over again. Not so the biblical authors, who are endlessly creative.

To make our point clearer, consider for a minute Revelation 12. The woman clothed with the sun can be seen to be both Mother Zion (i.e., the OT people of God configured as a woman) and Mother Mary, who gives birth to a male child destined to rule the nations. Satan (aka old dragon-breath) seeks to destroy the mother and child, unsuccessfully, and indeed, so unsuccessfully that the child ends up sitting on a throne in heaven, and Satan ends up cast out of that selfsame heavenly realm. Unable to kill the child prodigy savior figure, he turns his wrath on the woman, who meanwhile had fled into the wilderness. While Satan seeks to flood her out, she is protected there in the wilderness. Now wilderness is certainly not an image of heaven. It is rather an image of a lost earth, no longer in harmony with its original creation design. Not for John the theology of rapture, or "Beam me up, Scotty." No, the people of God will be protected from Satan's wrath on earth, not by escaping to heaven. Unable to destroy the woman, even while she is on earth, Satan stomps off in a huff to attack her children.

Here is a cautionary tale meant to warn the converts in Asia that they are under attack from the powers of darkness, but that God will not allow the gates of Hades to prevail against the church. The church will endure and prevail. While this is a Christian story, it is a story that draws on both OT imagery (notice the rainbow from the Noah story) and ancient combat myths. Here it is the angel Michael who does battle with Satan and casts him to earth.

A warning to interpreters of Revelation: If you do not know and understand the underlying and undergirding stories here, you will misread the plot and the way John uses these stories. In other words, doing theology in a narratological way even in a postmodern setting does not give us permission to ignore the historical contexts of our NT stories. There are both good and bad ways to retell these NT stories, and in this regard good and bad theologizing happens when we do so. Even though it is story, it is important to get the story straight. But where does all this storytelling lead us? Shall we just lie down and sleep contently, having heard a good bedtime tale? Or is there a strategy we could pursue in a postmodern situation? We address this question in our next chapter.

CHAPTER 12

And So?

In the last chapter we took a short odyssey through the storied world of the NT, in order to help us to begin to rethink what we mean by theology and theologizing. I am saying it has everything to do with story and storytelling, and that we need to get beyond both ancient and modern ways of handling the text that strip away the story, leaving a mass of quivering ideas and concepts that we then are free to rearrange in any order that pleases us. That may be an intellectually satisfying exercise for some, but in fact it turns out to be a way of neutralizing the story, and not allowing it to have its effect on us. It is in fact a power trip, an attempt to take control over these stories before they fully take hold of us. If that is what thinking theologically and doing theology amounts to, we need a moratorium on thinking and doing theology.

In fact, however, I would call us not to a sabbatical from theology but rather to do our theologizing in the very same manner as Jesus and the biblical authors—using story and, of course, especially the story of Jesus. I would offer the encouragement that our postmodern situation gives us a new opportunity to re-present the story in vivid new ways.

Whatever we may have thought about the flaws in Mel Gibson's movie *The Passion of the Christ*, and there were plenty, it was a compelling presentation. The emotional power of its dramatizing of the story carried the day for many in the audience, leaving some numb and others deeply moved. My point is simply that in the postmodern age where visual symbol and sign, and story and narrative are poignant and pregnant and speak volumes, we would be foolish indeed not to use them in an age of visual learners to tell and retell the old, old story. In fact, Jesus and his followers will rise up and call us blessed if we do so, for by creatively retelling the story as a way of doing theology, we will be following in the sacred footsteps of our inspired forebears.

OUT OF THE STORY AND INTO MANY WORLDS

The theologizing which is done in the NT is done out of various paradigmatic stories, but it is done into a variety of contexts or subcultural worlds. This theologizing is very much ad hoc in character, by which I mean it is intended to be words on target for various first-century audiences. The theological strategy and method Paul follows with the Corinthians differs somewhat from the rhetorical strategy he pursues with the Romans. The way Jesus addresses his disciples deliberately differs from the way he speaks to crowds or the Pharisees. One needs to consider not only the source of the theologizing but also the target audience being addressed. The theological ideas are the link between the storied world of the author and the worlds of the audience.

Of course, it is true that many of the same concepts are found in a variety of NT books, not least in the area of Christology where Son of God, Son of Man, and Lord ideas are found in many layers of the tradition and in numerous different texts. However, it is no accident that we hear so much in 1 Corinthians about resurrection and so much in Romans about the future of Israel. The theologizing is tailored to the situation of the audience being addressed. This is not just true of the letters of the NT but also of the other texts in the canon.

It is therefore important to consider the theological strategies and the kind of theological rhetoric being used in these different situations addressing differing audiences, if we are to take the measure of what is going on in these texts. Let us consider an example. Paul in 1 Corinthians, as in 1 Thessalonians, is writing to a largely Gentile audience, whose perceptions of and beliefs about the afterlife were shaped by pagan ideas most of their lives. In order to understand why Paul says what he does in 1 Corinthians 15 about proxy baptism for the dead, and why the Corinthians were resorting to such a practice, and the reason he goes to such lengths to reassure the Thessalonians about their deceased fellow Christians, one needs to understand something about pagan views of the fate of the dead.

HAVE A NICE AFTERLIFE

Gentiles who had not been exposed to Judaism before they became followers of Jesus would have found the whole idea of resurrection more than a little strange. It would have sounded more like the idea of standing up of corpses than some positive form of afterlife, more like *Night of the Living Dead* than the blessed hope. They were used to the Greek notion of the immortality of the soul, but that did not include with it the notion of a person coming back from the dead in new and improved flesh, or at least not normally.[1] What then would have been the concerns of the Corinthian or Thessalonian Christians about their deceased brothers and sisters in Christ? Was it just a concern about them being left behind or left out when Christ returned?

Greco-Roman peoples of various sorts did believe that the person survived death and went into the underworld (see Plato, *Gorg.* 52D). Coins would be placed on the eyes to pay the boatman Charon to carry the person down and across the river Styx, avoiding the obstacles along the way (e.g., Cerberus the dog, who guarded the gate into the underworld). There were stories such as the myth of Adonis, in which the child Adonis was so beautiful that Aphrodite hid him in a coffin and gave him to Persephone, the queen of the underworld. Aphrodite later wanted him back, and Zeus was lobbied and agreed to strike a deal whereby Adonis, would spend one-third of the year with Persephone, one-third with Aphrodite, and one-third to himself. Adonis chose to add his third to Persephone's, and so she could spend two-thirds of the year on Olympus and one-third in the underworld. While this story, unlike the story of Persephone, does not seem to be about the crop cycle, it is also not about what happens to normal human beings in the afterlife. As R. Bauckham also notes: "The festival in July at which Adonis' death was mourned by women seems to have played no particular emphasis on his return from the underworld."[2]

We may leave out of account the stories of visions of the otherworld and the afterlife, because they do not involve an actual death, nor do the stories of shamans who in some ecstatic state, after a ceremony of ritual death and rebirth, have their souls freed to journey to the underworld. The shaman characteristically goes on this journey to serve as a sort of shepherd or guide of an actually deceased person's soul, or, in the case of the story of Orpheus, to rescue a deceased soul who is desperately missed (in this case, the soul of Orpheus's wife).[3] What this story does show is the degree of sorrow and anxiety often expressed in the pagan world over the loss of a mate or another family member, something we can also readily see in the many many grave inscriptions found in *Inscriptiones Graecae*, and the depictions of sorrow in the grave art of the Greco-Roman world.[4] If Paul had read any of these inscriptions or seen any of the tomb art, it is no surprise that he might speak of pagans as being those without a viable future hope.

Various other phenomena in the Greco-Roman world, however, attest to another side of what pagans believed about the afterlife. There was, for instance, the attempts to obtain advice from the dead. We have the famous story of Odysseus going to Hades (Book 11) to consult the dead seer Teiresias, a story later revised by Virgil, who tells of Aeneas going to Hades to get advice from his father Anchises, who just happens to prophesy the future history of Rome (*Aen.* 6). These stories bear a certain resemblance to 1 Samuel 28:6–25, although that story is about necromancy, not about journeys to Hades. What such stories share in common is that the Hebrew concept of Sheol seems no more positive than the Greek notion of Hades. There was of course the White Isles or Elysium, but that was for the "few, the proud, the brave." These were the happy dead referred to by Pindar and Plato (cf. *Phaed.* 112A– 114C). As Bauckham points out, the function of all the stories of special journeys to Hades by illustrious figures was to give information about the fate of the dead, presumably because there was no little concern about what had happened to them in the afterlife.[5]

On the other hand there were the pagan parties held at the tomb on the birthdays of the deceased, complete with pouring tube to pour some wine into the tomb in hopes the deceased could also participate in the celebration (see *Corpus Inscriptiones Latinae* 6.26554).[6] The spirits of the dead were sometimes thought to stay in a sort of semi-existence near or in the tombs.[7] This practice is probably what Justin Martyr is referring to in his second-century apology when he writes of pagan magic at tombs, including the calling forth of spirits of one's deceased ancestors (*1 Apol.* 18). From a Roman point of view, of course, there was also the belief in the *genius*—the spirit of the *paterfamilias* who might be prayed to or consulted, or was believed able to inspire one and guide one to do the right thing. The Roman home shrines with death masks reflect this sort of belief structure, but this tells us nothing about whether the afterlife is viewed as pleasant for the deceased.

S. Dill rightly stresses: "No small part of old Roman piety consisted in a scrupulous reverence for the dead, and a care to prolong their memory by solid memorial and solemn ritual, it might be to maintain some faint tie of sympathy with the shade which had passed into a dim and rather cheerless world. The conception of that other state was always vague, and *often purely negative*. It is not often that a spirit is sped on its way to join a loved one in the Elysian fields, and we may fear that such phrases, when they do occur, are rather literary and conventional."[8] This sort of conclusion seems to be borne out by the famous inscription, "I was not, I am not, I care not,"[9] which in fact seems to suggest annihilation awaits us all.

On the whole the conclusion of Bauckham seems warranted:

> The old Homeric view was that the existence of the dead is undifferentiated: all share the same joyless gloom. The exceptions—on the one hand, Tantalus, Tityos, Sisyphus, who are punished eternally for their crimes against the gods, and on the other hand, a very few heroes of divine descent, like Menelaus, who are exempted from the common lot and dwell in the bliss of Elysium—are exceptions that prove the rule. But the descent into Hades [stories], so far as we can tell, reflected and encouraged a growing belief in retribution after death. The damned, who may

be regarded either as those guilty of heinous crimes or as those who have not been initiated in the mysteries, suffer punishments, while the blessed enjoy themselves in a sunlit paradise.[10]

The function of the mystery rites, particularly the Eleusinian ones, seems to have been to assure the person of a tolerable or even blessed afterlife, one that missed the punishments. The idea that there were such punishments for the wicked no doubt also increased the concern about the fate of the dead. Theocritus ably sums up the prevailing pagan attitude about death and the afterlife: "Hopes are for the living, but the ones who die are without hope" (*Id.* 4.42). Catullus (5.4–6) is equally succinct: "The sun can set and rise again / But once our brief light sets/ There is one unending night to be slept through" (cf. Homer, *Il.* 11.241). Lastly in the papyri (P. Oxy. 115, second century A.D.), we read, "I sorrowed and wept over your dear departed one as I wept over Didymus . . . but really, there is nothing one can do in the face of such things. So please comfort each other." This expression is typical, as was the elaborate and often lengthy period of mourning, the hiring of professional mourners to play sad music and weep at the grave (I call them "town criers"), and the like in both the more Semitic and the more Greco-Roman parts of the Empire.[11] It is striking that while in pagan literature there is the bemoaning of the fact that even the crops rise again and renew themselves, as seemingly also the sun did, but not humans who simply die (and so nature mocks humans with its resiliency), by the time Christians begin to use these nature analogies about dying and rising (see 1 Cor 15:35–44; Clement of Rome, para. 20), they are used in a positive way, as pointing forward to the greater glory of resurrection.[12]

It may be added as well that since there was a variety of opinions about the afterlife in early Judaism—that if, as is probable, a few of Paul's converts in Corinth or Thessalonike were exposed to Jewish beliefs about the afterlife in the synagogue service—one would still have to posit that Pharisaic beliefs must have been present for there to have been a meaningful point of contact with what Paul is saying here (cf. the confusion in Corinth indicated in 1 Cor 15 where some were actually saying "there is no resurrection of the dead"). More likely the vast majority of Corinthian and Thessalonian converts heard about these ideas first from Paul and his coworkers, and now Paul is further clarifying matters for them in this part of the "exhortation."

In this sort of largely pagan environment, it is understandable that Paul as a pastor would take some pains to counter inconsolable grief and reassure his converts that, for Christians, the afterlife would be a positive one—indeed, it would be like a large family reunion and would involve a form of life not less, but rather more vital and alive than the one they were currently experiencing. The spirit of the Christian belief, as opposed to the pagan belief, about the afterlife is aptly expressed by Chrysostom: "If then you seek [the deceased Christian], seek him where the King is, where the army of angels is; not in the grave, not in the earth" (*Hom. 2 Cor. 1:6*).

It is not necessary then to posit that Paul had failed to teach his converts about the afterlife—when he was present with them—because he assumed the parousia was so imminent that such teaching was superfluous. His teaching on the unknown timing of a thief breaking in during the night makes that suggestion highly improbable. More likely is the suggestion that we need to bear in mind both Paul's premature exit from Thessalonike, forestalling the adequate teaching he would have liked to have done while he was there, and also the fact that some Thessalonians had unexpectedly and suddenly lost their lives after Paul left, raising questions about the afterlife.[13]

In Corinth, on the other hand, Paul must respond to a report that some Corinthians were actually saying, "there is no resurrection of the dead." Notice that Paul does not need to reassure the Thessalonian audience that the parousia is coming. They already know about times and seasons of such an event (i.e., that it is unpredictable). What he does need to do is offer further teaching about that event, and first-time teaching about the fate of the dead as well, and more particularly he needs to show the connection between the fate of the dead in Christ, the resurrection of those dead, and the return of Jesus.[14]

In 1 Corinthians Paul must focus more clearly on the nature and fact of the future resurrection of believers, as well as the importance of the past resurrection of Jesus. In other words, what Paul chooses to say in these two letters—talking about basically the same subject matter, resurrection of believers and the return of Christ—differs in the two letters because of the differing situations and concerns he must address. Though both of the audiences are overwhelmingly Gentile, and so both need a short course in resurrection and parousia theology, the Thessalonians had actually lost loved ones due to persecution, whereas the Corinthian concern seems to have been about deceased non-Christians as well as Christians. There was likely concern that without the ritual of baptism some of the deceased might not be saved. This is hardly surprising when it was precisely through the pagan mystery rituals that a positive afterlife was assured.

What should we conclude from all this? That Paul tailors what he says to the situation and what he knows about the character and knowledge of the audience. He is not writing theological treatises: he is dealing with social and theological problems as a pastor should and would. Knowledge of the Gentile world illuminates the text and helps us to understand the strategies and goals of Paul in this situation. If one asks why we do not find Paul doing theology by means of telling Jewish parables like those of Jesus, it has everything to do with Paul's audience, not the limitations of his theological lexicon and literary abilities. But there is one more component to the new approach to the theologizing of the NT authors I am advocating. It has to do with what we do with the material once we have recognized the storied world from which the theologizing is done, and the contextualizing of the material so that it becomes a word on target.

CALLING ALL ARMCHAIR THEOLOGIANS

It is time, indeed it is well past time, to recognize that "theology" is what *we* do to and with the text. By this, I mean that the comparing of texts, synthesizing of concepts, drawing of analogies, dividing material into topics, analyzing them according to Calvinistic or Dispensational or Arminian categories and predilections, and declaring one or another idea or concept as more important and others as less important are all activities we do to the text. Of course, there are theological ideas in the NT. But what we do not have is Jesus' *Institutes*, or Paul's *Institutes*, or John's *Institutes*. Their material is not arranged according to modern ways of framing theological discussions, nor do they address all the topics we might find helpful or interesting. Theology is only one part of what these authors are interested in. There is also the small matter of what we call ethics, which really cannot be radically separated from the theologizing since the imperatives are built upon and presuppose the indicative statements. Indeed, they are the practical implications of the theological remarks insofar as they affect how Christians are to live.

So, in part, this section of our discussion is a call to realize that we are active readers of these texts, that we bring our own training and education and biases with us when we read them, and frequently we are guilty of anachronism, of reading things into the text, especially when we start trying to systematize and order the theological content we find in these documents. I am not suggesting that we should not try, for example, to figure out what Lukan theology or Pauline theology is all about, which requires comparison and synthesis. I am simply saying that we need to do it with more critical awareness and self-awareness.

But before you decide that you are capable of doing theological work on the New Testament, let me first suggest there are several prerequisites to attempting such a task. These are my equivalent to the Ninety-five Theses of Luther, only these are limited to a desideratum list when it comes to doing NT theology:

(1) You need to be able to read the text in its original language, since every translation is already an interpretation.

(2) You need to have studied the text in its original contexts (literary, historical, archaeological, theological, rhetorical). If you are not a scholar, then you must be able to do the hard work of reading commentaries and gaining some critical acumen so you can sift the material.

(3) If you are an Evangelical, then it is imperative that you interact with non-Evangelical treatments of the text, and also listen to what was said about the text by church fathers, who studied it in the original Greek before the time of Augustine and the Latinizing of the church. In other words, you need to get out of your own bubble and comfort zone and allow yourself to be challenged by the text and by others.

(4) As J. Bengel says, you need to apply the whole of yourself to the text. This cannot be a part-time or pastime kind of thing. The theologizing that goes on in the NT is complex and multifaceted. It takes one's full attention, and it takes a long period of study to grasp the height, depth, and breadth of the theological material in the NT.

(5) The text needs to not be watered down or dumbed down. Rather, one needs to ratchet up one's attention level and degree of devotion to the text, not to mention one's attention to detail.

6) New Testament theology, like translating the Bible, should be done in a community context. By this, I mean it should be done in close consultation with others working in the field, exchanging ideas and critiquing one another's work. It should not be done in isolation, lest the results be idiosyncratic or just plain quirky. The new is not necessarily the true, and the latest is not necessarily the greatest, despite our culture's predilections. Theology should be done in the context of the living Body of Christ.[15] It also should be done by a person who is open and listening to the guidance of the Holy Spirit. In other words, it should not be a mere intellectual exercise. It should be prayed over and guided by God.

(7) Western theologians who live in an individualist society that does not understand a collectivist biblical culture, much less an honor-and-shame one, need to do NT theology with the help of those in two-thirds of the world who do live in such cultures.

(8) The theologizing in the NT is theology written to and for a minority, often an oppressed one. We must listen to those sorts of voices, the voices of the least, last, and lost, to understand what theologizing by and for the poor, the hungry, and

the disenfranchised really looks like. Then perhaps we can avoid the tendency to spiritualize so many things that actually have to do with taking care of those less fortunate than ourselves. Similarly, the world is still largely a patriarchal place, as was the biblical world, and so we need to listen to the voices of all sorts of Christian women, learning how they read the text and do theology. Doing NT theology needs to no longer be an almost exclusively male activity.

(9) Biblical theology, and in this case NT theology, needs to be the basis not only of popular Evangelical theology, but also of systematic theology. In other words, systematic theology needs to never be done in isolation from deep exegetical treatments of the Bible. It needs to never be done simply by being in dialogue with other systematicians or theologians. It is the Bible, not Karl Barth or any other profound theologian, that needs to be the basis of systematic theology, and if the Bible is silent on some issue and there are no general ideas or principles from which one can extrapolate something, then one needs to resist the tendency to invent such material and then systematize it.

(10) This theologizing needs to be done across denominational and theological lines. In fact, perhaps it is time to recognize that denominations are a result of Protestant differing and bickering. They are children of the Protestant Reformation. They are also the result of profoundly weak ecclesiology on our part, and they reflect and are based upon the biblically weakest aspects of our theology—namely our distinctives, as this study has repeatedly pointed out.

(11) Above all, this enterprise of discovering and doing NT theology requires humility, not hubris. It requires a willingness to say "I don't know how to hold these things in tension," a willingness to resist the Evangelical lust for certainty, a willingness to embrace the mystery and be willing to accept some paradoxes.

(12) Perhaps, too, it is time for us to redraw the boundaries, and not just continue to nurture and appreciate our differences, theologically speaking. The world is laughing at us because our witness is so divided and we speak with forked tongues. Perhaps all Evangelicals need to spend more time sitting at the same table, sharing communion, serving one another, serving together in missions, listening to one another, loving one another, and leaving behind triumphalism based on our ecclesiological and theological differences.

If what divides us shapes us *more* individually than what theologically unites us as Evangelicals, something is wrong with this picture. Perhaps it is time to start over, and as Paul said, "to know nothing amongst ourselves but Christ and him crucified," and of course the Bible as the Word of God. On these central matters we ought to be able to agree. Indeed, on these sorts of central matters the salvation of the world hangs, and since we believe it is a lost world, we need to get on with sharing both the Word Incarnate and the Word written. We need to stop creating churches that essentially serve ourselves and nurture our own way and style of living, and do missions only as a bonus. We need to offer the world Christ once more, the real Christ of the NT. But this implies that we in turn know him in a profound way, have studied the Word deeply, have encountered the Word personally, have embraced the Word passionately.

CODA

Rebirth of Orthodoxy or Return to Fundamentalism?

Like it or not, the parent of modern Evangelicalism was by and large nineteenth and twentieth century Protestant fundamentalism. If we have been paying attention, lately there has been a rise in, and growing influence of, fundamentalism in all three major monotheistic religions in the world, including in America. This is in many ways a reactionary thing, a reaction to the drift of world affairs and the trajectory various cultures seem to be pursuing. It is to a large degree a product of fear rather than faith, because various things have raised the "fear factor" in our and in other cultures, including both terrorism and the war on terrorism. In light of this, I cannot stress enough that we should not be doing theology in reaction to anything and should not be reading the NT through the lens of fear rather than faith. The Left Behind syndrome should be left behind. We should be proactive, and deal with the positive substance of our vibrant Christian faith.

The vision and plan I am lifting up calls us to go forward not backward. There is a revision of an old hymn that goes like this—"like a mighty turtle / moves the church of God / brothers we are treading / where we've always trod / not united brethren / not one body we / we shall all be standing here until eternity / backward Christian soldiers / marching as to war. . . ." It will not be enough in the twenty-first century either to stand still and watch the world pass us by, or in reaction to the world go backwards into the benighted condition of fundamentalism, which reflects the closing of the American mind, not its enlightenment. It is no good praying fervently that next year will be 1955 all over again. It is not going to happen. Those who do theology while constantly looking longingly into the rearview mirror are going to crash sooner or later.

Again I say, we need to do our theologizing out of faith not fear. We have not been helped by the fundamentalist takeover of some of our major schools and seminaries, nor by the media attention given to fundamentalist televangelists, which makes most of us look like people who have zeal without knowledge, even of the Bible. This has not helped the progress of orthodoxy amongst Evangelicals. Let me tell you a story to illustrate what I do and do not have in mind.

In 1969, a friend of mine from High Point, N.C. and I were driving on the Blue Ridge parkway in the mountains of N.C. I had borrowed my father's 1955 Chevy Bel-Air, two tone, column shift. We were having a great time until the clutch blew out and as the Bible says, "my countenance fell." I knew there were no gas stations on the parkway, so we managed to push it down a ramp off the parkway and into a Texaco station. The mechanic there was clueless, and so we decided we needed to hitchhike home to the middle of the state. The very first people who picked us up were an elderly mountain couple who were "Flat-landers." We learned this when we began to talk about the recent landing on the moon by Neil Armstrong, and how his craft had also circled the earth. The man who was driving rejoined that this was all malarkey and a TV stunt. Everyone knew that the world was not round. Dumbfounded by this, and prone to be argumentative (he is now a lawyer), my friend did not recognize invincible ignorance when he saw it. So while I was telling him to hush he kept pressing the issue of why the man thought the world was not round. Finally the man said: "It says in the book of Revelations that the angels will stand on the four corners of the earth. The world couldn't have four corners if it was round. Thus, the world is not round because the Bible says so."

Now of course we should be wary of anyone who begins a sentence with "it says in the book of Revelations": this is not in fact the name of the last book of the Bible—it is Revelation singular. But more to the point, what was the man's main error? The problem was *not* that the man wanted to take the Bible seriously, but that he was attempting to take metaphorical and poetic apocalyptic prophecy literally. But John of Patmos was not trying to teach cosmology in that verse, he was just saying that God's messengers would go to or come from all points on the compass, from all directions. The language is certainly referential, but it is not meant to be interpreted literally. Notice how Nicodemus in John 3 takes Jesus' words literally about being "born again" and this leads to misunderstanding, rather than understanding. Such is the case with a good deal of Scripture.

Literalism, and a return to literalism when the intention of the biblical author was *not* to speak literally, is a violation of the character of such biblical material, not a faithful adherence to it. In other words, literalism in the service of a truth that is expressed metaphorically or imagaically is an error, a violation of that truth. It turns art into a lifeless artifact. We cannot afford to go back to a day when we ignore the various types or genres of literature in the Bible and interpret them all as if they were newspaper prose.

Nor can we go back to a day when we strive to be consistent in our inconsistencies by being only selectively literal! "Yes, the Ten Commandments do mention something about covetousness and greed, but no, this should not be taken literally if it calls into question our lifestyles of acquisition and conspicuous consumption." Such seems to be the logic of some fundamentalist and Evangelical preachers. Obviously selectivity is the character of every human discourse, but we must not baptize selective literalism and call it good, especially when the Bible quite literally begs us to widen our appreciation and understanding of various kinds of literature.

Nor can we afford the anachronism of reading into the text various modern concerns, and then proclaiming them biblical. I am thinking for example of the attempt to read America foreign policy into the Bible. NT theology has something to say about war and peace matters in a mostly indirect way, but most of us will not be comfortable hearing it. It calls for disciples of Jesus to love their enemies, not engage in retaliation or revenge taking, and there are blessings on peacemakers, not war promoters.

You know something is badly wrong with your NT theology when you oppose Middle East peace plans and efforts because it messes up your eschatological timetable. Didn't Jesus come riding into Jerusalem as the Prince of Peace? Didn't he call us to a gospel of peacemaking, reconciliation, healing, suffering and dying for the cause, not killing for it? Didn't Jesus command his disciples to stop the violence in the Garden of Gethsemane and didn't he heal the ear of the high priest's slave? Aren't we supposed to be imitating the conduct of Jesus and, on their better days, the earliest Christians? These are at least the kinds of questions Evangelicals should be wrestling with, not simply baptizing the policies and values of our culture and calling them good, whether those policies involve war or godless capitalism and hedonism and the like.

When I say we must go forward into a better grasp and embracing of biblical orthodoxy, I am not talking about a renouncing of critical thinking, a ceasing to dialogue with those with whom we disagree, or a repristinizing of various conservative cultural agendas of some Christians, such as the prevention of women from doing ministry. The NT does not endorse any of those sorts of renunciations or retrenchments.

The NT instead calls us to the constant renewal of our minds, and a recommitment to the biblical practices of the early church, which involved men and women working as coworkers in various sorts of ministries, as the examples of Priscilla and Aquila, or Andronicus and Junia and many others listed in Romans 16 (cf. Acts 18) show.[1] In fact, a careful reading of the NT shows that the authors of the NT, including Paul, were busily revising the patriarchal structures of their day within the Christian community with the goal, as Ephesians 5:21 makes clear, of mutual submission of all Christians to each other, without gender limitations.[2] Galatians 3:28 is in the NT, and it tells us that neither race, nor social situation, nor gender should be allowed to determine who we are in Christ. No, we are all one in Christ Jesus.

Biblical orthodoxy requires that we not only read the household codes in their proper contexts, but see the advice in those codes as it was intended, moving in a direction that goes *against* the flow of that male-dominated culture. These Christian codes reflect a Christian overhaul of a preexisting patriarchal system, but of course they have to start with the audience where they are in their existing situation, which involves an extant patriarchal household structure. Paul no more endorses that structure than he endorses slavery, and when the time and timing is right, Paul will make clear to a close friend and convert like Philemon, that to accept Onesimus back as a brother means accepting him *no longer as a slave* (Phlm 16). The same applies to what Paul says about relationships between men and women in Christ. Occasionally the goal of his advice is made clear as in Galatians 3:28 or Ephesians 5:21. There is indeed a radical social agenda in the NT, and even Paul is party to it. If we want to be faithful to the NT, indeed to the whole of it since it is all the inspired Word of God, then we had better get on with infusing grace into the existing fallen structures of our Christian community and families, and turn "to desire and dominate" (the effect of the curse or the fall; see Gen 3:16) back into "to love and to cherish."

But even if such practical NT theology is not your cup of tea, the orthodoxy I am talking about involves a generosity of spirit, a willingness to listen and learn, a willingness to admit that you might be wrong in your interpretation of the NT. This is why I have insisted that NT theology not be done in the isolation of one's private study, but in community, in dialogue with other Evangelicals, and in prayerful communion with God, listening to the guidance of the Holy Spirit.

One must especially be ready to embrace the remarkable literary diversity of the NT, which involves ancient biographies and histories in its first five books, various kinds of letters and homilies, and an apocalypse at the end. One must be prepared to accept that truth can as ably be expressed through a literary fiction like a parable as a historical account, through poetry as through prose, through oracles as through imperatives, through beatitudes, aphorisms, proverbs, and the like as through apodictic statements.

Indeed, when we are dealing with a reality as huge as God, and as profound as the Lord Jesus Christ, poetry is often the language which can best convey the *mysterium tremendum*. As Linda Greg puts it— "God, who thinks about poetry all the time, breathes happily as He repeats to Himself: 'There are fish in the net, lots of fish this time in the net of the heart.'"[3]

Since Evangelicals are at heart evangelistic, perhaps it is time to realize that at least for the sake of evangelism we need to be able to convey the truths once given, in ways that a postmodern audience will not merely understand but even wholeheartedly embrace. We need a rebirth of wonder and a whole new more poetic vocabulary to express NT theology these days, as I have suggested in the immediately preceding section of this book.

Lest someone worry that I am suggesting playing fast and loose with orthodoxy, I would simply say that I am not talking about watering down any of the key points of orthodoxy. The Apostle's Creed needs to be affirmed without fingers being crossed and without a redefinition of what virginal conception and bodily resurrection and the Trinity mean, without denying the second coming or fudging on original sin, and without vitiating the historical substance of the Gospels and Acts and other parts of the NT. I am however saying that we tell the old old story in new and compelling ways. I am saying we listen to new ways of expressing the old and abiding truths.

Part of this is constantly reminding ourselves of the sort of mistakes we have made before such as: 1) selectivism. Choosing our favorite texts, the ones we most naturally resonate with, and basing our theologizing on them; 2) filling in the gaps in the text with unbiblical ideas, and even making some of these ideas the hermeneutical keys to interpreting the whole Bible; 3) connecting the dots of individual NT ideas in eccentric ways. We may all be connecting dots on the same theological picture, but we connect them differently, and too often we do it in isolation from one another. In other words we need to look at each other's drawings, and ask not only "what's wrong with this picture" (meaning the other person's) but also "what's wrong with my picture." Theologizing should be a collegial, communal activity, not shots fired in anger or anxiety from our own private citadels. Perhaps most importantly we must recognize 4) that it is so often in our distinctives that we have the least exegetical basis for our theology.

We must recognize the wisdom that has come from our predecessors in doing theology. What has been believed "everywhere, by everyone, all the time" to use a phrase from ancient church history, is more likely to be true and biblically on the mark than the latest fad theology, or something that has only been believed lately and by one stream of Christian tradition alone. NT theology should be based on what the text says in a variety of places, not on a disputed reading of an isolated text, much less on a theological deduction based on the silence of the text about this or that or the other. Then too, we must know not only the position but the direction in which the rhetorical arguments of NT authors are moving, so that the trajectories we pursue will be moving with the text and not against its flow. Yet with all these provisos I am not suggesting we should give way to the paralysis of analysis and throw up our hands and abandon doing theology.

I am saying that the one who said, "Behold I make all things new," is constantly encouraging and inspiring us to try again to understand, embrace and promulgate in fresh and compelling ways the truth once given. For Jesus is not coming back to rescue us from the world, but to safely ensconce us in a new earth accompanied by all the company of heaven. At the messianic banquet we will be sitting down with some uncomfortable dining partners speaking strange languages and wearing strange garb, with whom we will be compelled to converse and will be called even to embrace.

It makes sense then that we should get on with the conversing and embracing now, especially when it comes to a subject we hold so dear— NT theology. There is a theology in and of the NT which is both bigger and better than our distinctive theological systems, indeed *that* biblical theology calls those systems to account and says "it is in your distinctives that you are least faithful to the Word, not most faithful." It is my hope that we may realize this here at the cusp of the twenty-first century and heed the twin cries once more of *semper reformanda* and *sola Scriptura*. May it be so in my lifetime, and in our children's lifetimes.

Notes

Overture

1. It is interesting that at the same time Dispensationalism began to rise to prominence in the nineteenth century in America, Joseph Smith was busy producing the *Book of Mormon*, precisely because of the concern that the Bible did not address or refer to the New World and its history.

2. When the title of this book speaks of "the problem of Evangelical theology," I am referring of course to what I view as the biggest problem—its insufficient grounding in the Bible, particularly the New Testament. Obviously there are other problems, but this one in my view is the most crucial and fundamental.

Chapter 1

1. A theology which suggests, if it does not come right out and say, that there are things that God does not know, and that his knowledge is still evolving, is at the end of the day too much like process theology. This is a rather classic example of doing theology without careful attention to what the Bible says about God's omniscience, for the biblical God is a God who knows all realities as well as all possibilities. But knowing something in advance is not the same thing as predetermining it, as a moment's reflection on God's foreknowledge of our sin will show.

2. See especially T. J. Deidun's helpful summary of the data, "Romans," in *A Dictionary of Biblical Interpretation* (ed. R. J. Coggins and J. L. Houlden; Philadelphia: Trinity Press, 1990), 601–4. Also helpful is J. Godsey, "The Interpretation of Romans in the History of the Christian Faith," *Int.* 34 (1980): 3–16.

3. On Erasmus's rejection of the Augustinian view see pp. 6–7 above and n. 13 below.

4. Deidun, "Romans," 601.

5. Ibid.

6. Ibid., 602.

7. Some of this material appears in another and much longer form in B. Witherington and D. Hyatt, *Paul's Letter to the Romans: A Socio-Rhetorical Commentary* (Grand Rapids: Eerdmans, 2004), 141–206.

8. It is interesting that a variety of manuscripts and church fathers, including Chrysostom, have an additional "and" after the word *gift*, thus distinguishing the gift from the righteousness. The text without the additional *kai* is, however, very well supported and is probably original.

9. This in turn means we should see the argument in 5:1–11 as both retrospective and prospective.

10. See C. E. B. Cranfield, *A Critical and Exegetical Commentary on the Epistle to the Romans,* 2 vols. (ICC on the Holy Scriptures of the Old and New Testaments 32; Edinburgh: T&T Clark, 1975–1979), 1:272.

11. For the argument that each person is their own Adam cf. *2 Bar.* 54:15: "Adam is therefore not the cause, save only of his own soul, but each of us has been the Adam of his own soul."

12. See the discussion in R. H. Bell, "Rom 5:18–19 and Universal Salvation," *NTS* 48 (2002): 417–32. He (mistakenly) concludes that Paul is also affirming universal salvation here.

13. Erasmus had an opinion on this matter which proved controversial in view of the enormous influence of Augustine and also Ambrosiaster, who argued all persons sinned in Adam, because they were seminally present in him. In his annotations on the Latin text of the NT, his long marginal note about Romans 5:12 urged that the *in quo* of the Latin, when traced back to the Greek original *eph ho,* meant "because" or "for that" rather than "in whom" (i.e., in Adam). This seems to call into question the doctrine of original sin. See *Erasmus' Annotations on the New Testament: Acts–Romans–I and II Corinthians* (ed. A. Reeve and M. A. Screech; Leiden: Brill, 1990), xiii, 366–77, for the actual Erasmean notes on the text.

14. See C. M. Talbert, *Romans* (Smyth and Helwys Bible Commentary; Macon, Ga: Smyth & Helwys, 2002), 148. He, however, prefers the Orthodox rendering which is "wherefore, from which it follows"; in other words, a logical inference is indicated by this phrase: since death passed to all, therefore it follows that all sinned. But this is not how Paul uses the phrase elsewhere.

15. N. T. Wright, "The Letter to the Romans," in *Acts—First Corinthians* (vol. 10 of *The New Interpreters Bible*; ed. L. Keck; Nashville: Abingdon Press, 2002), 393–770, here 529.

16. For discussion and further illumination on these texts see Talbert, *Romans,* 147–48.

17. This is an important point because in Romans 7:7–13 Paul will also personify sin when he deals with the story of the fall. See pp. 20–21 below.

18. Again we have the use of commercial rather than forensic language. The term means "put in a ledger."

19. It is worth noting that Paul does not suggest Christ is the antitype of Moses. When discussions about Jesus' faithfulness, even unto death, get started it is important to remember the point of comparison that Paul makes here. Christ's faithfulness is not covenant faithfulness to the Mosaic Law. It is simply faithfulness to enact the divine will, the plan of salvation that God intended. Christ is the last Adam, not the last Moses, nor Israel reduced to one person. In other words, Paul insists that Christ stands in a more universal relationship to all of humanity, including Gentiles, than Moses or Israel did. It is not an accident

that Paul chooses Abraham and Adam as his points of comparison in these chapters. Christ is, as we shall see in the discussion of Romans 10 (see pp. 150–54 below), the end of the Mosaic Law.

Furthermore, Christ is not in covenant relationship with God, like Israel was. He is not obliged to keep the Adamic, Abrahamic, Mosaic, or Davidic covenants. To the contrary, in Pauline theology he brings in or enacts through his death and resurrection the new covenant which at one and the same time fulfills the Abrahamic one and ends the Mosaic one. All these covenants, including the new one, are between God and his people, not between God and Christ.

20. Cranfield, *Epistle to the Romans*, 1:283.

21. C. K. Barrett, *From First Adam to Last: A Study in Pauline Theology* (New York: Scribner, 1962), 5.

22. Ambrosiaster, *Pauline Commentary* 15.84 says that the acquittal will not be universal like the condemnation is, for the very good reason that not all believe.

23. R. F. Collins, *1 & 2 Timothy and Titus: A Commentary* (Louisville: Westminster/John Knox, 2002), 311. The whole discussion on pp. 308–18 is helpful and has been drawn on here.

24. See D. R. de Lacey, "Jesus as Mediator," *JSNT* 29 (1987): 101–21, and A. T. Hanson, "The Mediator: 1 Timothy 2:5–6," in *Studies in the Pastoral Epistles* (London: SPCK, 1968), 56–77. Hanson is clearly wrong when he writes that *mediator* suggests someone inferior to God. This is a term referring to a function, not ontology. See W. Mounce, *The Pastoral Epistles* (WBC 46; Nashville: Nelson, 2000), 88.

25. See L. T. Johnson's brief but very insightful commentary, *Letters to Paul's Delegates: 1 Timothy, 2 Timothy, Titus* (New Testament in Context; Valley Forge, Pa: Trinity, 1996), 192. For those wanting his insights on the other two pastoral letters one should use his fuller commentary in the Anchor Bible Series (*The First and Second Letters to Timothy: A New Translation with Introduction and Commentary* [Anchor Bible 35A; New York: Doubleday, 2001]).

26. Especially when you have both *anti-* and *huper* in this phrase. See G. D. Fee, *1 and 2 Timothy, Titus* (NIBCNT; ed. W. W. Gasque; Peabody, Mass.: Hendrickson, 1988), 30.

27. T. C. Oden, *First and Second Timothy and Titus* (Int; Louisville: Westminster/John Knox, 1989), 47.

28. J. Jeremias, *Die Briefe an Timotheus und Titus* (NTD 9; Göttingen: Vandenhoeck & Ruprecht, 1975), 20.

29. See J. N. D. Kelly, *A Commentary on the Pastoral Epistles: I Timothy, II Timothy, Titus* (BNTC; London: A&C Black, 1963), 62–63 on what the Fathers said about these verses.

30. Johnson, *Letters to Paul's Delegates*, 197.

31. Note C. K. Barrett's *The Epistle to the Romans* (BNTC 6; rev. ed.; Peabody, Mass.: Hendrickson, 1991), 107 comment: "but it would be as wrong to deduce from these passages a rigid universalism as to suppose that they meant 'many' and therefore not 'all.'"

32. See pp. 11–12 above.

33. J. Fitzmyer, *Romans: A New Translation with Introduction and Commentary* (AB 33; New York: Doubleday, 1992), 421.

34. P. Achtemeier, *Romans* (IBC; Atlanta: John Knox, 1985), 96.

35. Barrett, *Romans*, 109.

36. See rightly, Fitzmyer, *Romans*, 422.

37. See pp. 21–37 below on Romans 7.

38. See A. K. Grieb, *The Story of Romans: A Narrative Defense of God's Righteousness* (1st ed.; Louisville: Westminster/John Knox, 2002), 66: "Later (in 7:7–25) Paul will argue that the law cannot control sin; all it can do is count it."

39. Grace here is also personified. Paul is using rhetorical techniques here which he will pick up again in Romans 7 when he retells the story of Adam, using the dramatic device of the first person. We will discuss the rhetorical use of personification on pp. 19–21 below when we reach Romans 7. Personification falls under the heading of figures of thought. See Quintilian, *Inst.* 9.2.30.

40. Fitzmyer, *Romans*, 422.

41. Barrett, *Romans*, 111.

42. James D. G. Dunn, *Romans 1–8* (Dallas: Word, 1988), 307–8.

Chapter 2

1. Talbert rightly notes that "impersonation" was also a rhetorical device used to train those learning to write letters (*Romans*, 2002, 186). See also Theon, *Progymnasta* 2.1125.22.

2. See W. G. Kummel, *Römer 7 und das Bild des Menschen im Neuen Testament* (Munich: Kaiser, 1974).

3. S. Stowers, *A Rereading of Romans: Justice, Jews, and Gentiles* (New Haven: Yale University Press, 1994), 264–69.

4. Unfortunately we have only fragments of Origen's Romans commentary. See the careful discussion in Stowers, *Rereading of Romans*, 266–67. Origen rightly notes that: (1) Jews such as Paul do not speak of a time when they lived before or without the Law; (2) what Paul says elsewhere about himself (cf. 1 Cor. 6:19; Gal 3:13 and 2:20) does not fit this description of life outside Christ in Romans 7.

5. Stowers, *Rereading of Romans*, 268–69.

6. It appears that the better a commentator knew both Greek and rhetoric, the more likely they were to read Romans 7 as an example of impersonation.

7. See pp. 8–9 above and pp. 148–52 below.

8. See Quintilian, *Inst.* 9.2.30–31: "By this means we display the inner thoughts of our adversaries as though they were talking with themselves . . . or without sacrifice of credibility we may offer conversations between ourselves and others, or of others among themselves, and put words of advice, reproach, complaint, praise or pity into the mouths of appropriate persons."

9. The sensitive analysis by J. N. Aletti, "The Rhetoric of Romans 5–8," in *The Rhetorical Analysis of Scripture: Essays from the 1995 London Conference* (JSNTSup 146; eds S. E. Porter and T. H. Olbricht; Sheffield: Sheffield Academic, 1997), 294–308, here 300, deserves to be consulted. He makes clear that Paul is not talking about Christians here.

10. It is telling that some of the most thorough recent treatments of Romans 7, even from the Reformed tradition have concluded that Paul cannot be describ-

ing the Christian experience here; cf. D. Moo, *The Epistle to the Romans* (NICNT; ed. G. D. Fee; Grand Rapids: Eerdmans, 1996), 443–50; Wright, "Romans," in *NIB* 10, 551–55 (who changed his mind from his earlier opinion that Christians were in view in Romans 7:14–25); cf. Fitzmyer, *Romans*, 465–73; Talbert, *Romans*, 185–209.

11. There are no real textual problems in this section of Romans.

12. It is not surprising that some early Jews saw the commandment given to Adam and Eve as a form of one of the Ten Commandments, specifically the one having to do with coveting. See Ben Witherington III, *Paul's Narrative Thought World: The Tapestry of Tragedy and Triumph* (Louisville: Westminster/John Knox, 1994), 14.

13. See now the very helpful treatment of Paul's rhetorical use of "I" here by J. N. Aletti, "Rm 7.7–25 encore une fois: enjeux et propositions," *NTS* 48 (2002): 358–76. He is also right that Paul reflects some understanding of both Jewish and Greco-Roman anthropology in this passage.

14. Stowers, *Rereading of Romans*, 269–70.

15. As even Cranfield, *Epistle to the Romans*, 1:337 has to admit, Paul in Romans 7:6 and in 8:8–9 uses the phrase *in the flesh* to denote a condition which for the Christian now belongs to the past. It is thus hopelessly contradictory to say on the one hand, "We no longer have the basic direction of our lives controlled and determined by the flesh" (337), and then turn around and maintain that Romans 7:14–25 describes the normal or even best Christian life, even though 7:14 says "we are fleshly, sold under sin" which comports only with the description of pre-Christian life in 7:6 and 8:8–9. This contradicts the notion that the believer has been released from "the flesh" in a moral sense.

16. E. Käsemann, *Commentary on Romans* (trans. and ed. G. W. Bromiley; Grand Rapids: Eerdmans, 1980), 192–212.

17. P. Gorday, *Principles of Patristic Exegesis: Romans 9–11 in Origen, John Chrysostom, and Augustine* (New York: Mellen, 1983), 164.

18. Notice that it was a Latin, rather than a Greek, church father who made this identification, and only after the strong influence of Manicheanism on him. It does not appear to me that Augustine was all that aware of rhetorical devices and techniques in the Greek tradition.

19. See the famous essay by K. Stendahl, "Paul and the Introspective Conscience of the West," in *Paul among Jews and Gentiles, and Other Essays* (Philadelphia: Fortress, 1977).

20. Note that Paul's frequent expressions of pathos in his letters, including in Romans, have regularly to do with his concern for his converts, or his fellow Jews, and not with his own personal moral struggles as a Christian. The absence of expressions of guilt about his current conduct, unless Romans 7 is an exception, is noteworthy. Furthermore, Philippians 3:6 strongly indicates that Paul did not have a guilt-laden conscience when he was a non-Christian Jew either.

21. Paul is retelling the story of Adam because of its relevance for his audience's understanding of themselves. They are not to go back down the Adamic road.

22. See *4 Ezra* 7:11; B.T. *Sanh.* 56b; and on the identification of Torah with the preexistent wisdom of God see Sir 24:23; Bar 3:36–4:1.

23. See Käsemann, *Romans*, 196: "Methodologically the starting point should be that a story is told in vv. 9–11 and that the event depicted can refer strictly only

to Adam. . . . There is nothing in the passage which does not fit Adam, and everything fits Adam alone."

24. Barrett, *Romans*, 132 points out the difference between here and Romans 3:20 where Paul uses the term *epignosis* to refer to the recognition of sin. Here he simply says "know."

25. See the earlier discussion of this view at some length by S. Lyonnet, "L'histoire du salut selon le chapitre 7 de l'épître aux Romains," *Bib* 43 (1962): 117–51.

26. Barrett puts it vividly: "The law is not simply a reagent by which the presence of sin is detected: it is a catalyst which aids or even initiates the action of sin upon man" (*Romans*, 132).

27. It simply complicates and confuses the matter to suggest Paul is also talking about Israel as well as Adam here. Paul is addressing a largely Gentile audience who did not identify with Israel, but could understand and identify with the progenitor of the whole human race. That Israel might be included in the discussion of those who are "in Adam" in 7:14–25 is certainly possible, but even there Paul has already described earlier in Romans 2 the dilemma of a Gentile caught between the Law and a hard place. My point would be that even in vv. 14–25 he is not specifically focusing on Jewish experience, or the experience of Israel.

28. On which see pp. 27–29 below. This has confused those who are unaware of this rhetorical convention, and who have taken the outburst, "Thanks be to God in Jesus Christ," to be a cry only a Christian would make, and that therefore Romans 7:14–25 must be about Christian experience. However, if 7:14–25 is meant to be a narrative of a person in Adam who is led to the end of himself and to the point of conviction and conversion, then this outburst should be taken as Paul's interjected reply or response with the gospel to the heartfelt cry of the lost person, a response which prepares for and signals the coming of the following argument in Romans 8 about life in Christ.

29. Cranfield, *Epistle to the Romans*, 1:351–52.

30. As we shall see, there is also nothing in Romans 7:14–25 to suggest that his complaint is specifically with Jews. It is sin and death, and their effects on humankind, and also the Law's effect, whether on Gentiles or Jews, that is critiqued. Furthermore, Paul, despite Luther's insistence, is not critiquing here the self-righteousness of Jews or others caught between a rock and a hard place when they know what they ought to do but are unable to do it. Sometimes in order to hear the text without the baggage of later interpretations, one has to deconstruct the later interpretations first.

31. Barrett: "Sin in its deceitful use of the law and commandment, is revealed not merely in its true colors but in the worst possible light" (*Romans*, 136).

32. The diatribe format used earlier in Romans has prepared for this with the "I" who is not Paul raising the question, and Paul providing the Christian answer.

33. Käsemann, *Romans*, 211–12. It will be remembered that Kasemann so struggled with this half verse that he said it must be a gloss, or if not, he would have to rethink his whole reading of Romans 7. This angst could have been avoided if he had examined the issue from a rhetorical perspective.

34. See Stehdahl classic essay in *Paul among Jews and Gentiles*.

35. Notice how clear it is in Philippians 3:6 that Paul is talking about righteous behavior, not just right standing before God. Righteous behavior by Paul must be what *dikaiosune* refers to there. This is made especially apparent because in

the same verse he has just mentioned his zealous behavior: persecuting Christians.

36. The view that Paul is describing the so-called carnal Christian here, who is on the road to apostasy, will not work, not only because Paul does not believe the Christian is under the Mosaic Law, but also because in Romans 8 he will address his whole audience as those who have been set free from the "rule" of sin and death. It is of course possible for a Christian to commit apostasy and even act like the description of the Romans 7 person, but Paul would stress that such behavior is: (a) not acceptable; (b) not inevitable; and (c) not a legitimate option for the believer. There is no legitimate excuse for sin in the believer's life. The bottom line of Cranfield's view of Paul's view of sanctification is that sanctification means, not empowerment of the will to resist sin and have victory over it, but apparently only renewal of the mind, for Cranfield says we become increasingly aware of sin as sanctification proceeds. This is of course true, but Paul is talking about the liberation of the human will from bondage, not merely release from condemnation for one's sins, or increasing awareness of one's spiritual condition. Paul's point is that the believer can, by drawing on the grace of God, overcome the temptation to sin, and indeed can obey and be faithful to God. As Charles Wesley's hymn says, conversion "loosed the power of canceled sin/he set the prisoner free." But see Cranfield, *Epistle to the Romans*, 1:341–47.

37. See pp. 211–16 below on Wesleyan ideas of perfection.

38. Barrett, *Romans*, 139.

39. S. R. Llewelyn, ed. *A Review of the Greek Inscriptions and Papyri Published in 1980–81* (vol. 6 of *NewDocs*; Grand Rapids: Eerdmans, 1993), 52–53. I owe the finding of the Seneca reference to him.

40. For a modern reassertion of the older Augustinian and Lutheran view of Romans 7:14–25, see J. I. Packer, "The 'Wretched Man' Revisited: Another Look at Romans 7:14–25," in *Romans and the People of God* (ed. S. K. Soderland and N. T. Wright; Grand Rapids: Eerdmans, 1999), 70–81.

41. That Jews could occasionally, though exceptionally, describe their condition in a fashion similar to what we find in Romans 7 is clear from 1QS 11:9–10: "As for me, I belong to the wicked humankind, to the company of ungodly flesh. My iniquities, rebellions, and sins, together with the perversity of my heart, belong to the company of worms and to those who walk in darkness." But far from this justifying reading Romans 7:14–25 as referring to the Christian, it rather argues for the opposite, for the person who wrote 1QS 11:9–10 was certainly not a follower of Jesus. J. D. G. Dunn, however, points out: "The illogicality of arguing that the passage here expresses with Christian hindsight the existential anguish of the pious Jew—which as a pious Jew he did not actually experience and as a Christian he still does not experience!—is not usually appreciated" (*Romans 1–8*, 394). Dunn has a point, however, since Paul is not describing day-to-day pre-Christian experience, he is offering a Christian description of a crisis experience in the life of a non-Christian. In this regard it could well be the experience of a pious Jew, such as that from Qumran described above, or a pious Gentile at the point of conversion. There is nothing illogical about such a view. What is illogical is claiming after what Paul clearly says in Romans 7:5–6, and what he will go on to say in Romans 8, that Romans 7:14–25 is a description of Christian life.

42. Certainly proselytes and God-fearers could be in view, who were now Christians, but Paul's view of the Law of God is such that he can even be refer-

ring to Gentiles who, while outside the Law, still had the Law written on their hearts.

43. There is certainly precedent in Greek usage for the sense rule or principle, even if it is not generally used this way elsewhere in the NT. See H. Räisänen, *Paul and the Law* (Philadelphia: Fortress, 1983), 50, n. 34.

44. See Cranfield, *Epistle to the Romans*, 1:364–67.

45. See pp. 10–13 above.

46. On this sort of bifurcated interpretation of the self and the Law even in the case of Christians, see especially Dunn, *Romans 1–8*, 388–89. But the Mosaic Law does not belong to the epoch of Christ, in Paul's view, anymore than the "I" in bondage to sin belongs to the story of the Christian life.

47. See Käsemann, *Romans*, 205–6.

48. See pp. 70–72 above.

49. Against Dunn, *Romans 1–8*, 396–97.

50. See Achtemeier: "it represents non-Christian life under the Law seen from a Christian perspective" (*Romans*, 122). His helpful survey of the issues can be found in pp. 118–30. As he says, one of the sure signs of a mistaken interpretation of a text is when Paul is made to say the exact opposite of what he seems to say. For example, he points to Calvin's reading of v. 17. Paul says: "It is no longer I that do it but sin that dwells in me." Calvin comments, "Paul here denies that he is wholly possessed by sin; nay he declares himself to be exempt from its bondage." Or again Paul says in v. 16, "I do what I do not want." Luther reads this to mean that Paul "does not do the good as often and to such an extent and as readily as he would like" (Achtemeier, 120–21). Something is clearly wrong with these readings of Paul's words, for they flatly deny the prima facie meaning of the text.

Chapter 3

1. See my discussion in B. Witherington, *Grace in Galatia: A Commentray on St. Paul's Letter to the Galatians* (Grand Rapids: Eerdmans, 1998), 287–90.

2. Some of the material in this portion of this chapter has appeared before in another form in my *Grace in Galatia* (Edinburgh: T&T Clark, 2004, 2nd printing). Just the bibliography on this subject takes up an enormous amount of space. See now J. D. G. Dunn, ed., *Paul and the Mosaic Law* (WUNT 89; Tubingen: Mohr, 1996), presenting the papers from the 1994 Durham conference on the Law. Pages 335–41 have an excellent beginning bibliography on the discussion of the subject between 1980–1994. For a sampling of the discussion from a variety of positions one may wish to compare and contrast J. D. G. Dunn, *Jesus, Paul, and the Law: Studies in Mark and Galatians* (Louisville: Westminster/John Knox, 1990); H. Hubner, *Law in Paul's Thought* (trans. J. C. G. Greig; ed. J. Riches; Studies of the New Testament and Its World; Edinburgh: T&T Clark, 1984); H. Räisänen, *Paul and the Law*; E. P. Sanders, *Paul, the Law, and the Jewish People* (Minneapolis: Fortress, 1983); F. Thielman, *Paul and the Law: A Contextual Approach* (Downers Grove: InterVarsity Press, 1994); S. Westerholm, *Israel's Law and the Church's Faith:Paul and His Recent Interpreters* (Grand Rapids: Eerdmans, 1988). Note that there are entire letters, such as 1 Thessalonians or Philippians, where the matter can hardly be said to be discussed at all. This reminds us that this sub-

ject was not constantly on Paul's mind, and that the Law comes up because the subject was prompted by something that was going on in Paul's churches.

3. The vast majority of scholars agree that Galatians precedes Romans, whatever chronology they may otherwise adopt. If, as I hold, it precedes all the other letters, then it becomes an even more key text, aiding our understanding of Paul's views early in his ministry while there was still fairly close contact and relationships with the Jerusalem church.

4. On which see pp. above.

5. That a Jewish Christian, indeed Paul himself, might choose to follow some of the Law for a variety of mostly prudential or missionary reasons is clear enough from a text like 1 Corinthians 9:19–23. It is also clear that in this same passage Paul says that he is no longer "under the Law," that is, no longer obligated to keep it. I would suggest the reason Paul says this is that he believes that the Mosaic covenant is no longer the covenant God's people are under, no longer seen by Paul as the necessary *modus vivendi* ("way of living") for Jew or Gentile in Christ.

6. In fact Paul reverses the equation in Galatians 5–6. If the Galatians go so far as to keep the Law, it will prove to be their means of "getting out," of committing apostasy.

7. See pp. 3–7 above.

8. On sects, see pp. 93–97 above.

9. To put it a slightly different way, in Paul's view the fulfillment of the Law comes about because the Holy Spirit works in the believer the essential qualities God has always wanted in his people (love of God and neighbor).

10. Thielman, *Paul and the Law*, 140, although he goes on to rightly qualify this remark by saying that to obey the summary of the Law in the love commandment is to complete the requirements of the Mosaic Law in some ultimate and eschatological sense. Obviously, one cannot say that Christians who do not submit to circumcision, do not keep kosher, probably do not observe the sabbath, do not in general observe rules about Levitical purity, do not pray the Jewish hours of prayer, do not follow the Law's teaching on oaths, do not observe the Law's stipulations about foreigners within the believing community, and do not do a host of other things have *kept* the entire Law. There must then be some distinction in Paul's mind between fulfilling the ultimate and eschatological sense of the Mosaic Law and keeping it all.

11. See pp. 46–50 below on this text.

12. See Sanders, *Paul, the Law, and the Jewish People*, 6.

13. Galatians 5:4, especially in view of v. 5 ("the hope of righteousness"), would seem to be about final not initial justification.

14. There is however a clear difference between blamelessness (which involves no standing law having been violated) and innocence before God. Paul says all have sinned and fallen short of God's glory, and that includes himself. What he does not say is that all have transgressed the Law. In the first place this would not be true for various Gentiles who were not under the Mosaic covenant. They were sinners, not transgressors. In the second place, avoiding transgression is not the same as fulfilling or keeping all the positive commandments of the Law. "Falling short" of positive requirements is not identical with violation of an existing statute. "Works of the Law" has to do with doing the positive things the Law says must be done. Transgression is obviously not a work of the Law! The curse falls on all who do not observe or obey all that the Law

requires (Gal 3:10), and therefore in Paul's view the curse falls on all who are under the Law (cf. his modified quotation of Psalm 143:2 in Galatians 2:16). Paul is not saying in Philippians 3:6 that while a Pharisee he observed all the positive statutes of the Law to perfection; he is saying that no one could accuse him of transgression on the basis of the Law's standards of righteousness. The old distinction between legally blameless and morally blameless is one Paul affirms and understands. In Paul's theology, no one is morally blameless, all are sinners, but not all are legally blameworthy, if one is speaking of the violation of a known statute.

15. It is precisely texts such as this that Paul is likely thinking of when he says that whoever submits to the Mosaic covenant sign is obligated to keep all the Law (cf. Gal 5:3).

16. While Dunn may be right that most scholars think that Second Temple Judaism did not teach the need for perfect Law-keeping (*Romans 1–8*, 312), there are dissenting voices; cf. T. R. Schreiner, *The Law and Its Fulfillment: A Pauline Theology of Law* (Grand Rapids: Eerdmans, 1993), 71, 181. The issue however is not what Second Temple Judaism taught or believed on this subject, but what the OT in fact says or commands.

17. See Sanders, *Paul, the Law, and the Jewish People*, 22, where he argues that Paul cites Habakkuk 2:4 to prove that no one can be "righteoused" by the Law.

18. Thielman, *Paul and the Law*, 127–28.

19. Against F. Watson, *Paul, Judaism, and the Gentiles: A Sociological Approach* (SNTSMS 56; Cambridge: Cambridge University Press, 1986), 61ff.

20. See Dunn: "Although some elements of legalism in Second Temple Judaism cannot be denied, we also cannot conclude that Second Temple Judaism as a whole is to be branded as 'legalistic' (that is, that salvation or life in the world to come is earned by obedience to Torah)" (*Paul and the Law*, 311).

21. Thielman, *Paul and the Law*, 142.

22. Ibid., 141.

23. On this important phrase see my Romans commentary listed in n. 7 of ch. 1.

24. Thielman, *Paul and the Law*, 141.

25. See Mark 15:21 for Simon of Cyrene as an example of one impressed to be a burden bearer. The difference is that the Johannine Jesus is exhorting his disciples to take on such burdens freely and of their own choice, as is Paul in Galatians 6:2.

26. See pp. below.

27. Thielman, *Paul and the Law*, 141.

28. Ibid., 239. I would demur from his further statement that the period of the restoration of Israel has dawned already, if by Israel he means Israel after the flesh. Paul's argument in Romans 9–11 is that the period of real restoration for that Israel will not come until the full number of the Gentiles come in. See my *Jesus, Paul, and the End of the World: A Comparative Study in New Testament Eschatology* (Downers Grove: InterVarsity Press, 1992), 99ff. Until then Paul expects only some Jews, a distinct minority, to be converted.

29. And as we will see in the next section of this book, the failure to come to grips with this fact is one of the most fundamental flaws in Dispensationalism. See pp. 89–132 below. For a thorough expose on C. I. Scofield and his shady dealings see J. M. Canfield, *The Incredible Scofield and His Book* (Vallecito, Calif.: Ross House Books, 1988).

30. Dunn, ed., *Paul and the Mosaic Law,* 313.

31. One can find all of this in ibid., 309–34.

32. James D. G. Dunn, *The Theology of Paul the Apostle* (Grand Rapids: Eerdmans, 1998), 95.

33. Thielman, *Paul and the Law,* 139.

34. Dunn, *Theology of Paul the Apostle,* 75. Cf. his *Jesus, Paul, and the Law*: "For what he is attacking is a particular *attitude* to the law as such, the law as a whole in its social function as distinguishing Jew from Gentile" (45).

35. Note that Paul is well familiar with this tradition. Not only do we find it quoted in 2 Corinthians 6:17, but notice Paul's quotation of the continuation of this same address to Jerusalem at Galatians 4:27 where Isaiah 54:1 is drawn on.

36. See M. Abegg, "Paul, 'Works of the Law,' and MMT," *BAR* 20, no. 6 (1994): 52–55, 82. Cf. this discussion to James D. G. Dunn, "4QMMT and Galatians," *NTS* 43 (1997): 147–53.

37. So Abegg, "Paul, 'Works of the Law,' " 52–53.

38. See J. Barclay, *Obeying the Truth: Paul's Ethics in Galatians* (Minneapolis: Fortress, 1988), 82, n. 18.

CHAPTER 4

1. G. F. Moore, *Judaism in the First Centuries of the Christian Era: The Age of the Tannaim* (3 vols.; Schocken Paperbacks on Jewish Life and Religion; New York: Schocken, 1971), 456.

2. I. H. Marshall, "Election and Calling to Salvation in 1 and 2 Thessalonians," in *The Thessalonian Correspondence* (ed. R. F. Collins; Leuven: Leuven University Press, 1990), 259–76, here 262.

3. See the discussion in B. Witherington and D. Hyatt, *The Letters to Philemon, Colossians, Ephesians* (Grand Rapids: Eerdmans, 2006), ad loc.

4. See the discussion of Romans 9–11 in Witherington and Hyatt, *Paul's Letter to the Romans,* 246–49.

5. See Marshall, "Election and Calling," 263.

6. Ibid., emphasis added.

7. Marshall, "Election and Calling," 259–76, and J. M. Gundry Volf, *Paul and Perseverance: Staying in and Falling Away* (Louisville: Westminster/John Knox, 1990).

8. Gundry Volf, *Paul and Perseverance,* 267–71.

9. Ibid., 271, 273–74.

10. Marshall, "Election and Calling," 261.

11. Ibid., 265.

12. Ibid.

13. See on this text Witherington and Hyatt, *Paul's Letter to the Romans,* 227–31.

14. Gundry Volf, *Paul and Perseverance,* 20–27.

15. Ibid., 24.

16. Ibid., 21.

17. See Marshall, "Election and Calling," 266–68.

18. Ibid., 269.

19. Gundry Volf, *Paul and Perseverance,* 83; see 81–83.

20. Marshall, "Election and Calling," 272–73. On the paraenetic context and content of various of these intercessory prayers, see G. P. Wiles, *Paul's Intercessory Prayers: The Significance of the Intercessory Prayer Passages in the Letters of St. Paul* (SNTSMS 24; Cambridge: Cambridge UniversityPress, 1974).

21. Marshall, "Election and Calling," 274.

22. Gundry Volf, *Paul and Perseverance,* 81, and 76–78.

23. See Witherington and Hyatt, *Paul's Letter to the Romans,* 234–35.

24. G. Beale, *1–2 Thessalonians* (IVPNT Commentary Series 13; ed. G. R. Osborne; Downers Grove: InterVarsity, 2003), 151.

25. As is well known, Greek verbs focus more on the kind rather than the time of action, and the aorist normally conveys the sense of punctiliar activity or the onset of something, whether it begins in the past or the present. Notice, for example, how at 1 Thessalonians 5:10 the aorist verb *zesomen* refers to a future event, and it may be ingressive there—"we will begin to live with him." By contrast the present tense often conveys ongoing activity; "I believe" means "I continue to believe/keep believing." In hortatory contexts, participles are often used to exhort the audience to do something or to continue to do something.

26. Beale, *1–2 Thessalonians,* 153.

27. Ibid., 152.

28. The word *peripoiesis* is rare, and often refers to a possession (Eph 1:14; 1 Pet 2:9), but in 2 Thessalonians 2:14 and Hebrews 10:39 it refers to obtaining.

29. See pp. 56–59 above.

30. I. H. Marshall, *1 and 2 Thessalonians: Based on the RSV* (NCBC; Grand Rapids: Eerdmans, 1983), 139–40.

31. One may compare 1 Timothy 2:6—"he died on behalf of all." Jesus did not just die for the elect.

32. See M. D. Hooker, "Interchange in Christ" *JTS* 22 (1971): 349–61; and Hooker "Interchange and Atonement," *BJRL* 60 (1977–78): 462–81.

33. Marshall, *1 and 2 Thessalonians,* 141.

34. Ibid.

35. The parallels include references to Jesus' death in 4:14 and 5:10, the phrase "together with" in 4:16 and 5:10, and, of course, the identical closing exhortation to encourage one another. See Beale, *1–2 Thessalonians,* 155.

36. On which see the next major section of this book pp. 89–108 below.

37. Beale, *1–2 Thessalonians,* 182, emphasis added.

38. It is possible that the original reading here is "God works all things together . . .," which is supported by some important witnesses including p46 A, B, and others. The shorter reading which omits *o theos* is even better supported, however, and is probably original.

39. However, as Fee avers, the subject may be God the Spirit, since Paul has been discussing the role of the Spirit immediately prior to this section. See G. D. Fee, *God's Empowering Presence: The Holy Spirit in the Letters of Paul* (Peabody, Mass.: Hendrickson, 1994), 587–91.

40. See J. D. G. Dunn, *Romans 1–8* (Edinburgh: T&T Clark, 1975), 481–82.

41. In his helpful summary of the evidence from the fathers Gerald Bray, ed., *Romans* (ACCSNT 6; ed. T. C. Oden; Downers Grove: InterVarsity, 2000), 233, says this:

> Apart from Augustine, who embraced it wholeheartedly, most of the Fathers found it somewhat puzzling to accept the apostle's teaching at face value. They did not want to deny that the world was planned and ordered by God, but neither did they want to suggest that there were some people whom God had predestined to damnation. They were convinced that predestination did not remove human free will. God's call to salvation was generally understood to be universal. The fact that not all responded was their fault entirely and the result of a deliberate choice on their part.

Bray (244) adds, "Only Augustine, and then only in his later writings, was prepared to accept the full implications of divine predestination." A sampling of what the fathers say shows that Augustine was by no means the only voice in the choir, and in fact it appears he was frequently singing solo. For example, Diodore in the *Pauline Commentary from the Greek Church* says about Romans 8:28–30: "This text does not take away our free will. It uses the word 'foreknew' before 'predestined.' Now it is clear that foreknowledge does not by itself impose any particular kind of behavior. . . . Whom did he predestine? Those whom he foreknew, who were called according to his plan i.e. who demonstrated that they were worthy to be called by his plan and made conformable to Christ" (cited by Bray, 235). Theodoret in his *Interpretation of the Letter to the Romans* puts it this way: "Those whose intention God foreknew, he predestined from the beginning" (Bray, 237). Or again Cyril of Alexandria in his *Explanation of the Letter to the Romans* says: "He calls everyone to himself, and no one is lacking the grace of his calling for when he says everyone he excludes nobody" (cited in Bray, 237). (Cyril is discussing Romans 8:28 in light of Jesus' saying "Come unto me all who labor.") Finally there is the much maligned Pelagius, who says in his *Commentary on Romans*: "Those whom God knew in advance would believe, he called. A call gathers together those who are willing to come, not those who are unwilling . . . Paul says this because of the enemies of the faith, in order that they may not judge God's grace to be arbitrary" (cited in Bray, 237). A few voices took a line closer to Augustine's, particularly Origen, but it was a minority opinion even in Augustine's day.

42. Dunn, *Romans 1–8*, 482, argues that the use of "foreknow" here "has in view the more Hebraic understanding of 'knowing' as involving a relationship experienced and acknowledged." This however makes no sense. You cannot have a relationship with someone who does not yet exist, and more particularly you especially cannot have the experience of a relationship that does not yet exist. You can, however, know something in advance without yet experiencing it, and this is what Paul has in mind here. Cf. Acts 26:5; 2 Pet 3:17.

43. Achtemeier, *Romans*, 144.

44. One point which Dunn, *Romans 1–8*, 485, and others seem to have clearly missed is that we continue to have reference to the same *ous* once in v. 29, and three times in v. 30. The import of this is twofold: (1) Paul is deliberately talking about a group of people—"those who." He does not for instance address individuals as we saw him doing with the "you" singular in 8:2. Election is seen as a corporate matter by Paul. There is an elect group (see below on v. 33);

(2) even more importantly, since vv. 29–30 must be linked to v. 28, the "those who" in question are those about whom Paul has already said they "love God," i.e. Paul makes perfectly clear that he is talking about Christians here. The statement about them loving God *precedes* and determines how we should read both the *ous* in these verses, and the chain of verbs. God knew something in advance about these persons, namely that they would respond to the call of God in love. For such people, God goes all out to make sure they in the end are fully conformed to the image of Christ. These verses would have had a very different significance had they read "and those God predetermined would love him, he then justified. . . ." But this is not what Paul says or suggests, not least because it does not comport with his theology of the nature of love.

45. See Käsemann, *Romans*, 244–45.

46. Cranfield, *Epistle to the Romans*, 1:434–35.

47. Käsemann, *Romans*, 246–47.

48. It is telling that it takes a tour de force, full-length argument in a monograph to suggest that Paul had some other view of apostasy than was the dominant one in early Judaism. But see Gundry Volf, *Paul and Perseverance*: "Me thinks she protesteth too much." The warning in 1 Timothy 1:19 to Timothy, coupled with living examples of those who had shipwrecked their faith, is a real one. It is telling that the author of this lengthy monograph does not even properly deal with this text, nor with similar texts such as Hebrews 6:4–6 which seem to have come out of the Pauline circle as well. The point that must be stressed about 1 Timothy 1:19 is this: one cannot make shipwreck of a faith one does not have, and Paul or the later Paulinist would not speak of making shipwreck of a false faith while urging Timothy to keep that same faith.

49. Käsemann, *Romans*, 248–49.

50. Cranfield, *Epistle to the Romans*, 1:440–41.

51. P. Melanchthon, *Commentary on Romans* (trans. F. Kramer; St. Louis: Concordia, 1992), 183–84.

52. See pp. 25–29 above.

53. See the summary of usage in H. Hoehner, *Ephesians: An Exegetical Commentary* (Grand Rapids: Baker, 2003), 173–74. He rightly concludes that we do have the local sense here. The problem with his treatment is that he tries to impose grammatical precision on an epideictic sermon which involves the language of the heart in long, effusive sentences. This is like trying to impose mathematical precision on the meter of a poem or song. Hoehner is trying to argue that the text must mean God chose "us" before the world began because the grammatical diagram of the sentence suggests such a conclusion. As Hoehner admits, however, even Calvin seems to have agreed that God's choosing "us in Christ" means Christ is the Elect One chosen before the world began and believers are "in him." Barth's view is of the same ilk as Calvin's. Hoehner also rejects Chrysostom's suggestion that God chose us through faith in Christ, because this would limit or even destroy God's freedom of choice (176). But the NT teaches repeatedly that divine condescension is the way of the biblical God, and that God accepts all kinds of limitations in order to have a relationship with human beings; the incarnation is a clear example of divine self-limiting (see Phil 2:5–11), as is Christ's death on the cross. There is therefore nothing surprising at all about the notion that an unconditionally loving God might limit his absolute freedom in order to allow humans to respond to his love freely by means of the aid of divine grace. God treats his people as persons who will be held responsible for their life choices. A loving response to

God cannot be coerced or predetermined, if it is to be personal and free. Indeed, it is also the case that for any behavior to be truly virtuous or loving, it must involve the power of contrary choice.

54. See the exposition of Chrysostom, *Hom. Eph. 1*, who is followed by Cassian and others. A non-Augustinian interpretation of this text has a long pedigree, in fact predating the rise of the dominant Augustinian reading of Paul, especially Paul's Romans and Ephesians.

55. Contrast this with what we find at Qumran where both the righteous who will be elected and the wicked who will be condemned are determined prior to creation of the universe (CD 2:7; 1QS 3:15–17). E. Best aptly observes that predestination is a concept dealing with God's purpose from all eternity rather than about individual salvation. See E. Best, *A Critical and Exegetical Commentary on Ephesians* (ICC on the Holy Scriptures of the Old and New Testaments: Edinburgh: T&T Clark, 1998), 119–20. Note the total lack of discussion of the predestination of the wicked here. Ephesians does not depict election as that which divides the human race, but rather as that which unites it in Christ, hence the strong contrast with the Qumran language about the election and salvation of the few righteous in contrast to the majority of the race.

56. See P. T. O'Brien, *The Letter to the Ephesians* (Pillar NTC; Grand Rapids: Eerdmans, 1999), 98, n. 49: "The idea of the incorporation of many into the representative head (using the preposition *en*) appears in the Septugint in relationship to Abraham (Gen 12:30) and Isaac (Gen 21:12) as well as in Paul with reference to Adam (1 Cor 15:22)."

57. A very helpful study of Paul's and the other NT authors' conceptions of election and perseverance is found in I. H. Marshall's *Kept by the Power of God: A Study of Perseverance and Falling Away* (2d ed; Minneapolis: Bethany Fellowship, 1974).

58. See C. C. Newman, "Election and Predestination in Ephesians 1:4–6a: An Exegetical-Theological Study of the Historical, Christological Realization of God's Purpose," *RevExp* 93 (1996): 237–47.

59. R. Schnackenburg, *Ephesians: A Commentary* (Edinburgh: T&T Clark, 1991), 51–52. He rightly adds that Paul is not talking about the personal preexistence of believers in heaven. What is being discussed is our election in the preexistent Christ, by which is meant believers are chosen in him, and believers were in God's plan from the beginning, in the plan God enacted in Christ.

60. Notice that Paul entirely avoids speaking of "mysteries" plural, perhaps because he wants to avoid comparison with the mysteries in mystery cults. Initiation in the Christian sense involved an open secret proclaimed to all, not a hidden revelation given only to those who had been initiated into the cult.

61. *Oikonomia* refers to the management or administration of something, or the basis of such administration, namely a plan. Whereas in Colossians 1:25 it refers to a plan or stewardship administered by Paul, here God is the one who does the administering and has a plan.

62. Schnackenburg, *Ephesians*, 65.

63. Fee, *God's Empowering Presence*, 669. This was also the view of Chrysostom and Ambrosiaster.

64. P. Perkins, "The Letter to the Ephesians," in *2 Corinthians–Philemon* (vol. 11 of *The New Interpreter's Bible*; ed. L. Keck; Nashville: Abington Press, 2000), 376.

65. Ibid.

66. G. B. Caird, *Paul's Letters from Prison: Ephesians, Philippians, Colossians, Philemon, in the RSV* (The New Clarendon Bible; Oxford: Oxford University Press, 1976), 40.

67. See Witherington, *Conflict and Community in Corinth: A Socio-Rhetorical Commentary on 1 and 2 Corinthians* (Grand Rapids: Eerdmans, 1995); Witherington and Hyatt, *Paul's Letter to the Romans*; Witherington, *Grace in Galatia*.

68. On which see pp. 135–50 below.

<h2 align="center">Chapter 5</h2>

1. We will have more to say about the problems Calvinism raises in our discussion of Romans 9–11 (pp. ## below) since some of the problems with that theological system overlap with those of Dispensationalism, not least when the Dispensational interpreter is a Calvinist.

2. There are in addition numerous collateral problems when the Reformed system is combined with the Dispensational system, resulting, for example, in the denial of various gifts of the Spirit being given and authentically used in the church today, coupled with the denial that women might be gifted by the Spirit to perform various forms of ministry. G. D. Fee, *Gospel and Spirit: Issues in New Testament Hermeneutics* (Peabody, Mass.: Hendrickson, 1991), 74, points out, for example, the glaring contradiction of insisting that 1 Corinthians 14:34–35 is eternally valid and bans women from speaking in the church today, while at the same time denying that what is said in this very same chapter about the validity of speaking in tongues still applies to the church in the present, even though 1 Corinthians 14:39–40 commands that no one should ever forbid speaking in tongues!

3. See the discussion in B. Rossing, *The Rapture Exposed: The Message of Hope in the Book of Revelation* (Boulder: Westview , 2004), 22, and the notes there.

4. See ibid., 23.

5. It is not possible to deal with all the enormous exegetical and theological problems that Dispensationalism presents us with, and so the reader is directed to Rossing, *The Rapture Exposed*, and to the fine and more general study of eschatology by C. Hill, *In God's Time: The Bible and the Fuure* (Grand Rapids: Eerdmans, 2002), 199–209 on the rapture. One point that should be stressed is that, as Hill points out, the Dispensational system is an everevolving thing, and now we even have "progressive" Dispensationalism—see C. A. Blaising and D. L. Bock, *Progressive Dispensationalism* (Wheaton, Ill.: BridgePoint, 1993)—which rejects the original idea of Darby that the Christian era was a mere parenthesis in between the two parts of the story of Israel, involving prophecy and its fulfillment. This theory suggests that the rapture removes the church from the earthly scene so the rest of the OT prophecies can come true literally for Israel. The problem, of course, with this is that various NT authors think these same prophecies are being fulfilled by Christ and in the new people of God, which is Jew and Gentile united in Christ. This theory of Darby's is especially ironic since Paul sees the Mosaic era and its legislation and prophecies as the parenthesis in between the Abrahamic and new covenants, the latter being the fulfillment of the former, and the promises to Abraham coming to fruition in Jesus. For a thorough expose on C. I. Scofield and his

shady dealings see J. M. Canfield, *The Incredible Scofield and His Book* (Vallecito, Calif: Ross House Books, 1988).

6. See Witherington, *Jesus the Seer: The Progress of Prophecy* (Peabody, Mass.: Hendrickson, 2000). The material in the next few pages of this book appears in another form in that study.

7. J. J. Collins, ed., *Apocalypse: The Morphology of a Genre* (Semeia 14; Missoula, Mont.: Scholars , 1979), 9. To this definition, D. Helholm added the suggestion that it is literature intended for a group in crisis with the intent of exhortation or consolation by means of divine authority.

8. One can begin to recognize the sea change in eschatology when one compares and contrasts Revelation with Hermas. See my *Jesus the Seer*, 371–78.

9. See my discussion in ibid., 353–57.

10. D. Potter, *Prophets and Emperors: Human and Divine Authority from Augustus to Theodosius* (Cambridge, Mass.: Harvard University Press, 1994), 104.

11. See C. Rowland, *The Open Heaven: A Study of Apocalyptic in Judaism and Early Christianity* (New York: Crossroad, 1982), on the otherwordly aspect of the book.

12. E. Schüssler Fiorenza, *The Book of Revelation—Justice and Judgment* (Philadelphia: Fortress, 1985), 149.

13. Marshall, *1 and 2 Thessalonians*, 200.

CHAPTER 6

1. Some Western and Byzantine witnesses (D, F, G, K, L, and others) have the perfect form of the participle ("have fallen asleep") here, conforming it to Matthew 27:52 and 1 Corinthians 15:20. The more unusual form is likely original. See B. M. Metzger, *A Textual Commentary on the Greek New Testament: A Companion Volume to the United Bible Societies' Greek New Testament* (3d ed; New York: United Bible Societies, 1971), 632.

2. A few manuscripts [A, B, *cop(boh)*] have *kleptas* ("thieves") in the accusative, and so the text reads "surprise you like thieves" ("do" or "are surprised"). This reading, while more difficult does not cohere with the context. See Metzger, *Textural Commentary,* 633; A. J. Malherbe, *The Letters to the Thessalonians: A New Translation with Introduction and Commentary* (AB 32B; New York: Doubleday, 2000), 293–94.

3. This is perhaps a small grammatical point in favor of the notion that Paul is not envisioning a necessarily imminent parousia, but rather a period of time when Christians will go on dying before Christ returns. But see the discussion in Malherbe, *Letters*, 263.

4. See the discussion of these matters in Witherington, *Jesus, Paul, and the End of the World*.

5. In fact one could read the phrase *the rest/remainder* to mean all non-Christians, Jews, or Gentiles, but perhaps Ephesians 2:12 should be our guide to Paul's meaning here, especially if the vast majority of his Thessalonian audience were formerly pagan.

6. See G. Beale, *1–2 Thessalonians*, 135.

7. See Marshall, *1 and 2 Thessalonians*, 124.

8. Here as in 1 Corinthians 15, Paul operates with a concept of the resurrection of the righteous. Thus in 1 Corinthians 15, he can talk about Christ being the firstfruits and those in Christ the latter fruits of the resurrection. This is, in part, because for Paul resurrection means for the believer full conformity to the image of Christ, something the dead outside of Christ will not receive when Christ returns. See the discussion in Witherington, *Jesus, Paul, and the End of the World.*

9. One thing this text probably does suggest is that Paul was in good health at this juncture and did not anticipate his imminent demise.

10. See the more detailed discussion in Witherington, *Jesus, Paul, and the End of the World*

11. E. Best, *A Commentary on the First and Second Epistles to the Thessalonians* (London: A&C Black, 1972), 195–96.

12. Notice that even in the Corinthians correspondence Paul considers either the possibility of being alive at the parousia, or the possibility of being raised from the dead (cf. 1 Cor 15:52 to 1 Cor 6:14; 2 Cor 4:14, 5:1, contrast Phil 1:20 where death seems possibly imminent but see Phil 4:5). It is interesting that Chrysostom suggested that Paul was not referring to himself but to those who would be alive at the parousia (*Hom. 1 Thess.*). But this resolves the tension in a way that Paul does not. Paul did, at least early in his ministry, conjure with the possibility of being alive when Jesus returns, or put another way, he certainly did not envision it happening a very long time after he had died. Even J. B. Lightfoot, *Notes on Epistles of St. Paul* (Winona Lake, Minn.: Alpha Publications, n.d.), 66, says:

> The Apostles certainly do speak as though there were a reasonable expectation of the Lord's appearing in their own time. They use modes of expression which cannot be otherwise explained. Such is the use of the plural here. . . . Nor does it imply more than a reasonable expectation . . . but nothing approaching to a certainty, for it is carefully guarded by the explanatory *hoi zontes, hoi perileipomenoi* which may be paraphrased, "When I say 'we,' I mean those who are living, those who survive to that day.'"

13. On this phrase not necessarily referring to a word of the historical Jesus see J. Delobel, "The Fate of the Dead according to 1 Thess 4 and 1 Cor 15," in *The Thessalonian Corrrespondence* (BETL 87; ed. R. F. Collins; Leuven: Leuven Universtiy Press, 1990), 340–47, here 341.

14. See, e.g., L. Morris, *The First and Second Epistles to the Thessalonians* (NICNT; Grand Rapids: Eerdmans, 1991), 140–41; J. Jeremias, *Unknown Sayings of Jesus* (trans. R. H. Fuller; London: SPCK, 1964), 80–83.

15. Here I am following Beale, *1–2 Thessalonians*, 137, and D. Wenham, *Paul: Follower of Jesus or Founder of Christianity?* (Grand Rapids: Eerdmans, 1995), 303–14, who should be consulted at length on the whole matter of Paul's use of the Jesus traditions. See also his "Paul and the Synoptic Apocalypse," in *Studies of History and Tradition in the Four Gospels* (vol. 2 of *Gospel Perspectives*; ed. R. T. France and D. Wenham; Sheffield: JSOT, 1981), 345–75.

16. This reassurance may have been particularly needed by any in Thessalonike who knew teaching such as that found in 2 Esd 13:24, which states that those who survive to the end are more blessed than those who die before it.

17. When one talks about a remainder, the implication seems to be that a minority of the total number is referred to. See Marshall, *1 and 2 Thessalonians*, 127.

18. Beale, *1–2 Thessalonians*, 135.

19. Cf. Prov 30:27 LXX; Thucydides, *Hist.* 2.92.

20. F. F. Bruce, *1 and 2 Thessalonians* (Waco, Tex.: Word, 1982), 103.

21. Notice as well that the going out to meet the dignitary is a great honor and is part of a public event, with the implication that this authority figure will deal with the dishonorable thereafter when he returns inside the city or home.

22. K. P. Donfried, "The Imperial Cults of Thessalonica and Political Conflict in 1 Thessalonians," in *Paul and Empire* (ed. R. A. Horsley; Harrisburg: Trinity, 1997), 215–23, here 217.

23. One has to wonder whether Paul was reflecting on the crackdown of Claudius on Jews and Christians in Rome in A.D. 49 and its aftermath as Claudius's reign deteriorated into bad government in his last years (i.e., A.D. 49–54), a crackdown which gave officials and others in a city like Thessalonike a license to treat Paul and his coworkers and converts as they apparently did.

24. H. Koester, "Imperial Ideology and Paul's Eschatology in 1 Thessalonians," in *Paul and Empire*, 158–66, see 158–59 esp.

25. N. T. Wright, "Paul's Gospel and Caesar's Empire," in *Paul and Politics* (ed. R. A. Hosley; Harrisburg: Trinity, 2000), 160–83, here 182–83.

26. See pp. 118–20 above.

27. See Marshall, *1 and 2 Thessalonians,* 129. The clear implication is that the parousia of Christ is the coming of God to earth.

28. The term *rapture* does not appear in the NT. It comes from the Latin term *raptus/rapio* which is a rendering of the Greek here, for *raptus* in Latin means "snatched." The idea is present in *4 Ezra* 6:26; 14:9. and also in Genesis 5:24 LXX, where it is used of Enoch being taken up into heaven. The word itself however, either in Greek or Latin, does not carry the connotation of "into heaven," as is made clear in texts which speak of death doing the snatching or the land of the dead being the place to which one was snatched.

29. Interestingly and ironically this verb is used in Plutarch, *Letter to Apollonius* 111C–D, 117B, and Lucian, *Funerals* 13 to refer to the action of death itself. Inscriptions as well refer to fate snatching away loved ones into the realm of the dead (*IG* II.1062a, 3; 11477, 9; IV620, 2; V.733, 12). *4 Ezra* 5:42 is interesting for it says "just as for those who are last there is no delay, so for those who are first there is no haste." Paul is using funerary language, another little clue that the rhetoric here is epideictic in character.

30. As Lightfoot, *Notes*, 69, makes very clear, the classical distinction between the pure ether of heaven and the atmosphere which has clouds in it is preserved here (see. e.g., Homer, *Il.* 8.558; 17.371; and we find it also in Christian writers, Athenagoras, *Leg.* 5 and Eph 2:2). "Thus then *eis aera* here denotes that the Lord will descend into the immediate region of the earth, where he will be met by his faithful people."

31. A. Smith, "The First Letter to the Thessalonians," in *2 Corinthians–Philemon* (vol. 11 of *New Interpreters Bible*; ed. L. Keck; Nashville: Abingdon Press, 2000) 671–738, here 725.

32. See, rightly, ibid., 725–26; See also T. Howard, "The Literary Unity of 1 Thessalonians 4:13–5:11," *Grace Theological Journal* 9 (1988): 163–90, rebutting the Dispensational reading of these texts.

33. Rightly noted by C. Wanamaker, *The Epistles to the Thessalonians* (NIGTC; Grand Rapids: Eerdmans, 1990), 177–78.

34. See, rightly, Lightfoot, *Notes*, 70–71. It is of course possible, since this is epideictic rhetoric, that Paul is using these terms as virtual synonyms here, and so we would have an example of pleonasm or fullness and redundancy of expression. See Marshall, *1 and 2 Thessalonians*, 132. However, throughout the history of Greek usage, including in modern times, these two words when juxtaposed had distinct meanings. Today *chronos* refers to the year, *chairos* to the time.

35. We may point out that Paul is capable of talking about events that must precede the parousia, as a way of making clear that the end is not yet at hand, but he does not speak of these events as sign markers or events that trigger the return of Christ and so must be closely juxtaposed in time with the parousia.

36. Here is where we point out that the Greek phrase *en taxei* can either be used adjectivally or adverbially. It can mean "soon," but it can also mean "suddenly." Too often scholars have simply ignored the possibility of translating the phrase "suddenly" (literally "in quickness"), overlooking the fact that the controlling metaphor when it came to discussing the coming of the Lord/Son of Man was "thief in the night," a metaphor which suggests a sudden break in, at an unexpected time.

37. See Marshall, *1 and 2 Thessalonians*, 133–34.

38. Of course he is probably not the first one to make this transfer. It seems to go back to Jesus and what he says about the coming of the Son of Man for judgment (Mark 14:62).

39. See the discussion in Witherington, *Jesus, Paul, and the End of the World*, 163–65.

40. Lightfoot, *Notes*, 71, takes this to mean that they knew the saying or parable of Jesus about this.

41. Wanamaker, *Epistles to the Thessalonians*, 178–79. The term *akribos* occurs only here and in Paul's Ephesians 5:15 and refers to investigating something with great care and so knowing beyond reasonable doubt. See Josephus, *Ag. Ap.* 2.175.

42. Malherbe, *The Letters to the Thessalonians*, 290.

43. See Lightfoot, *Notes*, 72.

44. See Wanamaker, *Epistles to the Thessalonians*, 180.

45. For more of this sort of evidence see the detailed discussion in K. Wengst, *Pax Romana and the Peace of Jesus Christ* (trans. John Bowden; Philadelphia: Fortress , 1987), 19–26, and in regard to our text 77–78.

46. On Revelation, see Witherington, *Revelation* (New Cambridge Bible Commentary; Cambridge: Cambridge University Press, 2003).

47. See Marshall, *1 and 2 Thessalonians*, 134–35.

48. Best, *First and Second Epistles to the Thessalonians*, 208.

49. Marshall, *1 and 2 Thessalonians*, 136.

50. See Lightfoot, *Notes*, 74, on this quote.

51. Best, *First and Second Epistles to the Thessalonians,* 210.

52. See Beale, *1–2 Thessalonians*, 144–45.

53. See pp. 59–89 above on Paul's conception of election.

54. Lightfoot, *Notes*, 75.

55. See Beale, *1–2 Thessalonians*, 149.

56. See Wanamaker, *Epistles to the*Thessalonians*, 184.

57. See Malherbe, *Letters*, 295.

58. Ibid., 295.

59. Drunkenness during the day was less common and considered more reprehensible (cf. Isa 5:11; Acts 2:15; 2 Peter 2:13).

60. Wanamaker, *Epistles to the Thessalonians*, 185.

61. Notice in this verse how faith and love are grouped together in connection with the metaphor of the breastplate. Lightfoot, *Notes*, 76, points out that faith is not fulfilled except by love. Malherbe, *Letters*, 298, notes the singular position of "hope" here. It is probably singled out because hope is what these converts under fire were most in need of at this juncture.

62. Bruce, *1 and 2 Thessalonians*, 112. Notice the reference in Galatians 5:5 to awaiting the hope of righteousness. The consummation of everything for the believer comes when Christ returns and they are transformed into his likeness. This is clearly not a reference to Christ's righteousness, but to the believers', which they will not fully obtain or reflect until the return of Christ and the bodily transformation of believers.

63. See Malherbe, *Letters*, 298.

64. The word *peripoiesis* is rare, and often refers to a possession (Eph 1:14; 1 Peter 2:9), but in 2 Thessalonians 2:14 and Hebrews 10:39 it refers to obtaining.

65. Marshall, *1 and 2 Thessalonians*, 139–40.

66. The parallels include references to Jesus' death in 4:14 and 5:10, the phrase *together with* in 4:16 and 5:10, and of course the identical closing exhortation "encourage one another." See Beale, *1–2 Thessalonians*, 155.

67. Smith, "First Letter to the Thessalonians," in *NIB* 11, 727.

68. See Hill, *In God's Time*, 205.

69. See Lightfoot, *Notes*, 108. See also Beale's critique, *1–2 Thessalonians*, 198.

70. See Bruce, *1 and 2 Thessalonians*, 163.

71. Beale, *1–2 Thessalonians*, 138–40.

72. The detailed and careful discussion of the parousia in B. Rigaux, *Saint Paul: Les Épîtres aux Thessaloniciens* (Paris: J. Gabalda, 1956), 195–280 should be consulted.

73. See the excursus of Best, *First and Second Epistles to the Thessalonians*, 349–54.

74. Ibid., 354.

75. Malherbe, *Letters*, 273.

CHAPTER 7

1. This material appears in a somewhat different and much fuller form in Witherington and Hyatt, *Paul's Letter to the Romans*, 236–79.

2. Some good manuscripts (p46, B, D, and others) have the singular, "covenant," but the plural is even better attested (Aleph, C, K, and many others). It is certainly more likely that a plural would be altered to a singular than vice versa, because the plural might be thought to involve theological difficulties. See Metzger, *Textual Commentary*, 459. In fact, however, Paul does speak of covenants plural, as Galatians 4:24 shows. He does not believe that God gave only one covenant in several adminstrations or forms. Indeed, he sees the

Mosaic covenant as an interim one between the Abrahamic and new covenants, with the latter being the fulfillment or completion of the Abrahamic covenant.

3. This citation from Isaiah is meant to be hopeful, and there is no justification for inserting the word "only" before the word *remnant* in the text. No Greek manuscript supports such an insertion.

4. Cranfield, *Epistle to the Romans*, 2:445–50.

5. In these last two sentences Wright is critiquing Stendahl, and also J. G. Gager, *The Origins of Anti-Semitism: Attitudes toward Judaism in Pagan and Christian Antiquity* (New York: Oxford University Press, 1983), and L. Gaston, *Paul and the Torah* (Vancouver: University of British Columbia Press, 1987). A decisive rebuttal to the view that Paul opts for a two covenant/two ways of salvation theory can now be found in H. Räisänen, "Paul, God, and Israel: Romans 9–11 in Recent Research," in *The Social World of Formative Christianity and Judaism: Essays in Tribute to Howard Clark Kee* (ed. J. Neusner et al.; Philadelphia: Fortress, 1988), 178–206.

6. N. T. Wright, "Romans," in *NIB* 10, 621.

7. Ibid., 622.

8. Ibid., 623–24.

9. Wright, "Romans," in *NIB* 10, 623–24.

10. Barrett, *Romans*, 165.

11. Which makes rather clear that Cranfield, *Epistle to the Romans*, 2:451–594, and others cannot be right in suggesting that Paul views non-Christian Jews as already saved persons apart from faith in Christ. Paul would not be wishing himself cut off for their sake if he believed that there was no need for such a heroic gesture since they were not in fact lost or cut off from God's people. What he believes is that they are cut off, but only for a time. His is an eschatological argument, not a purely theological one, for it brings future events into the mix.

12. Notice that Paul counts the Law, in principle, in the blessing or asset column.

13. As I have said in *Jesus, Paul, and the End of the World*, 115, Paul is probably thinking through a logical historical sequence in this list. Israel was made sons and daughters in the exodus; they saw the glory cloud; God then made a series of covenants with them; having done so, then the Law and divine worship were set up, and God obligated himself to the promises in the covenants; this in turn leads to mentioning the patriarchs who received the promises, and of course finally to the Promised One—the Messiah.

14. See the discussion in C. Bryan, *A Preface to Romans: Notes on the Epistle in Its Literary and Cultural Setting* (Oxford: Oxford University Press, 2000), 170–71.

15. The detailed arguments of Metzger, *Textual Commentary*, 459–62, are telling. Note especially that if the clause which begins with *ho hon* was intended to be an asyndetic doxology to God, then the word *hon* is totally pointless and superfluous. It would be more likely the text would have read *ho epi panton theos* if God were being distinguished from Christ here. Furthermore Pauline doxologies are never ever asyndetic (cf. Gal 1:5; Rom 1:25; 2 Cor 11:31; Rom 11:36; Phil 4:20).

16. Wright, "Romans," in *NIB* 10, 630.

17. While I agree with Wright, ibid., 635, that Paul does argue in Galatians 3–4 that Christ turns out to be the remnant, in the sense of being the seed of

Abraham, Paul is not arguing that way in this context. Jesus is not equated in these chapters with Israel; rather Jesus is said to be Israel's Messiah, which is not the same thing.

18. It is a mistake to argue, as Wright and others do, that Paul has two different definitions of Israel running in Romans 9–11. This is simply not true. Paul's concept of Israel involves the wider notion of the elect, and the narrower notion of those Jews selected for special purposes; but the latter is but a subset of the former, and in any case Paul is always talking about ethnic Jews. Unfaithful Israelites are still considered Israelites, though they are temporarily broken off, and faithful Gentiles are still considered Gentiles before or after they are saved. Jewish Christians are still seen as Jews as well as being Christians. The olive tree is indeed a symbol used to refer to Jew and Gentile being part of the same people of God. But Israel, or Jews, are not equated with the church, nor is Israel said to contain Gentile Christians. Paul is using the term "Israel" in this discussion in an ethnic sense, just as he uses the term "Gentile" in this context. That some Israelites are not "Israel" in the select or true sense does not mean that Paul has redefined Israel to mean the church. It is interesting that while D. Moo, "The Theology of Romans 9–11: A Response to E. Elizabeth Johnson," in *Romans* (vol. 3 of *Pauline Theology;* ed. P. M. Hay and E. C. Johnson; Minneapolis: Fortress, 1995) 240–58, rejects Wright's "two definitions of Israel" (one of which refers to the church) theory (see 252), he still maintains Calvin's "two definitions of election" theory, one corporate and one individual (255). But this theory is equally problematic if one wants to urge that individual election is to salvation. At least one of the individuals Paul refers to early in his argument in Romans 9—namely Pharaoh, whom God had elected for a specific historical purpose, is certainly not said to be elected to salvation. So then, do we have both individual election for historical purposes and a separate individual election for salvation? This theory has as many problems as the two-Israel theory of Wright.

19. See Cranfield, *Epistle to the Romans*, 2:480–84.

20. See the helpful discussion by G. B. Caird, "Expository Problems: Predestination—Romans ix–xi," *ET* 68 (1956–57): 324–27.

21. See rightly, Achtemeier, *Romans*, 157–59.

22. Cranfield, *Epistle to the Romans*, 2:493–96.

23. See the helpful and nuanced remarks of Achtemeier, *Romans*, 160–65, esp. 164–65:

> The difficulty lies in the fact that those who have understood these verses to be statements of eternal truth about how God deals with each individual, rather than a statement of how God has dealt with Israel in pursuing his plan for the redemption of a rebellious creation, have also tended to understand these verses in terms of a rigid and symmetrical predeterminism. God had determined before each individual was born whether or not that person would be saved or damned. Nothing that individual could do would alter that fact. Those who were damned got what they deserved as rebellious creatures. Those who were saved were saved only by grace. . . . That is simply not what Paul is saying in this passage. He is not writing about the fate of each individual. He is making a statement about how God dealt with Israel, and continues to deal with it, even when it rejects his Son; namely he deals with it in mercy, even when it deserves wrath. That is why one so badly distorts Paul's point if one assumes

these verses tell me about my fate, or anyone else's, before God: damned or saved. Rather, what these verses tell me is that the same gracious purpose at work in the election of Israel is now at work in a new chosen people to whom I can now belong, by that same gracious purpose of God. The passage is therefore about the enlargement of God's mercy to include Gentiles, not about the narrow and predetermined fate of each individual.

24. Barrett, *Romans*, 171.

25. Wright, "Romans," in *NIB* 10, 638, helpfully puts it this way: "the status of being God's promise-bearing people has in the last analysis nothing to do with whether Israel intends to do what God wants . . . or whether Israel expends energy on the task. . . . What matters, what carries the saving plan forward even though all human agents let God down, is God's own mercy."

26. See ibid., 639.

27. See rightly, R. Hays, *Echoes of Scripture in the Letters of Paul* (New Haven: Yale University Press, 1989), 66:

> Thus the allusion to Jeremiah 18 in Romans 9:20–21, like other allusions and echoes earlier in the text, anticipates the resolution of Paul's argument in Romans 11. The reader who recognizes the allusion will not slip into the error of reading Romans 9:14–29 as an excursus on the doctrine of the predestination of individuals to salvation or damnation, because the prophetic subtexts keep the concern with which the chapter began—the fate of Israel—sharply in focus.

28. Wright, "Romans," in *NIB* 10, 639.

29. Ibid., 641.

30. See the discussion by Bryan, *Preface to Romans*, 163–64, on the different verbs and deliberately different ways these two sets of vessels are described.

31. Ibid., 163. Cf. 2 Corinthians 9:5 on the use of this verb by Paul.

32. See rightly Cranfield, *Epistle to the Romans*, 2:496–97.

33. Paul enunciates here a double problem. On the one hand the Gentiles have obtained what they did not seek, and on the other hand Jews have not obtained though they sought righteousness through the Law. It is both Gentile belief and Jewish unbelief that constitute the problem here.

34. Käsemann, *Romans*, 279.

35. See Bryan, *Preface to Romans*, 171–72.

36. The translation by Stowers of this portion of Romans 10, *Rereading of Romans*, 311, is worth pondering: "I pray to God that my fellow Jews might be saved from God's anger. They want to do God's will but they are ignorant about God's plan for making things right. They have tried to work out a plan of their own for making things right instead of accepting God's plan. For Christ is the Law's goal with respect to God's plan for making things right, for all who believe [not just Israel]."

37. Thus the translation "goal" in itself is not adequate. But see Wright, "Romans," in *NIB* 10, 645–46.

38. Barrett, *Romans*, 184.

39. On the interpretation of this verse by the church fathers, see R. Badenas, *Christ, the End of the Law: Romans 10.4 in Pauline Perspective* (JSNTSup 10; Sheffield: JSOT , 1985), 515–20. Many of them do interpret Paul to mean goal

or culmination, but by no means all of them, and this ignores the way Paul uses the term elsewhere.

40. For a strong argument for the "goal" interpretation, see Wright, "Romans," in *NIB* 10, 656–57.

41. This, of course, does not mean that Paul thinks the Law, as part of Scripture ceases to have a function for believers or ceases to tell the truth. His regular citation of it in support of his arguments proves otherwise. The function it has, however, is as witness to the truth and promises of God, not as moral code, or Mosaic covenant that the believer is under and obliged to keep.

42. See my discussion in *Grace in Galatia*, 235–37.

43. As Barrett, *Romans*, 185, suggests, Paul may be saying here that humans could not have precipitated the incarnation. If so we have a reference to the preexistence of Christ here.

44. See rightly, Hays, *Echoes*, 80–83.

45. Barrett, *Romans*, 187.

46. Ibid., 188.

47. Paul seems to be drawing on Joel 2:32 (3:5 in the LXX). The interesting thing about that verse is that it also speaks of deliverance of those God called happening on Mt. Zion and in Jerusalem. In other words, it seems to relate to Paul's scripture quotation at 11:26a, which in the main has been associated with Isaiah 59:20–21 and Isaiah 27:9.

48. The issue in Paul's view is "delay" not "displacement," and so Paul's theology in regard to Israel should not be seen as supersessionistic.

49. On the structure of Romans 11 see D. G. Johnson, "The Structure and Meaning of Romans 11," *CBQ* 46 (1984): 91–103.

50. Nor does foreknowledge mean foreordination in Romans 8:29, where Paul distinguishes the two concepts.

51. Romans 11:2 must be compared with Romans 8:29. It leads to hopeless contradictions to suggest either that: (1) "foreknew" is used in a restrictive sense of the final elect in Romans 8:29, but not in 11:2; or (2) that "foreknew" simply means God's predetermined choosing in both places. Gundry Volf, *Paul and Perseverance*, 170–71, recognizes that Paul does use "foreknew" in 11:2 in a nonrestrictive sense, but then has no adequate explanation of how this comports with her view (see pp. 9–10) that something else is going on in Romans 8:29. The simple way to resolve this dilemma is to recognize that Paul does not mean "predetermined" by "foreknew," as should be clear from 8:29 where two different terms are used to convey what Paul wants to say.

52. As Barrett, *Romans*, 193, says, he gives the sense of it, not directly quoting.

53. C. H. Talbert, "Paul, Judaism, and the Revisionists," *CBQ* 63 (2001): 1–22.

54. The word has both senses, and Paul may be playing on this fact.

55. Stowers, *Rereading of Romans*, 312–15, takes the whole passage to refer to a footrace in which some Jews have temporarily stumbled but have not fallen out of the race, and will one day complete the race. Paul does use such a metaphor here, but only briefly, and the more important point is that he expects the turnaround of the Jews to transpire when Christ comes, not by continued striving on their part.

56. Both at Romans 11:12 and 11:16 we have elliptical sentences where the predicate must be supplied.

57. *Kosmos* here means not just the inhabited world, but the Gentile world as it is parallel to *ethne* Gentile nations in the next clause.

58. Barrett, *Romans*, 198, helpfully suggests the translation "full strength" contrasting the cutting down of the numbers of Israel to the fact that they will later be brought up to full strength once more.

59. E. E. Johnson, *The Function of Apocalyptic and Wisdom Traditions in Romans 9–11* (SBLDS 109; Atlanta: Scholars, 1989), 124.

60. Käsemann, *Romans*, 304–6, 312–14.

61. Ibid., 306–7.

62. As Cranfield, *Epistle to the Romans*, 2:561, says, Paul expects an eschatological act and result of God's plan, but he neither states nor implies that he sees his own work as the last-ditch effort before the end of the world that will produce this "all Israel."

63. Barrett, *Romans*, 199.

64. Cranfield, *Epistle to the Romans*, 2:562.

65. Origen and many of the fathers understood this to be a reference to the literal resurrection here. See Bryan, *Preface to Romans*, 187.

66. Cranfield, *Epistle to the Romans*, 2:484–88.

67. Ibid.

68. Ibid., 564–65.

69. See A. G. Baxter and J. Zeisler, "Paul and Arboriculture: Romans 11.17–24," *JSNT* 24 (1985): 25–32.

70. See Barrett, *Romans*, 201.

71. See my discussion in *Jesus, Paul, and the End*, 117.

72. Something Paul is attempting to do for his Gentile audience in Romans 9–11. He wants them to embrace and appropriate this heritage, as well as gain new-found respect for Jews and Jewish Christians.

73. On the use of this analogy or metaphor see J. C. T. Havemann, "Cultivated Olive—Wild Olive: The Olive Tree Metaphor in Romans 11:16–24," *Neot* 31 (1997): 87–106.

74. Käsemann, *Romans*, 311–12.

75. Ibid., 312–13.

76. It is clear from Bray's survey of the evidence from the early church fathers (*Romans*, 297–302) that the majority opinion was that after the full number of Gentiles were saved, then "all Israel" would be saved, which was understood to mean many Jews, if not all, and this would transpire when Jesus returned. For example, Theodoret, *Interpretation of Romans* says: "After the Gentiles accepted the Gospel, the Jews would believe, when the great Elijah would come to them and bring them the doctrine of faith." On the meaning of the "all" in the "all Israel" phrase, Diodore, *Pauline Commentary*, says: "[This] does not mean that every one of them will be but that either those who were understood by Elijah or those scattered all over the world will one day come to faith." Pelagius, *Commentary on Romans*: "Christ will come again to set them free." Cyril of Alexandria, *Explanation of Romans*, says: "Israel will be saved eventually, a hope which Paul confirms by quoting this text of Scripture. For indeed Israel will be saved in its own time and will be called at the end, after the calling of the Gentiles" (all cited by Bray, 298–99). Finally, we may quote Ambrosiaster, who says of the future of Jews in his *Commentary*

on Paul's Epistles: "they will be received with joy when they return to the faith, because God's love for them is stirred up by the memory of their ancestors" (cited in Bray, 299). It is true that Augustine believed "all Israel" here meant Jews and Gentiles united in one people (*Letters* 149), but as usual his is a minority opinion.

77. See the full-length monograph on the subject by F. Refoulé, ". . . *Et ainsi tout Israël sera sauvé:*" *Romains 11, 25–32* (Paris: Cerf, 1984).

78. P. W. van der Horst, "Only Then Will All Israel Be Saved. A Short Note on the Meaning of *kai houtos* in Romans 11:26," *JBL* 119 (2000): 521–25.

79. Ibid., 523–24.

80. Ibid., 524.

81. Ibid.

82. See the discussion by Wright, "Romans," in *NIB* 10, 690–91.

83. J. D. G. Dunn, *Romans 9–16* (WBC 38B; Dallas: Word, 1988), 681.

84. See Talbert, *Romans*, 264.

85. Gundry Volf, *Paul and Perseverance*, 185, thinks Paul has in mind the great mass of Jews who have either responded positively or negatively to the gospel in the gospel era. But this makes a mockery of the bold pronunciation that all Israel will be saved, because in fact Paul would only be talking about a small minority of the many generations of Jews.

86. See Barrett, *Romans*, 206.

87. Against the special pleading of Wright, "Romans,"in *NIB* 10, 692–93. It is interesting that Theodoret of Cyr was very clear on this matter: "After the Gentiles accepted the Gospel, the Jews would believe, when the great Elijah would come to them and bring them the doctrine of faith." See Bray, *Romans*, 298.

88. Cranfield, *Epistle to the Romans*, 2:578–79.

89. See Chrysostom, *Hom. 19*: "None of these things is immutable; neither your good nor their evil." See Bray, *Romans*, 295.

90. See Talbert, *Romans*, 265–67.

91. Käsemann, *Romans*, 315.

92. Dunn, *Romans 9–16*, 699.

93. Barrett, *Romans*, 211.

94. Hill, *In God's Time*, 208.

95. G. Carter, *Anglican Evangelicals: Protestant Secessions from the Via Media, c. 1800–1850* (Oxford Theological Monographs; Oxford: Oxford University Press, 2001), 220, 226.

96. See pp. 93–97 above.

CHAPTER 8

1. R. E. Chiles, *Theological Transition in American Methodism: 1790–1935* (New York: Rowman & Littlefield, 1983).

2. I once gave a quiz on Wesley and Calvin to several of my theological professors at the seminary I attended, with quotes from each, to see if they could identify who said what, particularly on matters of soteriology. They failed the

quiz, invariably mistaking Calvin's remarks for those of Wesley and vice versa. This shows that Wesley and Calvin were close on many key theological topics, particularly on Christology and some aspects of soteriology.

3. For a more detailed treatment of this section of this essay see my *Jesus, Paul, and the End of the World*, 51–72.

4. The next few pages have appeared in another form in a volume edited by P. Chilcote for Abingdon, entitled "Living in the Reign: The Dominion of God in the Wesleyan Tradition," in *The Wesleyan Tradition* (Nashville: Abingdon, 2002), 52–65. On Wesley's eschatology see my essay "*Praeparatio Evangelii*: The Theological Roots of Wesley's View of Evangelism," *Theology and Evangelism in the Wesleyan Heritage* (ed. J. C Logan; Nashville: Abingdon, 1994), 51–80, here 71–75.

5. John Wesley, *Sermons II: 34–70* (vol. 2 of *The Works of John Wesley*; ed. Albert C. Outler; Nashville: Abingdon, 1985), 499.

6. See, for example, the very late sermon, "The Signs of the Times" (1787).

7. Found now in John Wesley, *Sermons IV: 115–151* (vol. 4 of *The Works of John Wesley*; ed. Albert C. Outler; Nashville: Abingdon, 1985), 215–23.

8. On which see pp. 196–96 below.

9. Wesley, *Sermons IV*, 219.

10. Ibid., 220.

11. All references are to John Wesley, *Sermons I: 1–33* (vol. 1 of *The Works of John Wesley*; ed. Albert C. Outler; Nashville: Abingdon, 1985), here 218.

12. Ibid., 218–19.

13. Ibid., 223.

14. Ibid., 224.

15. Ibid., 230.

16. Ibid., 232.

17. *Notes on the New Testament* (London: Methodist Publishing House, n.d.).

18. Ibid.

19. This material appears in a somewhat different form in my *The Realm of the Reign: Reflections on the Dominion of God* (Nashville: Discipleship Resources, 1999), 83–93.

20. See pp. 171–73 above.

CHAPTER 9

1. The next few pages appear in another and much fuller form in a volume entitled *Conversion in the Wesleyan Tradition*, and my essay therein, "New Creation or New Birth? Conversion in the Johannine and Pauline Literature" (ed. K. Collins and J. Tyson; Nashville: Abingdon, 2001), 119–42.

2. See my essay "*Praeparatio Evangelii*," 51–80.

3. See my "The Waters of Birth: John 3:5 and 1 John 5:6–8," *NTS* 35 (1989): 155–60.

4. John Wesley, *Sermons on Several Occasions* (London: Wesleyan Methodist Book Room, n.d.), 236, emphasis added.

5. The old debate of whether *anothen* in John 3 means "again" or "above" is not finally a matter that can be settled, though the former rendering makes better

sense in the context of the discussion between Jesus and Nicodemus. The author makes clear by other means that he is referring to a birth that comes from God.

6. "The Marks of the New Birth," in John Wesley, *Standard Sermons* (2 vols.; 5th annot. ed.; ed. and annot. E. M. Sugden; London: Epworth, 1961), 1:248–49.

7. Ibid., 247.

8. It is an interesting fact that in the Standard Sermon entitled "The Means of Grace," Wesley lists prayer, searching the Scriptures, and receiving the Lord's Supper, but not baptism. This cannot be because he assumed everyone in his audience was baptized as an infant, for there were non-Conformists (e.g., Quakers) in his audience for whom this was not true. It rather reflects where the heart of the matter was with Wesley—namely, it had to do with spiritual experience that comes through faith.

9. I. H. Marshall, *The Epistles of John* (NICNT; Grand Rapids: Eerdmans, 1978), 186.

10. "The Great Privilege," in *Standard Sermons*, 1:248.

11. Ibid., 249.

12. Ibid., 252.

13. Ibid., 258.

14. Marshall, *Epistles of John*, 184–85.

15. See pp. 19–35 above.

16. Here I am relying on the telegraphic exposition of Romans 7 found in Wesley's *Notes on the New Testament*.

17. Emphasis added.

18. See the discussion now in Witherington and Hyatt, *The Letters to Philemon, Colossians, Ephesians*.

19. See pp. 59–89 above.

20. See Wesley, "Salvation by Faith," in *Standard Sermons*, 1:10–11.

21. See the more in-depth discussion of this in Witherington and Hyatt, *Paul's Letter to the Romans*, 99–139.

22. Wesley, "Justification by Faith," in *Standard Sermons*, 1:62–63.

CHAPTER 10

1. See pp. 127–30 above.

2. There is a difference between momentary inspiration from the Spirit to speak God's word, such as happened to the prophets throughout the ages (see the depiction of the women and men in Luke 1–2), and the actual bestowal of the Spirit becoming "indwelling" in the believer. This only begins to happen, according to Luke, at Pentecost.

3. See the discussion in B. Witherington, *The Acts of the Apostles: A Socio-Rhetorical Commentary* (Grand Rapids: Eerdmans, 1998), 128–63.

4. See Witherington, *Conflict and Community in Corinth*, 276–90.

5. See the wonderful and exhaustive study done by Fee, *God's Empowering Presence*.

Chapter 11

1. Another form of this section will appear in a collection of essays for Maxie Dunnam to be published by Abingdon.
2. See my *Jesus the Sage: The Pilgrimage of Wisdom* (Minneapolis: Fortress, 2000).
3. See Witherington and Hyatt, *Paul's Letter to the Romans*.
4. On the nature of apocalyptic prophecy, see my *Revelation*.

Chapter 12

1. There was, of course, the myth of Persephone being taken into the underworld by the god Hades, and being allowed back into the world after her mother Demeter lobbied Zeus for her return. This is an allegory about the seasons, and the compromise result was Persephone was allowed to return to earth for two-thirds of the year, but had to be in the underworld with her husband Hades the rest of the year. It is this myth that was reenacted in the Eleusinian mysteries.
2. R. Bauckham, *The Fate of the Dead: Studies on the Jewish and Christian Apocalypses* (NovTSup 93; Leiden: Brill, 1998), 21.
3. See I. M. Linforth, *The Arts of Orpheus* (Berkeley: University of California Press, 1941), 16–21; M. O. Lee, "Orpheus and Eurydice: Myth, Legend, Folklore," *Classica et Mediaevalia* 26 (1965): 402–12.
4. I am thinking particularly of a sculpture in the Athens Museum of the soldier who dies in Asia Minor and never returns home. He is depicted on the tomb as sitting on a hill, with his helmet off, looking towards Greece with absolute despair and sorrow on his face.
5. Bauckham, *Fate of the Dead*, 29.
6. On the evidence for the drinking tubes in tombs, see K. Hopkins, *Death and Renewal* (Sociological Studies in Roman History 2; Cambridge: Cambridge University Press, 1983), 201–55, here 232.
7. R. M. Ogilvie, *The Romans and Their Gods in the Age of Augustus* (London: Chatto & Windus, 1969), 75. There were various sorts of rituals for the dead that might be performed (see Horace, *Odes* 1.28–34), and it may be that proxy baptism in Corinth should be seen in light of such practices. See Witherington, *Conflict and Community in Corinth*, 294.
8. S. Dill, *Roman Society from Nero to Marcus Aurelius* (London: Macmillan, 1904), 256–57, emphasis mine.
9. R. MacMullen, *Paganism in the Roman Empire* (New Haven: Yale University Press, 1981), 55.
10. Bauckham, *Fate of the Dead*, 29.
11. See W. K. C. Guthrie, *The Greeks and Their Gods* (London: Methuen, 1950), 174–82, 260–95, 368–70.
12. See Lightfoot, *Notes*, 64.
13. See Wanamaker, *Epistles to the Thessalonians*, 164–66.
14. See rightly, ibid., 166.
15. However, I do not think this should be done in an insular way. Dialogue and discussion should be had with non-Christians as well, and in detail, not least because they do not approach the text within the same circle of reflection, and

we need outsider views in various ways, not least because Christian theology is supposed to be done in the service of a God who loves the world, and as an evangelistic missionary task.

CODA

1. See Witherington and Hyatt, *Paul's Letter to the Romans.*
2. See the forthcoming Witherington and Hyatt volume, *The Letters to Philemon, Colossians, and Ephesians.*
3. L. Gregg, "Fishing in the Keep of Silence," in *Good Poems* (selected and intro. by G. Keillor; New York: Penguin, 2002), 433.

Works Cited

Abegg, M. "Paul, 'Works of the Law,' and MMT." *Biblical Archaeology Review* 20, no. 6 (1994): 52–55, 82.

Achtemeier, P. *Romans*. Interpretation: A Bible Commentary for Teaching and Preaching. Atlanta: John Knox, 1985.

Aletti, J. N. "The Rhetoric of Romans 5–8." Pages 294–308 in *The Rhetorical Analysis of Scripture: Essays from the 1995 London Conference*. Edited by S. E. Porter and T. H. Olbricht. Journal for the Study of the New Testament: Supplement Series 146. Sheffield: Sheffield Academic, 1997.

———. "Rm 7.7–25 encore une fois: enjeux et propositions." *New Testament Studies* 48 (2002): 358–76.

Badenas, R. *Christ, the End of the Law: Romans 10:4 in Pauline Perspective*. Journal for the Study of the New Testament: Supplement Series 10. Sheffield: JSOT, 1985.

Barclay, J. *Obeying the Truth: Paul's Ethics in Galatians*. Minneapolis: Fortress, 1988.

Barrett, C. K. *From First Adam to Last: A Study in Pauline Theology*. New York: Scribner, 1962.

———. *The Epistle to the Romans*. Rev. ed. Black's New Testament Commentaries 6. Peabody, Mass.: Hendrickson, 1991.

Bauckham, R. *The Fate of the Dead: Studies on the Jewish and Christian Apocalypses*. Supplements to Novum Testamentum 93. Leiden: Brill, 1998.

Baxter, A. G., and J. Zeisler. "Paul and Arboriculture: Romans 11.17-24." *Journal for the Study of the New Testament* 24 (1985): 25–32.

Beale, G. *1–2 Thessalonians*. IVP New Testament Commentary Series 13. Edited by G. R. Osborne. Downers Grove: InterVarsity, 2003.

Beasley-Murray, G. R. *The Book of Revelation*. New Century Bible. London: Marshall, Morgan and Scott, 1974.

Bell, R. H. "Rom 5.18-19 and Universal Salvation." *New Testament Series* 48 (2002): 417–32.

Best, E. *A Critical and Exegetical Commentary on Ephesians*. International Critical Commentary on the Holy Scriptures of the Old and New Testaments. Edinburgh: T&T Clark, 1998.

————. *A Commentary on the First and Second Epistles to the Thessalonians*. London: A&C Black, 1972.

Blaising, C. A., and D. L. Bock. *Progressive Dispensationalism*. Wheaton, Ill: BridgePoint, 1993.

Bray, G., ed. *Romans*. Ancient Christian Commentary on Scripture: New Testament 6. Edited by Thomas C. Oden. Downers Grove: InterVarsity, 2000.

Bruce, F. F. *1 and 2 Thessalonians*. Waco, Tex.: Word, 1982.

Bryan, C. *A Preface to Romans: Notes on the Epistle in Its Literary and Cultural Setting*. Oxford: Oxford University Press, 2000.

Caird, G. B. "Expository Problems: Predestination—Romans ix–xi." *Expository Times* 68 (1956–57): 324–27.

————. *Paul's Letters from Prison: Ephesians, Philippians, Colossians, Philemon, in the Revised Standard Version*. The New Clarendon Bible. Oxford: Oxford University Press, 1976.

————. *The Revelation of St. John the Divine*. Peabody, Mass.: Hendrickson, 1966.

for a thorough expose on C.I.

>Scofield

Canfield, J. M. *The Incredible Scofield and His Book*. Vallecito, Calif: Ross House Books, 1988.

Carter, G. *Anglican Evangelicals: Protestant Secessions from the Via Media, c. 1800–1850*. Oxford Theological Monographs. Oxford: Oxford University Press, 2001.

Chiles, R. E. *Theological Transition in American Methodism: 1790–1935*. New York: Rowman & Littlefield, 1983.

Collins, A. Y., ed. *Apocalypse: The Morphology of a Genre*. Semeia 14. Missoula, Mont.: Scholars , 1979.

Collins, R. F. *1 & 2 Timothy and Titus: A Commentary*. Louisville: Westminster/ John Knox, 2002.

Cranfield, C. E. B. *A Critical and Exegetical Commentary on the Epistle to the Romans*. 2 vols. International Critical Commentary on the Holy Scriptures of the Old and New Testaments 32. Edinburgh: T&T Clark, 1975–1979.

Deidun, T. J. "Romans." Pages 601–4 in *A Dictionary of Biblical Interpretation*. Edited by R. J. Coggins and J. L. Houlden. Philadelphia: Trinity, 1990.

DeLacey, D. R. "Jesus as Mediator." *Journal for the Study of the New Testament* 29 (1987): 101–21.

Delobel, J. "The Fate of the Dead according to 1 Thess 4 and 1 Cor 15." Pages 340–47 in *The Thessalonian Correspondence*. Bibliotheca ephemeridum theologicarum lovaniensium 87. Edited by R. F. Collins. Leuven: Leuven University Press, 1990.

Dill, S. *Roman Society from Nero to Marcus Aurelius*. London: Macmillan, 1904.

Donfried, K. P. "The Imperial Cults of Thessalonica and Political Conflict in 1 Thessalonians." Pages 215–23 in *Paul and Empire*. Edited by R. A. Horsley. Harrisburg: Trinity, 1997.

Dunn, J. D. G. "4QMMT and Galatians." *New Testament Studies* 43 (1997): 147–53.

——. *Jesus, Paul, and the Law: Studies in Mark and Galatians*. Louisville: Westminster/John Knox, 1990.

——, ed. *Paul and the Mosaic Law*. Wissenschaftliche Untersuchungen zum Neuen Testament 89. Tubingen: Mohr, 1996.

——. *Romans 1–8*. Word Biblical Commentary 38A. Dallas: Word, 1988.

——. *Romans 9–16*. Word Biblical Commentary 38B. Dallas: Word, 1988.

——. *The Theology of Paul the Apostle*. Grand Rapids: Eerdmans, 1998.

Erasmus, Desiderius. *Erasmus' Annotations on the New Testament: Acts–Romans–I and II Corinthians*. Edited by A. Reeve and M. A. Screech. Leiden: Brill, 1990.

Fee, G. D. *1 and 2 Timothy, Titus*. New International Biblical Commentary on the New Testament. Edited by Ward W. Gasque. Peabody, Mass.: Hendrickson, 1988.

——. *God's Empowering Presence*. Peabody, Mass.: Hendrickson, 1994.

——. *Gospel and Spirit: Issues in New Testament Hermeneutics*. Peabody, Mass.: Hendrickson, 1991.

Fitzmyer, J. *Romans: A New Translation with Introduction and Commentary*. Anchor Bible 33. New York: Doubleday, 1993.

Gager, J. G. *The Origins of Anti-Semitism: Attitudes toward Judaism in Pagan and Christian Antiquity*. New York: Oxford University Press, 1983.

Gaston, L. *Paul and the Torah*. Vancouver: University of British Columbia Press, 1987.

Godsey, J. "The Interpretation of Romans in the History of the Christian Faith." *Interpretation* 34 (1980): 3–16.

Gorday, P. *Principles of Patristic Exegesis: Romans 9–11 in Origen, John Chrysostom, and Augustine*. New York: Mellen, 1983.

Gregg, L. "Fishing in the Keep of Silence." Page 433 in *Good Poems*. Selected and introduced by G. Keillor. New York: Penguin, 2002.

Grieb, A. K. *The Story of Romans: A Narrative Defense of God's Righteousness*. Louisville: Westminster/John Knox, 2002.

Gundry Volf, J. M. *Paul and Perseverance: Staying In and Falling Away*. Louisville: Westminster/John Knox, 1990.

Guthrie, W. K. C. *The Greeks and Their Gods*. London: Methuen, 1950.

Hanson, A. T. "The Mediator: 1 Tiimothy 2:5-6." Pages 56–77 in *Studies in the Pastoral Epistles*. London: SPCK, 1968.

Havemann, J. C. T. "Cultivated Olive—Wild Olive: The Olive Tree Metaphor in Romans 11:16-24." *Neotestamentica* 31 (1997): 87–106.

Hays, R. *Echoes of Scripture in the Letters of Paul*. New Haven: Yale University Press, 1989.

Hill, C. *In God's Time: The Bible and the Future.* Grand Rapids: Eerdmans, 2002.

Hoehner, H. *Ephesians: An Exegetical Commentary.* Grand Rapids: Baker, 2003.

Hooker, M. D. "Interchange and Atonement." *Bulletin of the John Rylands University Library of Manchester* 60 (1977–1978): 462–81.

———. "Interchange in Christ." *Journal of Theological Studies* 22 (1971): 349–61.

Hopkins, K. *Death and Renewal.* Sociological Studies in Roman History 2. Cambridge: Cambridge University Press, 1983.

Howard, T. "The Literary Unity of 1 Thessalonians 4:13–5:11." *Grace Theological Journal* 9 (1988): 163–90.

Hübner, H. *Law in Paul's Thought.* Translated by J. C. G. Greig. Edited by J. Riches. Studies of the New Testament and Its World. Edinburgh: T&T Clark, 1984.

Jeremias, J. *Die Briefe an Timotheus und Titus.* Das Neue Testament Deutsch 9. Göttingen: Vandenhoeck & Ruprecht, 1975.

———. *Unknown Sayings of Jesus.* Translated by Reginald H. Fuller. London: SPCK, 1964.

Johnson, D. G. "The Structure and Meaning of Romans 11." *Catholic Biblical Quarterly* 46 (1984): 91–103.

Johnson, E. E. *The Function of Apocalyptic and Wisdom Traditions in Romans 9–11.* SBL Dissertation Series 109. Atlanta: Scholars Press, 1989.

Johnson, L. T. *The First and Second Letters to Timothy: A New Translation with Introduction and Commentary.* New York: Doubleday, 2001.

———. *Letters to Paul's Delgates: 1 Timothy, 2 Timothy, Titus.* New Testament in Context. Valley Forge, Pa.: Trinity, 1996.

Käsemann, E. *Commentary on Romans.* Translated and edited by G. W. Bromiley. Grand Rapids: Eerdmans, 1980.

Kelly, J. N. D. *A Commentary on the Pastoral Epistles: I Timothy, II Timothy, Titus.* Black's New Testament Commentaries. London: A&C Black, 1963.

Koester, H. "Imperial Ideology and Paul's Eschatology in 1 Thessalonians." Pages 158–66 in *Paul and Empire: Religion and Power in Roman Imperial Society.* Edited by R. A. Horsley. Harrisburg: Trinity, 1997.

Kummel, W. G. *Römer 7 und das Bild des Menschen im Neuen Testament.* Munich: Kaiser, 1974.

Lee, M. O. "Orpheus and Eurydice: Myth, Legend, Folklore." *Classica et Mediaevalia* 26 (1965): 402–12.

Lightfoot, J. B. *Notes on Epistles of St. Paul.* Winona Lake, Minn.: Alpha Publications, n.d.

Linforth, I. M. *The Arts of Orpheus.* Berkeley: University of California Press, 1941.

Llewelyn, S. R., ed. *New Documents Illustrating Early Christianity: A Review of the Greek Inscriptions and Papyri Published in 1980–81.* Vol. 6 of *New Documents Illustrating Early Christianity.* Grand Rapids: Eerdmans, 1993.

Lyonnet, S. "L'histoire du salut selon le chapitre 7 de l'épître aux Romains." *Biblica* 43 (1962): 117–51.

MacMullen, R. *Paganism in the Roman Empire*. New Haven: Yale University Press, 1981.

Malherbe, A. J. *The Letters to the Thessalonians: A New Translation with Introduction and Commentary*. Anchor Bible 32B. New York: Doubleday, 2000.

Marshall, I. H. "Election and Calling to Salvation in 1 and 2 Thessalonians." Pages 259–76 in *The Thessalonian Correspondence*. Edited by R. F. Collins. Leuven: Leuven University Press, 1990.

———. *The Epistles of John*. New International Commentary on the New Testament. Grand Rapids: Eerdmans, 1978.

———. *1 and 2 Thessalonians: Based on the Revised Standard Version*. New Century Bible Commentary. Grand Rapids: Eerdmans, 1983.

———. *Kept by the Power of God: A Study of Perseverance and Falling Away*. 2d ed. Minneapolis: Bethany Fellowship, 1974.

Melanchthon, P. *Commentary on Romans*. Translated by F. Kramer. St. Louis: Concordia, 1992.

Metzger, B. M. *A Textual Commentary on the Greek New Testament: A Companion Volume to the United Bible Societies' Greek New Testament*. 3d ed. New York: United Bible Societies, 1971.

Moo, D. *The Epistle to the Romans*. New International Commentary on the New Testament. Edited by G. D. Fee. Grand Rapids: Eerdmans, 1996.

———. "The Theology of Romans 9–11: A Response to E. Elizabeth Johnson." Pages 240–58 in *Romans*. Edited by David M. Hay and E. Elizabeth Johnson. Vol. 3 of *Pauline Theology*. Minneapolis: Fortress, 1995.

Moore, G. F. *Judaism in the First Centuries of the Christian Era: The Age of the Tannaim*. 3 vols. New York: Schocken, 1971.

Morris, L. *The First and Second Epistles to the Thessalonians*. New International Commentary on the New Testament. Grand Rapids: Eerdmans, 1991.

Mounce, W. *The Pastoral Epistles*. Word Biblical Commentary 46. Nashville: Nelson, 2000.

Newman, C. C. "Election and Predestination in Ephesians 1:4–6a: An Exegetical-Theological Study of the Historical, Christological Realization of God's Purpose." *Review and Expositor* 93 (1996): 237–47.

O'Brien, P. T. *The Letter to the Ephesians*. Pillar New Testament Commentary. Grand Rapids: Eerdmans, 1999.

Oden, T. C. *First and Second Timothy and Titus*. Interpretation. Louisville: Westminster/John Knox, 1989.

Ogilvie, R. M. *The Romans and Their Gods in the Age of Augustus*. Ancient Culture and Society. London: Chatto and Windus, 1969.

Packer, J. I. "The 'Wretched Man' Revisited: Another Look at Romans 7:14-25." Pages 70–81 in *Romans and the People of God*. Edited by Sven K. Soderlund and N. T. Wright. Grand Rapids: Eerdmans, 1999.

Perkins, P. "The Letter to the Ephesians." Pages 349–466 in *2 Corinthians–Philemon*. Vol. 11 of *The New Interpreters Bible*. Edited by L. Keck. Nashville: Abingdon, 2000, 11:376.

Potter, D. *Prophets and Emperors: Human and Divine Authority from Augustus to Theodosius*. Revealing Antiquity 7. Cambridge, Mass.: Harvard University Press, 1994.

Räisänen, H. "Paul, God, and Israel: Romans 9–11 in Recent Research." Pages 178–206 in *The Social World of Formative Christianity and Judaism: Essays in Tribute to Howard Clark Kee*. Edited by J. Neusner, et al. Philadelphia: Fortress, 1988.

———. *Paul and the Law*. Philadelphia: Fortress, 1983.

Refoulé, F. ". . . *Et ainsi tout Israël sera sauvé*": *Romains 11, 25-32*. Paris: Cerf, 1984.

Rigaux, B. *Saint Paul: Les Épîtres aux Thessaloniciens*. Paris: J. Gabalda, 1956.

Rossing, B. *The Rapture Exposed: The Message of Hope in the Book of Revelation*. Boulder: Westview, 2004.

Rowland, C. *The Open Heaven: A Study of Apocalyptic in Judaism and Early Christianity*. New York: Crossroad, 1982.

Sanders, E. P. *Paul, the Law, and the Jewish People*. Minneapolis: Fortress, 1983.

Schnackenburg, R. *Ephesians*. Edinburgh: T&T Clark, 1991.

Schreiner, T. R. *The Law and Its Fulfillment: A Pauline Theology of the Law*. Grand Rapids: Eerdmans, 1993.

Schüssler Fiorenza, E. *The Book of Revelation—Justice and Judgment*. Philadelphia: Fortress, 1985.

Smith, A. " The First Letter to the Thessalonians." Pages 671–738 in *2 Corinthians–Philemon*. Vol. 11 of *The New Interpreter's Bible*. Edited by L. Keck. Nashville: Abingdon, 2000.

Stendahl, K. "Paul and the Introspective Conscience of the West." In *Paul Among Jews and Gentiles, and Other Essays*. Philadelphia: Fortress, 1977.

Stowers, S. *A Rereading of Romans: Justice, Jews, and Gentiles*. New Haven: Yale University Press, 1994.

Talbert, C. H. "Paul, Judaism, and the Revisionists." *Catholic Biblical Quarterly* 63 (2001): 1–22.

———. *Romans*. Smyth and Helwys Bible Commentary. Macon, Ga.: Smyth & Helwys, 2002.

Thielman, F. *Paul and the Law: A Contextual Approach*. Downers Grove: InterVarsity, 1994.

Van der Horst, P. W. "Only Then Will All Israel Be Saved: A Short Note on the Meaning of *kai houtos* in Romans 11:26." *Journal of Biblical Literature* 119 (2000): 521–25.

Wanamaker, C. *The Epistles to the Thessalonians*. New International Greek Testament Commentary. Grand Rapids: Eerdmans, 1990.

Watson, F. *Paul, Judaism, and the Gentiles: A Sociological Approach*. Society for New Testament Studies Monograph Series 56. Cambridge: Cambridge University Press, 1986.

Wengst, K. *Pax Romana and the Peace of Jesus Christ*. Translated by John Bowden. Philadelphia: Fortress, 1987.

Wenham, D. *Paul: Follower of Jesus or Founder of Christianity?* Grand Rapids: Eerdmans, 1995.

———. "Paul and the Synoptic Apocalypse." Pages 345–75 in *Studies of History and Tradition in the Four Gospels*. Gospel Perspectives 2. Edited by R. T. France and D. Wenham. Sheffield: JSOT, 1981.

Wesley, J. *Notes on the New Testament*. London: Methodist Publishing House, n.d.

———. *Sermons on Several Occasions*. London: Wesleyan Methodist Book Room, n.d.

———. *Sermons I: 1–33*. Vol. 1 of *The Works of John Wesley*. Edited by Albert C. Outler. Nashville: Abingdon, 1984.

———. *Sermons II: 34–70*. Vol. 2 of *The Works of John Wesley*. Edited by Albert C. Outler. Nashville: Abingdon, 1984.

———. *Sermons IV: 115–151*. Vol. 4 of *The Works of John Wesley*. Edited by Albert C. Outler. Nashville: Abingdon, 1984.

———. *Standard Sermons: Consisting of Forty-four Discourses, Published in Four Volumes in 1746, 1748, 1750 and 1760 (Fourth Edition, 1787) to Which Are Added Nine Additional Sermons, Published in vols. I to IV of Wesley's Collected Works, 1771*. Edited and annotated by Edward H. Sugden. 5th annotated ed. 2 vols. London: Epworth, 1961.

Westerholm, S. *Israel's Law and the Church's Faith: Paul and His Recent Interpreters*. Grand Rapids: Eerdmans, 1988.

Wiles, G. P. *Paul's Intercessory Prayers: The Significance of the Intercessory Prayer Passages in the Letters of St. Paul*. Society for New Testament Studies Monograph Series 24. Cambridge: Cambridge University Press, 1974.

Wilken, R. *The Spirit of Early Christian Thought*. New Haven: Yale University Press, 2003.

Witherington, B. *The Acts of the Apostles: A Socio-Rhetorical Commentary*. Grand Rapids: Eerdmans, 1998.

———. *Conflict and Community in Corinth: A Socio-Rhetorical Commentary on 1 and 2 Corinthians*. Grand Rapids: Eerdmans, 1995.

———. *Grace in Galatia: A Commentary on St. Paul's Letter to the Galatians*. Grand Rapids: Eerdmans, 1998.

———. *Jesus, Paul, and the End of the World: A Comparative Study in New Testament Eschatology*. Downers Grove: InterVarsity, 1992.

———. *Jesus the Sage: The Pilgrimage of Wisdom*. Minneapolis: Fortress, 2000.

———. *Jesus the Seer: The Progress of Prophecy*. Peabody, Mass.: Hendrickson, 2000.

———. "Living in the Reign: The Dominion of God in the Wesleyan Tradition." Pages 52–65 in *The Wesleyan Tradition: A Paradigm for Renewal*. Edited by P. Chilcote. Nashville: Abingdon, 2002.

———. "New Creation or New Birth? Conversion in the Johannine and Pauline Literature." Pages 119–42 in *Conversion in the Wesleyan Tradition*. Edited by K. Collins and J. Tyson. Nashville: Abingdon, 2001.

———. *Paul's Narrative Thought World: The Tapestry of Tragedy and Triumph*. Louisville: Westminster/John Knox, 1994.

————. "*Praeparatio Evangelii*: The Theological Roots of Wesley's View of Evangelism." Pages 51–80 in *Theology and Evangelism in the Wesleyan Heritage*. Edited by J. C. Logan. Nashville: Abingdon, 1994.

————. *The Realm of the Reign: Reflections on the Dominion of God*. Nashville: Discipleship Resources, 1999.

————. *Revelation*. New Cambridge Bible Commentary. Cambridge: Cambridge University Press, 2003.

————. "The Waters of Birth: John 3:5 and 1 John 5:6-8." *New Testament Studies* 35 (1989): 155–60.

Witherington, B., and D. Hyatt. *The Letters to Philemon, Colossians, Ephesians*. Grand Rapids: Eerdmans, 2006.

————. *Paul's Letter to the Romans: A Socio-Rhetorical Commentary*. Grand Rapids: Eerdmans, 2004.

Wright, N. T. "Paul's Gospel and Caesar's Empire." Pages 160–83 in *Paul and Politics*. Edited by R. A. Horsley. Harrisburg: Trinity, 2000.

————. "The Letter to the Romans." Pages 393–770 in *Acts–First Corinthians*. Vol. 10 of *The New Interpreters Bible*. Edited by L. Keck. Nashville: Abingdon, 2002.